THE ANCIENT N

ROUTLEDGE HISTORY OF THE ANCIENT WORLD

General Editor: Fergus Millar

THE ANCIENT
NEAR EAST
c. 3000–330 BC
Volume One

Amélie Kuhrt

London and New York

First published 1995
by Routledge
11 New Fetter Lane, London EC4P 4EE

Simultaneously published in the USA and Canada
by Routledge
29 West 35th Street, New York, NY 10001

First published in paperback 1997

Typeset in Garamond by
Ponting–Green Publishing Services, Chesham, Bucks
Printed in Great Britain by
T.J. International Ltd, Padstow, Cornwall

British Library Cataloguing in Publication Data
A catalogue record for this book is available from the
British Library

Library of Congress Cataloguing in Publication Data
Kuhrt, Amélie
The Ancient Near East / Amélie Kuhrt.
2 v. cm. — (Routledge history of the ancient world)
Intended audience: Students and scholars working in
history of this region.
Includes bibliographical references and index.
Contents: v. 1. From *c.* 3000 BC to *c.* 1200 BC –
v. 2. From *c.* 1200 BC to 330 BC
1. Middle East–History–To 622.
I. Title.   II. Series.
DS62.23.K87   1995
939′.4—dc20   94—41951

ISBN 0–415–01353–4 (Volume 1, hbk)
ISBN 0–415–16763–9 (Volume 1, pbk)
ISBN 0–415–12872–2 (Volume 2, hbk)
ISBN 0–415–16764–7 (Volume 2, pbk)
ISBN 0–415–01352–6 (2 volume set, hbk)
ISBN 0–415–16762–0 (2 volume set, pbk)

CONTENTS

Volume Two

CONTENTS

FIGURES

MAPS

TABLES

ABBREVIATIONS

AA	*Archäologischer Anzeiger*
AAAS	*Annales Archéologiques Arabes de Syrie*
AAASH	*Acta Antiqua Academiae Scientiarium Hungaricae*
AASOR	Annual of the American School of Oriental Research
ABAW	*Abhandlungen der Bayerischen Akademie der Wissenschaften*
ABC	A.K. Grayson *Assyrian and Babylonian Chronicles* (TCS 5) Locust Valley, NY 1975
ABL	R.F. Harper (1892–1914) *Assyrian and Babylonian Letters belonging to the Kouyounjik Collection of the British Museum* (14 vols) London, Chicago
AchHist 1	*Achaemenid History 1: Sources, Structures, Synthesis* (H. Sancisi-Weerdenburg ed.) Leiden 1987
AchHist 2	*Achaemenid History 2: The Greek Sources* (H. Sancisi-Weerdenburg, A. Kuhrt eds) Leiden 1987
AchHist 3	*Achaemenid History 3: Method and Theory* (A. Kuhrt, H. Sancisi-Weerdenburg eds) Leiden 1988
AchHist 4	*Achaemenid History 4: Centre and Periphery* (H. Sancisi-Weerdenburg, A. Kuhrt eds) Leiden 1990
AchHist 5	*Achaemenid History 5: The Roots of the European Tradition* (H. Sancisi-Weerdenburg, J.-W. Drijvers eds) Leiden 1990
AchHist 6	*Achaemenid History 6: Asia Minor and Egypt: Old Cultures in a New Empire* (H. Sancisi-Weerdenburg, A. Kuhrt eds) Leiden 1991
AchHist 7	*Achaemenid History 7: Through Travellers' Eyes* (H. Sancisi-Weerdenburg, J.-W. Drijvers eds) Leiden 1991
AchHist 8	*Achaemenid History 8: Continuity and Change* (H. Sancisi-Weerdenburg, A. Kuhrt, M.C. Root eds) Leiden 1994
ActSum	*Acta Sumerologica*
ADFU	Ausgrabungen der Deutschen Forschungsgemeinschaft in Uruk-Warka
ADOG	Abhandlungen der Deutschen Orient Gesellschaft
AfO	*Archiv für Orientforschung*
Äg. Abh.	Ägyptologische Abhandlungen

Ägyptische Inschriften	*Ägyptische Inschriften aus den Königlichen Museen zu Berlin* (2 vols) Leipzig 1913–1924
AION	*Annali del'Istituto Universitario Orientale di Napoli*
AJA	*American Journal of Archaeology*
AJAH	*American Journal of Ancient History*
Akk.	Akkadian
AMI	*Archäologische Mitteilungen aus Iran*
ANET	*Ancient Near Eastern Texts relating to the Old Testamant* J.B. Pritchard (ed.) (3rd rev. edn) Princeton, NJ 1969
AnOr	Analecta Orientalia
AnSt	*Anatolian Studies*
AOAT	Alter Orient und Altes Testament
AOF	*Altorientalische Forschungen*
AOS	American Oriental Society
APAW	Abhandlungen der Preussischen Akademie der Wissenchaften
Ar.	Aramaic
ARAB	D.D. Luckenbill *Ancient Records of Assyria and Babylonia* (2 vols) Chicago 1926–7
ARCE	American Research Center in Egypt
ARE	J.H. Breasted *Ancient Records of Egypt* Chicago 1906
ARM	Archives Royales de Mari
ArOr	*Archiv Orientalni*
AS	Assyriological Studies
ASAE	*Annales du Service des Antiquités de l'Égypte*
ASNP	*Annali della Scuola Normale di Pisa*
BaF	*Baghdader Forschungen*
BaM	*Baghdader Mitteilungen*
BAR	British Archaeological Reports
BAR	*Biblical Archaeological Review*
BASOR	*Bulletin of the American Schools of Oriental Research*
BibArch	*Biblical Archaeologist*
BiOr	*Bibliotheca Orientalis*
BMFA	*Bulletin of the Museum of Fine Arts* Boston
Bo.	Symbol for Boghazköy-Texte
BSAG 4 and 5	*Bulletin of Sumerian Agriculture* vols 4 and 5: *Irrigation and Cultivation in Mesopotamia* (parts I and II) Cambridge 1988–90
BSFE	*Bulletin de la Société Française d'Égyptologie*
BSOAS	*Bulletin of the School of Oriental and African Studies*
CAD	*The Assyrian Dictionary of the University of Chicago* Chicago 1956–
Camb.	*Inschriften von Cambyses, König von Babylon (529–521 v. Chr.)* (Babylonische Texte 8–9) J.N. Strassmaier, Leipzig 1890
CBQ	*Catholic Bible Quarterly*

CAH	*Cambridge Ancient History*
CDAFI	*Cahiers de la Délégation Archéologique Française en Iran*
CH	Codex Hammurabi
CHI	*Cambridge History of Iran*
CRAIBL	*Comptes Rendus de l'Académie des Inscriptions et Belles-Lettres*
CT	Cuneiform Texts from Babylonian Tablets in the British Museum
CTH	E. Laroche *Catalogue des textes hittites* (Études et Commentaires 75) Paris 1971
CTN	Cuneiform Texts from Nimrud
DHA	*Dialogues d'histoire ancienne*
D.S.	Diodorus Siculus *The Library of History*
EA	J.A. Knudtzon *Die El-Amarna-Tafeln* (Vorderasiatische Bibliothek 2) Leipzig 1907–15. For completely new translations (with notes, commentary and introduction) see now W. Moran 1987 *Les Lettres d'el Amarna: correspondance diplomatique du pharaon* (LAPO 13) Paris (English version, with some revisions and updating, Baltimore, MD 1992)
EES	Egypt Exploration Society
EI	*Eretz Israel*
El.	Elamite
Encyclopedia	*Encyclopedia of Archaeological Excavations in the Holy Land* (eds M. Avi-Yonah and E. Stern) Oxford 1975–1978
Enclr	*Encyclopaedia Iranica* (ed. E. Yarshater) London, Boston 1985–
EpAn	*Epigraphica Anatolica*
FAOS	Freiburger Altorientalische Studien
FGrH	F. Jacoby *Die Fragmente der Griechische Historiker* Berlin 1923–
GM	*Göttinger Miszellen*
HdO	Handbuch der Orientalistik
Hdt.	Herodotus, *Histories*
HUCA	*Hebrew University College Annual*
IEJ	*Israel Exploration Journal*
IOS	*Israel Oriental Series*
IrAnt	*Iranica Antiqua*
IsMEO	Istituto per il Medio o Estremo Oriente
JA	*Journal Asiatique*
JANES	*Journal of the Ancient Near Eastern Society*
JAOS	*Journal of the American Oriental Society*
JARCE	*Journal of the American Research Center in Egypt*
JCS	*Journal of Cuneiform Studies*
JEA	*Journal of Egyptian Archaeology*
JEOL	*Jaarbericht van het Vooraziatasch-Egyptisch Genootschap 'Ex Oriente Lux'*

JESHO	*Journal of the Economic and Social History of the Orient*
JHS	*Journal of Hellenic Studies*
JNES	*Journal of Near Eastern Studies*
JSOT	*Journal for the Study of the Old Testament*
JTS	*Journal for Theological Studies*
JTVI	*Journal of the Transactions of the Victoria Institute*
K	Symbol for texts from the Kouyunjik Collection in the British Museum
KAH II	O. Schroeder *Keilschrifttexte aus Assur historischen Inhalts, Zweites Heft* (WVDOG 37) Leipzig 1922
KAI	H. Donner, W. Röllig *Kanaanäische und Aramäische Inschriften* (3 vols) Wiesbaden 1973–9
KBo	Keilschriftexte aus Boghazköy
KTU	M. Dietrich, O. Loretz, J. Sanmartin *Die keilalphabetischen Texte aus Ugarit einschliesslich der keilalphabetischen Texte ausserhalb Ugarits* I (AOAT 2, 4) Kevelaer, Neukirchen-Vluyn 1976
KUB	Keilschrifturkunden aus Boghazköy
LAPO	Littératures Anciennes du Proche-Orient
LÄ	*Lexikon der Ägyptologie* Wiesbaden 1975–86
LKA	E. Ebeling, K. Köcher *Literarische Keilschrifttexte aus Assur* Berlin 1953
MAD	Materials for the Assyrian Dictionary
MAOG	*Mitteilungen der Altorientalischen Gesellschaft*
MARI	*Mari: Annales de Recherches Interdisciplinaires*
MCS	*Manchester Cuneiform Studies*
MDAIK	*Mitteilungen des Deutschen Archäologischen Instituts in Kairo*
MDP II	V. Scheil *Textes élamites-sémitiques, première série* (Mémoires de la Délégation en Perse II) Paris 1900
MDP IX	V. Scheil *Textes élamites-anzanites, troisième série* (Mémoire de la Délégation en Perse IX) Paris 1907
MDP XI	V. Scheil *Texts élamites-anzanites, quatrième série* (Mémoire de la Délégation en Perse XI) Paris 1911
MIO	*Mitteilungen des Instituts für Orientforschung*
MVAeG	Mitteilungen der Vorderasiatisch-Aegyptischen Gesellschaft
NABU	*Notes Assyriologiques Brèves et Utiles*
NAPR	*Northern Akkad Project Reports*
NEB	New English Bible
NL	Nimrud Letters
OA	*Oriens Antiquus*
OBO	Orbis Biblicus et Orientalis
OIP	Oriental Institute Publications
OLA	Orientalia Lovaniensia Analecta
OLZ	*Orientalistische Literaturzeitschrift*

OP	Old Persian
Or.	*Orientalia*
PAPhS	*Proceedings of the American Philosophical Society*
PBS 5	A. Poebel *Historical and Grammatical Texts* (University of Pennsylvania Museum, Babylonian Section 5) Philadelphia 1914
PBS 13	L. Legrain *Historical Fragments* (University of Pennsylvania Museum, Babylonian Section 13) Philadelphia 1922
PBS 15	L. Legrain *Royal Inscriptions and Fragments from Nippur and Babylon* (University of Pennsylvania Museum, Babylonian Section 15) Philadelphia 1926
PCPS	*Proceedings of the Cambridge Philological Society*
PEQ	*Palestine Exploration Quarterly*
PRU	Palais Royal d'Ugarit (Paris)
RA	*Revue d'Assyriologie*
REA	*Revue des Études Anciennes*
RIM	Royal Inscriptions of Mesopotamia
RIDA	*Revue international des droits de l'antiquité*
RLA	*Reallexikon der Assyriologie* Berlin 1928–
RSO	*Rivista degli studi orientali*
SAA 1	S. Parpola *The Correspondence of Sargon II* Part I: *Letters from Assyria and the West* (State Archives of Assyria 1) Helsinki 1987
SAA 2	S. Parpola, K. Watanabe *Neo-Assyrian Treaties and Loyalty Oaths* (State Archives of Assyria 2) Helsinki 1988
SAA 3	A. Livingstone *Court Poetry amd Literary Miscellanea* (State Archives of Assyria 3) Helsinki 1989
SAA 4	I. Starr *Queries to the Sungod: divination and politics in Sargonid Assyria* (State Archives of Assyria 4) Helsinki 1990
SAA 5	G.B. Lanfranchi, S. Parpola *The Correspondence of Sargon* Part II: *Letters from the Northern and Northeastern Provinces* (State Archives of Assyria 5) Helsinki 1990
SAA 6	T. Kwasman, S. Parpola *Legal Transactions of the Royal Court of Nineveh* Part I: *Tiglath-pileser III through Esarhaddon* (State Archives of Assyria 6) Helsinki 1991
SAA 7	F.M. Fales, J.N. Postgate *Imperial Administrative Records* Part I: *Palace and Temple Administration* (State Archives of Assyria 7) Helsinki 1992
SAA 8	H. Hunger *Astrological Reports to Assyrian Kings* (State Archives of Assyria 8) Helsinki 1992
SAA 10	S. Parpola *Letters from Assyrian and Babylonian Scholars* (State Archives of Assyria 10) Helsinki 1993
SAAB	*State Archives of Assyria Bulletin*
SAOC	Studies in Ancient Oriental Civilization

SBT	Studies in Biblical Theology
SDB	*Dictionnaire du Bible: supplément*
SCO	*Studi classici e orientali*
SSEA Journal	*Society for the Study of Egyptian Antiquities Journal*
StBoT	Studien zu den Boghazköy Texten
StIr	*Studia Iranica*
StOr	*Studia Orientalia*
Sum.	Sumerian
TAPhA	*Transaction of the American Philosophical Society*
TCL	Textes cunéiformes du Louvre
TCS	Texts from Cuneiform Sources
Theban Tombs	The Theban Tombs Series (London 1915–)
Thuc.	Thucydides *History of the Peloponnesian War*
TIM I	*Old Babylonian Letters, part 1* (Texts from the Iraq Museum) Baghdad 1964
TMO	Travaux de la Maison de l'Orient
TTAED	*Türk Tarih Arkeloji ve Etnografya Dergisi*
TUAT	*Texte aus der Umwelt des Alten Testament* (O. Kaiser *et al.* Hsg) Gütersloh 1982–
UET 1	C.J. Gadd, L. Legrain, S. Smith *Royal Inscriptions* (Ur Excavation Texts 1) London 1928
UET 3	L. Legrain *Business Documents of the Third Dynasty of Ur* (Ur Excavation Texts 3) London 1947
UET 5	H.H. Figulla *Letters and documents of the Old Babylonian period* (Ur Excavation Texts 5) London 1953
UET 8	E. Sollberger *Royal Texts* part II (Ur Excavation Texts 8) London 1965
UF	*Ugarit Forschungen*
Urk. I	K. Sethe *Urkunden des Alten Reiches* (2nd edn) Leipzig 1933
Urk. III	*Urkunden des ägyptischen Altertums, Abt. III Urkunden der älteren Äthiopenkönige* (H. Schäfer ed.) Leipzig 1905
Urk. IV	*Urkunden des ägyptischen Altertums, Abt. IV: Urkunden der 18. Dynastie* (K. Sethe, W. Helck eds) Leipzig, Berlin 1906–1958
UVB	*Vorläufige Berichte über die von der Notgemeinschaft der Deutschen Wissenschaft in Uruk-Warka unternommenen Ausgrabungen*
VAB	Vorderasiatische Bibliothek
VAT	Vorderasiatische Abteilung Tontafeln, Berlin
WO	*Welt des Orients*
WVDOG	Wissenschaftliche Veröffentlichungen der Deutschen Orient Gesellschaft

WZKM	*Wiener Zeitschrift für die Kunde des Morgenlandes*
Xen.	Xenophon
YNER	Yale Near Eastern Researches
YOS I	Clay A.T. *Miscellaneous Inscriptions in the Yale Babylonian Collection* New Haven 1915
YOS X	Goetze A. *Old Babylonian Omen Texts* New Haven 1947
YOSR	Yale Oriental Series: Researches
ZA	*Zeitschrift für Assyriologie und verwandte Gebiete*
ZÄS	*Zeitschrift für Ägyptische Sprache und Altertumskunde*
ZAW	*Zeitschrift für alttestamentliche Wissenschaft*
ZDPV	*Zeitschrift des Deutschen Palästina-Vereins*
ZSS	*Zeitschrift der Savigny-Stiftung*

PREFACE

This book is intended as an introduction to ancient Near Eastern history, the main sources used for reconstructing societies and political systems, and some historical problems and scholarly debates. It is emphatically *not* a history in the conventional sense of the word, for two reasons: first, as I have emphasised at several points, it is impossible to write a narrative history of events; second, I am not a specialist in all areas and periods of the complex Near Eastern region. I have tried to treat the periods and areas usually studied in universities, which means that, inevitably, my coverage is selective. My treatment of Egypt has been kept brief deliberately, as there are plenty of good studies of Egyptian history at all levels.

A general bibliography accompanies the Introduction (referred to in references as chapter 0) and is arranged thematically, so that it can serve as an overall orientation. Each thematic section bears a letter of the alphabet (e.g. 0A, 0B etc.) and items are arranged alphabetically within it. Where appropriate (in the text and in the more detailed references to each chapter) I have referred to works in the introductory bibliography in square brackets (e.g. Bottéro *et al.* 1967a [0B]). Similarly, references provided in the chapter bibliographies are subsequently referred to thus: Powell 1978 [chapter 1]. All dates, unless indicated otherwise, are BC. I have not aimed at a single consistent system in the spellings of names, but have used the most familiar forms. When transliterating Akkadian, Hittite and Egyptian words š = 'sh'. In Akkadian, Sumerian and Hittite every 'h' is hard (i.e. like the 'ch' in Scottish 'loch'); this is not true of modern Arabic, classical Hebrew and Egyptian, so in these I have indicated hard 'h' by 'kh'. The convention for transcribing Sumerian (to differentiate it from Akkadian) is to write the word 'spaced out', e.g. l u g a l; where the reading of a word is not known, the sign-name is written in capitals (e.g. UruKAgina); where Hittite uses an Akkadian word, the convention is to transcribe it in italic capitals, e.g. *HAZANNU*. Some Old Persian words have been reconstructed from loanwords in Aramaic, Elamite and Greek; since they are not attested in Old Persian texts, the reconstructed word is indicated by an asterisk, e.g. *ganzabara-.

I completed the first draft of the book in summer 1992, and feel reasonably confident that I managed to pick up most of the important publications up to that point. It has taken another two years to revise, rewrite and correct the manuscript. In the mean time, a lot more has appeared; I have been able to incorporate some additional material, but I know that I have omitted others (e.g. D. Frayne's publication of the Old Akkadian royal inscriptions – part of the Royal Inscriptions of Mesopotamia (RIM) project – appeared early this year, but as it has not yet reached any of the libraries accessible to me in England, I have not been able to include it). The fate of a book such as this is to be out of date in several respects as soon as it is published – I hope it will, nevertheless, still prove useful to undergraduates and classical ancient historians (at whom it is aimed primarily).

Finally, I should like to express my gratitude to the people who have helped me by reading the manuscript, or individual chapters, at various stages and who have offered invaluable advice and constant support. My thanks go to Pierre Briant, Margaret Drower, David Hawkins, Alan Lloyd, Fergus Millar, Alan Millard, Richard Stoneman and Susan Sherwin-White. I must also thank David Saxon for drawing many of the figures. I am grateful to Routledge for its editorial work on a difficult text and for the help it has provided in preparing the maps.

Amélie Kuhrt
University College London
September 1994

INTRODUCTION

The region

The area embraced by the 'Near East' in this book extends from Turkey (Anatolia) and Egypt in the west through the Levant (a term that includes the territory of the modern states of Israel, Lebanon, Jordan, and Syria west of the Euphrates) to Mesopotamia (north Syria east of the Euphrates, and Iraq) into Iran. The last is separated from the low-lying Mesopotamian area by the Zagros mountains, where the land rises in a series of high ridges to dip gently to the Iranian plateau. From here routes lead north into Central Asia, east to Afghanistan, and south-east into India. A fairly recent development has been increased archaeological exploration of the Arab-Persian Gulf and the Arabian peninsula; so this region should also be included. In a very general sense, the area of the Near East corresponds with the modern term 'Middle East'. The divergence in academic and modern political usage is the result of scholars sticking, by and large, to the old European terminology, developed in the fifteenth century, in order to define areas east of Europe beginning with the Ottoman empire. The British coinage of the term 'Middle East', reflecting strategic interests in the first decades of the twentieth century, was not adopted as it had little bearing on the historical and cultural concerns of scholars.[1] The scholarly terminology is not very precise: as exploration has progressed, 'Near East' has come tacitly to embrace Iran, with its close links to ever more distant cultural networks; and it excludes Greece which, logically, is part of it. But one fact is obvious: the ancient Near East is a vast territory that dwarfs Europe in size and was, not surprisingly, infinitely varied both geographically and culturally.

This roughly defines the area. But it would be difficult, indeed false, to draw hard and fast boundaries for the 'Near East', as there were continuous and important contacts in all directions. Anatolia, the Levant and Egypt were frequently in direct contact with the Aegean, while for long periods Egypt maintained close relations with the Red Sea and the Horn of Africa, as well as some, albeit distant and indirect, links with sub-Saharan Africa via the Sudan (ancient Nubia, Adams 1975 [0Gg]). Mesopotamia, especially the southern region, had regular trading links with the Arab-Persian gulf and

1

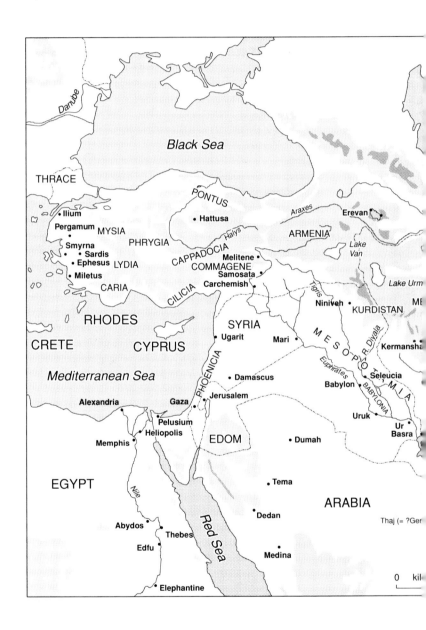

Map 1 General map of the Near East

eastern Arabian peninsula, particularly Bahrain and Oman. This was also the main route through which Mesopotamia and India maintained communications (Potts 1990 [0Gf]). From the east, Mesopotamia imported the prized, blue, semi-precious stone lapis lazuli, mined in north-east Afghanistan (Badakhshan, Herrmann 1968 [0Gk]), as well as finished soapstone vessels from Kirman in eastern Iran (Tepe Yahya, Kohl 1975 [0Gk]). Within this far eastern region there flourished highly developed urban cultures in the third and second millennia, centred on south-central Asia (former Soviet Turkmenistan and Uzbekistan), Seistan and the Indus region, which were in direct, close communication with one another – a fairly recent insight (Masson and Sarianidi 1972 [0Gh]; Kohl in Rowlands *et al.* 1987 [0E]; Tucci 1978 [0Gi]; Lamberg-Karlovsky 1972 [0Gk]).

In the Near East, different areas were in close contact with each other, sometimes in unexpected ways. For example, the Assyrians ran a long-distance trade network in central Anatolia (*c.* 1900–1830; chapter 2b), and an expatriate Hittite community lived under Egyptian rule in north Syria *c.* 1450. The typical Arab-Persian Gulf seal impression found on the *bulla* which had sealed a bale of goods at Acemhüyük, near the Great Salt Lake in Turkey, points to trade links between central Anatolia and the Gulf communities in the early second millennium (Potts in al-Khalifa and Rice 1986 [0Gf]: 389–390). All this simply serves to give some idea of how extensive and complex the interconnections in the area were. It is important to be aware that the Near East has never been a neatly definable, coherent entity, but rather represents a series of overlapping economic, political and cultural systems.

Languages and writing

Two aspects of this diversity are the number of languages (about fifteen) known to have been in use at various times, and the number of writing systems (approximately seven: *World Archaeology* 1986 [0H]; Hooker 1991 [0H]). Naturally, some languages and systems of writing dominate the historical picture: Egyptian was largely limited in use to that country, but the language and script were adopted by the Nubian rulers of dynasty XXV (chapter 12a) for their inscriptions far to the south of Egypt. It has been argued that a form of the Egyptian hieroglyphic system was adapted to render a local language of the Sinai peninsula and perhaps also the Semitic language of Byblos (cf. Diringer 1948 [0H]), although this now seems doubtful (*World Archaeology* 1986 [0H]). Akkadian, a Semitic language spoken in Mesopotamia and using a cuneiform script, was widely used in the second millennium, and had the status of a *lingua franca*: the Egyptian and Hittite kings regularly communicated with each other in Akkadian, and the Egyptians conducted some of their imperial affairs in the Levant in that language (chapters 4–7). The cuneiform script was also adapted to render the Indo-European language spoken by the Hittites in Turkey (chapter 5). Of comparable, if not even greater, importance was Aramaic, also a member of the Semitic language-group but using an alphabetic script. Aramaic spread rapidly in the first millennium and, once adopted by the Achaemenid Persians (550–330: chapter 13) as an administrative language for their huge empire, it was used from western Turkey (Daskyleion, Lycia) to Afghanistan (Ai Khanoum, Kandahar); it eventually influenced the written form of Middle Iranian (Naveh 1982 [OH]). Aramaic is one of the very few ancient Near Eastern languages (others are the Coptic form of Egyptian and modern Persian) that has continued in use until the present day within a restricted number of communities. Hebrew, of course, is another. It also belongs to the Semitic language family and is closely related to Aramaic; written Aramaic, indeed, influenced the classic Hebrew letter forms. Although biblical Hebrew is immensely important culturally in the modern world, given the profound influence exercised by the Hebrew Bible and Jewish beliefs on Christianity and Islam, it was restricted in use as a spoken language to the small kingdoms of Israel and Judah. Although Hebrew continued to be written and classical texts studied, it looks as though Aramaic was increasingly adopted by Jews for day-to-day speech from the Achaemenid period onwards.

The dominant writing systems used in the third and second millennia (Mesopotamian cuneiform and Egyptian hieroglyphs) were a complicated mix of ideograms and syllabic signs. In the course of the second millennium, there are hints that a local script developed in the Levant, which used one sign to render a single sound (chapter 6b). This much simpler system is a forerunner of the alphabet that came into general use in the course of the first millennium. But the earliest clearly alphabetic system, with links to the later Greek, and ultimately the Roman, alphabet, is not found until around the middle of the eleventh century in a Phoenician inscription at Tyre (chapter 8c(i)). How and when this Phoenician writing system was introduced into, or adopted by, the Aegean region is still a matter of considerable scholarly dispute (for general discussion, cf. Healey in Hooker 1991 [OH]; for a recent extreme stance, see M. Bernal, *Cadmean Letters*, Winona Lake, IND, 1990).

The widespread use of writing in most areas of the Near East means that considerable quantities (though by no means all) of the rich literature and mythology of the peoples of the region can be, and is continuously being, recovered. Extensive literary interconnections within and beyond the region have become evident, which have changed perceptions of the uniqueness of some classic texts. Great public excitement was generated, for example, in 1872 when George Smith identified a Mesopotamian flood-story, in many ways directly comparable to the one in the Old Testament, among the cuneiform tablets dug up at the Assyrian capital, Nineveh. A Babylonian text describing the secret birth and exposure in a reed-basket of the infant Sargon of Agade, later to become one of the most famous 'world-conquerors' (see chapter 1c), closely resembles the Moses story; Freud (*Moses and Mono-theism*, Amsterdam, 1939; trans. London, same year) used it to point out that such themes are pervasive and not peculiar to Judaism. Hittite literature, when deciphered, was found to contain stories (such as the Kumarbi myth, which is actually of Hurrian origin) that seem to have influenced Hesiod's image of successive generations of gods in the *Theogony* (Walcot, *Hesiod and the Near East*, Cardiff, 1966). Recently, one scholar has argued that the background to the emergence of Greek *historia* in the fifth century might be sought in a developed Anatolian historiographic tradition continuously traceable from the thirteenth to the end of the fifth century (Uchitel, *SCO* 10 (1989/90)). Conversely, the details of the Egyptian myth of Isis and Osiris, clearly circulating in Egypt at a very early date and intimately linked to Egyptian kingship, are only known from much later Greek accounts (Plutarch). Many Egyptian texts only allude to, and select episodes from, myths, perhaps because they were composed for use in cultic contexts (for the great Hymn to Osiris, the longest extant Egyptian version of the Osiris story, cf. Erman 1927 [OI]; Lichtheim 1973–80 [OI], vol. 2). The complex genres of Near Eastern literary texts, with their sophisticated poetic and metrical forms, are only gradually being defined, and literary analysis is still in its infancy (generally, see Röllig 1978 [OJ]; Vogelzang and Vanstiphout 1992 [OJ]).

The environment

Before considering some of the problems encountered in writing the history of the early Near East, some general points about the physical conditions should be made, as the constraints of climate and terrain have influenced patterns of life. Crucially important are the levels of rainfall in the area: in the north and west (Turkey, Levant, north Mesopotamia, north Iran) enough rain falls to grow crops without the need for regular irrigation, but in south Mesopotamia and Egypt the annual rainfall is very low, so that agriculture is totally dependent on irrigation using the great rivers (for the Iranian plateau, see Beaumont, Blake *et al.* 1976 [ON]: 88–92). But there the similarity between the two countries ends: before the construction of the great Aswan dam the Nile flooded the valley from mid-July to September, i.e. after the harvest, and receded again just at sowing time; while in south Mesopotamia the Tigris and Euphrates flood in the springtime at the very moment when the crops are ready to be harvested. A lot of energy, therefore, has to be expended on clearing and constructing canals to control the floodwaters.

The most important crops for human consumption throughout the region are wheat and barley, with vetch and clover grown as feed for large cattle and the draught animals essential for agriculture and military purposes (oxen, donkeys and, increasingly from *c.* 2000 on, horses). The maturing season for these crops, however, varies from April to July in the highland areas of Iran and Turkey to February to May in what is often called the 'Fertile Crescent', i.e. Mesopotamia, Levant, Egypt. The important thing to note in the latter case is that the harvest is over by summertime. Apart from animals kept for special purposes, sheep and goats were the main livestock. Because the areas of suitable arable land are limited, herding has always tended to be restricted to the margins of the farming zones, and the availability of grazing lands varies according to the seasonal rainfall. As a result, a lot of herding in the Near East is traditionally fully or partially transhumant, i.e. herders are forced to move their flocks from season to season to where there is water and suitable grazing. Another animal that became increasingly important is the camel, which can be bred successfully in the full desert and makes the crossing of very large tracts of arid land possible. The date of its domestication is still debated (Ripinsky, *JEA* 71 (1985), very early, versus Bulliet 1990 [ON] and *RLA* 5: 330–332), but what is clear is that its military and economic potential remained insignificant before the early first millennium.

Understanding Near Eastern history

By far the greater part of the history, literature, society and culture of the ancient Near East has to be reconstructed on the basis of excavated material, including large, albeit variable, quantities of texts (clay tablets in Mesopotamia and Hittite Anatolia; papyri in Egypt). The evidence is, therefore, incomplete and there are great gaps in our knowledge, partly because total excavation is an impossibility, partly because excavated texts are often fragmentary. There are king-lists, chronicles, annals and (auto)biographical texts (bibliography [OK]), which allow us to reconstruct the history and chronology of some regions at some periods. But such material is patchy, hence so is our knowledge of Near Eastern history. Another problem is that the majority of documents are administrative notes and legal transactions, i.e. they are embedded in a specific historical and cultural milieu which, by their very nature, they do not need to explain. An analogy would be that of attempting to write the history of Britain using worm-eaten records found in a monastery (cf. the papyri of the funerary endowment of Neferirkare *c.* 2400), a civil service department (cf. the Drehem archives relating to supplies of cattle-pens *c.* 2100), a gentleman's private study (cf. the texts from the house of the 'purifier' and administrator at Ur *c.* 1800) and perhaps a section of the British Library (cf. the enormous archives from the great temple at Boğazköy *c.* 1400–*c.* 1200), all separated by centuries from each other. The difficulties of trying to write any kind of history on this basis are obvious: one scholar (Powell 1978 [chapter 1]) has remarked, aptly, that years of painful study of such documents are needed in order to establish a single detail of social behaviour, which is encapsulated in a casual remark in Herodotus' *Histories* – if only we had a comparable work. Unfortunately, we do not. The Old Testament compensates us for the absence of such a narrative history to some degree, but we must remember that its focus is very narrow and slanted, given the theological message it was compiled to carry for one tiny Near Eastern community.

Because of the sheer complexities of studying the texts, which are scattered (as a result of excavation and random acquisition on the antiquities market) through the world's major museums (as well as private collections[2]), volumes of published texts, let alone translations and commentaries, are only very gradually, albeit continuously, being produced.[3] A good deal of primary text-publication has appeared in article-form in the many academic journals[4] and essay collections,[5] and they are the major forum for detailed discussion of material. Some valuable selections of texts in translation aimed at a wider audience do exist or are in progress ([0I]), but they represent only the tip of the iceberg in terms of the written material available. This makes it hard for the beginner to gain an impression of the range of documents; but the situation for the informed scholar is not much easier. For example, the discovery of enormous quantities of tablets (over 8,000) at Tell Mardikh (ancient Ebla) in north Syria in 1975, dating to the mid-third millennium, completely changed the prevailing view of the peoples of this region as non-literate Amorites at the time (cf. Liverani in Wiseman, 1973 [0A]): the Ebla texts show that the language was not Amorite and the inhabitants the very opposite of illiterate. One scholar (Veenhof 1985 [chapter 2]) presented an important analysis of the chronologically tricky sequence of political events in the large state of Mari *c.* 1800, which was immediately shown to be partly untenable by a simultaneously published text. Similarly, early in 1989 an important south Mesopotamian city previously known only from texts (Mashkan-Shapir) was identified on the ground (see *The Times* 21.3.1989; Stone and Zimansky, 1992 [chapter 2]). Unfortunately, the editors of the standard Assyriological reference work, now in process of compilation (*Reallexikon der Assyriologie* [0Q]), had just completed final proofs of the volume containing the article on Mashkan-Shapir, and were thus unable to include even a mention of this important discovery: until the addenda volume appears, which is unlikely to happen this century, the layperson could be quite unaware of this important discovery.

Another factor that cannot be stressed too much is the enormous time-span of traceable history in some parts of the Near East. By the time of Alexander of Macedon's conquest of the Persian empire (334–324), the peoples of Egypt and Mesopotamia could look back on a history of about 3000 years – the length of time that separates us now from the fall of Troy. They maintained traditions and stories about their earliest history, kings and sages, as well as subsequent important events, as is demonstrated by the historical works in Greek of Berossus of Babylon (cf. P. Schnabel, *Berossus und die babylonisch-hellenistische Literatur*, Leipzig, 1923; S. Burstein, *The Babyloniaca of Berossus*, Malibu, Cal., 1978) and Manetho of Sebennytos in Egypt (Loeb edn, 1940), both written in the early third century, and both only surviving in tiny fragments. Despite the fact that most general books end their surveys of Near Eastern history with either the Persian or the Macedonian conquests, there is no reason to assume that these events were felt by the inhabitants to represent a political change of greater significance than earlier invasions. Recent studies have emphasised, rightly, the elements of cultural and institutional continuity throughout the region in the Hellenistic period.[6] The only reason, then, for ending this introduction to Near Eastern history with Alexander is the structuring of the series in which it is published, which reflects the European perspective on ancient history.

An important concomitant of the immense length of time covered in this introductory book, and the problems of recovering historical sequences, is the tendency to compress events: a 100-year period can only too easily be dismissed as of no importance by a scholar accustomed to ranging over millennia. But, of course, the fact that *we* may not know much of what was going on at a particular time is only a reflection of the unevenly distributed evidence. It is frequently in the periods for which scholars have no material that the most important changes were taking place (e.g. the period 1600–1500 when the Kassites were established in Babylonia (see chapter 7a) and the Mitannian state came into being (see chapter 6a)). The tendency to compress events can give an impression of a confusing sequence of unidentifiable peoples dominating the area in a random and meaningless way. This book is intended to help to dispel the perception of Near Eastern history as an incomprehensible cycle of events occurring beyond the edge of the familiar world.

Histories of the Near East usually start around 3000: this coincides, in conventional archaeological periodisation, with the beginning of the Near Eastern 'Bronze Age' lasting to *c.* 1200, the beginning of the archaeological 'Iron Age'. The terminology derives from the so-called 'Three-Age System' of stone, bronze and iron devised by the Danish scholar Thomsen early in the last century in order to classify a collection of prehistoric finds in his museum. It reflects the increasingly advanced technology in the production of cutting tools and weapons, but its underlying concept of a linear evolution of societies is no longer generally accepted. The three-age system is of limited practical value now, but the terminology is so well established that it has continued in use, though with many modifications and refinements. It will not be employed much in this book, as most of the material allows closer chronological definitions. However, regions whose cultures can only be defined in archaeological terms were in contact with those where developments can be more closely monitored, so that terms such as 'Middle Bronze Age' and others will occasionally appear.

Although the evolutionary framework implied by the three-age system is to be rejected, it remains the case that the beginning of the 'Bronze Age' in the Near East *c.* 3000 approximately coincides with the establishment of fully urban, relatively stable, developed societies not only in Mesopotamia and Egypt, but also, during the third millennium, in the Levant, Iran, Central Asia, the Indus valley and Anatolia (Troy, Alaca Hüyük), with related developments in the Arab-Persian Gulf. The appearance of writing in some regions at this time is particularly important for the historian. The most sustained and continuous scribal developments occur in Egypt and southern Mesopotamia, although it is now clear that forms of notation on clay were already in use during the fourth millennium in an area stretching from north Syria to eastern Iran (cf. Walker in Hooker 1991 [0H]). The availability of written records, together with later documentary evidence such as king-lists, makes it possible gradually to delineate historical processes in terms of a more precise chronology of events, names of peoples and individuals, languages, the political, social and economic structures of these complex societies, and something of their specific cultural concepts: in other words it becomes increasingly possible to identify the actors and begin to discern what the characteristic traits of different regions are in a way that bald descriptions of archaeological levels and artefacts do not allow. As Mortimer Wheeler so aptly summed it up: 'the archaeologist may find the tub but altogether miss Diogenes' (quoted by Allchin and Allchin 1982: 299 [0Gj]).

Problems of evidence

Despite the almost continuous records available from southern Mesopotamia and Egypt from about 3000, not all periods are equally well represented in the evidence, or equally well understood. This problem is related both to the types of source available and the particular circumstances of their recovery. Thus, excavation in many parts of the Near East is on 'mounds' (called variously *tell, tepe, hüyük, kom*), which represent accumulated settlement debris. In southern Mesopotamia the most conspicuous mounds are often the remains of temples, which tended to be rebuilt on the same spot. Because these mounds promise rich rewards to the archaeologist, a disproportionate number of finds comes from large sanctuaries, while relatively little is known of the remainder of the cities. This is true, for example, of Woolley's exploration of Ur, about which a French scholar remarked:

> the excavator left to one side an area covered by houses which he found too 'poor' to attract his attention. In doing that he completely falsified the urban picture of Ur crowded within its walls, and denied his successors the possibility of a sociological and economic study of the population of Ur who used the dwellings.
>
> (M.T. Barrelet, *BiOr* 35 (1978): 274)

A further limiting factor is that certain areas are very difficult to excavate for a variety of reasons. One is that a site may still be inhabited, as is the case with Aleppo (north Syria), which was the centre of an important kingdom in the first half of the second millennium; Erbil (ancient Arbela), one of the major cities of the Assyrian empire; and Ecbatana (modern Hamadan), capital of the Medes. Another is that an ancient city may have been located on valuable arable land still in use: this is most striking in Egypt, whose early urban life is very poorly known, since most material comes from tombs located on the edges of the desert in agriculturally marginal land. Only very recently has a project been started to survey the territory of the old Egyptian capital, Memphis, and excavate some of the mounds dotted among the villages and fields.[7] Local topographical features can also create difficulties: the city of Babylon, for example, has yielded scarcely any material antedating the Neo-Babylonian period (626–539) because of the very high water-table at the site: water fills excavation trenches if they are dug below a certain level; so only a tiny fraction of the city in Hammurabi's time – a thousand years earlier – has been reached by the spade. Another important factor is financial constraints, which allow very few sites ever to be completely excavated. The great city of Uruk (modern Warka), which covered an area of over 9 km² by the end of the fourth millennium, has been actively investigated by German teams since before the First World War, yet exploration of the city is nowhere near total even now. It is important to remember how partial the picture of most sites is bound to be.

A somewhat different problem in reconstructing a picture of the past is that of identifying sites. For example, it was known from inscriptions that an important centre of the Elamite state was Anshan, the main identified capital of which was Susa in south-west Iran (Khuzistan) not far from southern Mesopotamia; it was, therefore, assumed that Anshan must be located somewhere a little to the east of Susa (cf. map in Hinz 1972 [chapter 7]). The identification of Tall-i Malyan in Fars as Anshan in 1972 (cf. Lambert 1972 [chapter 7]) led to a fundamental revision of perceptions of the size and power of Elam because Malyan lies about 320 km to the east, close to later Persepolis (cf. Vallat 1980 [chapter 7]). This illustrates the important implications of the precise location of places: a particular gap in this respect is the still unlocated city of Agade, centre of the first Mesopotamian empire (cf. chapter 1b), although some agreement concerning its probable siting, based on deductions made from texts, now exists (G. McEwan, *AfO* Beiheft 19: 8–15). Still the most disputed is the location of Washshukanni, capital of the important state of Mitanni, which flourished in north Syria between 1550 and 1350 (chapter 6a).

The chronological framework

The use of *circa* and 'approximately', as well as alternative chronological tables and varying dates for the reigns of kings, will recur regularly in this book. It is possible to reconstruct a relatively precise chronological outline for Egypt, using astronomical observations and king-lists, back to dynasty I. There are disagreements, however, about the exact interpretation of astronomical data, the length of some reigns, and the extent of overlap of rival rulers in periods of political disunity. As a result there are contending dating schemes: in recent years most Egyptologists have tended to prefer a chronology somewhat lower than that used in the revised edition of the *Cambridge*

Ancient History vols I and II [0B].[8] Generally, I have used these lower dates, but have also indicated alternative dates as appropriate.

A similarly more or less precise chronology is reconstructable for Mesopotamia, using the Assyrian records of annual eponyms (officials who gave their names to the years) and the Assyrian King List. On the basis of synchronisms with Babylonian rulers to the south, a chronology based on a number of different king-lists can be set up reaching back to 2400. Before that, Mesopotamian chronology is imprecise, and it is usual to stick to relative archaeological sequences: writing became important in the Uruk 3 phase (*c.* 3100–2900), and the succeeding periods are called Early Dynastic I (2900–2700), II (2700–2600), III (2600–2300). These phases obviously provide only a crude yardstick. There is considerable scholarly disagreement and variation in dating them, and in using the terminology. I have simply indicated the most widely used conventions.

The dating of events in other parts of the Near East (Anatolia, Levant, Iran) is dependent on correlations with Mesopotamian and/or Egyptian dates. A crucial area of debate among scholars is the date of Hammurabi of Babylon, on which hinges the whole chronology of the Near East in the second millennium. The so-called 'Middle Chronology', used by most standard works (e.g. *CAH*, rev. edn [0B]), places Hammurabi in 1792–1750, but there are attractive arguments in favour of lower and higher chronologies. Both high (Hammurabi = 1848–1806, cf. Huber 1982 [0O]) and low (implied date for Hammurabi = 1728–1686, cf. Gates 1981 [0O]) dates have been proposed, and continue to be debated and modified (cf. Na'aman 1984 [0O]). On the whole, I have followed the middle chronology for the sake of convenience, and indicated other datings where relevant; more discussion of the chronology is contained in each chapter. In general it is true to say that the further back one moves in time the less precise the dating and the greater the divergences between the different chronologies.[9]

The Neolithic background

The immediate forerunners of the complex states in Egypt and southern Mesopotamia can be traced back to *c.* 4500 in Egypt and *c.* 6000 in Mesopotamia, while elsewhere in the Near East settled centres are found in some areas reaching back almost to the end of the last ice age (*c.* 10,000). The period is broadly subdivided into the Neolithic (until about 5000) and Chalcolithic phases (*c.* 5000–3000). It was in these periods that a series of crucial developments took place: the development of farming techniques (now argued to have begun even before 10,000, cf. Unger-Hamilton 1985 [0P]), building skills, craft traditions such as pottery, trade networks; the establishment of village and town life (Çatal Hüyük, Jericho) and the initial exploitation of metals (copper). It is this process, obviously a long and complex one, for which Gordon Childe coined the term 'Neolithic Revolution' (cf. McNairn 1980 [OP]: 78–80), by which he sought to define the major changes in socio-economic organisation and political development which resulted from people settling in permanent communities and controlling their food supply through the domestication of animals and plants. On present evidence this development seems to have occurred earliest in the Near East, although the greater quantity of data now available emphasises how long drawn out and complicated it was, and the term 'revolution' is no longer found very useful (cf. Oates and Oates 1976 [OP]). Why these changes should have taken place is, by its very nature, bound to remain hypothetical (for a conspectus of theories, see Redman 1978; Maisels 1990 [chapter 1]); but why they should have happened at this particular time in this particular part of the world is easier to answer. The Near East was an area less drastically affected than many others by the climatic changes which took place at the end of the last glaciation, so the ecological base for subsistence was not fundamentally disrupted. The wild varieties of barley and wheat and the wild ancestors of sheep, goat, large cattle, pigs and camels were all indigenous to the region. These are the species that were successfully domesticated, and have formed the staple commodities and basic livestock in the area ever since, with only a few more recent additions such as rice, sugarcane and, among domestic animals, horses. The fact that rain-fed farming was feasible in the foothills of the high mountain ranges and the Mediterranean littoral may well have encouraged the first experiments in farming; however, the sizable (c. 4.5 ha, 11 acres) settlement at Jericho which flourished between c. 8000 and 6000 and is located in an extremely hot and arid locale near the Dead Sea suggests that some form of irrigation was already in use, aided by a perennial spring (Kenyon 1972 [OP]; Oates and Oates 1976 [OP]).

Although most of the excavated sites of this period are villages, a number of factors counsel caution in assuming that the prevailing mode of community life was that of simple and isolated villages: the size (c. 15 ha) of Çatal Hüyük in Turkey, dated to around 6000, its closely clustered houses, elaborate decoration (wall-paintings) and objects (e.g. a spectacular flint knife with carved handle) argue for a previously unsuspected sophistication in the political, socio-economic, artistic and intellectual spheres. Jericho is a similarly complex, even earlier, town site, enclosed by a massive stone wall and ditch incorporating a large circular stone tower with an internal staircase. Its socio-political organisation can only be guessed at, but can scarcely have been 'simple'. Evidence of the far-flung interrelations already existing in this period has been provided by obsidian analysis (Dixon et al. 1972 [OP]). Obsidian is a black volcanic glass, which has the properties of very high quality flint and is found in only a limited number of places; analysis of the sources of the obsidian used in the production of objects from this period thus illuminates the complexity of communication networks. The obsidian used for some objects at Jericho, for example, appears to have come from the Kayseri area of central Turkey.

All the prerequisites for growth on a large scale, then, were already present when in south Mesopotamia and Egypt the important developments took place that led eventually to the establishment there of politically sophisticated states. At present it looks as though these two regions adapted techniques perfected in various parts of the Near East and, possibly because of particular physical constraints as well as advantages (Maisels 1990 [chapter 1]), came eventually to outstrip those other areas of settlement in both size and complexity.

Notes

1 For the setting up of the strategic region of the Middle East, cf. H.V.F. Winstone *Gertrude Bell*, London 1978; for a brief discussion of the terminology, see A. Gunter, *Asian Art*, I/2 (1988): 3–5.

2 As recently as 1988, a substantial private collection of clay tablets, seals and inscriptions, few of them known to scholars, was put up for auction by Christie's of London (catalogue: *Ancient Near Eastern Texts from the Erlenmeyer Collection*, Tuesday, 13 December 1988).

3 For Hittite texts, see the series: Studien zu den Boğazköy Texten, Texte der Hethiter; for West Semitic texts, see Donner and Röllig 1973–9 [chapter 8], Gibson 1971–5 [chapter 8]; for Neo-Assyrian texts, cf. the series: State Archives of Assyria; for various categories of Mesopotamian texts, see the series: Texts from Cuneiform Sources; Royal Inscriptions of Mesopotamia; for Sumerian inscriptions, see Cooper 1986 [chapter 1]; Steible and Behrens 1982 [chapter 1]; Steible 1991 [chapter 1]; for Egyptian documents and inscriptions, see *Urkunden des ägyptischen Altertums*; for Mari, see Archives Royales de Mari; for Ugarit, Palais Royal d'Ugarit.

4 For example, fifty-eight Late Babylonian texts, part of a large private collection, were published by H.G. Stigers in *JCS* 28 (1976).

5 For example, O.R. Gurney, 'Three contracts from Babylon' in the *Festschrift* for the Russian Assyriologist, I.M. Diakonoff (1982) [OE].

6 See, for example, S.B. Downey, *Mesopotamian Temple Architecture: Alexander through the Parthians*, Princeton, 1988; A. Kuhrt and S. Sherwin-White (eds), *Hellenism in the East*, London, 1987; D.J. Thompson, *Memphis under the Ptolemies*, Princeton, 1988; S. Sherwin-White and A. Kuhrt *From Samarkhand to Sardis*, London, 1993 . Books devoted exclusively to Egyptian culture and history often include the period right up to AD 395.

7 The Survey of Memphis is carried out under the auspices of the Egypt Exploration Society; it began in 1981. For regular reports, see *JEA* 69 (1983) and subsequent volumes.

8 An extreme low chronology has been proposed recently by a group devoted to revising the absolute chronology of the Mediterranean and Western Asia: P. James *et al.*, *Centuries of Darkness*, London, 1991; similar, though slightly diverging revisions, are upheld by another group, too, and partly published in the journal *Ancient Chronology Forum*. The hub for the dating of other cultures is Egypt, so much of the work of both groups focuses on Egyptian evidence. Many scholars feel sympathetic to the critique of weaknesses in the existing chronological framework presented in these volumes, but most archaeologists and ancient historians are not at present convinced that the radical redatings proposed stand up to close examination (see the balanced review of James *et al.*, by A. Dodson in

PEQ 124 (1992): 71–72; and the detailed criticisms by a number of specialists in *Cambridge Archaeological Journal* 1/2 (1991): 227–253).

9 Detailed discussions of a whole range of specific chronological problems can be found in Aström, 1987–9 [OO]. A survey of key evidence and sites has been regularly presented in *AJA* by E. Porada, to keep scholars abreast of developments crucial for dating. A revised version of the classic compendium on chronology (Ehrich 1992 [OO]) is now available.

Part I

THE DEVELOPMENT OF STATES AND CITIES
(*c*. 3000–*c*. 1600)

1

MESOPOTAMIA IN THE
THIRD MILLENNIUM BC

1a The background (*c.* 6000–*c.* 2900)

Environment

At the time that the first written documents begin to yield some coherent sense (*c.* 3200, see Green 1980), Mesopotamia had been inhabited for well over 2000 years. At that time (*c.* 5000) the shoreline at the head of the Arab-Persian Gulf extended further south, although a rise in sea-level had shifted it northwards by at least 4000, if not earlier. A number of books show the Gulf coast extending much further north in antiquity than it does today, reflecting a view held early this century. But it was argued in the early 1950s (Lees and Falcon 1952) that this was not the case. The Tigris and Euphrates rivers deposit most of their sediment before reaching the sea, which causes problems with irrigation and can result in ancient sites becoming totally buried under silt (as in the case of the important prehistoric site of Ras al-'Amiya in northern Babylonia), but would have left the coastline virtually unchanged for the last six thousand years or so. More recently, again, doubts have been voiced about the Lees and Falcon hypothesis (Adams 1981; Sanlaville 1989), and some scholars are once more accepting that the Gulf coast lay further north in antiquity than it does today. Whatever view is adopted, it seems that Ur and Eridu were probably always the most southerly of the Mesopotamian cities, for between them and the sea stretch the marshes of Iraq, which are not capable of supporting large communities.

The marshes have always been an important factor in Mesopotamian history by providing a refuge for rebels, as they are difficult to control. They also represent an important resource, providing tall reeds for roofing and reed products such as baskets and mats, as well as food items such as fish, waterfowl and wild boar. Some of the earliest iconographic motifs on items such as cylinder seals[1] are elaborate reed huts, directly comparable to the splendid guesthouses constructed by the modern Marsh Arabs (W. Thesiger, *The Marsh Arabs*, London, 1964), and what appear to be reed bundles associated with the Sumerian goddess Inanna. Another important resource

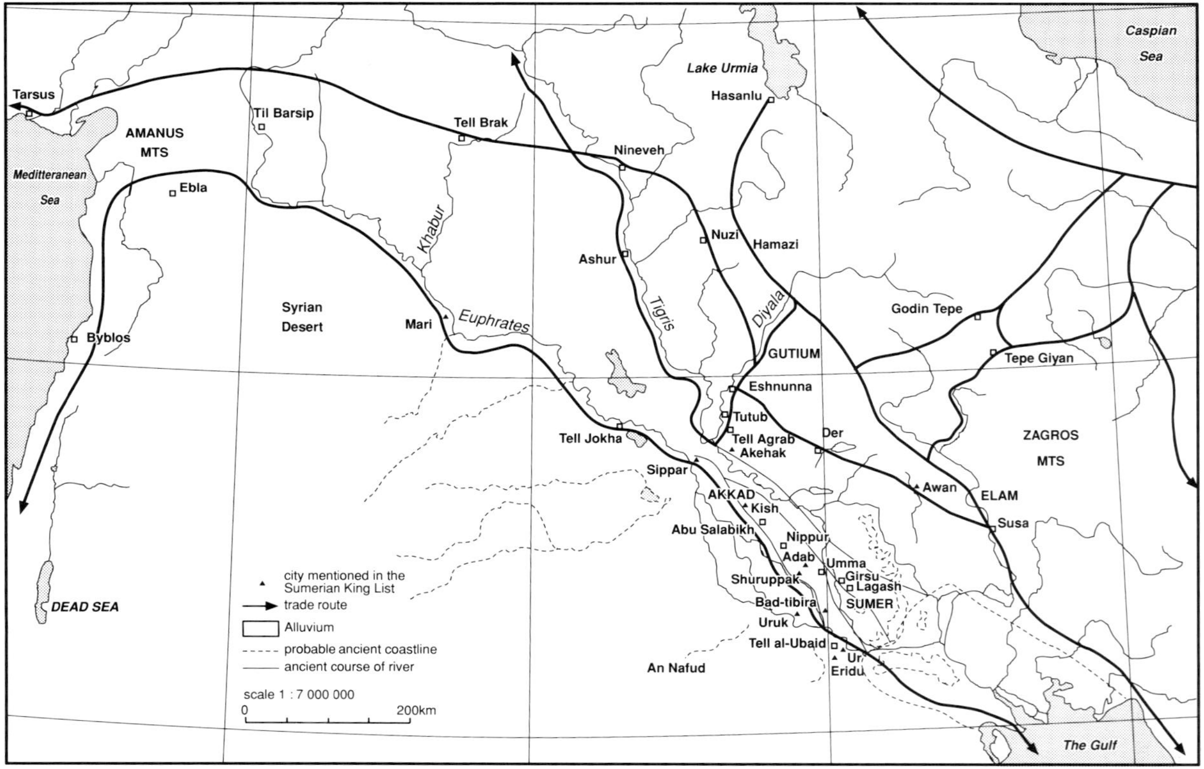

Map 2 Early Mesopotamia

that grows well in the lower reaches of the two rivers is the date-palm, whose fronds can be used for roofing and its fibrous trunk for ropes and light constructions. But it is valued above all for its fruit, which ripens in the autumn to supplement the spring crops, can be easily stored and provides excellent nutrition. For successful cropping, the trees need careful cultivation and artificial pollination. Their important role in the south Mesopotamian economy is reflected in later Assyrian texts that refer to the cutting down of date-palms as a strategic measure by invading armies. At least as important as these local resources is the lack of other important raw materials, which all had to be imported. South Mesopotamia has no sources of metals, no trees that produce suitable timber for larger constructions and only insignificant amounts of stone. The focus of much documented Mesopotamian commercial and imperial activity is the acquisition of these items.

The courses of the two rivers draining the flat south Mesopotamian plain are not always stable, and have changed from time to time. This fact, together with their spring flooding (at ripening and harvest-time) and the deposition of great quantities of silt, makes their use for irrigation into a particularly hard task (cf. *BSAG* 4 and 5). A further hazard is the rapid evaporation of surface water, causing salinisation of the soil which, it was argued in an influential paper in 1958 (Jacobsen, *Science* 128: 1251–1258; cf. Jacobsen 1982), could result in declining crop yields and was exacerbated by irrigation, thus triggering political crises. While it is certainly true that there is a problem with salt in the area, it has now been shown, fairly conclusively, that the authorities of the Mesopotamian cities always recognised the problem of soil salinity and had techniques of dealing with it (Powell 1985). The Euphrates and Tigris flow at very different rates (the Tigris is much faster flowing): the former is by far the easier to use for irrigation, and the settlement pattern reflects this. Cities and villages are generally located on canals leading east from the Euphrates, but there is very little urban settlement along the Tigris below Baghdad.

The development of settled life

The earliest 'culture' (reflecting a distinct artefactual assemblage) related to south Mesopotamia is the Samarran of the sixth millennium, identified on sites located mainly in east Iraq near the Iranian border and slightly north of Baghdad (see table 1). Rain-fed farming is not feasible here, and at two sites (Choga Mami, Tell es-Sawwan; see Oates and Oates 1976 [OP]; Helbaek 1972) evidence for artificial irrigation has been found. This is thought to have been organised on a community, or possibly family, basis, as the sites are quite small and did not expand significantly.

An analogous development was also taking place around this time further south, shown by the French excavations of a flourishing agricultural village at Tell 'Oueili (near later Larsa; Huot 1991; 1992), which represents a forerunner of the well-attested farming culture of the south, the 'Ubaid

Table 1 Early Mesopotamia: chronology of main archaeological phases

	North	*South*
6000	Hassuna	
		Samarra
5500	Halaf	'Oueili
5000		'Ubaid 1 (Eridu)
		'Ubaid 2 (Hajji Mohammed)
4500		'Ubaid 3 ("Ubaid 1')
		'Ubaid 4 ("Ubaid 2')
4000	Tepe Gawra	
		Early Uruk
3500		Late Uruk/Uruk IV
		Uruk III/Jemdet Nasr
3000		
2900		Early Dynastic period (ED I)
2700		ED II
2600		ED III

(*c.* 5000–4000). The 'Ubaid culture is named after the site near Ur where it was first identified by Woolley in the 1920s. Its cultural sequences were clarified by Oates (1960), who defined four main phases. The distinctive elements of 'Ubaid 3 have been found well beyond the confines of southern Iraq, in north Iraq, Syria, Iran, many (about forty) sites in Saudi Arabia, where it represents an intrusive element, and in the Arab-Persian Gulf. How should we interpret this evidence? Oates has suggested that it may reflect the attempt by people in south Mesopotamia to control and exploit trade routes in order to acquire the resources so signally absent there. Some support for this hypothesis may be found in the fact that a number of the northern 'Ubaid sites are distributed along the route leading to the Ergani Maden copper mines in south Turkey. But how such control might have been exercised is unknown. One other significant find should be noted: at Eridu a sequence of sanctuaries underlies the large, later sacred precinct of 2100–2000, providing a continuity of temple-building in the same spot from 'Ubaid 1 right through into the historical period. This is important evidence for cultural continuity despite the techno-logical and political changes that occurred over 3000 years.

The cultural phase succeeding the 'Ubaid, the Uruk (*c.* 4000–2900), is marked by a change in pottery: a fairly plain wheel-made ware replaced the painted 'Ubaid ones. The culture takes its name from the site of Uruk/Warka, which has provided the main, indeed almost the sole, evidence for all its stages, although the earliest sequences are still rather poorly known. The different name does not imply that the Uruk phase (during the latest periods of which the great urban centres using writing develop) represents a fundamental change in culture, reflecting a new population. The changes that mark its appearance are rather determined by new technologies and materials, such as the use of the wheel, increased metal production, and the development of stone-working for vessels. This is an important point, since many have tried to associate the Uruk phase with the arrival of the Sumerians, whose language (which cannot be linked to any of the known language families) is the earliest fully readable one identified in the Uruk tablets (Jones 1969; Oates 1960). At present there is no persuasive evidence that the Sumerians moved into the area of south Iraq at any particular point or that they were ever the sole ethnic group in the region (Oates 1960). As far as the obviously limited material for tracing answers to this question goes at present, Sumerians probably lived in this region together with other peoples (at least one group must be related to the later speakers of Semitic Akkadian) from the earliest times.

The Late Uruk period

Towards the end of the Uruk phase (Uruk 4: *c.* 3500–3200) the first written records appear, using pictograms, usually, although not exclusively (Gelb 1969), representing accounts (Green and Nissen 1987). The cuneiform that can be read as Sumerian developed from these early pictograms during the succeeding Uruk 3 period (*c.* 3200–2900; also known as 'Jemdet Nasr').[2] At the same time there appear immense ceremonial complexes at the sanctuary sites of Eanna and Anu in Uruk: they are set on large platforms, with elaborate approaches and layouts, and some are built of stone. The walls have intricate niches and the buildings contain enormous (2m diameter) columns, free-standing and attached ('engaged'). The column drums, like the walls, are decorated with mosaic patterns made up of small cones. The points of the cones are fitted into the wall and the flat, visible ends are coloured yellow, black or red. This phenomenon is not exclusive to Uruk – a similarly elaborate, painted structure has been revealed at 'Uqair to the north (near Kish), and remnants of another at Ur; and there are similar developments at Susa in western Elam. Associated with these structures is a range of objects with characteristic decoration, such as stone vases, inlaid or worked in relief, or a finely carved trough. The excavators also found some beautifully sculpted objects, such as a marble mask which originally had its eyes and brows inlaid with precious materials, and other decorations applied to the hair (Strom-menger and Hirmer 1965 [0M] pls. 30–31). It is possible that this was originally part of a statue or relief, in which case the complete figure would have been almost life-size. A significant find from this period is a basalt stele with the relief of two figures hunting lions: one wields a spear, the other shoots with a bow. As the two figures are identically dressed, bearded and coiffed, it is possible that the same person is being shown using different weapons. A similarly dressed person is depicted on a number of objects from Uruk: he appears repeatedly on the large, finely worked cylinder seals of this period, where he is the dominant figure in complicated scenes, and, most strikingly, he is almost certainly shown at the culminating point of the complex of activities depicted on the large Uruk vase (fig. 1).

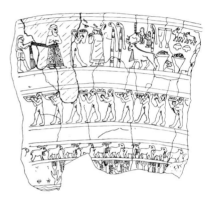

Figure 1a Uruk vase (Iraq Museum; drawing by D. Saxon, after Strommenger and Hirmer, 1965 [0M])

Figure 1b Scene on Uruk vase (drawing by D. Saxon)

What does this evidence add up to? The appearance of writing, the elaborate buildings, the use of imported materials, sophisticated art-works and the population increase reflected in the size of settlements, all signal the emergence of substantial urban communities with developed socio-economic structures. Nothing else can explain the materials, techniques and scale of buildings. But their precise origins, as well as specific character, remain a matter for speculation. The evidence points to a highly evolved political system in place: the figure dominating so many of the pictorial scenes probably stands at the head of this society, and is presumably the ruler; the fact that he appears repeatedly as the most prominent actor in ceremonial contexts suggests that the important ideological and religious activities of the state are in his care and under his control. The rare items (stone in considerable quantity, precious materials for inlays) used for constructing the large complexes and their associated equipment were imported from afar; successful commercial activities can therefore be assumed to exist, as well as a high degree of technical mastery. This in turn implies the ability to mobilise labour successfully and the existence of an expanded and stable agricultural base. The importance of the latter is mirrored by the recurrent imagery of ears of wheat alternating with cattle, found on cylinder seals, stone vessels and the Uruk vase (figs. 1 a-b). A long-current assumption is that the ceremonial complexes, or temples, were in some sense the primary socio-economic institutions, which stimulated urban development, and that the ruler figure represents a 'priest-king'. As an explanation it leaves too many questions unanswered, e.g., What kind of community built the temples and how did it develop? Where did the resources come from? How did the 'clergy' gain sufficient power for their chief to wield political power? In his analysis of early Mesopotamian burial-practices (c. 5000–2900), Forest (1983) approached the question of early Mesopotamian social and political development differently: he defined the presence of competing lineage groups, who cemented their power by constructing prominent buildings, such as temples, which gave the south Mesopotamian cities their typical form. According to Forest's view, state development took place within a society that had no temples or clergy, but was dominated by rivalry between clans. The increase in population, the development of organised religion, social differentiation, control of scarce resources, technical developments and the expansion of irrigation must all be seen as one of the effects of political rivals trying to outdo each other. Elaborate temple buildings and finely worked prestige objects were just some of the many elements used by emerging power groups to underpin their pre-eminent position.

Since the 1960s substantial evidence of the external contacts, implied by the materials used at Uruk, has been accumulating (Algaze 1993). These contacts were probably organised directly by some of the large city states that had emerged in south Mesopotamia and Elam. Sites in north Iraq and north Syria, most strikingly Habuba Kabira on the Euphrates (Strommenger 1980) and

25

perhaps Tell Brak (D. Oates in Curtis 1982 [0Gb]: 63–64), as well as in Turkey, represent some kind of trading establishments existing alongside the indigenous culture (Weiss 1985 [0Gc]: 77–82). A similar pattern of commercial settlement initiated by Susa can be observed in Iran along the routes leading north and east (Weiss and Young 1975; Carter and Stolper 1984: 126–131). Common pictographic signs, found throughout the region used on *bullae* and small clay tablets for accounting, support the view that these places were linked to one another (cf. Schmandt-Besserat, 1977; 1983; 1992 [0H]).

In the case of Iran, the texts are written in what is known as 'Proto-Elamite', which remains largely undeciphered (Carter and Stolper 1984: 5–9). But by the Uruk 3 phase in south Mesopotamia (*c.* 3200–2900) the tablets can be read as rendering the Sumerian language, as already mentioned. The system then develops fairly rapidly into a reasonably effective tool for recording speech. It is known as cuneiform (wedge-shaped) because of its characteristic later shape. Although the language of the largest number of these early texts is Sumerian, it is important to realise that some Semitic words appear in them from the earliest periods; there is a working assumption at present that, while Sumerian may have been the dominant language spoken in the area south of ancient Nippur, the Semitic language known as Akkadian predominated in the area to the north. The lack of any substantial use of Akkadian before *c.* 2300 may then reflect partly the relative dearth of text finds from more northerly sites, partly perhaps a less widespread use of writing. One problem with this view is the find of Uruk 3 period Sumerian texts from Jemdet Nasr, near Kish. Whatever the explanation, there is little to support the assumption that the speakers of Semitic Akkadian represent some kind of later population movement into the area around the middle of the third millennium (Gelb, 1977), and nothing at all in favour of a notion of a 'racial conflict' between 'Semites' (Akkadian speakers) and 'Sumerians' at any time (Jacobsen 1939a).

To sum up: by *c.* 2900 the techniques of irrigation agriculture and the exploitation of supplementary food supplies (dates, fish, wildfowl) had been successfully harnessed by power groups emerging in a number of cities to provide a fairly reliable food supply that could yield a substantial surplus. This long-drawn-out development had resulted in an articulated social structure, with a supreme ruler in each city probably controlling most resources, such as land, specialised craft production, exotic goods and precious materials obtained by trade, as well as symbolically and ideologically important community institutions such as temples. The growing complexity of this urban organisation is reflected by the development of writing to cope with the volume and diversity of activities, and by the evidence for trading establishments on routes along which materials rare in Mesopotamia were obtained. Many important details of the society remain unclear, such as: How large was the area of land directly owned by the ruler and his kin in comparison to that belonging to other members of the community? To what extent did the ruler initiate foreign mercantile activities? How far did he simply make use of existing trading networks and merchants? How did he maintain control of the city? What were the chief symbolic supports of his power? How large a role was played by other wealthy families, and how did they interact with the ruling family? How were administrative personnel recruited? Were they permanent office-holders or simply called to act in certain specific capacities as occasion required? Answers to all these crucial questions, which in turn beg many more, are at present unknown. Although this period and the later Early Dynastic III (ED III: *c.* 2600–2300) share certain iconographic and cultural elements, the many years that separate them rule out reading interpretations of the later period back into the earlier one: while a recognisable cultural framework exists, the specificities of socio-economic and political organisation could be subject to important temporal, as well as regional, variations.

1b The cities (*c.* 2900–2340)

Sources and the problems of using them

Much more varied and extensive documentation is available for the period which succeeds the late Uruk, generally called the 'Early Dynastic' (ED), 'pre-Sargonic' or 'Old Sumerian' period (table 2). The ED terminology, with its three main subdivisions (ED I, II, III), is based on an archaeological sequence first established by the Oriental Institute (Chicago) in the Diyala area, to the east of Baghdad. Despite the fact that it has been recognised for some time that this region displays several features not typical of the area further south, including a sparsity of written material, the terminology continues in use. Some modifications, however, have become necessary: an important recent one is the recognition, on the basis of the excavations at Nippur, that ED I,

Table 2 The Mesopotamian cities *c.* 2900–*c.* 2340

2900	Early Dynastic I	
2800		
2700	Early Dynastic II	
2600	Early Dynastic III	Enmebaragesi of Kish
2500	Lagash: Ur-Nanshe	Mesalim 'king of Kish'
	Akurgal	
2450	Eanatum	
	Enanatum I	
2400	Enmetena	
	Enanatum II	
	Enentarzi	
	Lugalanda	
2350	Uruinimgina	
	(= UruKAgina)	
	Lugalzagesi of Umma and Uruk	

which had been grudgingly assigned a life of about one hundred years by the Diyala team, and considered to be scarcely definable (Strommenger 1960; Hansen 1963), was quite a long and important phase of perhaps 200 years' duration (2900–2700) underrepresented in the Diyala region. The evidence has not as yet been published, but the basic results are being incorporated in studies, and are profoundly affecting the image of this period (cf. Winter, *JCS* 36 (1984)).

There is a wealth of material available from a range of urban centres in the form of building remains, large carved plaques, charming stone figures often depicted in attitudes of worship, cylinder seals, pottery, inscriptions on stone and documents on clay. Most striking must surely be the rich remains unearthed in tombs at Ur (Woolley 1934) dating to ED III (*c.* 2600–2340), which comprised quantities of elaborately worked objects in such precious materials as gold, silver and lapis lazuli. There is also evidence of the practice of retainer burial there at this time. But understanding the historical significance of all these finds is difficult (Moorey 1977; Pollock 1991).

The written material is unevenly distributed through the period, consisting as it does of groups of tablets from various sites and different periods. The main sites that have produced collections are Ur in the ED II period (*c.* 2700–2600); Shuruppak (modern Fara) and Abu Salabikh (ancient name not known) in the ED IIIA period (*c.* 2600–2500, see Pomponio 1983; Martin 1988; Biggs 1974); and Girsu (modern Tello: one of the centres of the state of Lagash), whose rich archives date to the very end of the period (2430–2340). Outside the region, the large Ebla archives, dating to *c.* 2450–2350, now provide valuable information on one of the cities developing to the north-west of the traditional 'cradle of civilisation' in south Iraq.[3] Further smaller groups of texts are known from other sites, but their dating is more problematic (see Alberti and Pomponio 1986: 11, for a complete list). The texts illustrate the administration of large estates (Girsu), the military and labour organisation of the palace (Shuruppak; Ur), and literary and scribal activities (Shuruppak; Abu Salabikh).

One problem that has haunted Mesopotamian history for far too long must be laid to rest. The first major (and still very valuable) work on the Girsu archives was done by the pioneer Sumerologist, Deimel (1931). He assumed that the repeated references to the property and estates of the goddess Baba (or Bau) appearing in the texts indicated that they were part of a temple archive. The picture of the society that he reconstructed, on this basis, was one in which the temples owned all land throughout the entire state of Lagash (to which Girsu belonged). All inhabitants were effectively temple-servants of various ranks. The ruler was merely the deputy of the main patron deity of Lagash, Ningirsu, while the ruler's wife occupied a similar position *vis-à-vis* Ningirsu's divine consort, Baba (Bau). Private property, particularly private land, did not exist at all. This reconstruction was dubbed the 'theocratic temple-state'. It has been extremely influential, especially among theorists of state-formation (e.g. Wittfogel, *Oriental Despotism*, New Haven, Conn., 1957), and was accepted with only few modifications by Assyriologists for a long time (Adams in Kraeling and Adams 1960 [OE]; Falkenstein 1954). Already in 1959 this reconstruction was being challenged by the Soviet scholar Diakonoff (1959/1974), who demonstrated that the area covered by the state of Lagash was far larger than Deimel had argued, and that the territory not surfacing in this 'temple archive' was independently owned by family groups. Much more recently, Sumerologists analysing the crucial terminology of the documents have reached yet more radical conclusions and have argued, persuasively, that the estates of the various gods were in fact the property of the city-ruler and his family, and not temple estates at all (Foster 1981; Pomponio 1984; Tunca 1986; van de Mierop 1989).

Two quite different kinds of textual material have been thought to be useful for reconstructing something of the historical outline of the Early Dynastic period. First, and most important, is the 'Sumerian King List', compiled, in its present form, not before the late nineteenth century, but purporting to list the rulers of different cities from the beginning of time. The pattern of presentation is to list a sequence of kings ruling in one city, followed by a group from another one. The lengths of reign of the earliest kings are immense, and clearly belong to purely legendary time, an assumption confirmed by the fact that they are presented as ruling 'before the flood'. After the flood, the list continues and kings eventually are credited with seemingly realistic reigns. The kings are represented as rulers of a particular city which holds some kind of hegemony over the rest; this they have taken over from another city and so initiated a new period of rule (Sum. b a l a), in which they and their descendants wield power until they in turn lose it to yet another dynasty. Thus:

> After the flood had swept thereover, when kingship was lowered from heaven the kingship was in Kish.
> In Kish, Ga . . . ur(?) became king and reigned 1,200 years.
> (This is followed by 20 kings of Kish with different long reigns; then:)
> Enmebaragesi, the one who carried away as spoil the weapons of the land of Elam, became king and reigned 900 years;
> Aka, son of Enmebaragesi, reigned 625 years.
> 23 kings reigned its 24,510 years, 3 months and 3½ days. Kish was smitten with weapons; its kingship was carried to Eanna (Uruk).
> In Uruk, Mes-kiag-gasher, son of Utu (sun-god), became e n ('lord') and king and reigned 324 years. Mes-kiag-gasher went into the sea and came out from it to the mountains.
> Enmerkar, son of Mes-kiag-gasher, king of Uruk, the one who built Uruk, became king and reigned 420 years;
> divine Lugalbanda, a shepherd, reigned 1,200 years;
> divine Dumuzi, a fisherman(?) – his city (was) Ku'a(ra) – reigned 100 years;

divine Gilgamesh – his father was a *lillû*-demon – e n of Kullab (Uruk), reigned 126 years;
Urnungal, son of divine Gilgamesh, reigned 30 years;
Utu-kalamma, son of Urnungal reigned 15 years;
Laba . . . ir reigned 9 years;
En-nun-dara-Anna reigned 8 years;
MES(?)-HE, a smith, reigned 36 years;
Melam-Anna reigned 6 years;
Lugal-ki-tun(?) reigned 36 years.
12 kings reigned its 2,310 years. Uruk was smitten with weapons; its kingship was carried to Ur.
In Ur, Mes-Anne-pada became king and reigned 80 years (etc.)
(Jacobsen 1939b: 76–93, i, 40–iii, 40)

For the dynasties of Agade and Ur III (see chapter 1c and 1d), i.e. after the end of ED III, the king-list seems fairly reliable as far as royal names and lengths of time ruled are concerned. Is the list, therefore, a guide to historical reality at any point in the Early Dynastic period too? An enormous amount of energy and effort was invested by Jacobsen (1939b) in demonstrating how it might be turned into a historically usable tool for the period, at least from ED II onwards. He related the royal names appearing in ED inscriptions to names in the king-list, thus setting up several synchronisms, and argued for a series of overlapping dynasties that were presented later as sequential periods of rule. His approach is perhaps best clarified by an example: two short inscriptions of (En)-me-barage-si of Kish, the father of Aka, exist; a later short epic poem recounts a battle between Aka of Kish and Gilgamesh of Uruk, in which Gilgamesh was victorious; it is, therefore, arguable that Aka was effectively the last king of the Kish dynasty to wield hegemony in south Mesopotamia (see quotation, p. 29), and was succeeded by Gilgamesh of Uruk. Gilgamesh's predecessors were simply included in the list because the compiler had all that material to hand; they would themselves have been only local kings. Working back from the chronologically more secure Agade dynasty could, then, be a way of using the list to reconstruct a skeleton outline of rulers.

Several factors undermine the validity of such a procedure. First, the material included is extraordinarily disparate, and seems frequently to have been culled from stories current, presumably, at the time of compilation, rather than from sober sources such as local date-lists. Second, the number of rulers that appear in inscribed material, as well as in the list, is only six so far – a minuscule proportion of the many listed. This makes one wonder how many were real kings and how many were mythical characters associated with a particular city. Third, it is clear that a calendrical or strictly historical interest was not the aim of the work – rather its purpose was to present an image of continuity of rule over the south Mesopotamian region by only one city at any one time, in a sort of god-given rotation, from time immemorial. It is thus much more likely that the particular ideology that informed this compilation reflects the need for legitimation of the rulers under whom it was carried out rather than any concern with the strict accuracy of a, by then, very remote past. In the words of one scholar: 'Since the king-list is not a reflection of real events but is, rather, a depiction of an *idea* of reality, the text should forever be banished from reconstructions of early Mesopotamian history' (Michalowski 1983: 243).

Other material that has been pressed into service, in the hope that it might illuminate events, structures and institutions of the Early Dynastic period, is the later epics centring on early rulers of Uruk, such as Gilgamesh. The cycle of stories about these kings makes exciting reading: Enmerkar's dispute with the ruler of Aratta in Iran (Cohen 1973) has been thought to reflect a pattern of trade in the ED II period (following Jacobsen 1957); the story of conflict between Gilgamesh and Aka of Kish, in which the headstrong Gilgamesh consults on his course of action, first with a council of elders who advise caution, and then a council of young warriors who want to rush into battle, has been thought to provide evidence for civic assemblies and a royal obligation to deliberate with them before taking action (Jacobsen 1943; Römer 1980). But to read such late literary texts in the hope of obtaining concrete evidence is bound to mislead. While there can be no doubt that the Mesopotamian cities maintained far-flung trading relations in order to acquire exotic goods, their specific mode of organisation is not illuminated by the Enmerkar story, which focuses more on the motif of demonstrating the moral superiority of Enmerkar, king of Uruk, than anything else. Uruk traded grain for precious stones including lapis lazuli – these are recurring goods in trade inventories that do not clarify a particular historical exchange-system. Similarly, it is clear from other documents that councils of elders formed one of the organs of government in Mesopotamian cities, and can be found throughout most of their history in some form. But the device of paralleling this with a council of fighting men, whose advice contradicts that of the elders, is a literary one (cf. Rehoboam: 1 *Kings* 12. 6–11) serving to enhance Gilgamesh's proposed bolder course (Berlin 1983; Katz 1987). It does not illuminate institutional features peculiar to early Mesopotamian society.

Political and social organisation

What kind of picture of this long, important and formative period can be built up despite all these uncertainties? First, there is the pattern of urban settlements, which increase in density and size from the late Uruk into the ED III period, so that by 2500 it looks as though 80 per cent of the population resided in substantial cities of more than 40 ha (100 acres). A good example is ancient Shuruppak (modern Fara), excavated early this century, but only analysed recently in a careful study (Martin 1988). There is no sign here of settlement earlier than *c.* 3000 (Uruk 3 = Jemdet Nasr). By the end of ED I the settlement covers 70 ha, and steadily increases in size to reach a maximum of 100 ha in the ED IIIA phase, enclosed by a city wall and with an estimated population of 15,000 to 30,000. Sealings and tablets indicate that it had a well-organised military and agricultural organisation able to supply the fighting, food and industrial needs of a complex state. The city was ruled by a king (although royal names are not known), and a number of officials are mentioned whose functions are uncertain; there is no evidence for a major temple-complex, although that probably reflects the method of excavation rather than a real absence. Finds of tablets in a large house indicate that here was a substantial household controlling about 120 ha of arable land, divided for cultivation among twenty-six individuals. The dating of texts is not by the king's name, but by 'periods' (Sum. b a l a), the meaning of which is unclear.

Another group of tablets from Shuruppak contain literary texts and scribal exercises, illustrating the high accomplishments of a society that was not merely literate but valued its poetic traditions and set store by learning through reading and writing. This image is corroborated by the astonishing find of literary tablets at Abu Salabikh dating to around the same period (2600–2500), some of which duplicate the Shuruppak material. The Abu Salabikh finds include a very early version of a temple-hymn, also known from later texts (Biggs 1974; Sjöberg and Bergman 1969), and a collection of proverbs (Alster 1974), of which again later versions are known. An extract from them will serve to give the reader a flavour of this popular genre of early literature:

> The intelligent one, who knew the (proper) words, and was living in
>   Sumer,
> Shuruppak, the . . .,
> the intelligent one, who knew the (proper) words, and who was living
>   in Sumer,
> Shuruppak gave instructions to his son:
> 'My son, let me give you instructions,
> May you pay attention to them!
> (next line fragmentary)
> Do not buy a prostitute, it is horrible (?),
> Do not make a well in a field, the water will do damage to you (?)
> Do not give evidence against(?) a man, the city will . . .
> Do not guarantee (for someone), that man will have a hold on you' (etc.)
>   (Alster 1974: 11ff.)

It is interesting that, while all the literary compositions are in Sumerian, about half the personal names of the Abu Salabikh scribes who wrote the texts are Semitic.

Kings and cities

The many documents from Girsu (modern Tello) show that in the state some land was owned by the king, some assigned to temples and some in private ownership. But the precise interrelationship of the three sections of the community still requires clarification, as does the precise economic status of those people who have no land. A key to beginning to understand the socio-political structure is to see the ruler as protector of the city in the name of the city's tutelary deity, for whom he therefore cared by building and maintaining temples. His privileged relationship with the deity ensured divine help, blessing and plenty for the city in return for the ruler's constant attention to his (or her) needs. This is exemplified by part of an inscription from the city-state of Lagash, dating from c. 2450, where the king is described as created and nurtured by the gods:

> Ningirsu (patron-god of Lagash) implanted the semen for Eanatum (king of Lagash) in the womb [. . .] rejoiced over Eanatum. Inanna (a goddess) accompanied him, named him Eana-Inanna-Ibgalakakatum (his full name: 'worthy in the (temple) Eana of Inanna of Ibgal'), and set him on the special lap of Ninhursag (a mother goddess). Ninhursag [offered him] her special breast. Ningirsu rejoiced over Eanatum, semen implanted in the womb by Ningirsu. Ningirsu laid his span upon him, for (a length of) five forearms he set his forearm upon him: (he measured) five forearms (cubits), one span! Ningirsu, with great joy, [gave him] the kin[gship of Lagash].
> (E. Sollberger, *Corpus des inscriptions 'royales' présargoniques* Ean. 1: iv–v; Sollberger and Kupper 1971: 1C5acf.; Cooper 1983: 45)

Most inhabitants of the city, including the ruler himself, played a role in relation to divine cult, whether as cult-singer, weaver, baker, shepherd or small farmer whose basic products were used for offerings. Performing the various necessary functions for the deity and his/her home carried with it emoluments in the form of either landholdings or rations, so that any one task provided an income. Most (male) citizens were probably obliged to perform some of these duties and they were almost certainly a source of social status. It seems unlikely that temple staff had only cultic duties and were distinct from the citizen-body; rather, such religious service was only one aspect of a life that might otherwise be engaged in commerce, textile production or farming for personal survival and gain. It is crucial to remember that the king was responsible for seeing that everything connected with divine worship was satisfactorily performed: it was he alone who could increase or diminish a temple's estates, appoint persons to prestigious cultic office, embellish a temple with exotic materials, and organise the manpower to construct sacred buildings. This is illustrated in part by an inscription, again from the state of Lagash (c. 2500):

Ur-nanshe, king of Lagash, son of Gunidu, 'son' of (the town) Gursar, built the temple of Nanshe (goddess), fashioned (the statue of) Nanshe, dug the canal . . ., for Nanshe he made water fill (the canal) . . ., made (a statue of) Esir.
He chose Ur-nimin by means of liver-omens (as) husband (i.e. high cultic official) of Nanshe.
He built the A-edin ('house of the desert'), built the Nin-gar, built the E-gidri (all these are shrines), built the walls of Lagash, fashioned (the statue of) Lugal-uru.
The boats of Dilmun (region of Bahrain), from (this distant) land brought the wood (for him).

(Steible and Behrens 1982: Urn. 24; Cooper 1986 La 1.17)

Here we plainly see the king building temples, making divine statues, appointing a high-ranking cult-official, undertaking irrigation works, fortifying his kingdom and importing timber via the Gulf. Another Ur-nanshe text records the feasting organised by the king to mark the completion of a temple: 'When he built the temple of Ningirsu, he had 70 gur (30,800 kilos) of barley distributed for consumption in the temple' (Cooper 1986: La 1.20). These pious works, then, were simply part of a whole range of royal activities affecting all aspects of city life. It is essential to remember at all times that the cultic staff did not have better access to divine knowledge than the king. So they were not in a position to claim a god-given authority greater than his. There were no separate religious and secular spheres with competing interests. All aspects of life were intertwined, and at the head of the political-religious order stood the king himself, conceived, nourished and physically fashioned by the gods.

One aspect of city rule in this period that continues to present difficulties is the variety of terms used to designate the head of the state, which may indicate that the origin of the office differed from place to place. The two most common titles used are 'l u g a l' = literally 'big man', and 'e n s i' = 'governor'; a third term is used at Uruk: 'e n', which is usually translated 'lord', but in some contexts designates a temple function. We must, however, exercise due caution before concluding that this indicates that the office of ruler at Uruk originated within the temple. In fact, the few contemporary inscriptions from Uruk indicate that the term 'l u g a l' was used, with 'e n' appearing only in the abstract noun 'lordship'. The only context in which rulers of Uruk are regularly called 'e n' is in the later epic stories about them, and they do not constitute admissible evidence for reconstructing historical realities.

Royal courts

The definition of the royal family, court and administrative structure is problematic. Some of the artefacts of the ED III period illustrate aspects of this, such as the 'standard of Ur' – a wooden object (now in the British Museum) of uncertain function inlaid with elaborate scenes in shell and lapis lazuli (Strommenger and Hirmer 1965 [OM] pl. 72). One side depicts people bringing what may be booty from the war shown on the reverse: teams of donkeys, well-filled sacks, sheep and oxen are shown being driven, as well as a man carrying fish in either hand. In the top register (see fig. 2), at the climax of the scene, a banquet is taking place, with a figure who is probably the king, seated on a carved stool. He is slightly taller than the rest, grasping a cup and facing a group of his courtiers, similarly seated and holding cups in their raised hands. The feasting group is attended by servants and entertained by a singer accompanied by a lyre-player. Full-scale examples of the bull-headed lyre played by the musician were found at Ur, made of both silver and gold with inlaid decoration. The bulls have hair, beard and eyes of lapis lazuli. From the size of the sounding-box and from reconstructed stringing, it is evident that the sound produced by the lyre had the range and tone of a cello. Court life in the Mesopotamian cities obviously included refined and sophisticated pleasures.

The Ur standard is the most elaborate depiction of its type, but the so-called 'votive plaques' (possibly used as elaborate locking devices: Hansen, 1963) show analogous scenes. An inscribed plaque of Ur-nanshe of Lagash is particularly interesting (Strommenger and Hirmer, 1965 [OM] pl. 73; Steible and Behrens 1982: Urn. 20; Cooper 1986: La 1.20). The text, commemorating

Figure 2 Banquet scene from the Ur standard (British Museum; drawing by D. Saxon)

temple building and timber transport, is rather brief, but the sculptured scenes are revealing. In the upper one Ur-nanshe, depicted as very tall and carrying the royal basket of building bricks on his head, faces a row of people who are identified by labels as members of his family: his wife (or daughter?), ÁB-da, and four sons, including the heir to the throne, Akurgal; behind him stands his cup-bearer, Anita. In the lower one Ur-nanshe is seated, holding a cup; another cup-bearer is behind him, and facing him stands a functionary entitled 'head snake-charmer', who is followed by three more royal sons. The 'snake-charmer' appears in lists of musicians, and this is perhaps his titular court function; why this should be so is puzzling. Cup-bearers, as royal advisers and confidantes, are common in many societies and periods, although it is not obvious why two appear on the Ur-nanshe plaque. The naming and depicting of Urnanshe's wife (probably) and children is striking. It is clear from other, later material from Lagash that the ruler's wife controlled large estates, organised their exploitation, engaged in commercial activities and corresponded personally with the spouses of rulers in other cities (Lambert 1953; Asher-Grève 1985; van de Mierop 1989); the king's children also had specific estates set aside for them. So the king, his wife and the royal children were the chief landowners of the state, which allowed them to reward or recruit loyal supporters by grants of land (Charvát 1978). Those royal sons who did not become king in their turn were probably appointed to lucrative high-status offices in the city, among which were posts in the temple (Cooper 1983b: 10; 30–33). There is thus every reason to assume that a majority of the most important functions of state were filled by members of the royal family and their relatives.

War

An undoubtedly crucial factor in the pre-eminent status of the king was his prominent military role. The best-known inter-city conflict is that between Umma and Lagash, which provides the fullest information, both textually and pictorially, on how war was conducted. The fact that war was probably organised in similar fashion in other cities is supported by artefacts from other sites, especially Ur (the 'war side' of the Ur standard) and Mari, away to the north-west. But nothing compares to the detailed evidence (a combination of narrative and pictorial represention, cf. fig. 3) of the 'Vulture stele' of Eanatum of Lagash (*c.* 2450).[4] The dispute in this instance was caused by Umma's infringement of an old-established boundary agreement. Eanatum's first move, having established the *casus belli*, was to point this out to Ningirsu (city-god of Lagash) and ask him to strike the enemy down. In response, Ningirsu came to him in a dream, promising victory in the battle to come. This is followed by the battle itself, led by the king in person, who is shown in his chariot leading the army, and again on foot, leading into battle the dense phalanx of footsoldiers, who are trampling the fallen enemy under foot. The victory over Umma is symbolised by the vultures at the top of the stele carrying off the heads of the dead (Winter 1985), and expressed in the text by a description of Eanatum's construction of twenty burial mounds for the fallen enemy. The longest part of the text is reserved for the oaths that the defeated king of Umma was obliged to swear on the battle-nets of the major gods. These nets are not shown in use by the king or his army and were perhaps a specifically divine weapon (Cassin 1987 [OE]: 229); one is depicted on the obverse of the stele, held by the god Ningirsu, who smites the enemy caught in his net. The soldiers on the stele, wearing distinctive pointed (leather?) helmets and carrying spears, present an impregnable wall with their gigantic, overlapping rectangular shields.

At Ur and Mari the soldiers' equipment is similar, except that, after the

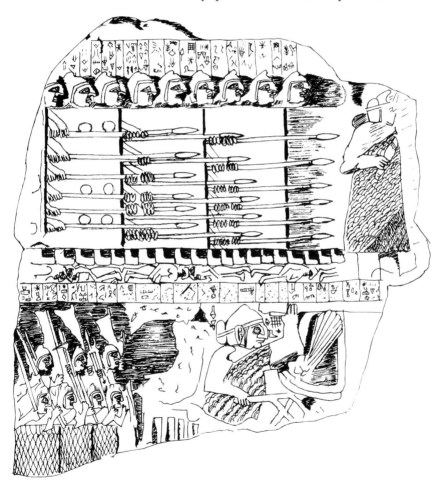

Figure 3 Vulture stele from Girsu (Louvre; drawing by D. Saxon)

battle, the soldiers are shown wearing long cloaks over their skirts and sometimes carrying battle-axes. The taking of prisoners is not referred to by Eanatum, although it is virtually certain that this happened regularly (Gelb 1965), and indeed the Ur standard appears to show people being bound and prodded, although the scene is not very clear. Better evidence comes from Mari, where a man is shown with his arms painfully pinned behind his back and tied at the elbows in a manner that was standard for captives in succeeding periods (Strommenger and Hirmer 1965 [OM]: pl. 75). The donkey-drawn chariots, carrying a driver and spearman, had four solid wheels and leather sides (cf. fig. 4). They represent a sophisticated technical achievement, and illustrate the level of wealth at the king's disposal. The donkeys, dependent on supplementary feeding and requiring special training, represent another major resource concentrated in the hands of the king. It is interesting here to note that many of the Shuruppak texts relate to the activities of what may have been a palace department specialising in the care of donkeys. The composite bow was very important, extremely accurate and powerful in delivering arrows: Eanatum is described as being struck in the eye by an arrow in the battle with Umma; the royal figure on the earlier Uruk stele (see p. 23) uses one to shoot a lion, and in succeeding periods it became a regular

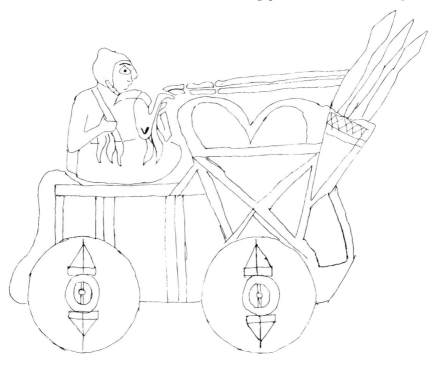

Figure 4 Sumerian war-chariot (from Ur standard British Museum; drawing by D. Saxon)

attribute of kings triumphant (e.g. Naram-Sin stele, fig. 5). The complexity of its construction (length of time, special materials) has been carefully analysed recently (Miller *et al.*, *World Archaeology* 18 (1986); Haas, *Nikephoros* 2 (1989)), and this helps us to grasp what careful planning and immense resources must have gone into the preparations for war.

Society

A range of different social and professional groupings appears in texts, and there is debate as to how precisely they should be understood. Some terms clearly refer to gangs of labourers (g u r u š), but beyond this general description it is quite uncertain what their status was: Was it legally defined and different from that of other people (Gelb 1965)? Or did it simply describe all those who made up a particular workforce which might have been conscripted for a limited period? This is an insoluble problem at present, and it is by no means clear that such people were dependent serfs, as is often assumed. Other terms appear in a famous document from Tello (ancient Girsu), which is very hard to understand: the 'Uruinimgina reforms',[5] dating from the very end of ED III. The text describes a situation in the state of Lagash 'in former times', when things were bad, and then the changes introduced by Uruinimgina intended to put things right. It is the first example of what was to become a regular activity of the king in his role as the righter of social wrongs and defender of the weak:

> Uruinimgina solemnly promised Ningirsu that he would never subject the waif and the widow to the powerful.
> (Steible and Behrens 1982: Ukg. 1, 4–5, 6; Cooper 1986: 9.1–3)

In the reform text, two less privileged individuals are defined: one is the š u b – l u g a l, holder of a land-parcel, who could clearly be put under pressure by people of superior status such as the 'foreman' (u g u l á) and 'aristocrat' (l ú – g u – l a – b i); he was protected from physical violence at the hands of these superiors by the reforms. The š u b – l u g a l in turn was in a more powerful position than the i g i n u d u (literally 'blind man'), whose labour the š u b – l u g a l could use, for example, for irrigation. These two social groups are in turn differentiated from the 'poor man' and debtors – a situation that could be the result of straight failure to discharge outstanding obligations, or punishment for theft and murder. The reform text also regulated payments for a number of services, such as divination, burial and mourning ceremonies; and certain taxes, such as for divorce and betrothal (or marriage), were abolished. The pre-eminent position of men over women was guaranteed by the king, who ordered that a woman guilty of speaking disrespectfully to a man shall have her mouth crushed with a baked brick; the brick was to be displayed at the city-gate. An interesting, but particularly tricky, passage runs as follows:

Women in former times each had two men, but women of today have been made to give up that crime.

(Steible and Behrens 1982: Ukg. 6; Cooper 1986: La 9.3)

Suggested interpretations have ranged from the practice of a woman marrying two brothers (Edzard, *Genava* 8: 256f.) to persuasive arguments for seeing the text as related to the practice of *ius primae noctis* (Glassner in Lesko 1989 [OE]), which was abolished by the reform.

Uruinimgina's text does not mention slaves. They certainly existed, but possibly not in economically significant numbers at this time. Much more evidence comes from the period *c.* 300 years later (i.e. the Third Dynasty of Ur, see chapter 1d), when two-fifths of slaves figuring in sales are local people (e.g. parents selling children). Where they came from in the Early Dynastic period is not certain. Were they prisoners-of-war, or foundlings?

Slaves formed one of the many items whose purchase was recorded in the sale documents of the period (Edzard 1968). But not all sales were recorded in written form. The sale document appears in this, as in later periods, to have been used to support the testimony of witnesses, but did not constitute evidence of sale by itself (Steinkeller 1989). An interesting feature of the procedure in sales of *immobilia* (orchards, houses, land), well attested for this period, was the practice of solemnising the transaction by presenting gifts and additional payments, over and above the agreed purchase price, to the seller, his kinsmen, the witnesses and officials in attendance. This was followed by the buyer giving a feast in his home for all the participants in the transaction, during which they ate, drank and anointed themselves with oil (Steinkeller 1989: 142–144; Glassner 1985: 39–48; Cassin 1987 [OE]; Foxvog 1980). The sale of landed property, in which all family members usually have an interest, is a major decision not lightly undertaken, especially in societies where land is the main resource. In early Mesopotamia, this elaborate purchase ceremony served to stress the importance of the act. Further, ethnographic analogies suggest that it may also have been intended to create a symbolic bond between the purchaser and the seller and his relatives. The practice was not limited to this period or area, but is also attested later in regions to the north and west (*c.* 1800: Eshnunna, Mari; *c.* 1350–1200: Emar).

Inter-state relations

How did the complex urban societies of the ED period interact with each other and the surrounding world? Some pieces of suggestive evidence exist, none particularly easy to understand. From the ED I period come a number of seal-impressions bearing names of cities, which, it has been suggested, reflect the institutionalisation of inter-city trading relations, although precisely how it worked is unknown (Nissen 1988). From the later ED III period comes evidence for gifts exchanged between the wife of the ruler of Lagash and the wife of the ruler of Adab to the north-east, as well as other evidence for exchanges of imported goods coming ultimately from Iran and the Gulf. Beyond the immediate confines of southern Mesopotamia, evidence for contacts is impressive, and recent work, in particular in Syria, has expanded the picture enormously. The Mari evidence for military equipment virtually identical to that in southern Mesopotamia has already been mentioned; and the stylistic parallels in statuary from there and the site of Ashur with the south Mesopotamian material are striking. A hoard of finely worked, precious items was found in a jar at Mari: beautifully carved figurines in stone, gold and lapis lazuli beads. Some of them are certainly of south Mesopotamian manufacture, such as a long lapis lazuli bead with an inscription of Mesanepada, king of Ur. It is not necessary to interpret the entire treasure as a royal gift from that city, however, since the evidence for similar craft and artistic traditions at Mari is well documented (Kohlmeyer in Weiss 1985 [0Gc]: 133).

It is clear that by 2500 a number of sites in north Mesopotamia and Syria had expanded very rapidly. In addition to Ashur and Mari, there are the sites of Tell Taya (north of Ashur), Tell Leilan (on the Khabur river), Tell Khuera (on the western fringe of the Khabur plain), and Ebla (modern Tell Mardikh, south-west of Aleppo). Some of the cities that developed here are over 100 ha (250 acres) in size, easily rivalling, even outstripping in some cases, the south Mesopotamian centres. Why this development occurred is unclear, but the discovery of well over 8,000 tablets at Ebla has shown that Ebla was in close contact with Mari (which seems to have wielded extensive political power (Michalowski 1985)), with Kish and perhaps other cities in the Mesopotamian south. From this area Ebla adapted the writing system for recording its own Semitic language; how many other cities did so is unknown at present (cf. note 3). This vast material is only now being published, but some indication of the kind of city Ebla was has already emerged. At the head of the city was a *malikum* (prince/king) and a body of elders – references to neighbouring states indicate that they were similarly governed. It commanded immense resources in the form of agricultural products (wool and textiles, olive oil, wine, barley, flax for linen) and extensive commercial wealth: gold and silver appear to have been available in large quantities and were used as a means of exchange not only by the palace; further, Ebla had access to valuable tin-bronze (Muhly 1983) because it controlled the routes from Anatolia. The kingdom was not enormous, but it included Carchemish on the Euphrates and the Antioch plain to the north, and maintained active contacts not only with Mari but also with places throughout north Mesopotamia as far as the Tigris.

In south Mesopotamia, the cities seem to have been linked to each other in yet another way, which is not well understood. According to some of the ED III inscriptions, certain rulers from a variety of cities occasionally included in their titulary the element 'king of Kish'. The title appears to imply that the holder has some sort of ill-defined hegemony over other political centres. Thus, Mesanepada, king of Ur, also calls himself 'king of Kish'. But the best evidence for the manner in which the institution may have functioned relates to King Mesalim, whose own city is not known (Der?) and who held the title *c.* 2600. First, a bowl from Adab commemorates the performance of a temple-ritual there by 'Mesalim, king of Kish . . . while Nin-kisal-si was ruler of Adab' (Sollberger and Kupper 1971: IA3b); second, an inscribed stone mace records that 'Mesalim, king of Kish, builder of the temple of Ningirsu, brought (this mace) for Ningirsu, (while) Lugal-sha-engur (was) ruler of Lagash' (Sollberger and Kupper 1971: IA3a). Clearly, then, Mesalim carried out royal acts in these centres although they had their own kings. Some of the later inscriptions of the Lagash rulers are particularly illuminating: for about 150 years, from *c.* 2500, Lagash was involved almost continuously in a territorial dispute with the neighbouring state of Umma. Time and again the kings of Lagash, recording victories over Umma, traced the dispute back to its origins and took as justification for their own position a ruling by Mesalim 'king of Kish', who had acted as arbitrator in the conflict between the two states and established the boundary. One of the crimes of which Umma was accused was that of not respecting his decision. Thus:

> Enlil (chief of Sumerian pantheon), king of all lands, father of the gods, by his authoritative command, demarcated the border between Ningirsu (patron-god of Lagash) and Shara (patron-god of Umma). Mesalim, king of Kish, at the command of Ishtaran (Mesalim's god, associated with the city of Der, east of the Tigris), measured it off and erected a monument there. Ush, ruler of Umma, acted arrogantly: he smashed that monument and marched on the plain of Lagash.
> (E. Sollberger, *Corpus des inscriptions 'royales' présargoniques de Lagash*: Ent. 28–29; Sollberger and Kupper 1971: IC7i; Cooper 1983b: VI. 6 (49))

This indicates that one of the ways in which the person laying claim to the kingship of Kish functioned was to regulate inter-city conflicts. But how did a king qualify for this position? A clue is provided by another Lagash inscription in which the ruler, Eanatum, claims to have conquered Elam, Urua (probably in the vicinity of Elam), Umma, Uruk, Ur and Ki-Utu (a city in the south); to have raided successfully three further Elamite border towns, killing the prince of one of them; and to have put down a revolt by the king of Akshak (a city to the north). After this, says Eanatum:

> To Eanatum, who occupies the thoughts of Ningirsu, to Eanatum, the ruler of Lagash, Inanna (important goddess associated particularly with Uruk), because she loves him, gave over and above the rulership of Lagash, the kingship of Kish.
> (E. Sollberger *Corpus des inscriptions 'royales' présargoniques de Lagash*: Ean. 2; Sollberger and Kupper 1971: Ic5b)

According to the text, Eanatum then consolidated and expanded his military victory so that regions to the east, north and west (Mari on the Euphrates) were all subject to him in some not clearly specified sense. This is one of the clearest indications that, while there were strong cultural, religious, artistic and commercial links between the cities, political rivalry led to serious conflicts. It was probably this competition for dominance that resulted in the formation in late ED III of larger political units: the state of Lagash itself included the centres of Girsu and Nina in addition to the eponymous city (Hansen 1992); Umma, its hostile neighbour, also included the important town of Zabala; to the west and south of Lagash, Uruk and Ur were united under the rule of Lugalkiginedudu shortly before 2400, and expanded later to absorb the whole state of Umma as well. This move effectively isolated Lagash, and perhaps contributed to its eventual defeat (Cooper 1983b: 8–9). It is possible, although the evidence is less full, that Kish and Akshak further north had also formed a political coalition a little earlier than that of Ur and Uruk. The culmination of the struggle came with Lugalzagesi, ruler of the Uruk-Ur-Umma unit, who eventually claimed overlordship of the entire region. With lengthy phrases and elaborate epithets, he presented himself as appointed by the patron-deities of various conquered cities to rulership of the land, set over the whole country by the head of the Sumerian pantheon, Enlil of Nippur, and claiming to control the road 'from the Upper Sea (Mediterranean) to the Lower Sea' (the Gulf). The bitter sentiments of the defeated king of Lagash, Uruinimgina, now reduced to ruling a mere rump state at Girsu, are also preserved:

> The man of Umma (Lugalzagesi), because he has destroyed Lagash, has sinned against Ningirsu! May the hand he has used against him (i.e. the god) be cut off! Uruinimgina, king of Girsu, had committed no sin! May Nidaba, the goddess of Lugalzagesi, ruler of Umma, carry this sin on her neck!
> (E. Sollberger, *Corpus des inscriptions 'royales' présargoniques de Lagash*: Ukg. 16; Sollberger and Kupper 1971: IC11m; Steible and Behrens 1982: Ukg. 16; Cooper 1986: La 9.5)

* * *

The 500- to 600-year period of Mesopotamian history from 2900 to 2340 can only be reconstructed very imperfectly. the period down to 2600 (ED I and II) is mainly represented by archaeological material – the presence of written material hints at the complexities of social organisation, but is too sparse and abstruse to fill out the archaeologically derived picture. In the succeeding period (ED III), a time when the cities expanded enormously in size, the documentation becomes much more varied and dense. Although the textual information is still not very full, and translating the written word a process fraught with problems, it is possible to grasp something of the configurations of power, and of the ideological, economic and social systems. But how far scholars still are from comprehending this culturally rich and important historical phase, in which many of the fundamental patterns of city life emerge, is best illustrated by the mass of material found in the graves at Ur (Woolley 1934; 1982): individual items shed considerable light on Mesopotamian society, and the accumulation of sheer wealth and fine craftsmanship indicates clearly that immense resources were available; but the reason for the burial of important individuals, apparently together with their retainers, furniture and treasures, remains speculative (Moorey 1977; Pollock 1991). Were they kings and queens? Were they people who had participated in a particular ritual? Were they high-level priestesses? Was the practice of multiple burials unique to Ur or more widespread? It is a measure of our present ignorance that the significance of the richest find of the period is still completely baffling.

1c The Empire of Agade

Introduction to sources and chronology

The period succeeding the Early Dynastic in Mesopotamia is named after the first successful attempt to centralise power by bringing the various cities of Mesopotamia under the permanent control of one dynasty of rulers. In many respects, it can be seen as the culmination of the escalating inter-city rivalries that had marked the preceding hundred years in the south. Lugalzagesi eventually claimed extensive political control and began to consolidate it through land grants made to local rulers (Charvát 1978), thereby turning them into dependent governors and so laying the foundations of an administrative system for his new domain.

The precise dates of the Agade period are disputed: a standard dating makes it extend from 2340 to 2159 (*CAH* dates: 2370–2189), but an alternative, lower date has been proposed more recently by Glassner (1986), with dates from 2296 to 2105 (see tables 3i–ii). Given the lack of precision of the ED datings, there are no particular obstacles to accepting a later starting date for the Agade dynasty; the late end point has interesting implications. Alternative terms for the period are 'Old Akkadian Empire', the 'Akkadian period' and the 'Sargonic period'. The last is derived from the name of the founder of the dynasty, Sargon; the others relate to alternative spellings of the name of Sargon's capital, Agade/Akkade, which has not so far been certainly located, although it is known that it was in the northern part of the south Meso-potamian plain. One suggestion is that it may have been at Ishan Mizyad, a few kilometres from Kish, where there is a large unexplored mound (Weiss 1985 [0Gc]: 125); later textual evidence suggests that it was near the con-fluence of the Tigris and Diyala (McEwan, *AfO* Beiheft 9). An important point to note about Agade is that it was essentially a new foundation – it had not existed as an important urban centre in the ED period (when it was probably just a small settlement) and all sources are unanimous in describing

Table 3i Chronology of Agade rulers and their successors

Agade	Uruk	Lagash	Gutians	Kish
	Lugalzagesi	(Uruinimgina?)		Urzababa
Sargon (2340–2284)				
				(5 more rulers?)
Rimush (2284–2275)				
Manishtushu (2275–2260)				
Naram-Sin (2260–2223)				
Sharkalisharri (2223–2198)			Sarlagab	
Igigi Nanum Imi Elulu (2198–2195)	Ur-nigin	Lugal-ushumgal		
Dudu (2195–2174)	Ur-gigir		(total = 21 kings)	
Shu-durul (2174–2159)		Ur-Baba Gudea Ur-Ningirsu Pirigme Ur-ni		
	Utu-hegal	Nammahani	Tirigan	

2113 = beginning of the Third Dynasty of Ur ('Ur III')
(see Table 3ii, p. 46, for an alternative chronology)

it as the foundation of Sargon. It continued to exist as a town, certainly into the early Hellenistic period (third century), although it never again played a prominent political role. It is usually assumed that in later times the territory in present-day Iraq, stretching roughly from Baghdad to Nippur, was named 'Akkad' after the city, while the area extending from Nippur to the Gulf was called 'Sumer'. Evidence supporting this assumption is slight – nothing indicates that the term 'Sumer and Akkad', which comes to be used regularly of the south Mesopotamian plain in the succeeding centuries, refers to tightly defined geopolitical units, although sketch-maps can make this assumption appear a fact. It is just as plausible to assume that the term refers to the linguistic, cultural and political diversity of the area.

Table 3ii Alternative chronology of Agade kings (*source*: Glassner 1986)

Agade	Uruk	Lagash	Gutians	Kish
	Lugalzagesi	Uruinimgina		Urzababa
Sargon (2296–2240)				
Rimush (2239–2230)				
Manishtushu (2229–2214)				
Naram-Sin (2213–2176)		Lugal-ushumgal		
		Puzur-Mama	Erriduwazir	
Sharkalisharri	Ur-nigin	Ur-Utu	Sarlagab	Shar-addi-
(2175–2150)		Ur-Mama		qubbishin
Igigi		Lu-Baba	Elulmesh	
Nanum	Ur-gigir	Lu-gula		
Imi		Inim-ku	La-'arab	Beli-ishar
	Kuda	Ur-Baba		
Elulu		Gudea	Puzur-Sin	
	Puzur-ili			
Dudu	Ur-Utu	Ur-Ningirsu	Iarlakan	
		Pirigme	Si'um	
Shu-durul	Utu-hegal	Ur-ni	Tirigan	
		Nammahani		

On this chronology, kings are still ruling in Agade at the time when Ur-nammu (founder of Ur III) establishes himself in power.

With the creation and expansion of the Agade empire, the Semitic language spoken in this region, known as Akkadian after the city, came to be written much more extensively. It is this language which dominates Mesopotamian history for the next almost two thousand years: the particular form of the language in this period is known as 'Old Akkadian'. Although Sumerian continued to be used, to some degree, for administrative, legal and, above all, literary texts, for at least another six hundred years (and certain Sumerian liturgies and prayers continued to be recited in rituals well into the Hellenistic period: Kuhrt and Sherwin-White, *JHS* 111 (1991)), it probably declined in use as a widely spoken language from this time (Cooper 1973).

The reason why scholars are quite well informed about the Agade period and some of the achievements of, at least, its first five rulers is that documentation (which includes several royal inscriptions) is relatively rich (Gelb 1961; Hirsch 1963; Michalowski 1980b; Kutscher 1989; Gelb and Kienast 1990): it ranges from votive texts on vases, statue-bases and stone plaques to brief legends on seals. All the Agade rulers, save four ephemeral kings, are mentioned in these texts, and the largest number of texts, as well as the longest ones, are those of Naram-Sin, Sargon's grandson. The majority of the royal inscriptions exist in later copies only; they were copied in the Old Babylonian period (c. 2000–1595) from monuments dedicated in temples, above all the temple of Enlil at Nippur (the 'Ekur'), which, as the home of the head of the Sumerian pantheon of gods, occupied a particularly important position. Collections of documents relating to administrative matters and economic transactions have been recovered primarily, but not exclusively, from south Mesopotamia (Umma, Lagash), and scribal texts illustrating developments in the language were found in the Diyala area.

The organisation of a large political unit required a uniform system for dating, and in this period the practice of naming years after a particular event was introduced; it remained the standard method of dating for the next seven hundred years or so. Scribes made collections of such 'year-names' for their own use, and they can provide valuable historical information as well as a chronological framework. The collections of year-names were almost certainly among the sources used by the compilers of the Sumerian King List (see pp. 29–31) for this period; this accounts for the greater reliability of the list for the Agade dynasty.

A consequence of the dynasty's enormous impact on Mesopotamian history is the composition, later, of stories about some of the Agade kings, which purport to be copies of royal votive inscriptions, but are clearly later compositions with a didactic purpose. Because they imitate the form of inscriptions, the term 'narû literature' is applied to this distinctive genre (Güterbock 1934/1938; Goodnick-Westenholz 1983; Galter 1986); narû is Akkadian for 'stele', i.e. a stone memorial set up by a king. The most famous example of this genre is the Sargon 'birth-legend', the extant copies dating no earlier than the late Assyrian period (720–610; Lewis 1980; Glassner 1988). The seemingly sudden rise of the Agade dynasty, its far-flung conquests and expeditions and its apparently sudden fall led to the rapid creation of an extensive body of legendary and epic material, in both Sumerian and Akkadian. The stories focus particularly on the founder of the empire, Sargon, and his famous grandson, Naram-Sin, who is sometimes confusingly presented as the last ruler, who ultimately brought the dynasty his grandfather had created to a catastrophic end (Cooper 1983).[8] These stories continued to circulate, and to be copied, reshaped and read well into the Hellenistic period. While they illustrate, dramatically, the ideological and symbolic importance of the Agade kings, they cannot be considered reliable historical sources for the period; the temptation to treat them so is not always resisted. The dynasty's enduring fame is further illustrated by the so-called 'historical omens' of the Old Babylonian period. In Mesopotamia, it was believed that the sun-god 'wrote' the future on the entrails of sheep. The innards were examined and studied, and certain shapes were invested with a particular meaning (this process is known as extispicy). In a number of compilations listing such forms and their significance, certain features are said to signify exploits of the Agade rulers. For example: 'If the "palace-gate" (part of the liver) is doubled, the kidney trebled, and there are two breaches on the right side of the gall-bladder, it is an omen of the ruler of Apishal, whom Naram-Sin took prisoner upon breaching the wall of his city' (YOS X 24: 9). Finkelstein (1963) argued that, given the nature of divination, such correlations must derive from contemporary observations of actual events and that the omens, therefore, constituted a valuable, primary historical source. This cannot be accepted; both the type of information appearing in omen contexts, and the now clearer understanding of how the collections of omens were compiled and transmitted, indicate that they are merely anecdotal material reflecting the popularity of stories told about the Agade kings and no more (Cooper 1980).

The rise and fall of Agade

Sargon's origins and rise to power are totally obscured by the various romances associated with him later. According to the very late 'birth-legend', employing the worldwide popular motif of the culture-hero exposed at birth, it was a 'rags to riches' story (the earliest preserved text comes from eighth-century Nineveh):

> Sargon, mighty king, king of Agade, am I;
> My mother was an *ēntum* (cultic functionary of very high status), my
>   father I knew not;
> My father's brother(s) dwell(?) in the mountains;
> My city is Azupiranu, situated on the banks of the Euphrates;
> My mother, the *ēntum*, conceived me, in secret she bore me;
> She placed me in a basket of rushes, she sealed 'my door' (i.e. the lid)
>   with bitumen;
> She cast me into the river which did not rise over me;
> The river bore me up and carried me to Aqqi, the water-drawer.
> Aqqi, the water-drawer, lifted me out as he dipped his ewer;
> Aqqi, the water-drawer, adopted me, brought me up;
> Aqqi, the water-drawer, set me up as his gardener.
> As a gardener, Ishtar (Akkadian goddess of sex and war) loved me;
> For [56] years I exercised kingship.
>
> (King 1907: appendix I; *ANET*: 119; Lewis 1980)

Earlier material (from the first half of the second millennium), presumably derived from folktales,[7] gives Sargon a slightly different background: Sargon's birth was humble; his father was perhaps a date-grower (there is no hint of a high-born mother as in the late version); he somehow entered the court of Urzababa, the king of Kish, and rose in his service to become royal cupbearer. For an unknown reason, the gods decreed the downfall of his royal master and, despite the machinations of Urzababa, Sargon became king, founded a city and ruled 'the world' (Cooper and Heimpel 1983).

The only features of Sargon's early history that seem fairly well established are that Agade was a newcomer on the political scene and that both Urzababa and Lugalzagesi were his contemporaries and, certainly in the case of the latter, opponents. Everything else is uncertain; even Sargon's name, which means literally 'the legitimate/true king', inspires suspicion. What seems possible is that, having established himself as an independent ruler, Sargon undertook expeditions to western Iran, campaigned to the north and, perhaps economically and politically most significant, conducted victorious campaigns against the powerful states of Mari, Ebla and further west 'as far as the Cedar Forest and the Silver Mountain' (Sollberger and Kupper 1971: IIA1b; for the problem of the location of Iarmuti, cf. *RLA* 5: 266–267). How far, and in what manner, these regions were incorporated at this stage into Sargon's realm is difficult to determine. One problem is the date of Sargon's conquest of the south Mesopotamian cities. Although a number of factors can be put forward in favour of a relatively late date in his reign (Jacobsen 1957), it is best to admit that the evidence is simply insufficient to resolve this. All that is known comes from an inscription copied in the Old Babylonian period at Nippur:

> [Sargon, the king of Agade, the . . . of Inanna, king of Kish, anointed of Anu (sky-god), king] of lands, governor of Enlil, conquered the city of Uruk and destroyed its walls. He challenged (the man of) Uruk in battle and took Lugalzagesi, the king of Uruk, prisoner in the course of the battle; he led him in a wooden collar to the gate of Enlil.
>
> Sargon, king of Agade, challenged (the man of) Ur in a battle and defeated the city and destroyed its walls. He defeated E-Nin-kimara (town probably between Ur and Lagash) and destroyed its walls and conquered its land from Lagash to the sea. He washed his weapons in the sea. He challenged Umma in a battle [and he defeated the city and destroyed its walls].
>
> To Sargon, king of lands, Enlil gave no rival; Enlil gave him the Upper Sea and the Lower Sea. From the Lower Sea, citizens of Agade held the government. Mari and Elam were subject to Sargon, king of lands. Sargon, king of lands, restored Kish and made (its fugitive inhabitants ro)occupy the city.
>
> (PBS 5: 34 & 41 and PBS 15: 41; Sollberger and Kupper 1971: IIA1a)

It is clear from the unfortunately broken end of the tablet that the original monument depicted Sargon together with his defeated enemies, with Lugalzagesi at their head. The reference to governors of Agade exercising control, presumably replacing the captured kings, is quite clear although there is a little evidence to suggest that, in some cases, local rulers were left unmolested. The reference to the rebuilding and resettling of Kish is tantalising, suggesting as it does that the city had been devastatingly defeated at an earlier date. The 56-year-long reign (although cf. Foster 1982a) of Sargon must have been fully occupied with his innumerable campaigns and subsequent administrative restructuring. The large, later corpus of temple-hymns offers an intriguing glimpse into one of Sargon's moves to consolidate his control. The composition of the hymns is attributed to Enheduanna, the daughter of Sargon, in particular the cultic poems in favour of Inanna (Hallo and van Dijk 1968). An incribed, limestone disc (Winter 1987b) and the literary material make it certain that Enheduanna was installed as the cultic 'bride' (*ēntum*) of the moon-god, Nanna, at Ur. It is probable that the office already existed, but it certainly increased in importance, with the holder of the office now, and for the next 500–600 years, always being the daughter of whichever Meso-potamian king, who held (or claimed to hold) a power greatly superior to that of a mere city-ruler. Enheduanna's prime duties were to pray for the well-being of the king, her father. The wider, political implications of the appointment are less clear. It has been suggested that Enheduanna not only acted as the 'bride' of Nanna at Ur, but may also have played a prominent role in certain rituals at Uruk (Hallo and van Dijk 1968). If so, then the permanent presence of such a close relative of the king, together with her retinue, in two places at the heart of the power-base of Sargon's chief enemy, Lugalzagesi, must have worked to strengthen Agade's hold on southern Mesopotamia.

Sargon was succeeded by two of his sons, Rimush and Manishtushu. In spite of the obvious problems involved in succeeding to the control of a newly formed empire, they appear to have managed to maintain their father's conquests intact and successfully to consolidate the dynasty's hold. This is suggested not only by inscriptions and the distribution of finds (Nissen 1988), but also by their bestowal of land to followers after conquest (Rimush: Foster 1985) and by means of direct purchase (Manishtushu: MDP II: 1ff.). Their hold on the north Iraq area (Ashur; Nineveh) and the Khabur area (Tell Brak) is particularly well attested.

The empire reached its apogee under Naram-Sin. For his reign much more written material is available, including quite long royal inscriptions (many in later copies). Its organisation at this time can be fairly well delineated: garrisons are known from north Syria to west Iran; there is evidence for the continuation of Sargon's policy of appointing a royal daughter to the position of *ēntum* at Ur; other members of the royal family were deployed to fill cultic offices elsewhere (e.g. at Mari); the king was involved in extensive temple-construction; and royal relatives were installed as governors. Beyond the immediate boundaries of this quite tightly controlled empire, rock-reliefs at Pir Huseyn (north-east of Diyarbakir, Turkey) and Darband-i-Gaur in the Zagros (south-east Kurdistan) commemorate Naram-Sin's more distant exploits. Three inscriptions refer to campaigns in the west against Ebla, which raises the question of how far this area was integrated into the realm.

The most dramatic development in Naram-Sin's reign was the change in royal titulary as it appears on items belonging to, or dedicated by, his servants. The legend on the seal of an Agade official impressed on two tablets found at Tello (ancient Girsu) reads:

> Naram-Sin, the strong male, god of Agade, king of the four quarters
> (i.e. of the universe): Lugal-ushumgal, scribe, governor of Lagash
> (F. Thureau-Dangin, *Recueil des tablettes chaldéennes*, 1903: 165, 166;
> Sollberger and Kupper 1971: IIA4p)

The divine element is mirrored in the way Naram-Sin is represented on contemporary victory monuments: he is much taller than the rest of humanity (in contrast to earlier depictions) and wears on his head a horned helmet, the exclusive attribute of gods (fig. 5). The question of Naram-Sin's divinisation has been illuminated in a surprising way by the inscription on a cast copper statue, found near Dohuk in north Iraq (Al-Fouadi 1976), which adds to the already rich repertoire of very fine Agade period art (Amiet 1976):

> Naram-Sin, the mighty king of Agade: when the four corners of the world opposed him with hostility, he remained victorious in nine battles because of the love of Ishtar and even took the kings who had campaigned against him prisoner. Because he succeeded when heavily pressed in maintaining his city in strength, his city (i.e. its inhabitants) implored Ishtar of Eanna, Enlil of Nippur, Dagan of Tuttul (near confluence of Balikh and Euphrates), Ninhursanga of Kesh, Enki of Eridu, Sin of Ur, Shamash of Sippar, Nergal of Kutha to have him as the god of their city Agade and they built him a temple in the midst of Agade.
>
> (Farber 1983)

Many later stories of Naram-Sin concern a major revolt against him, and invasions, in some cases led by demonic forces, over which he eventually triumphs. Here, then, is an indication that his ultimate success in the face of a major threat to the realm was, at least according to the text, greeted with such joy by his relieved subjects that they begged to be allowed to honour him publicly as a god – a practice without known precedent in Mesopotamia, but one that continued, sporadically, into the Old Babylonian period.

That the cohesion of the empire was threatened at times is not surprising, but whether it was outside pressure that led eventually to its collapse is unclear. The traditional explanation for the collapse of the dynasty of Agade – that the Gutians from the Zagros region destroyed Agade – has been shown to be in large part a mirage created by *post eventum* speculations intended to explain the glorious dynasty's abrupt demise after Naram-Sin (Hallo 1971; Michalowski 1983; Glassner 1986). In fact, the dynasty retained control right through the reign of Naram-Sin's successor, Shar-kali-sharri, who reigned for a respectable twenty-five years, although there are hints of strain (Glassner

Figure 5 Naram-Sin victory stele from Susa (Louvre; drawing by D. Saxon)

1986), and he may have had to fend off attacks on his frontiers. That all had not been well is implied by the fact that his reign was followed by a short period of anarchy, breaking the regular succession of the dynastic family at Agade. At the same time, a number of local rulers re-established their independence in the south Mesopotamian centres (Lagash, Kish, Uruk), and the Gutians built up a small power-base in the Diyala region. Thus, by the time the power struggle within Agade was resolved, the territory left to its last two rulers (Dudu and Shudurul, with a combined total reign of forty-six years) had shrunk to the city's immediate vicinity.

King and country

Because the sources are fragmentary and our knowledge of the empire is therefore limited, it is only too easy to get the impression that it was no more than a sudden, brief burst of glory with little attempt by the kings to create any kind of imperial structure. This is a distortion: the time from Sargon's accession to the death of Shar-kali-sharri was 140 years; during at least a hundred years of that the Agade kings held a large territory (including most of Mesopotamia and parts of western Iran and Elam) under their direct rule. Moreover, despite the often frustrating nature of the evidence, it is clear that there was a quite deliberate policy of centralisation. Thus, Agade became 'the city' *par excellence* (see the Naram-Sin inscription, p. 51), the residence of the king, which symbolised the empire and was exalted above all other cities ('Agade is king'; 'divine Agade'). The extant archives indicate that agricultural surpluses were produced for, and sent to, Agade; similarly, the activities of craftsmen were demanded and absorbed by the capital; as the king, royal family and dignitaries were located there, Agade became the major centre of consumption. The royal inscriptions also emphasise its role as the chief centre towards which long-distance trade was oriented:

> Sargon . . . caused the boats of Meluhha (= India), the boats of Magan (Oman), and the boats of Dilmun (Bahrain/Gulf) to dock at the quays of Agade.
>
> (PBS 15: 41 and 34; Sollberger and Kupper 1971: IIA1b)

The close commercial links with the Indus Valley in this period are well established, not least by the presence in Mesopotamia of an Indian (Meluhhan)-language interpreter (Edzard 1968–9: no. 33). Agade was likewise the main recipient of exotic booty:

> Manishtushu, king of Kish, when he had conquered Anshan and Sherihum, caused the Lower Sea to be crossed in boats . . . The cities on the other side of the sea, 32 (of them) combined for the battle. But he was victorious and conquered their cities, he killed their princes [and] took away . . . From the mountains beyond the Lower Sea he extracted black stones; he loaded (them) onto boats and had them dock at the quay of Agade.
>
> (MDP XV: 1–3; Sollberger and Kupper 1971: IIA3b)

The establishment of a centralised administrative machinery is reflected in the increasing standardisation, throughout the period, of script, weight systems, calendar (the year-names, see p. 47) and archive-keeping (Foster 1986). The government of conquered areas was in the hands of royally appointed governors (e n s i), while some places also had a military commander heading a small garrison force. Although at times it was a local ruler who was appointed, or confirmed in office, as governor by the Agade kings (e.g. Susa:

Carter and Stolper 1984: 14–15), the fact that he ruled only by their permission or with their agreement is a measure of the strength of Agade's hold. Sargon's reference to the citizens of Agade controlling all the land from the Lower Sea (see p. 49), as well as the evidence from Naram-Sin's reign, suggests that the members of the imperial government came from the Agade court as well as the royal family; this is paralleled by the close control of temple institutions at key centres primarily through royal kin (see p. 50). Both archaeological evidence (Tell Brak: Nissen 1988; Jidle: Mallowan, *Iraq* 8 (1946)) and textual references (Sikamanum: Hirsch 1963, Naram-Sin b5: IV 20–V 16) show that many places were established as fortresses and citadels for military defence and control; royal involvement in their foundation is reflected by the fact that a number were named after the dynasty or founder, e.g. 'Dur-Rimush' = 'Fortress of Rimush', 'Dur-Akkade' = 'Stronghold of Agade'.

The position of the king reflects the political centralisation. His importance as the central, unifying figure is illustrated by the appearance of personal names that praise him, e.g. 'The-King-is-my-Fortress' (Westenholz 1979: 111); by the fact that oaths were sometimes sworn by him, rather than by gods (Edzard 1974); and by his role as the ultimate arbiter (Glassner 1986: 13). His unrivalled supremacy is reflected by his titulary: sometimes he was simply 'king' without qualification. As the ideology ascribed ultimate power to him, his presence throughout the realm was physically and symbolically crucial: the king thus travelled through the realm with his retinue (Foster, 1980), and his symbolic presence was marked the length and breadth of the empire by life-size royal statuary set up in city-shrines. Finally, the king was eventually exalted beyond the human sphere, and mediated between the world of the gods and that of his subjects: for them he was the provider of wealth, status and safety, like the gods themselves who had permitted him to join their ranks (see the Naram-Sin text, p. 51).

Throughout the reign of the first four Agade monarchs there is a continuous emphasis on the role of the king as warrior and triumphant conqueror. The epithets stress the universality of his control, and the inscriptions record ceaseless campaigning in places ever further afield and more exotic:

> Never since the appearance of men, did any king among the kings ravage Armanum and Ebla.
>
> (UET 1: 24A; Sollberger and Kupper 1971: IIA4e)

> Naram-Sin, king of Agade who . . . all the lands of Elam up to Barahshi and the lands of Subartu (north) up to the Cedar Forest; further, when he went to Talhatum, that road had never been taken by any king among the kings: Naram-Sin, king of Agade took it, and Inanna gave him no rival. The governors of Subartu and the lords of the high countries brought their tribute before him.
>
> (UET 1: 274; Sollberger and Kupper 1971: IIA4d)

The military organisation grew in size and complexity: levies from the cities were used, and pastoral groups living on the fringes, such as Amorites and Gutians, were recruited to form special contingents. Soldiers were supplied with rations of food, wool and weapons and some were given plots of land for subsistence. The personal responsibility of the king for all this is illustrated by a statement of Sargon:

> 5,400 (military) men I made to eat before me each day.
> (PBS 15: 34 & 41; Sollberger and Kupper 1971: IIA1b)

Booty from his far-flung campaigns flowed into the king's treasury and was redistributed in the form of magnificent presents to temples, favoured subjects and members of the royal family – serving to stress the ruler's pre-eminent position, since he both created and controlled this wealth through his military exploits. Another form of wealth acquired through the royal campaigns was land, which the king could use to augment his own estates and those of his relatives, or bestow as land-parcels on officials and soldiers (Foster 1985). His great wealth also enabled him to buy land from poorer farmers and redistribute it as he saw fit (Manishtushu obelisk, MDP II: 1ff.). Records of landed estates, usually worked by tenants, show the king, members of the royal family and high functionaries at court owned land throughout the region of south Mesopotamia (Foster 1982a).

Taken together, the evidence points to new and important developments in the position of the king that are directly linked to his wealth, political centrality and military leadership. An emphasis on his physical splendour is very marked – he wore special clothes, had a special hairdo, carried royal insignia, sat on an intricately carved throne and used weapons of superior craftsmanship. Although some elements of this equipment and ideology were present earlier, they were not as elaborate as they became at this time, reflecting directly the power and success of the Agade kings. At the same time, it is important to stress a strong element of continuity underlying the major transformations brought about by the Agade dynasty: the essence of political culture and ideology was still centred on the concept of one city dominating others; no new idea of a 'national' identity developed, apart from that of city affiliation, as is clear from the fact that the king of this extensive political conglomerate continued to be, first and foremost, the 'king of Agade', and beyond that 'king of lands' or 'of the four corners of the world', while the use of the traditional hegemonic title 'king of Kish' was retained from the preceding period. This is the political pattern that dominated Mesopotamian history for the next five hundred years or so; the Agade empire was seen by later kings as the major exemplar of the success that could be achieved by one city in imposing its control on the rest.

1d The Third Dynasty of Ur (2112–2004)

From the end of Agade to the rise of Ur

The picture of south Mesopotamia under the last Agade rulers and for a generation beyond (although cf. table 3ii) is reminiscent of the political pattern of the ED III period, when power was divided among several different local rulers; the main centres now were Uruk, Lagash, Kish, Agade and Gutians in the Diyala. Less than a century later, a literary text of this period depicted the whole area as dominated, indeed the collapse of Agade as brought about, by invading barbarians from the mountains in the east, the Gutians. They were presented as unleashed on the country by Enlil, head of the pantheon, because of a sacrilege committed by Naram-Sin: he was accused of removing goods and divine statues from Nippur, Enlil's city:

> Though they were not the goods of a plundered city,
> Large ships were docked at the temple,
> Large ships were docked at Enlil's temple, and
> The goods were removed from the city.
> As the goods were removed from the city,
> So was the good sense of Agade removed,
> The ships jarred the docks, and Agade's intelligence was displaced.
>
> The roaring storm that subjugates the entire land,
> The rising deluge that cannot be confronted,
> Enlil, because his beloved Ekur (Enlil's temple at Nippur) was destroyed, what should he destroy (in revenge) for it?
> He looked towards the Gutian mountains;
> He scoured all of the broad mountain ranges -
> Not classed among people, not reckoned as part of the land,
> Gutium, a people who know no inhibitions,
> With human instincts, but canine intelligence, and monkeys' features -
> Enlil brought them out of the mountains.
> Like herds of locusts they lie over the land,
> Their arms are stretched over the plains for him (sc.Enlil) like a snare for animals,
> Nothing leaves their arms,
> No one escapes their arms.
> Messengers no longer travel the highways,
> The courier's boat no longer takes to the rivers.
>
> (Cooper 1983a: ll. 142–63)

While there is some evidence that Gutians, who had served in the Agade armies, dominated a sector in the eastern region, this was not so much a cause of Agade's crumbling power as an effect. Their transformation into the divine

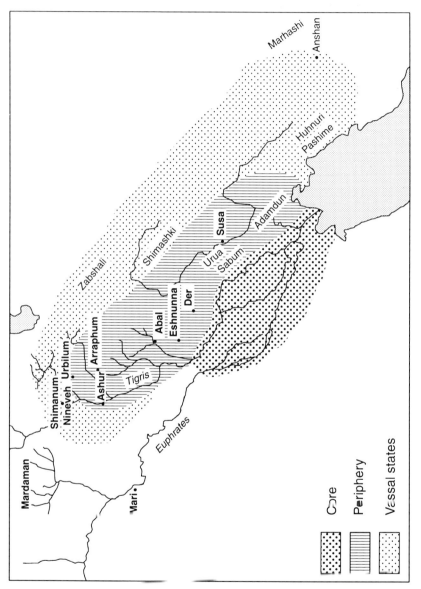

Map 3 The state of the Third Dynasty of Ur

tool that destroyed Agade probably reflects the ideological interests of the kings of the Ur III dynasty (2112–2004) – i.e. the period when the text was composed. In their explanation of the fall of the Agade empire, they cast themselves in the role of its heirs: the Agade kings had misused their power and the burden of Agade's physical destruction was placed on a culturally peripheral group. What is clear is that the text represents a distortion of historical events (Cooper 1983a).

The history of the period that separates the end of the reign of Shar-kali-sharri from the establishment of the Third Dynasty of Ur is not at all well known, but the competition among powerful, rival city-rulers for pre-eminence is quite plain. Gudea of Lagash is the most famous of them, at least now: a great number of beautifully sculpted, black diorite statues of him are known and so widely admired that several forged Gudea statues exist (Johansen 1978; cf. F. Tallon, *Asian Art* 5/1 (1992)). In addition to these and a series of fine carved stone vases, some of the longest and earliest Sumerian literary texts were written during Gudea's reign. They relate to his many temple-foundations and are among the finest examples of Sumerian poetry, celebrating the import of rare materials for temple-building from distant lands and the special favour bestowed by the gods on Gudea (Falkenstein 1966). But despite his wealth and claim to have brought timber from far up the Euphrates, Gudea's rule was limited to the area of his own city.

The development of the state of Ur III

The bulk of the evidence for the last century of the third millennium comes from south Mesopotamia, where a new political entity emerged victorious from the inter-city rivalries, replacing, and building on, the earlier Agade achievements, and reasserting very strongly the concept of political unity under a single king. This new, highly centralised political formation is known, after the Sumerian King List, as the 'Third Dynasty of Ur', or 'Ur III' for short. This is also the period embraced by terms such as 'Neo-Sumerian' and 'Sumerian Renaissance'.

The origins of the dynasty are obscure. Inscriptions indicate that some moves towards claiming hegemony over the south Mesopotamian cities were made by Utuhegal of Uruk, who is given a seven-year reign by the Sumerian King List, just preceding the establishment of Ur III. He also figures as the heroic protagonist of a splendid later poem concerning the expulsion of the Gutians from Mesopotamia (see Kupper and Sollberger 1971: IIK3a; *TUAT* I/4: 316–319). Two stelae from Ur indicate that Ur-Nammu/a, first king of the Ur III dynasty, was Utuhegal's governor there. Trying to deduce from this how Ur-Nammu came to establish himself as an independent king is difficult. It is possible to argue for a situation in which he revolted against his overlord at Uruk and eventually wrested control of the area from him (*CAH* I, ch. 22). But an alternative scenario has been presented (Hallo 1966; Sollberger 1954–6) whereby Ur-Nammu was actually a close relative of Utuhegal, governing Ur on his behalf. When Ur-Nammu's control of the region was threatened by Nammahani, ruler of Lagash, he defeated and killed him. It was this exploit that led to his taking the title 'king of Sumer and Agade' in his fourth regnal year. The details of what happened to Utuhegal are not known, but the Ur III kings did forge very close politico-cultural ties between Ur and Uruk, which played a symbolically crucial role in the kingship of Ur. Thus no hostility was ever expressed towards Utuhegal, and the close cultic relationship between the two cities was strengthened, with the main Uruk sanctuary being elaborately rebuilt and equipped with a magnificent high ziggurat by Ur-Nammu. It also seems plausible that the Uruk epics about Gilgamesh and other early kings were given their classic Sumerian form at this time (one is definitely attested: Hallo 1974: 189; Michalowski 1987: 52). The way in which different members of the dynasty repeatedly linked themselves to the earlier Uruk kings through mythical family ties is probably related to their interest in the epics: thus, Ninsun and Lugalbanda, Gilgamesh's mother and father, were revered as the divine parents of the Ur III kings, with Ninsun playing a prominent role (cf. Klein 1981a; 1981b), and Gilgamesh himself was presented as the brother of the Ur kings. The text known as 'The Death of Urnammu' (Kramer 1967) makes this clear: it describes Ur-Nammu presenting gifts in the underworld to 'his brother, Gilgamesh'.

The term 'Sumerian Renaissance' has been used of this period, implying that a specifically Sumerian cultural revival took place. This is understandable, given the marked flourishing of Sumerian literature and language. Virtually all administrative texts preserved from this time are written in Sumerian; there was a massive production of Sumerian literary texts in the schools where potential officials learned to write (e d u b b a, Michalowski 1987: 51–54; Sjöberg 1974); and an entirely new Sumerian literary genre, the royal hymn, was created at this time (Klein 1981a; 1981b). Does all this activity in Sumerian then represent the resurgence of a particular politico-cultural identity that had been suppressed and required reasserting and fostering? That is a hard position to maintain, since there is no evidence for a 'decline' in Sumerian in the preceding period. The evidence indicates, rather, that Sumerian developed now as a specifically literary, hence 'cultured', dead language which was boosted by the Ur III kings (Michalowski 1987: 52), perhaps because it had been the traditional language of the extreme south where the new power-centre was located. If there were a deliberate harking back to an early 'Sumerian' past we would also expect to see signs of a rejection of the Agade period. But there is nothing of the kind: the surviving evidence shows that the period of disaster was perceived to be that of the supposed Gutian rule. Nowhere do the Ur kings present themselves as embodying a contrast or opposition to the Agade dynasty (Cooper 1983a) – rather, their political ambitions were predicated on those of the Agade kings (Oates 1986 [OGb]), and indeed a cult of Naram-Sin was maintained at Nippur in this period.

Finally, not only is there an enormous number of Akkadian words in the Sumerian texts, but also the majority of personal and newly founded town names are Akkadian (e.g. Ishbi-Erra, Puzrish-Dagan); even more significant, all royal names and names of queens, daughters and sons of the royal family, save the first two, are in good Akkadian. The fact that Sumerian was the language of education and bureaucratic aspiration seems to have been a device that served to define and distinguish the educated élite; it could work in this way precisely because Sumerian was no longer commonly spoken (Cooper 1973; Michalowski 1987: 53; for a full discussion of the 'Sumerian Renaissance', cf. Becker 1985).

Reconstructing the state of Ur III

The sources for this period exist in their tens of thousands, the largest number by far represented by administrative documents, reflecting the state enterprises and state control which characterise the period (Steinkeller 1987a). Many still await a full analysis, although a large number of studies exists. They provide an unrivalled insight into tiny details of daily life, such as diet and clothing, and above all into the planning and organisation of the manufacturing industries and agriculture. They illustrate the enormous input of manpower required, the intricate constructions demanded by the highly efficient irrigation system, with its weirs, leaching of saline ground, patterns of sowing, harvesting, and fallow (Kang 1973; Powell 1985; Civil 1987), which could produce massive yields.[8] Another striking feature of the period on which there is rich documentation is the state production centres. The important textile industry at Ur itself, employing many women and children and producing wool and linen garments, some extraordinarily elaborate, has been intensively studied (Waetzold 1972); similar evidence exists for the metals industry (Limet 1960). Most astonishing is the evidence for the detailed central planning that was needed to organise all this, and which functioned quite efficiently for almost a hundred years, although the delicate balancing the system required made it vulnerable to crises. It was a unique attempt in Mesopotamian history by the state to organise and control production: 'never again did centralisation reach such a high degree' (Steinkeller 1987a: 22).

Many of the Ur III tablets were excavated clandestinely and sold through the antiquities market, so that archives have become scattered, their find spots are not certain and it is an enormous labour to arrange the texts into coherent groups (Jones 1974). The fact that most of the texts come from government offices or relate to the state's care of temple-estates constitutes another problem, in that private transactions are underrepresented. The interaction of individual households with the state economy and their contribution to it is therefore difficult to assess. It has become evident only fairly recently that, while the relative extent and significance of private property remains disputed (Gelb 1969; Steinkeller 1989), private land-ownership (as earlier too) is a factor to be reckoned with (Diakonoff 1971, Waetzold 1987). The level of production carried out in private households is also difficult to quantify (Gelb 1965; 1979b). The evidence for commercial activities run by independent merchants, who organised trading activities for the state by acting as creditors for government institutions, is more secure (Powell 1977). For these sophisticated transactions to work, a system of barter (usually, though loosely, assumed to be the way in which commerce was conducted) seems inadequate. It has been forcefully argued (Powell 1978) that metal coils (of gold, silver, bronze and copper) of standard weights were produced as a way of storing metals, from which pieces could be cut and weighed in order to provide currency for exchanges; or items could be manufactured from such units by smelting. This system of standardised currency is best illustrated by the Ur III material, but the terminology appears in the Agade period, and it seems plausible that it was already in use earlier.

The administrative picture of Ur III that emerges from this rich material is of south Mesopotamia divided into a number of provinces, each with a provincial city centre, governed by an e n s i (governor), probably recruited from the local élite. Families which obtained official standing in this way normally passed their positions on to descendants, as well as obtaining access to other important posts (Zettler 1984). Next to the governors stood military commanders (s a g i n), who, in some cases, commanded military units recruited from fringe groups (as in the Agade period) which made up sections of the permanent army. Military personnel in the highest position came either directly from the royal family or had married into it. It is possible that there was a careful separation of civil and military powers within the central provinces of south Mesopotamia (Steinkeller 1987a; see map 3), but this was certainly not always the case in the areas to the north (Ashur) and east (Zagros, Elam), which had been incorporated by conquest into the state. The primary control of this frontier zone, on which the safety of the Ur III state depended, was in the hands of the s u k k a l m a h; his position as virtual viceroy is exemplified by the fact that in Elam, after the disappearance of the Ur III dynasty, the local rulers took the title 's u k k a l m a h' as a quasi-royal one (Carter and Stolper 1984). The rich material from the new royal foundation near Nippur, Puzrish-Dagan (modern Drehem: Hallo 1960; Keiser 1971; Kang 1972; Steinkeller 1987a; Sigrist 1993) has demonstrated that a complex tax structure functioned during Ur III. There was a system of centrally located redistribution centres, into which provinces paid their dues (b a l a) and on which the central government drew for such things as supplying temples and paying those entitled to royal largesse or dependent on rations, as did the provinces for theirs. The system depended on a high level of central planning and accounting, and functioned to integrate the different provincial centres into a unified whole. One of the sources of supplies of livestock to the centre at Puzrish-Dagan was the g ú n m a-d a ('tax of the provinces'), payable in livestock by military personnel settled in the frontier zones.

How the labour, on which the state depended, was recruited is rather less clear, as are details of the social system. There are many areas of disagreement among scholars. Legal and sale documents show the unmistakable existence of private property. People sold orchards, houses, and slaves. Selling a house was publicised by the driving of a nail into the property to be sold (Malul 1987). Whether people were able to dispose of arable land is less certain. It is possible that the land that appears in the documents was held in return for services, i.e. essentially part of the crown's property. It remains a subject for debate whether this represents all available land, or whether the uneven documentation hides the existence of privately owned fields (Gelb 1969; Steinkeller 1989). Chattel slaves appear regularly in the sale documents: it is estimated that about two-fifths of their number were indigenous – poor families selling their children, indigent family groups (such as mothers with suckling babes), or even sons selling their mothers in times of stress. Slaves themselves could amass property and eventually redeem themselves, as shown by this document from Ur:

> Am[mazaza], the slave-woman of A['aduga] has redeemed herself from A['aduga]. 6½ mina of silver and a full-grown cow she has given him as her complete saleprice. As long as A'aduga and Ninabbana (his wife) live, she will do service for their children and their spouses. After (the death of) A'aduga and Ninabbana, Ammazaza can go wherever she wishes. No one will contest it. (Witnesses include a potter and several cultic functionaries).

(UET 3: 51; TUAT I/3: 201–202)

With respect to non-slave labour, it is possible to distinguish between people who were obliged to carry out specified work quotas in return for fields granted or rations received, and those who joined work-gangs as hired labourers and worked under no such compulsion (Waetzold 1987). It has been thought that the state of Ur III was marked by rigid social stratification and the existence of a dependent labour force of 'serfs' (g u r u š; e.g. Diakonoff 1974; Gelb 1979a). But arguments against this have been presented recently, based on an analysis of documents relating to a group of foresters at Umma (Steinkeller 1987b): they were employed in cutting, processing, planting and maintaining a variety of low-growing trees such as willows, riverine poplars and possibly wild licorice. What emerges is that there was some degree of social mobility between those forming labour-groups and those who fulfilled managerial functions. Moreover, the labourers could, and did, hold plots of land, and it was in return for that state-granted land that they worked, part of the year, on government projects (see also, for this pattern of part-time work, Uchitel 1984). The documentation also makes it plain that they lived and worked in family groups. Nowhere, in this case, are the workers landless, propertyless, kinless 'serfs' or 'helots'.

Royal rule and royal ideology

Other sources for this period provide information on aspects of royal ideology and policy, and show that, in several respects, there are parallels with the Agade period. Thus the system of year-names was used for dating throughout the realm, providing a uniform calendar for all. It is largely from these year-names that information on major campaigns, for example, derives. But more refer to the completion of building projects by the king and important cultic events, e.g. the continuing practice of installing royal daughters in the office of e n-priestess of the moon-god at Ur. Relations with client-states and neighbouring powers are illuminated by year-names referring to marriages of members of the royal family, usually daughters, to rulers in adjoining countries in order to avoid wars and/or strengthen alliances. The material mainly concerns princesses married to rulers in the east and north-east, who stood in a dependent relationship to the state of Ur III. There is one instance of a prince (Ur-Nammu's son) marrying the daughter of the

Table 4 Chronology of the Third Dynasty of Ur

conventional	low
Utuhegal: 2119–2113	Utuhegal: 2055–2048
Ur-Nammu: 2112–c. 2095	Ur-Nammu: 2047–2030
Shulgi (formerly read 'Dungi'): 2094–2047	Shulgi: 2029–1982
Amar-Sin (formerly read 'Bur-Sin'): 2046–2038	Amar-Sin: 1981–1973
Shu-Sin: 2037–2027	Shu-Sin: 1972–1964
Ibbi-Sin: 2026–2004?	Ibbi-Sin: 1963–1940

king of Mari, which was definitely not subject to the Ur state. This can only reflect the cementing of friendly relations between neighbours (Hallo 1976: 31; Michalowski 1975; *RLA* 4: 283, nos. 6–10). The fact that some of these political marriages are known from year-names is an indication of their prime political importance; the weddings are likely to have been publicly announced, and the great convoys, escorting the princess with her bridal trousseau to her husband's home, became the focus of wide popular attention.

Beyond the evidence of the year names, the 'history' of the Ur III period is very scantily known save for its rise and fall – and even these events bristle with problems and their details remain obscure. The year-names are an important witness to the emphasis placed on royal military exploits. Among the few things known about the Ur III kings is that one (Ur-Nammu) was killed in battle (Kramer 1967) – quite a rare event at any time and clearly illustrating the important role played by the king as warrior – and that another (Ibbi-Sin) was captured by the Elamites in an attack, taken to Elam and died in captivity (Jacobsen 1953). Other year-names tantalisingly refer to repeated victories in the Zagros mountains of western Iran, to military action against various, unfortunately ill-defined, pastoralists in the north-west ('Amorites'), and to attempts to regulate and control relations with some Amorites by the building of a fortified wall; but the precise details of these activities escape us.

The extant royal inscriptions are not nearly as informative as those from the Agade period; many are brief, votive texts dedicating a statue or object (Steible 1991). There are many inscribed 'foundation figurines', generally showing the king with the royal basket of bricks on his head (cf. Urnanshe of Lagash, p. 36), which formed part of the deposit placed in the foundations of buildings (R.S. Ellis, *Foundation Deposits in Ancient Mesopotamia*, New Haven, Conn., 1967), and vast numbers of bricks, stamped with the names of kings and used in royal construction projects. They provide helpful indicators of the extent of building undertaken by individual kings. They show that a major building programme was initiated by Ur-Nammu at Ur, particularly in the main temple area, where the magnificent ziggurat dates back to the Ur III period (fig. 6). Woolley's reconstruction of the upper stages of the ziggurat is purely hypothetical; there is no evidence for the domed gateways he included (Woolley 1954: fig. 16). However, the presence of vaulted 'mausolea' dating to this time (perhaps related to a funerary cult, but probably not the place where the Ur kings were buried, see Moorey 1984), and a pitched brick vault at the site of Rimah in north Iraq (Oates 1986 [OGb]: 48, fig. 28), indicate that, while Woolley's visualisation of the upper part of the ziggurat must remain speculative, it was not technologically impossible. Other constructions of sanctuaries are known at Uruk, Nippur, Eridu, Larsa, Kish, Lagash, Adab and Eshnunna in the Diyala. Much of this is temple-building, but the last site has produced a governor's residence with an attached shrine for the royal cult. Exactly where the palace and main residence of the kings were is not known. What the sources suggest is that, while Ur was certainly the chief dynastic centre, Uruk and Nippur played a very important role; and Eridu, too, seems to have had some symbolic significance for the rulers. Presumably this was related to the particular gods traditionally associated with these centres, and to the roles they played in the pantheon.

An important guide to royal activity and self-presentation is the earliest preserved 'law-code', directly comparable in its arrangement – a prologue followed by legal prescriptions – to the later, most famous Mesopotamian set of laws, the Hammurabi code. It is preserved in Old Babylonian copies from Nippur, Ur and Sippar. The promulgator of this code is now generally thought to be the second ruler of the dynasty, Shulgi, in whose long reign the consolidation of the empire of Ur took place (Kramer 1983b; Steinkeller 1987a). Written records and administrative procedure were standardised during his reign, the government reorganised and centralised, a standing army created, the tax and supply systems introduced, the king deified in his lifetime, and the official calendar devised. The prologue to the laws also mentions the institution of new divine offerings, the revitalisation of agricultural activities, the reopening

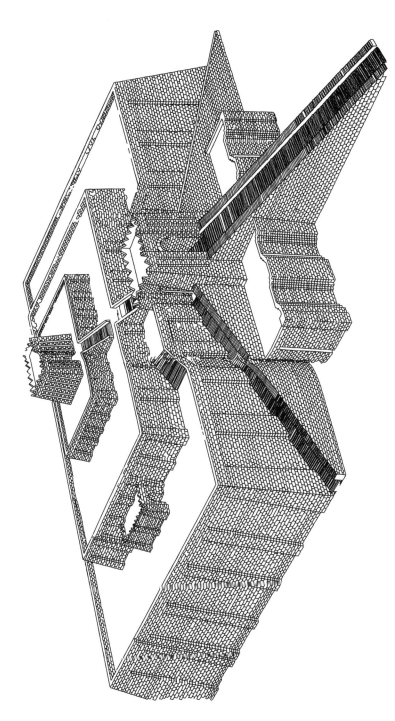

Figure 6 Ur ziggurat (reconstruction; after Roaf 1990 [0A])

of the Gulf trade, the establishment of 'freedom' (a m a – a r – g i$_4$ – b i) for some cities (presumably from certain labour-dues; cf. Yıldız 1981: 93 n. 20a) and the creation of new royal weight-standards. The image of the king as guarantor of all justice for his people is hammered home in the prologue:

> The orphan I certainly did not consign to the rich man, the widow I certainly did not consign to the powerful man, the 'man of 1 sheqel' I certainly did not consign to the 'man of 1 mina', the 'man of 1 sheep' I certainly did not consign to the 'man of 1 ox' . . . Hostility, violence, (and) lamentation to Utu (sungod, and god of justice) I caused to disappear definitively; I set justice in the land of the Sumer.
>
> (Finkelstein 1968–9; Yıldız 1981; *ANET*: 523ff.; *TUAT* I/1: 18ff.)

How the legal ordinances were administered is unclear, as is the king's role in the judicial process. From the extant legal documents, it appears that cases were normally decided at a local level by the *hazannum* (usually translated 'mayor'), although the provincial governor could override his decisions. The sale documents show symbolic solemnising acts taking place in this, as in earlier and later periods, in front of witnesses at the gate of a town quarter or temple precinct (Malul 1985). An indication that temple gates were particularly associated with legal transactions is a passage in the 'Lament over the Fall of Sumer and Ur', where the breakdown of law and order is described:

> Verdicts were not given in the Dublamah (gate of the temple of the moon-god at Ur), the place where oaths used to be taken
> The throne was not set up at its place of judgement, justice was not administered . . .
>
> (Michalowski 1989, ll. 438–439)

Did the king really function as the ultimate legal authority? References to the king as judge exist in literary texts (e.g. royal hymns, see pp. 68–69), which suggest that, in theory at least, the king was seen as the fount of justice and final arbiter.

Rather different information comes from the carved cylinder seals and accompanying legends, which record the personal names of the higher functionaries. The names were frequently compounds of the king's name, which functioned as the theophoric element. An illustration would be the name 'Simat-Shulgi' = 'Belonging to (the god-king) Shulgi' (cf. 'Simat-Ishtar' = 'Belonging to (the goddess) Ishtar'). The seal legends can be grouped into two main categories: one type is rather brief and gives name, office and descent of the owner – invaluable for studying the families of the officials. Others are much longer, such as:

> Shu-Sin, mighty king, king of Ur, king of the four quarters (of the world): Sur-ku-nunna, scribe, son of Lu-Ningirsu, the stockbreeder, is your servant.
>
> (Petrie Museum tablet, UC 36134)

These are expressions of loyalty to the king, and may be related to one of the most frequent images found on Ur III seals, the 'presentation-scene'. It shows the king seated, often with a small vessel in his hand, and being approached by a minor deity who brings a person into his presence (see fig.7). The figure brought before the king may well represent the seal owner, while the royal figure occupies the space that on earlier scenes of this type was occupied by a god. This, then, seems to reflect something of the divine aspect of the king, although it has been pointed out (Winter 1986; 1987a) that, apart from his position, he does not have any obvious divine attributes. The king is shown here as the just ruler, linked to early, legendary, divine kings, while the person being presented is in the position of petitioner protesting his loyalty to the throne. Possession of the seal itself is proof that the king has responded favourably and reciprocated by placing his trust in the owner. The seal-scenes thus illustrate the highly complex and delicately balanced interaction between the divine ruler and the upper echelons of the bureaucratic structure: the king at its apex forms a bridge between the human and divine spheres.

The divine nature of the king is also reflected in some 'letter-prayers'. These are petitions addressed to a deity or deified king by individuals. One striking example, beautifully composed in poetic form, is preserved in an Old Babylonian version, and may have been intended to address the statue of a dead king in the temple:

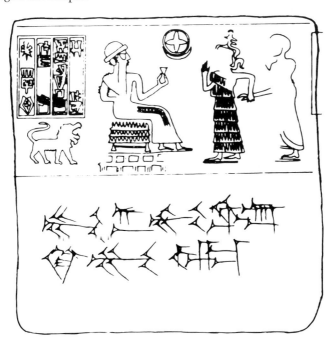

Figure 7 Seal-impression from an Ur III tablet (Petrie Museum, UC 36134)

To my king with varicoloured eyes, who wears a lapis lazuli beard
    speak;
To the golden statue fashioned on a good day
The . . . raised in a pure sheepfold, called to the pure womb of Inanna,
The lord, hero of Inanna, say:
'You (in) your judgement, you are the son of Anu
Your commands, like the word of a god, cannot be reversed,
Your words, like rain pouring down from heaven, are without number
Thus says Urshagga, your servant:
"My king has cared for me, who am a 'son' of Ur.
If now my king is (truly) of Anu,
Let not my father's house be carried off,
Let not the foundations of my father's house be torn away.
Let my king know."' (sc. 'This is my plea')
           (A. Falkenstein, *ZA* 44 (1934): 1–25; *ANET*: 382)

While it is not possible to maintain that this is how the Ur kings were actually addressed by petitioners, it may present a distant echo of such approaches.

The most remarkable evidence for the development of kingship ideology and its divine aspects in this period is the royal hymns. There are various types of hymn, some expressing prayers on behalf of the king and offered up in cultic contexts. But others appear to have been composed for specific occasions, to be sung in the course of court ceremonies; some elements seem to be refrains sung by a chorus, while others are in the first person and represent the king himself speaking. Because they are by and large preserved only in Old Babylonian versions, it has been doubted that they were composed in the Ur III period, but it now seems likely that they were indeed highly elaborate ceremonial poems performed at the courts of the Ur III rulers.[9] Although each hymn is different, they all contain the same essential elements (Hallo 1963) which emphasise the legitimacy of the king, through his royal descent, divinely born and appointed by the highest gods. His strength and physical beauty are also stressed: he is the perfect soldier and military commander, exceptionally strong and brave and an expert in handling all kinds of weapons. He always leads his troops into battle; the fame of his military triumphs is known throughout the world and inspires terror in his enemies. Occasionally there is a description of his exploits as a hunter of dangerous animals – he does not crouch in a pit to ensnare lions with nets, but fights them face to face and makes the land safe for the shepherd. Other themes are the king's care for the temples, the prosperity of the land, his justice and protection of the weak. These features are also taken up in the prologue to the law-code (see pp. 64–66); another text mentions the provision of a great canal by Ur-Nammu (Hallo 1966). In one of the Shulgi hymns there is also an interesting description of the construction of roads, equipped with resthouses, making communications both rapid and safe:

I (sc. Shulgi) enlarged the footpaths, straightened the highways of the
    land,
I made secure travel, built there 'big houses',
Planted gardens alongside of them, established resting-places,
Settled there friendly folk,
(So that) who comes from below, who comes from above,
Might refresh themselves in its cool (shade),
The wayfarer who travels the highway at night,
Might find refuge there as in a well-built city.

(ANET: 585; Klein 1981b: Shulgi, A 26–35)

The king's wisdom and learning are also duly emphasised: he is so wise
that all seek his advice in the assembly; when he decides a case he is able to
speak all the five languages used by his subjects without recourse to
interpreters (the languages were probably Akkadian, Sumerian, Amorite,
Elamite and perhaps Gutian). He is also the most expert diviner and knows
the liver-omen texts better than anyone else, so that when he inspects the
livers of sacrificial sheep the omen-experts look on in amazement at his skill.
His education is stressed:

As a youth, I studied the scribal arts in the tablet-house (i.e. school),
    from the tablets of Sumer and Akkad,
Of the nobles, no one was able to write a tablet like me,
In the place where the people attend to learn the scribal art,
Adding, subtracting, counting and accounting – I completed all (the
    courses);
The fair Nisaba (patron goddess of scribal arts),
Endowed me generously with wisdom and intelligence.

(G.R. Castellino, Two Shulgi Hymns (B, C), Rome: ŠB 196ff.; cf. Klein
1981a: 16 and n. 64)

The king also excels in music. He knows all hymns and melodies; he is
possessed of a pure, sweet voice; he is able to tune and play every instrument
(including antique ones); his music-making is so delightful that he makes his
subjects and the gods exceedingly happy. The king's reverence for the gods,
and his understanding of how to pacify them and pray to them on behalf of
his subjects, is also matchless. Given the many virtues and talents of the
king, his subjects respect him, as later generations are enjoined to do; the
hymns usually end by emphasising the unity and harmony of the country
under a single, supreme ruler.

    The king's special relationship to the gods was further enhanced by his
celebration of the 'sacred marriage' festival (RLA 4: 251–259; Kramer 1983a;
Frymer-Kensky 1992 [OL]: 55–59). Although the details of this ceremony
come from slightly later, references to it appear in the royal hymns, and there
is no reason to suppose it was not performed at this date. A number of aspects

of the ritual remain obscure, but it is likely that the king took the role of Dumuzi, the mortal husband of the goddess Inanna of Uruk; the role of Inanna herself was possibly played by a priestess. The king came to Inanna as her lover and 'slept' with her. Through this sexual act he approached the world of the gods more closely than other mortals and ensured the continuing beneficent partnership between humanity and the divine sphere. The ritual probably took place on the king's accession. It culminated in the bestowal of the royal insignia and the goddess' pronouncement of his 'destiny', in other words she publicly declared her support for him so that his reign would be long and successful.

The end of Ur III

The essential vulnerability of the system on which the elaborate super-structure of the Ur state rested has been mentioned. It depended on holding together a large stretch of territory, being able to maintain regular com-munications, collect taxes and tribute, protect long frontiers, and produce wealth in the form of finished products and regular agricultural surpluses. What configuration of events precipitated Ur's ultimate dramatic break-up is not clear, but signs of problems in the conquered territories, perhaps indicating a loss of control, began to appear in the reign of Shu-Sin (Steinkeller 1987a: 36 n. 55), and rapidly reached crisis proportions in that of Ibbi-Sin. A series of letters between Ibbi-Sin and two of his provincial governors[10] provides a vivid picture of the last Ur III ruler in dire straits: short of the crucial grain resources, with prices rising at fantastic rates, communication routes, and so supplies, disrupted by fringe groups of pastoralists ('Amorites'), cities in south Mesopotamia thrown on their own resources as a result of the failure of the central power to protect and provision them, and their gradual abandonment of the central calendar, Ibbi-Sin was left with a very diminished and probably undersupplied force to face a serious attack by combined forces from Elam and Shimashki (north-east Khuzistan, see Steinkeller 1988). The rapidly worsening situation is illustrated by this letter:

> After you have spoken to Ibbi-Sin, my king: 'This is what Ishbi-Erra, your servant, says: "I was ordered to make a journey to Isin (and) Kazallu in order to buy barley. The barley has a value of 1 (sheqel silver) per kor of barley (and) 20 talents of silver have been provided for the barley-purchase. Reports were received that hostile m a r t u (Amorites) entered your territory and I have brought 72 000 kor of barley, the entire barley, into Isin. Now the m a r t u have completely penetrated into the land of Sumer (and) have captured all the fortresses there. Because of the m a r t u I cannot give the barley to be threshed. They are stronger than I. I should be seized. May my king have 600 transport boats each of 120 kor capacity prepared . . . I shall assume (protection

of) the place where the boats dock, and thus all(?) the barley may be stored (and) transferred in its totality. Assuming that you let the barley diminish too much, I shall have barley brought in to you. My king, the Elamite has become bitter in battle, his barley-rations will soon be finished, you should not let (the strength of) your arm grow slack, you should not hasten to enter a servant-relationship with him, and you should not run after him! Barley for 15 years: your provisions of the palace and the city are all in my hand. The guarding of Isin and Nibru, my king, I am taking upon myself! May my king know (this)!'"

(PBS 13: no. 9; *TUAT* I/4: 344–346)

But despite such detailed information the complex sequence of events remains obscure. One approach is to see the 'nomadic' Amorites pressing in from the Syrian desert, breaking through the frontier wall (above p. 64) and descending to ravage the rich cities of the south Mesopotamian plain (Jacobsen 1953). But the evidence, which shows that many groups of Amorites formed an integral part of the Ur III state (Buccellati 1966), with others following a variety of subsistence patterns and forming small enclaves on and beyond the fringes of the state, suggests that there can never have been a unified 'barbarian horde' of Amorites, capable of wreaking havoc in a concerted move. A more subtle model of interaction must be posited: the marauding bands mentioned in the letters were separate groups (all dubbed 'Amorite' by the Ur III government), who took advantage of the collapsing imperial structure and probably made an already critical situation worse (Michalowski 1983). Certainly, the final devastating onslaught on Ur came from Elam and Shimashki, as is made clear by the famous 'Lamentations' over the destruction of Ur, composed not long after the disaster (Kramer 1940; Michalowski 1989). Although they are not eye-witness accounts, they nevertheless paint a moving picture of the ruin of a city:

Hunger filled the city like water, it would not cease,
(This) hunger contorts (people's) faces, it twists their muscles.
Its people are (as if) surrounded by water, they gasp for breath,
Its king breathed heavily in his palace, all alone,
Its people dropped (their) weapons, (their) weapons hit the ground,
They struck their necks with their hands and cried.
They sought council with each other, they searched for clarification:
'Alas, what can we say about it, what more can we add to it?
How long until we are finished off by this calamity?
Ur – inside it there is death, outside it there is death,
Inside it we are being finished off by famine,
Outside it we are being finished off by Elamite weapons,
In Ur, the enemy has oppressed us, oh, we are finished!'
They take refuge(?) behind it (i.e. the city walls), they were united (in their fear).

The palace that was destroyed by (onrushing) waters has been defiled,
    its bolt was torn out,
Elam, like a swelling flood wave, left only the spirits of the dead(?).
In Ur (people) were smashed as if they were clay pots,
Its refugees were (unable) to flee, they were trapped inside the walls,
Like fish living in a pond, they seek shelter.
The enemy seized the Ekishnugal of Nanna,
The statues that were in the treasury were cut down,
The great stewardess Niniagara ran away from(?) the storehouse,
Its throne was cast down before it, she threw herself down into the dust.
                (*ANET*: 611ff.; Michalowski 1989: ll. 390–412)

Interestingly, the fall of the powerful dynasty of Ur was not presented in the laments as due to royal sacrilege, as was the case with the fall of the Agade dynasty (Cooper 1983a: 29–30). It was simply accepted that its time had run out and the gods had decided to end its rule:

Who has ever seen a reign of kingship that would take precedence (for ever)?
The reign of its (sc. Ur's) kingship had been long indeed but had to exhaust itself.
O my Nanna (moongod and patron deity of Ur), do not exert yourself (in vain), leave your city!
                (*ANET*: 611ff.; Michalowski 1989: ll. 368–370)

Notes

1 Cylinder seals are a form of sealing peculiar to Mesopotamia (they were also used by adjacent societies at various times). They are small cylinders (usually of stone or paste) carved with often intricate scenes (sometimes also bearing inscriptions). When the cylinder was rolled over the damp clay of a tablet, the carved image was unfolded and impressed on the document. Many cylinder seals have been found, and many more impressions are known from tablets. They constitute one of the most important sources for the study of iconography and stylistic developments, as well as for social and governmental practices (for a good general introduction, see Collon 1987 [0M]; for sealing practices, cf. McG. Gibson and R.D. Biggs (eds), *Seals and Sealing in the Ancient Near East* (Bibliotheca Mesopotamica 6), Malibu, Cal., 1977).
2 On the problems of the terminology of the archaeological phases, cf. Crawford 1991; U. Finkbeiner (ed.) *Gamdat Nasr: period or regional style?*, Wiesbaden 1986; for a general discussion of Jemdet Nasr, cf. R.J. Matthews, 'Jemdet Nasr: the site and period' *BibArch* 55 (1992): 196–205.
3 Cf. now also the approximately contemporary site of Tell Beydar (*c.* 45 km west of Tell Brak, in the headwaters of the Khabur river). where a Belgian team have found about 65 documents (reported in the *Independent* 23.11.1993). All the personal names are Semitic; the texts have affinities with southern Mesopotamia. (The number of texts now stands at over 100.)
4 The stele (its surviving fragments are now in the Louvre) is of limestone, carved

with scenes on both sides; its original place of erection is not precisely known.

5 The name was originally read 'Urukagina'; it is now usually read 'Uruinimgina', although sometimes the uncertainty is signalled by writing UruKAgina.

6 It is now known that the great literary poem on the destruction of Agade in Naram-Sin's reign was already in existence in the Ur III period; Cooper, 1983a: 11.

7 The various strands of these tales surface in the Sumerian King List (Jacobsen 1939: col. vi. 31–35), the late 'Weidner Chronicle' (*ABC* 19: 46–48) and a Sumerian literary text (Cooper and Heimpl 1983).

8 The huge surpluses on which the state depended suggest that Herodotus' much later account of Babylonia's agricultural productivity, which he says his listeners refused to believe (Herodotus I 193), is likely to have been correct. The Ur III material certainly shows that such miraculous yields were *possible*.

9 The evidence for the existence of the royal hymns at the time of Ur III is a) the archaic spelling used in some passages (Klein 1981a; 1981b) and b) the identification of a fragment of an Ur III version of one hymn (Civil, *Or.* 54 (1985)).

10 The letters were copied and recopied in the later Old Babylonian schools and perhaps elaborated there (Michalowski 1980a).

2

MESOPOTAMIA *c.* 2000–*c.* 1600: THE OLD BABYLONIAN AND OLD ASSYRIAN PERIODS

Introduction

The period from the end of Ur III to the end of the first dynasty of Babylon (1595 according to the conventional 'middle chronology') is called broadly 'Old Babylonian'. This is really a linguistic terminology, describing the Akkadian language as it developed in south Mesopotamia at this time. In the north, by contrast, the earliest documents in the Assyrian dialect of Akkadian are found in this period ('Old Assyrian'). Akkadian was not the exclusive written language: as in the preceding period, a lot of material, especially literary texts, was still being composed in Sumerian, and a large proportion of the rich harvest of Sumerian literature is preserved in copies from this period; legal texts, too, used Sumerian formulae extensively. Obviously, the training in schools and in learned families (Sjöberg 1974; Charpin 1986) continued to stress the cultural value of reading and writing Sumerian. But later in the period there is a marked increase in Akkadian literary texts and inscriptions.

This is a time rich in very diverse documentation from a variety of cities and smaller sites. The material illuminates brilliantly an enormous range of activities in the numerous states of Mesopotamia, parts of the Levant and even Anatolia. The richest and most varied evidence of all is, undoubtedly, the huge Mari archives (modern Tell Hariri; *c.* 1800–1760). But the important archives from Kültepe (ancient Kanesh) in Anatolia, which provide a detailed picture of Assyrian long-distance trade (see chapter 2c), and the smaller archives from Shemshara (the Rowanduz area of north-east Iraq) and Rimah (the Sinjar region) also illustrate trade, politics and international relations at this time. The far-reaching interconnections between different regions illuminated by this material are known to have existed earlier, but only now can they be defined more precisely.

The dominant political pattern of the period is that of a multitude of independent city-states, forging alliances, trying to draw smaller cities into their orbit, and competing with each other for pre-eminence. Some of the states emerge as fairly large and powerful entities: places such as Eshnunna,

Mari, Isin, Larsa and Babylon. The political model which some of them strove to emulate was that of Agade and Ur III. In several centres, from the Levant to south Mesopotamia, dynasties with rulers bearing Amorite names were in control. Amorite was a Semitic language, closely affiliated to the western Semitic group to which later Hebrew belongs. Unfortunately, almost the only evidence for the Amorite language is provided by personal names, which suggests that it was never written. How the Amorite dynasties and people came to form such a significant element in the population of the area is not known. But their continuous presence in the armies and workforces of the Agade and Ur III empires is well attested (see pp. 55; 71), so they were not a new population group. Those Amorites who lived in the frontier zones of the Ur III state and had taken the opportunity, as it crumbled, to move into core regions probably swelled their number (see chapter 1d; for basic documentation, cf. Anbar 1991). Some of the new city-dynasties used royal titles that defined the king as a member of a particular Amorite tribe, such as: 'Sin-kashid, king of the Amnanum (tribe)', or simply as belonging to the Amorites, e.g.: 'Zabaya, chief of the Amorites (Sum. m a r t u = Akk. *amurru*)'. Such pedigrees seem to have played a crucial, albeit poorly understood, role in the royal ideology of this time. The Amorite 'royal genealogy', which was related to a royal ancestor cult, provides another hint of their importance (see Finkelstein 1966; Michalowski 1983; Yuhong and Dalley 1990).

It is not at present possible to present a connected political history of this period.[1] The available archives make it possible to glimpse a pattern of shifting power-centres within Mesopotamia. Thus we can see that in southern Mesopotamia the hegemony of the Isin dynasty (successors to Ur III) was successfully challenged by the city of Larsa, which in turn was defeated by Hammurabi of Babylon's expansionist policy. It is also possible to trace the creation by Shamshi-Adad I of a large, though fleeting, 'empire' in north Mesopotamia, which embraced important cities such as Mari, Ashur, Nineveh and Shubat-Enlil (possibly, though not certainly, Tell Leilan in the Khabur headwaters: Weiss 1985 [0Gc]; 1985; *MARI* 4 (1985)). Other important political powers, whose histories remain unfortunately fairly obscure, are Eshnunna in the Diyala valley, and Aleppo and Qatna in north Syria. Of these, the history of the powerful kingdom of Aleppo is perhaps the one most consistently illuminated by various documents. But none of the evidence comes from Aleppo itself, and it often serves simply to make us more aware of the depths of our ignorance. Ebla (Tell Mardikh IIIA and B) has yielded rich archaeological material (palaces, temples, a strongly fortified city-wall, subterranean tombs analogous to those found at Ugarit slightly later), which indicates its revival as an important urban centre. But very little textual material comes from Ebla in this period and its political relations with the larger powers remain obscure. However, the evidence of an inscribed royal statue indicates that here, too, an Amorite dynasty was in control (Matthiae 1984; Weiss and Kohlmeyer in Weiss 1985 [0Gc]).

2a South Mesopotamia c. 2000–c. 1800

The Sumerian King List and the 'royal correspondence of Ur' (see p. 70) show that the shrunken remnants of the Ur III state were held together by Ishbi-Erra, an official of Ibbi-Sin, who had established himself in the fortified city of Isin. By his twenty-second regnal year he was able to expel the Elamite garrison from Ur, and gain some control over the original core of the empire. But places like Eshnunna (Diyala valley) and Der (east Tigris) continued to be independent, although it was some time before their rulers laid claim to royal titles (Edzard 1957). Ashur and Elam (with Susa) also remained firmly outside Ishbi-Erra's realm. Nevertheless, the new king gradually adopted part of the Ur III titulary, such as 'king of the four quarters', and was, at least in some contexts, deified. There is, in fact, considerable evidence for continuity in royal and governmental traditions, despite the marked political changes (Stone 1987). Ibbi-Sin's daughter, for example, retained her position as *ēntum* of the moon-god at Ur until her death, when she was succeeded by Ishbi-Erra's daughter; in fact, much of the evidence for this office comes from this period (Weadock 1975). Some of the most magnificent royal hymns, developing and elaborating the themes of the Ur III hymns (see pp. 68–69), were composed for the Isin kings (Römer 1965). The fullest evidence for perform-ance of the sacred marriage ritual, with its emphasis on divine blessing of the occupant of the throne, also dates from this period (see pp. 69–70). In a rather different sphere, the marked similarity in administrative practices is striking, although this subject is only now beginning to receive full attention (van de Mierop 1987). The basic bureaucratic structure was the same and officials took names with, for instance, Ishbi-Erra as the theophoric element. The main political and economic base for Ishbi-Erra's power (however curtailed by comparison with Ur III) was his hold on the ideologically important cities of Ur, Uruk and Nippur and his control of the routes to the Gulf coast, which allowed him to take full advantage of the rich Arabian and Indian trade (Oppenheim 1954; Potts 1990 [0Gf]: I, chs. 6 and 7).

Many of the elements of royal ceremonial and ritual, which are a marked feature of the Isin dynasty, certainly down to 1932, can be interpreted as a deliberate emulation by the Isin kings of the Ur III imperial style, which was necessary in order to cement their position as the legitimate successors of the Ur III rulers. The promulgating of law-codes was another activity that may be classified as an important part of royal ideology, taken over by the Isin rulers from Ur III. Only fragments of copies of one of the codes are preserved (Steele 1948), but enough survives to show that its form was very similar to that of the Ur code. It was originally inscribed on a stele, perhaps set up in a temple, and presented the king in the now standard role of the just ruler. Such legal prescriptions were just one part of a mass of royal legal and govern-mental ordinances which emerge with relative clarity only in the next two to three hundred years. They can be shown to have formed part of a king's regular activities throughout the whole of Mesopotamia, parts of the Levant (north Syria) and Elam. It was usual for a king on, or soon after, his accession to affirm publicly his concern for social justice through an edict. His focus on that occasion was the righting of imbalances, particularly those created by debt. Careful study has made it possible to reconstruct in part how the process worked (Kraus 1984; Charpin 1986: 70ff.; Greengus 1988): torches were lit to signal to the population that a royal proclamation was to be made, local officials were summoned to the capital for briefing and written copies of the enactments distributed. The tablets that enshrined the debtors' obligations to their creditors were then collected and broken, thereby dissolving the debt. In cases where the contracting parties wished a particular agreement to continue in force, this had to be formally reaffirmed before the king's servants and judges (Kraus 1958; Charpin 1986: 169–173). Some features of these royal pronouncements are also found in the law-codes. This suggests that the codes and edicts were part of a range of royal legal decisions, which were re-enacted on a king's accession (or perhaps simply ratified) and sometimes formally repeated later in the reign (Kraus 1984).

The final compilation of the Sumerian King List (see pp. 29–31) at this time played a crucial role in showing that the Isin dynasty ruled in accordance with the divine will, which ordained that dynasties should rise and fall, and that it was a fit successor to the Ur III kings. The list presented the Isin kings as an integral part of the kaleidoscopic pattern of royal power since time began: famous kings, such as Sargon of Agade and Shulgi of Ur, were part of this divine lottery and now it was the turn of Isin's rulers (Michalowski 1983). The rebuilding of temples, destroyed by the Elamites and their allies from Shimashki (see pp. 70–71), was important in illustrating the divine harmony which obtained under the Isin kings: the two famous lamentations over the destruction of Ur were composed shortly after its fall and commemorated the restoration of its famous sacred buildings (Kramer 1940; Michalowski 1989). These 'historical' laments, as well as other similar ones, all describe the destruction and total break-down of civilised life as due to a divine decision which unleashed enemy invasions, made the hostile armies triumph and caused the abandonment of the city by its patron-deity. The restoration, therefore, of a city devastated at divine command, could only be undertaken once permission to rebuild it had been obtained from the gods; the divine granting of the go-ahead to a particular king confirmed that he enjoyed special favour from the gods. The Nippur Lament, commemorating the rebuilding there by Ishme-Dagan, king of Isin (1953–1935), illustrates this important aspect:

> He (Enlil) heard his prayer, and looked benevolently upon him.
> The words of Ishme-Dagan (king of Isin) pleased him.
> His submission and surrender moved him.
>
> (Vanstiphout 1983: 336)

The pride which the Isin kings took in this visible evidence of divine blessing was emphasised, from the reign of Ishme-Dagan (1953–1935) onwards, by the introduction of a whole string of new titles. Henceforth the kings were described as those 'who care for Ur, Nippur, Eridu, Uruk and Isin' – the major cities of ideological importance that they had rebuilt. Archaeologists have found some buildings at Isin, including the temple of Gula, Isin's patron-goddess and patroness of healing. However, the chronological sequences still need clarification before we can gain a full impression of the city in this period; as the German excavations on the site progress, they will eventually provide this (*RLA* 5: 189–192; Hrouda 1977–87).

Despite their elaborate ideology, the ultimate fragility of the Isin kings' hold on power is marked by the rise of a rival dynasty at Larsa, about 100 km to the south (1932, see table 5). This was one of the Amorite dynasties, as is evident from the names of its kings, and the occasional use of a title indicating their tribal affiliation (see p. 75). Gungunum (the first ruler of the independent Larsa dynasty, 1932–1906) and his father had, almost certainly, functioned as governors of the province of Lagash (which included Larsa) for the Isin rulers, which indicates the level of integration of many Amorites into the political fabric. Larsa's break with the Isin domain was marked by Gungunum's capture of Ur, which was not only of symbolic importance but, above all, the main port for the profitable Gulf trade; its loss robbed the Isin kings of an important source of revenue.

The reasons behind the secession of Larsa are completely obscure. An interesting group of texts (Walters 1970) suggests that a factor (probably only one among many) was the insufficient attention paid by the Isin rulers to the irrigation of the country beyond their own immediate environs. It is unclear whether this neglect was due to the smaller scale of the state economy and labour-force; but that squabbles about water were a recurring factor deter-mining political events in the south for a considerable time (about sixty years) seems certain. The dispute ended when kings Abisare (1905–1895) and Sumu-el (1894–1866) of Larsa effected a pincer movement around Isin, cutting it off almost totally from water by diverting its canals southwards to the Larsa region. The impact of this on the economy of Isin, combined with its loss of Ur, the connected Gulf trade and its eventual loss of control over Nippur, seems to have been drastic and Isin declined rapidly. Signs of this political catastrophe can be seen at Isin in a dynastic crisis, which brought a usurper to the throne (Enlil-bani 1860–1837) and ended the solid father–son succession that had prevailed earlier. Although kings continued to rule in Isin, their real political power waned dramatically. But their ideological claim to be rulers of the region must have continued to have some force: the city of Isin was not conquered and integrated into the Larsa kingdom until the last king of Larsa, Rim-Sin (1822–1763); and it was such an important achieve-ment that all Rim-Sin's remaining thirty-one years of reign were named after this event:

Table 5 Chronology of southern Mesopotamia *c*. 2000–1750

Isin	Larsa	Babylon
Ishbi-Erra (2017–1985)	[Naplanum 2025]	
	[Emisum 2004]	
Shu-ilishu (1984–1975)	[Samium 1976]	
Iddin-Dagan (1974–1954)		
Ishme-Dagan (1953–1935)	[Zabaya 1941]	
Lipit-Ishtar (1934–1924)	Gungunum 1932–1906	
Ur-Ninurta (1923–1896)	Abisare 1905	
Bur-Sin (1895–1874)	Sumu-el 1894	Sumuabum (1894–1881)
Lipit-Enlil (1873–1869)		Sumulael (1880–1845)
Erra-imitti (1868–1861)	Nur-Adad 1865	
*Enlil-bani (1860–1837)	Sin-iddinam 1849	Sabium (1844–1831)
	Sin-eribam 1842	
	Sin-iqisham 1840	
Zambiya (1836–1834)	Silli-Adad 1835	
Iter-pisha (1833–1831)	Warad-Sin 1834	
Ur-dukuga (1830–1828)		Apil-Sin (1830–1813)
Sin-magir (1827–1817)	Rim-Sin I 1822–1763	
Damiq-ilishu (1816–1794)		Sin-muballit (1812–1793)
		Hammurabi (1792–1750)

(This is the conventional 'Middle Chronology' used by, e.g., *CAH*; for the 'low chronology' all dates would have to be *lowered by 64 years*, giving a date for Hammurabi of 1728–1686; see Introduction, p. 12.)

* contemporary of Sinkashid of Uruk.

(Rim-Sin year 30): 'With the elevated weapon of Anu, Enlil and Enki the true shepherd, Rim-Sin, conquered the royal city Isin, and all its inhabitants, as many as there were, caused its many inhabitants to preserve their life, and made its royal name famous for all time.'

(year 31): 'The year following (the one in which) with the elevated weapon of Anu, Enlil, and Enki etc.'
(year 32): 'The year after the year following etc.'
(year 33): 'The fourth year of etc.'
(and so on until Rim-Sin's 60th year)

(RLA 2, s.v. 'Datenlisten': 152–153; 163–164)

The Larsa dynasty was by no means free from political challenges, as is shown by an unusual text composed by a later ruler of Larsa, Sin-iddinam (1849–1843). According to this, the territory of Larsa was invaded by enemies at the end of the reign of Sumu-el (1866) – the king responsible for building a barrage and successfully diverting the water from Isin (see p. 78). The invasion threatened the country with famine and so, in desperation, the population revolted against the king of Larsa by going over to the enemy. At this point, when all seemed lost, Utu (Sumerian sun-god, patron-deity of Larsa) chose a human helper to put matters right and appointed Nur-Adad, Sin-iddinam's father (1865–1850), whom he taught how to restore order in the kingdom of Larsa (van Dijk 1965). It is an intriguing tale, obviously composed to strengthen the hold of a king with no real genealogical claim to the throne, and it is our only, rather elusive, clue to the political problems encountered by Larsa in its attempt to establish an independent, secessionist state. Nur-Adad and Sin-iddinam seem to have been successful in setting the new kingdom on a more solid footing: an impressive palace was built in Larsa itself by Nur-Adad (*RLA* 6: 500–503; Margueron 1982). The recent discovery of Mashkan-Shapir (at Abu Duwari, p. 8; Stone and Zimansky 1992), second capital of the realm, shows that Larsa controlled territory on and to the east of the Tigris. Sin-iddinam enclosed this important city with a city-wall; it was crossed by four canals and contained a palace.

Although Larsa thus became a power to be reckoned with, it seems never to have succeeded in establishing itself as a larger, integrated state. A later text from Mari simply describes the great Rim-Sin of Larsa (1822–1763)[2] as ruler of the city and head of a coalition of ten to fifteen other cities (see p. 99). This suggests considerable political fragmentation within the region, with smaller states drawn into the orbit of more powerful ones. The disturbances at Larsa in the mid-nineteenth century were probably not an isolated incident. At approximately the same time, Uruk became independent under Sinkashid 'king of Uruk, king of the Amnanum (an Amorite tribe)'. The new ruler of Uruk established a dynasty, allied himself by marriage with the newly emergent rulers of Babylon (also Amorites) and claimed full royal titles. Eshnunna in the Diyala valley also extended its power around this time, probably culminating in a brief control of Ashur in *c.* 1830. By the late nineteenth century the great centralised state of Ur III lived on only as a distant memory.

2b Ashur in the Old Assyrian period (c. 2000–c. 1800)

Location and name

The site of Ashur is located about 100 km south of Mosul, on the west bank of the Tigris, occupying a northern spur of Jebel Hamrin. To the north and east the site was originally washed by rivers: the Tigris to the east and a canal to the north (cf. fig. 8). Ashur lies on the fringes of the rainfall zone, which means that farming is not completely dependent on irrigation; it is also in an excellent position to take advantage of important caravan routes running north to south, and east to west. The Ottoman sultan presented the site to the German emperor, Wilhelm II, and it was under his august auspices that the Deutsche Orientgesellschaft conducted excavations there between 1903 and 1913. Very little of the Old Assyrian period remains were investigated. This was due to the fact that a large section of the Ashur-temple lay under a

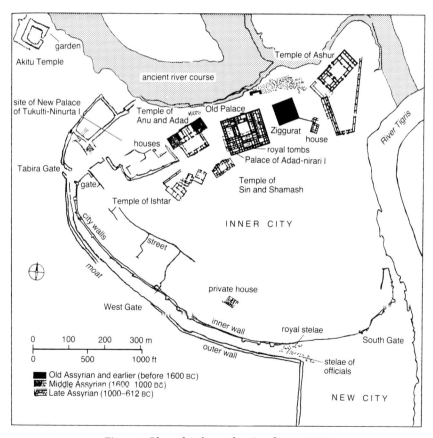

Figure 8 Plan of Ashur (after Roaf 1990 [OA])

Turkish police-post, while elsewhere later monuments and buildings from the great imperial phases of Assyria's history are too important, and simply too large, to make fuller excavation feasible. Some deep soundings were made, mainly on the site of the Ishtar temple. They provided a sequence of levels on which a relatively coherent picture of the chronology hinges (see table 6; Larsen 1976). It is not always easy to assign other structures, such as the city-walls, to a specific period. Some evidence for buildings is derived from inscribed bricks and royal building inscriptions. Private houses dating to the Old Assyrian period have been found, but are unfortunately not fully published (see generally Andrae 1938).

Table 6 Chronology of the Old Assyrian kings

	27 [Sulili	
	28 Kikkiya	(not attested in
c. 2015–	29 Akiya]	inscriptions)
c. 1939	30 Puzur-Ashur I	
	31 Shallim-Ahhe	
	32 Ilushuma	
1939–1900	33 Erishum I	
	34 Ikunum	(majority of *kārum*
	35 Sargon I	Kanesh II texts *c.* 1900–*c.* 1830)
	36 Puzur-Ashur II	
1900–1814	37 Naram-Sin	
	(4-year reign)	
	38 Erishum II	
	(1-year reign?)	
1813–1781	39 Shamshi-Adad I	(level Ib *kārum* Kanesh texts *c.* 1800–1780? or *c.* 1820–*c.* 1750?)

(Arabic Numbers refer to the Assyrian king list, see pp. 85–86.)

The name 'Ashur' is something of a problem (see Lambert in Wiseman 1973 [OA]), because the name of the chief god of the city and the name of the town are identical. The city-name, Ashur, appears already in texts of the Agade period (but not in the Ebla texts, cf. Geller *RA* 77 (1983)) and does not appear as a divine name until Ur III. Scholars have, therefore, argued that the place-name is the primary one and the god's name derived from it – a divine embodiment of the city. In much later periods the place-name was sometimes written BAL.TIL, which was, according to J. and H. Lewy, the original name of the site and showed that it was really Hurrian (*CAH* I, ch. 25); but it is now generally accepted that the spelling BAL.TIL is no more than a learned scribal archaism. The name for the later country of Assyria derives from the city Ashur; but, in the Old Assyrian and earlier periods, Ashur comprised no more than the city and its immediate environment. It always occupied a special place in Assyria right down to its destruction in

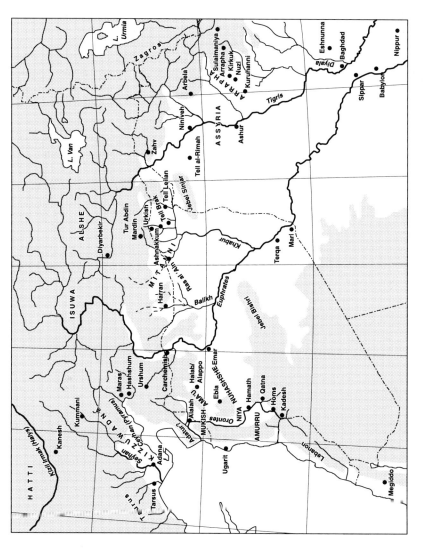

Map 4 Upper Mesopotamia and north Syria

614, even when other Assyrian towns developed into important political centres, because it was the original core of the country and centre of the Ashur-cult. Its territory was in later periods always referred to simply as 'the country' (*mātum*).

Sources for Ashur's history

The main contemporary sources for the city's history are the royal building inscriptions from Ashur which, with rare exceptions, are brief, and limited to noting repairs and embellishments of major monuments. They use the Old Assyrian dialect of Akkadian (quite distinct from Old Babylonian) and they only give the king a very simple title: '*išš'iak (dingir) Aššur*' = 'vicegerent (or governor) of the god Ashur'. A typical example is this text of Erishum I (1939–1900), found on bricks and on the stairway of the Ashur-temple:

> Erishum, vicegerent of the god Ashur, son of Ilushuma, vicegerent of the god Ashur, built the entire temple area of the temple of the god Ashur and the Step Gate, the courtyard, (and) the chapel of the god Ashur for the god Ashur, his lord, for his life and the life of his city.
> (B. Meissner, *Die Inschriften der altassyrischen Könige*, 1926: V, 8a–e; Grayson 1972: XXXIII no. 8; Grayson 1987: A.0.33.4)

The contemporary royal texts are complemented by the inscriptions of much later Assyrian rulers (from the Middle and Neo-Assyrian periods; see chapters 7b; 9) which mention building done by earlier kings. An important (albeit problematical) aspect of these texts is that they date such earlier work in relation to the later king, which provides potentially valuable chronological information (the technical term for them is 'Distanzangaben': Na'aman 1984 [OO]). Here, for example, is the Middle Assyrian king Tiglath-pileser I (1114–1076) recalling work done by his royal predecessors:

> At that time the temple of the gods An and Adad, the great gods, my lords, which Shamshi-Adad, vice-regent of Ashur, son of Ishme-Dagan, also vice-regent of the god of Ashur, had previously built: 641 years had passed, it had become dilapidated and Ashur-dan, king of Assyria, son of Ninurta-apil-Ekur, also king of Assyria, tore down that temple but did not rebuild (it) and for 60 years its foundation had not been relaid.
> (L.W. King, *Annals of the Kings of Assyria* 1 (1902), cyl. A: vii 60–70; Grayson 1976: LXXXVII 1 (§54); Grayson 1987: A.0.87.1)

The only ruler (before the fourteenth century) to depart from the tradition of a very simple titulary and use of the Assyrian dialect in inscriptions was Shamshi-Adad I (1813–1781). He introduced very long, elaborate royal epithets based on models from south Mesopotamia, and simultaneously started to use the Old Babylonian dialect for his inscriptions (Grayson 1971).

The political, economic and social situation in Ashur is mainly illuminated by the numerous Old Assyrian texts from the Assyrian trading establishment at Kanesh, near Kayseri, in central Anatolia, dating *c.* 1900–1830 (*kārum* Kanesh II: Özgüç 1963; *RLA* 5: 378–382; see chapter 2c). The only fully preserved royal edict comes from here; perhaps it was read out in public on the occasion of a formal oath-taking ceremony (Landsberger and Balkan 1950; Kraus 1984). The text is rather obscure in places, but reflects the role of Ashur's king as upholder of justice:

> (The god) Ashur (is) king. Erishum (is) vicegerent. Ashur (is like) reed swamps that cannot be traversed, districts that cannot be trodden upon, canals that cannot be crossed.
>
> The one who talks too much (i.e.tells lies) in the Step Gate, the demon of ruins will seize his mouth and his hindquarters; he will smash his head like a shattered pot; he will fall like a broken reed and water will flow from his mouth. The one who tells lies in the Step Gate, his house will become a house of ruin. He who rises to give false testimony, may the [Seven] Judges who decide legal cases in [the Step Gate give a false] decision [against him]; [may Ashur], Adad, and Bel, [my god, pluck his seed]; a place [. . .] may they not give him.
>
> [The one who . . .] . . . obeys me, [when he goes] to the Step Gate [may] the palace deputy [assist him]; [may he send] the witnesses and plaintiff (to the court); [may] the judges [take the bench] and give a proper decision [in Ash]ur.
>
> (Landsberger and Balkan 1950; Grayson 1972: XXXIII 9 (§§74–76);
> Grayson 1987: A.0.33.1).

More evidence for Assyrian trade and the political situation in the period of Shamshi-Adad I (1813–1781) comes from the Mari archives (see chapter 2d), the Shemshara tablets (Laessøe 1959; 1965; Eidem 1985; 1992), the Rimah texts (Dalley *et al.* 1976) and, most recently, the Tell Leilan material (Weiss 1985), all of which formed part of the great realm created by Shamshi-Adad I.

The most important, as well as most complicated, piece of evidence for this period is the Assyrian King List, of which several copies from the early first millennium exist. The relevant part of the text is the beginning:

> 1) Tudiya, 2) Adamu, 3) Yangi, 4) Kitlamu, 5) Harharu, 6) Mandaru, 7) Imsu, 8) Harsu, 9) Didanu, 10) Hanu, 11) Zuabu, 12) Nuabu, 13) Abazu, 14) Belu, 15) Azarah, 16) Ushpia, 17) Apiashal
> (the first twelve names should probably be discarded as they also appear in the Hammurabi genealogy, see Finkelstein 1966)
> Total: 17 kings 'who lived in tents'
>
> _____
>
> 26) Aminu the son of Ilu-kabkabi, 25) Ilukabkabi the son of Yazkur-ilu, 24) Yazkur-ilu the son of Yakmeni, 23) Yakmeni the son of Yakmesi, 22) Yakmesi the son of Ilu-Mer, 21) Ilu-Mer the son of Hayani, 20) Hayani the son of Samanu, 19) Samanu the son of Hale, 18)

Hale the son of Apiashal, 17) Apiashal the son of Ushpia (= no. 16 above)
Total: 10 kings 'who are ancestors'.
(The king-list moves backwards at this point; these individuals are in
fact the ancestors of Shamshi-Adad I. The intention seems to be to link
his father (no. 25 = Ilu-kabkabi) and brother (no. 26 = Aminu) to
Apiashal (= no. 17), the son of Ushpia (cf. Landsberger 1954).)

27) Sulili son of Aminu, 28) Kikkiya, 29) Akiya, 30) Puzur-Ashur (I),
31) Shallim-Ahhe, 32) Ilushuma
Total: 6 kings 'whose eponyms (*limmu* (cf. p. 89) are destroyed'.

33) Erishum (I) son of Ilushuma whose [. . .]; he ruled as king for 40 years

34) Ikunum son of Erishum; he ruled as king for [x years]

35) Sargon (I) son of Ikunum; he ruled as king for [x years]

36) Puzur-Ashur (II) son of Sargon; he ruled as king for [x] years

37) Naram-Sin son of Puzur-Ashur; he ruled as king for [x] years

38) Erishum (II) son of Naram-Sin; he ruled as king for [x] years
(for nos. 33–38), cf. table 6)

39) Shamshi-Adad (I), son of Ilu-kabkabi. In the time of Naram-Sin he
went to Kar-Duniash (i.e. Babylonia, northern part). In the eponymy
of Ibni-Adad, Shamshi-Adad came up from Kar-Duniash. He seized
the town of Ekallate (near Ashur). He stayed in Ekallate for three years.
In the eponymy of Atamar-Ishtar, he went up from Ekallate. He
removed Erishum (= no. 38), son of Naram-Sin (= no. 37) from the
throne. He seized the throne. He ruled as king for thirty-three years.

(N.B.: The numbers have been added for convenience; cf. table 6; I.J. Gelb,
JNES 13 (1954): 209ff.; *ANET*: 564–566; Larsen 1976: 34–40; *RLA* 6: 101–115;
Landsberger 1954)

The list has obviously undergone considerable manipulation in order to
accommodate Shamshi-Adad I – who was an Amorite conqueror and not
from Ashur at all – in a list of indigenous rulers (further discussion: Larsen
1976). The chronology for the Assyrian kings from about 2000 to Shamshi-
Adad (or, more correctly, Shamshi-Addu) that can be approximately established is given in table 6.
What are the main features of Ashur's history in this period, which we can
deduce from this material? First, it established its independence soon after
c. 2000, and was governed by local kings. Secondly, it had developed a
commercial network by c. 1900, as shown by the evidence for Assyrian traders
settled in central Anatolia between c. 1900 and c. 1830. Thirdly, the Amorite
chieftain Shamshi-Adad I (1813–1781) conquered Ashur late in the nineteenth
century.

Ashur's emergence on the international stage

The chances of reconstructing the history of the city of Ashur in any more detail on the basis of the material discussed are slight. Particularly puzzling is the question of how Ashur came to play a central role in the long-distance trade network. Texts of kings Ilushuma and his son, Erishum I (1939–1900), give a hint as to how it established itself in this position. The longer one (that of Ilushuma) is extant in numerous copies on bricks (plus one limestone fragment) and runs as follows:

> Ilushuma, vicegerent of Ashur, beloved of the god Ashur and the goddess Ishtar, son of Shallim-ahhe, vicegerent of Ashur, son of Puzur-Ashur, vicegerent of Ashur:
>
> Ilu-shuma, vicegerent of Ashur, built the temple for the goddess Ishtar, his mistress, for his life. A new wall ... I constructed and subdivided for my city house-plots. The god Ashur opened for me two springs in Mount Ebih and I made bricks for the wall by the two springs. The water of one spring flowed down to the Aushum Gate, the water of the other spring flowed down to the Wertum Gate.
>
> The 'freedom' (*addurāru*) of the Akkadians and their children I established. I 'purified' their copper. I established their 'freedom' from the border of the marshes and Ur and Nippur, Awal and Kismar, Der of the god Ishtaran, as far as the City (i.e. Ashur).
>
> (B. Meissner, *Die Inschriften der altassyrischen Könige*, 1926: IV, 2; Grayson 1972: XXXII 2 (§§40–42); Grayson 1987: A.0.32.2)

Contrary to an older view, according to which this related to a campaign of conquest in the south by Ilushuma (*CAH* I, ch. 25), Larsen (1976) has argued persuasively that the text reflects an attempt by Ilushuma to attract traders from south Mesopotamia to the Ashur market by giving them certain privileges. Ashur had managed to seize a controlling position in the tin trade with the east, and so served as an entrepot, where south Mesopotamian traders could go to buy tin and probably also to sell some of their copper (which came mainly from the Gulf). Following Ilushuma's decree, they preferred to do this as they could now get a much better deal in Ashur than in other centres. The places mentioned in the text, it is argued, may refer to the three major caravan routes from the south. One ran from Ur (the point of entry for copper from the Gulf) to Nippur then up to Ashur; the second ran perhaps along the Tigris; and the third went from Elam through Der, east of the Tigris, and then across to Ashur. If we accept this proposition and add the statement by Erishum, Ilushuma's successor (1939–1900), that he 'made tax-exempt silver, gold, copper, tin, barley, wool ...' (Grayson 1972: §62), we can see that the Assyrian kings deliberately introduced a policy intended to maximise the profits of their nodal position in trade.

To summarise: although the sources are sparse, Ashur seems to have developed into a substantial city-state soon after 2000: it had important sanctuaries; it was fortified by city-walls and well supplied with water; and it was ruled by a local dynasty from Puzur-Ashur I (some time before 1939) to c. 1830. Ashur was in control of a flourishing trade network in Anatolia between c. 1900 and 1830, which was run by family-based Assyrian merchant-houses (see chapter 2c). Ashur's importance in this commerce was probably due to its strategic position on routes, which its kings cleverly exploited by offering certain advantages to their trading partners, especially those in south Mesopotamia (see Leemans 1968). Ashur's Anatolian colonies served to extend the Assyrian market and stimulate its economy.

The highly profitable position, which Ashur had gained and consolidated between 1939 and 1830, made it into a target for Shamshi-Adad I (1813–1781; see pp. 86; 98), whose base lay to the west of Ashur. The history of his ambitions and successful expansion can be partially reconstructed using the Mari archives and the Assyrian King List (see p. 86). According to this, he seized the throne from his brother at home, then attacked the area around Babylon and Sippar, and finally turned north to take Ekallate (probably just north of Ashur) and Ashur, where he deposed the local king. He also conquered other places, such as Mari, at an unspecified date; it is likely that he seized the latter only around the middle of his long reign (Veenhof 1985, especially addendum 207). Eventually Shamshi-Adad's realm included the area of the Khabur headwaters, locality of one of his royal centres, Shubat-Enlil; the recently excavated site of Tell Leilan (probably Shubat-Enlil itself) demonstrates what a wealthy city from this period and in this area looked like (Weiss 1985). From there his kingdom stretched down to include Terqa and Mari on the Euphrates, east across the plain to Ekallate and to the now great city of Ashur. It also came to include the small, but flourishing, state of Karana (including the site of Tell Rimah) in the Jebel Sinjar, the large city of Nineveh further north than Ashur, and parts of the Zagros to the east, such as Shemshara (near Rowanduz) and Tukrish north of Elam. Shamshi-Adad's reign lasted thirty-three years. During that time he managed to hold this substantial territory together by dint of installing his sons as dependent kings at Mari (ruled by his younger son, Yasmah-Addu) and Ekallate (under his heir, Ishme-Dagan); smaller centres, such as Karana, remained under their indigenous rulers, now subjects of Shamshi-Adad, while Ashur, Nineveh and Shubat-Enlil were under the direct rule of Shamshi-Adad himself.

The city-state of Ashur

Is it possible to define any of the institutions of the city of Ashur beyond these bare bones? The material from the Old Assyrian trading quarter at Kanesh (modern Kültepe, cf. chapter 2c) provides some insights. The king was entitled simply 'vicegerent of the god Ashur' (p. 84), which probably relates to his role in cult, where he was conceived as acting on behalf of the god, as illustrated by the statement, found in some inscriptions (p. 85), that 'the god Ashur is king, X is his vicegerent'. The title is only used in the formal royal inscriptions, which shows its purely ceremonial nature. The usage in day-to-day documents is quite distinct: here the ruler was always called simply *rubā'um* or *bēlum* meaning, respectively, 'prince' and 'lord'.[3] These terms seem to define his position within the community as head of the royal family and so occupying a pre-eminent position *vis-à-vis* other families. They do not depict the king as an autocratic ruler. Shamshi-Adad I's conquest of Ashur transformed this situation dramatically: the king of Ashur was now termed *šarrum* ('king') as in the south, and he assumed lengthy, laudatory epithet in inscriptions, which is a measure of the profound internal dislocation experienced by Ashur in the wake of Shamshi-Adad's seizure of the throne.

The Old Assyrian documents also reveal the working at Ashur of 'the City' (*ālum*), by which a kind of city-assembly seems to be meant, probably made up the heads of the great merchant houses there (Larsen 1976). All important matters of policy seem to have been in the hands of 'the City': it was the city that took decisions binding on the community (*awat ālim* = 'the word/command of the city') and passed legal decisions (*dīn ālim* = 'the judgement of the city'). It controlled the diplomatic relations with the Anatolian principalities on, or near, whose territories the Assyrian merchant settlements were located. Through the agency of the city-herald (*šipru ša ālim*), it enforced general commercial policy; it probably fixed the export tax, which was levied on all trade caravans by the city at a specified rate, and their bales were sealed by the city. It is possible, though not certain, that this important body met in a specially designated building called the 'house of the city' *(bīt ālim)*. The other extremely important political institution (for the whole of Assyrian history indeed) is the *limmum*. This was the title of an official, chosen annually by lot, after whom each year was named and, at this period, the office seems never to have been held by the king (in contrast to the Middle and Neo-Assyrian periods, see chapters 7b and 9). Those eligible for the *limmu*-ship probably came from a select group, perhaps constituted by the heads of the major families of Ashur. It is possible that the chairman of the city-assembly was the current *limmum*; so the office rotated annually among a small, but powerful, group of citizens who effectively counter-balanced the powers of the king (Larsen 1976). The picture of the Ashur community (before Shamshi-Adad) that we obtain from this piecemeal evidence is that of a highly complex civic structure, largely run by a powerful group of businessmen, representing their family interests. The position of the ruler was largely restricted to that of acting for the community within the cultic and ceremonial spheres, undertaking public building projects and overseeing the exercise of justice.

2c The Old Assyian merchants in Anatolia (*c.* 1900–*c.* 1830)

Introduction

The bulk of our information for understanding the city of Ashur and its economic base comes from documents found about 1200 km to the northwest at *kārum* Kanesh, a site in central Anatolia. It lies near the Halys river (modern Kızıl Irmak), 20 km or so north-east of the modern city of Kayseri on the Anatolian plateau, close to the great circular mound of Kültepe, which rises about 20 m above the surrounding plain. Late in the last century explorers recognised Kültepe as an important site, and the probable source of many unusual texts appearing on the antiquities market, often called 'Cappadocian tablets'. Attempts to locate the precise find-spot of the tablets remained fruitless until the Czech scholar Hrozny discovered, in 1926, that the tablets were actually being dug up at a much smaller site about 90 m to the north-east of the main mound. This smaller site turned out to contain the settlement of merchants from Ashur, the *kārum*, hence the tablets are now known as 'Old Assyrian'. Since 1948 the site has been thoroughly excavated by Tahsin Özgüç, an eminent Turkish archaeologist, with the result that perhaps 12,000 tablets have been added to the 3000 or so available earlier, and the stratigraphy of the site has been clarified. It is now plain that the main site of Kültepe consists of a large circular city-area with a palace building on the citadel, which was the centre of the important Anatolian principality of Kanesh, while the merchant quarters of the *kārum* consisted of sizable, but not lavish, typically Anatolian, houses quite separate from the city of Kanesh.

Most of the texts held in museums before the start of the thorough Turkish excavations have been published (for a list, cf. Orlin 1970), but only a tiny handful of the many found more recently have been made available. This means that deductions based on the published material, which probably represents less than a quarter of all the texts, will only be validated when the texts found more recently are studied. Apart from this, at present insuperable, difficulty, other factors complicate the picture. One is that two levels of the *kārum* at Kanesh have produced tablets: level II, conventionally dated between 1900–1830, and Ib, which is contemporary with Shamshi-Adad I (1813–1781) and his successor. The dating of level Ib is still not firm: it was once considered to represent a relatively short span of time, but the discovery of more texts now makes it likely that it covered another fairly long period. However, given the present state of publication, the bulk of written material comes from the earlier level II period, and the later phase of the merchant settlement is very under-represented. There are also difficulties in under-standing precisely the Old Assyrian dialect and the specific terminology it developed for its uniquely documented long-distance overland trading enter-prises. The political situation in Anatolia presents another problem: it can only be inferred from references in the Assyrian merchant-documents themselves (p. 93; chapter 5a). The local Anatolian rulers at this period seem to have used the Old Assyrian dialect and the cuneiform writing-system to communicate among themselves, but finds of texts on the city-mound have so far been slight.

The chronology of *kārum* Kanesh has provoked considerable discussion. The levels of the city-mound extend from the early third millennium right through to c. 1200, but the four levels of the *kārum* are generally considered to have flourished mainly in the period between c. 2000 and 1600. This dating has been disputed by several scholars (e.g. Mellaart 1957), who think that the *kārum* was already established in the last quarter of the third millennium, perhaps contemporary with the Ur III state. But against this view has to be set the fact that the extensive Turkish excavations have found no material of this date in *kārum* Kanesh (T. Özgüç 1959; 1986), and no Anatolian cities are mentioned in the Ur III texts (Larsen 1976). So it seems more likely that the *kārum* quarter did not come into being until some time around 2000 (see table 7). What we should note, though, is that the quarter existed already well before the Assyrians, as far as we know, became such prominent traders there. It is thus possible that a local Anatolian trading station existed here already earlier, of which the Assyrians, by virtue of their extensive connections and advantageous commercial tariffs, became eventually the leading and most powerful members. But even in the *kārum* II phase the settlement was by no means exclusively inhabited by Assyrians, and the archaeological material is entirely Anatolian in type. Were it not for the texts, we would have no inkling that any Assyrians were present at all.

Although *kārum* Kanesh is the richest and most informative site for the Assyrian trade, it is unique only during the time of phase II. A number of

Table 7 Archaeological sequence of Kültepe in the Old Assyrian *kārum*-period

kārum Kanesh	Kanesh city-mound
virgin soil	building level
kārum IV (40–50 years?)	Middle Bronze I building level
kārum III (40–50 years?)	?
kārum II (62–80 years; destroyed by fire; tablets from reign of Erishum I–Puzur-Ashur II)	contemporary occupation level
kārum Ic (no occupation) (10–20 years?)	public building (Warshama king of Kanesh)
kārum Ib (30, 50 or 70/80 years? destruction by fire)	public building with Anitta spearhead
kārum Ia (deserted)	?
	Hittite Old Kingdom buildings (c. 1650–)

other Anatolian settlements have produced analogous remains, and occasionally even texts, contemporary with phase Ib, such as Alishar (level 10: probably ancient Amkuwa, Gelb 1935), Boğazköy IVd (ancient Hattusa, Bittel 1970), Karahüyük in the Konya plain (Alp 1968) and Acemhüyük near the Great Salt Lake (N. Özgüç 1980). The last site has produced an enormous number of clay-sealings, some inscribed, found in palace storerooms, which reveal the great volume of the trade and its extensive links with Syria, Mesopotamia and even the Arab-Persian Gulf (Potts in al-Khalifa and Rice 1986 [OGf]). It has been suggested that this large, important site should be identified with the prominent city of Purushhattum (Hittite Purushanda) mentioned in the Old Assyrian documents. But it is now thought more likely that Purushhattum was Karahüyük-Konya.

The organisation of the Assyrian trade

The documents show that two distinct types of trading establishment existed in Anatolia. The main one, and the best-known, is the *kārum*, a term that in origin means merely a quay, but, because most trade in Mesopotamia was water-borne, it came by extension to mean the harbour and trading quarter of a city, where merchants gathered for their business. When the Assyrians established permanent trading quarters far from home they simply applied the term to such settlements although they were now, of course, no longer located necessarily on river banks. The other type of trading centre was called *wabartum*, a term unique to the Old Assyrian merchants in Anatolia. The word seems to be linked to a term for 'guest'; it is therefore suggested that it may originally have designated a caravanserai, which eventually expanded into a more permanent residential and trading centre, although smaller and less autonomous than a *kārum*. Some evidence exists to suggest that *wabartum*-settlements were usually located adjacent to cities either less economically important or more difficult of access and so off the beaten track. The residents of a *wabartum* seem to have come under the administrative authority of the nearest *kārum*. But it must be admitted that some uncertainty exists in understanding fully this type of commercial settlement.

The numbers and the density of the trading centres can be recovered, more or less, from the documents. The situation in the *kārum* II period is more certain than in the Ib phase. In the earlier period there was probably a total of eleven *kārum*s and ten *wabartum*s; in level Ib the number of *kārum*-establishments increased to fourteen, and there is evidence that some of the settlements that earlier on had been smaller *wabartum*-stations developed at this time into fully organised *kārum*-centres. The most important *kārum* was the one at Kanesh (at least in level II), which formed the hub of the network of trading settlements, with routes radiating northwards as far as the Halys mouth on the Black Sea, north-east to the region of modern Sivas and south-west to the important Anatolian political centres of Purushhattum and

Wahshushana. A further group of colonies was located in the area to the southeast, along the routes leading into north Syria and Mesopotamia, and some were set at the northerly crossing points of the Euphrates. These were the routes along which the goods coming from the Arab-Persian Gulf, Carchemish and Mari were transmitted to Acemhüyük (level Ib).

How did the Assyrian colonies relate to the Anatolian principalities in which they were located, and whose agreement they needed in order to carry on their profitable business? In order to answer this central question, we must try to reconstruct a picture of the political structure of Anatolia (Liverani 1988 [OC]), which can only be done by using incidental references in the Old Assyrian texts. Independent city-states seem to have been the norm. They controlled the surrounding stretches of countryside and, in some instances, smaller urban centres. The majority of the population seems to have been 'Hattian' (the term used to describe the indigenous non-Indo-European population of Anatolia). I use the term 'seems' advisedly, because the evidence is limited to personal names: most are Hattian, but a very few Indo-European, Amorite and Hurrian names indicate that no certain conclusions about the ethnic make-up of Anatolia can be drawn (Garelli 1963). Three states, Purushhattum, Kanesh and Wahshushana, dominated politically, and controlled quite extensive areas defined in each case as a 'country' (*mātum*). The rulers of both the smaller states and the 'countries' were (as far as the evidence goes) all called *rubā'um* = 'prince', except for the ruler of Purushhattum who was called 'great prince'. This suggests that this westerly state was recognised as wielding some kind of greater power than the others.

It has been argued in the past (J. Lewy *HUCA* 27 (1956); *CAH* I, ch. 24) that the whole region where Assyrian colonies are found was subject to Ashur. This view was based on the fact that a few texts demonstrate that the Anatolian states were linked to the city of Ashur by oaths, administered by envoys from there. But recent reconsiderations of this hypothesis make it much more likely that the city of Ashur simply regulated its diplomatic relations with the Anatolian rulers through the city envoys, and that the oaths almost certainly related to the precise agreements under which the Assyrian traders could operate within the territory of the Anatolian centres. This conclusion is strengthend by other evidence, which shows that Assyrians could be clapped into prison by the Anatolian princes for smuggling restricted goods, that all Assyrian caravans were subject to a tax from the local ruler, and that he may have had first pick of the goods. The idea that Ashur wielded political control over Anatolia has now become untenable and is to be rejected (Orlin 1970; Larsen 1976).

The organisation of this astonishingly complex and far-flung Assyrian commercial system has been painstakingly recovered from the texts (at least for level II: Larsen 1976), although a certain number of uncertainties persist. It seems that the smaller *wabartum* settlement came under the authority of the nearest *kārum*, which deferred to *kārum* Kanesh, which in turn came under the direct supervision of Ashur with its city-assembly.[4] Kanesh was thus of central importance in the system, and some documents reveal that its own institutions were modelled on those of Ashur, with an assembly and officials, mirroring those of 'the City' (see chapter 2a).

The most striking feature of the Assyrian trade in Anatolia is the fact of permanence: merchant families (*bītum*: literally 'house', hence also 'family') in Ashur sent some of their male relatives to settle in one of the Anatolian colonies, where they directed and promoted the family trading business by selling consignments of goods, sending the profits back home and also adding to them by engaging in the internal Anatolian carrying trade. Sometimes a merchant in Ashur might make use of someone outside his family for a time in order to complete a particular transaction. In spite of the fact that business was basically a family matter, some of the capital funding for the trade came from shared, long-term investments which financed a particular trader over a period of several years; at the end of the time specified the investors received equal shares of the profit; the trader also gained a share, and provisions were made for cases of early withdrawal. These agreements were called 'sacks' (*naruqqu*), which derives from the original practice of placing actual goods in a trader's carrying sack (Veenhof 1987). Only one of these important contracts has been published so far (Landsberger 1940: 20–26; cf. Larsen 1976), but it seems likely that it represents a regular practice, which cut across the normal family-ties and united the interests of the great merchant-houses of Ashur.

The caravans of donkeys by which the goods were actually transported on the five- to six-week journey (Hecker 1980) were generally fairly small. Each donkey carried a load of textiles and a small amount of what is, almost certainly, to be interpreted as tin (Landsberger 1965; Larsen 1976; 1987). Ashur played a major role at this time in the acquisition and distribution of this metal from the east.[5] On arrival in Anatolia everything, including the donkeys, was sold, and the main import back to Ashur was silver and some gold. Within Anatolia itself the Assyrians, given their sophisticated and developed system of trading stations, were able to increase their profits by playing the dominant role in the internal carrying trade. They probably also organised the Anatolian inter-state trade in copper (Larsen 1967), which may have been mined at the rich deposits of Ergani Maden (near Elazığ, Turkey). The tin was, bulk for bulk, more valuable than the textiles, but it was the textiles which provided the main volume of the trade (Veenhof 1972; Larsen 1987), and the documents show that they were centrally important to Assyrian commerce and highly valued in Anatolia. The texts refer to special kinds of garments and certain types of cloth as being more popular at this or that moment, and the merchants were careful to watch the market and work out where their best chances for profit lay. Some, though not all, of the textiles were produced in Ashur itself by the female members of the merchant houses, as shown by this letter written to a woman in Ashur by her merchant husband in Kanesh:

Thus Puzur-Ashur, speak to Waqqurtum:

With 1 pound of silver – levy separately added, pay over completed – sealed by me, Ashur-idi is on his way to you. (Concerning) the fine cloth that you sent me: you must make cloth like that and send it to me via Ashur-idi, then I will send you (as payment) ½ pound of silver (per piece). Have one side of the cloth combed, but not shaved smooth: it should be close-textured. Compared to the textiles you sent me earlier, you must work in 1 pound of wool more per piece of cloth, but they must still be fine! The other side (of the cloth) must be just lightly combed: if it still looks hairy, it will have to be closeshaved, like *kutānu*-cloth (a very common textile, possibly a kind of sheet). As for the *abarnê*-cloth (originally named after the place, Abarne, which became the name of a type of cloth, cf. 'tweed') which you sent me, you must not send me that sort of thing again. If you do want to do so, then make it the way I used to wear it. But if you don't want to make fine textiles – as I have heard it they can be bought in quantity over there (i.e. where you are); buy (them) and send them to me. One finished (piece of) cloth, when you make it, should be nine ells long and eight ells wide (4.5 by 4 m).

(TCL 19: 17; cf. Veenhof 1972: 103v; 1983 [OI]: 84)

The rich evidence from *kārum* Kanesh reveals the details of the trading mechanism only for the Old Assyrian commerce in Anatolia. There are hints in other documents of the period that similarly elaborate merchant systems were in operation in other parts of the Near East. The Assyrian system is just one aspect of the commercial structures functioning at this time, which has, by chance, been recovered. It provides a vital glimpse into the pattern of highly complex regional interaction and its organisation at this time (Larsen 1987).

2d Mari and its world (c. 1810–c. 1760)

Introduction

The city of Mari is situated on the Euphrates, just downstream from its confluence with the Khabur river (not far from the modern Syria–Iraq border), at the site of modern Tell Hariri. Excavation, references in the Early Dynastic inscriptions and now the Ebla archives, show that it was a considerable political power in the period between 2600 and 2300. The names inscribed on small statues indicate that the language spoken and written in the area at that time was certainly a Semitic one, probably related to Akkadian (Gelb 1977). The French excavations, begun in the 1930s and still continuing, found an inscribed statue of an Early Dynastic king in 1934, which established the equation Tell Hariri = Mari. Despite the importance of Mari in the mid-third millennium, the term 'Mari Age', occasionally used in books, is applied to the period c. 1810–1760, i.e. the approximate date and time range covered by the justly famous archives found there. This material illuminates the last phase of Mari's existence as a typical state of the classical Old Babylonian period, before it was destroyed and absorbed, at least temporarily, by Hammurabi of Babylon (1792–1750). Mari is an example which illustrates, in immense detail, the internal structure and wider, external relations of one of the many principalities ruled by an Amorite dynasty, like so many others in this period. The Mari tablets also throw considerable light on the political picture of the greater part of Western Asia from the Levant (Lebanon, Syria, even briefly the northern part of Palestine (Malamat 1983)) in the west to the area of Mesopotamia (north and south) and western Iran in the east.

The physical remains at Mari, such as the temples, the magnificent palace (Margueron 1982) and associated finds (elaborate, brightly coloured frescoes, statuary: see fig. 9), and the layout of the town, which is now being explored (cf. generally Aynard and Spycket 1989; for regular excavation reports, see

Figure 9 Painted fresco of a royal investiture scene, Mari
(after A. Parrot, *Mari* II, Paris, 1958)

MARI 1ff.), provide extremely valuable information on the culture and architecture of the period, which is still only fairly sparsely attested for south Mesopotamia and the area of Assyria (north Iraq). Two other sites, differing both from Mari and each other, have produced approximately contemporary archaeological material, which shows that a fundamental cultural unity prevailed among the contending kingdoms. One is Tell Harmal (ancient Shaduppum, in a suburb of modern Baghdad), a tiny provincial centre which formed part of the kingdom of Eshnunna (Baqir 1959). Although it is smaller in scale and uses simpler materials and technology, the layout of its temple and its style of sculpture is similar to that of Mari (fig. 10). The collection of mainly scribal exercise tablets from Tell Harmal includes, uniquely, an extensive body of mathematical texts (for publications, see *RLA* 7: 533). Another important item found among the Harmal tablets is a copy of the Eshnunna law-code, showing that the Eshnunna kings, like other rulers of this period, presented themselves as protectors of the weak and righters of wrongs (*ANET*: 161–3; *TUAT*: 32–38; Yaron 1969). The other site is Tell Rimah in the Sinjar region of north Iraq, excavated by the British in the 1960s. Its ancient name is not absolutely certain (*RLA* 5: 405–407) – the most recent consideration of the problem makes it virtually certain that it is to be identified with Qatara, an important town in the small kingdom of Karana (Eidem 1985). Whichever identification is favoured, it is certain that Tell Rimah represents the remains of a substantial city of this autonomous, though tiny, state which fell for a while under the control of Shamshi-Adad I

Figure 10 Terracotta lion, one of a pair from Tell Harmal (courtesy of M.S. Drower)

(1813–1781; see chapter 2b) and, somewhat later, formed part of the dominions of Hammurabi of Babylon (1792–1750; see chapter 2e). The palace at Rimah has produced a quantity of interesting texts, including the archive of its last known queen, Iltani (Dalley *et al.* 1976). The most striking building is the large temple, its façade elaborately decorated with mud bricks cut as engaged spiral and diamond-patterned columns or palm-trunks. Other sites have produced some, but much less impressive, remains of this type of decoration (Larsa, Ur, Shemshara). The current excavations at Tell Leilan have now revealed substantial buildings decorated in the same style (Weiss 1985). The evidence for cultural homogeneity, despite political fragmentation, is growing.

The political scene

The history of Mari, before the time illustrated by the archives, is complex, and the chronology of rulers (see table 8) is exceedingly difficult to establish (Veenhof 1985; Kupper 1989). A text from the reign of Yasmah-Addu (*c.* 1782–1776) tells us that a certain Yaggid-Lim, king of Mari, and Ila-kabkabu, king of an unknown region to the west of Assyria and father of Shamshi-Adad I, had drawn up a treaty with each other. Yaggid-Lim was duly succeeded by his son, Yahdun-Lim, who tried to expand Mari's political control in the western Euphrates zone and north Syria. Mari's westward expansion led to a close alliance with the kingdom of Yamhad, centred on Aleppo, which was sealed by a dynastic marriage: Yahdun-Lim's son and heir, Zimri-Lim, married Shibtu, the daughter of the king of Yamhad, Yarim-Lim. This new compact probably threatened the balance of power agreed with Ila-kabkabu, now dead and succeeded by his son, Shamshi-Adad I (but see Charpin and Durand 1984). He, perhaps using the broken agreement as a pretext, attacked and defeated Yahdun-Lim and, in the ensuing chaos, a usurper (Sumuyamanum) seized the throne. He was probably rapidly eliminated by Shamshi-Adad, who thus added Mari to his already extensive realm as an autonomous state, ruled by his younger son, Yasmah-Addu, but owing him allegiance. The political edifice personally created by Shamshi-Adad largely collapsed when he died and his son, Ishme-Dagan, succeeded. As a result, Zimri-Lim, who had been biding his time in exile at the court of his father-in-law in Aleppo, was able to regain the throne of Mari, strongly supported by his in-laws. The elements of uncertainty loom large in this outline, but it gives us something of the flavour of shifting alliance, sudden expansion, intrigue and conflict that could, and did, occur in this period – but only the Mari archive provides sufficient detail to allow scholars to attempt a reconstruction.[6]

An oft-quoted report sent to the Mari ruler by one of his officials reflects the wider international political scene in the time of Zimri-Lim (*c.* 1775–1761). It illustrates well the delicate balance of alliances, which could lead to sudden, though precarious, expansion:

There is no king who is strong by himself: 10 or 15 kings follow Hammurabi of Babylon, as many follow Rim-Sin of Larsa, Ibalpiel of Eshnunna and Amutpiel of Qatna, while 20 kings follow Yarim-Lim of Yamhad.

(Dossin 1938: 117)

This letter is crucial in providing a list of what were considered to be the main

Table 8 First Dynasty of Babylon and contemporary kings (conventional 'middle' dates)

Babylon	Larsa	'Sealand'	Mari
Sumuabum (1894)	Sumu-el (1894)		
Sumulael (1880)			
	Nur-Adad (1865)		
	Sin-iddinam (1849)		
Sabium (1844)			
	Sin-eribam (1842)		
	Sin-iqisham (1840)		
	Silli-Adad (1835)		
	Warad-Sin (1834)		
Apil-Sin (1830)			
			Yaggid-Lim (1820)
Sin-muballit (1812)	Rim-Sin (1822)		Yahdun-Lim (1810)
Hammurabi (1792)			Sumu-Yaman (1794)
			Yasmah-Addu (1790)
			Zimri-Lim (1775)
Samsu-iluna (1749)	Rim-Sin II (1741)		
Abi-eshuh (1711)			
Ammi-ditana (1683)		Damiq-ilishu (1677)	
Ammi-saduqa (1647)		Ishki-bal (1641)	
Samsu-ditana (1625–1595)		Shushi (1616)	
		Gulkishar (1589)	

(On the 'low' chronology, dates for Hammurabi of Babylon are 1728–1686; the end of the first dynasty of Babylon is 1531.)

powers of the time in the Near East. It reveals, surprisingly to us, that by far the most powerful one was Yamhad, centred on Aleppo – a fact that would certainly never have been suspected, as Aleppo has been continuously inhabited, making excavation there difficult. There is, therefore, practically no material recovered from this important kingdom, and we are totally dependent on occasional references like this in order to grasp some hints of its role (Abdallah 1985). The letter also reveals that, at this time, only two kingdoms in south Iraq were considered of any importance: Larsa and Babylon; while Eshnunna, which controlled the main route leading from Mesopotamia to Iran, was seen as an important power immediately to the east. Ashur is omitted from the roster of powers – it had ceased to be a major player in the game of international politics with the death of Shamshi-Adad I.

The other state mentioned as politically significant is Qatna (modern Tell Mishrife, only partially excavated) situated on the Orontes in the present state of Syria. Relations with Yamhad/Aleppo and Qatna were of central interest to the kingdom of Mari, because the territories of the two states adjoined both each other and that of Mari (Klengel 1965–70: III, 146–147). The important caravan route, which ran from Mari through the oasis of Tadmor (classical Palmyra) on to Qatna, was controlled at its eastern end by Mari and in the west by Qatna. From Qatna, routes led south to Damascus and west, through the Homs-Tripoli gap, down to the Mediterranean and the great port of Byblos. The Euphrates route – important because a lot of goods, as the archives show, were shipped by river – led from Mari to Emar (modern Tell Meskene) and thence by land to Aleppo. Emar was also the terminus of a long overland route, which passed through the Jezira[7] (also partly under Mari's control) and crossed the Euphrates at Carchemish (Hallo 1964). Aleppo controlled other routes westwards to the coast, and we find the coastal city of Ugarit sending requests to the king of Mari via the king of Yamhad. In this situation, both Yamhad and Qatna were anxious to maintain good relations with Mari, but competed with each other for political advantage: the resulting tensions between the two neighbours could be manipulated by the Mari king. This can be seen fairly well by examining Mari's relations with the two states when it was under the rule, successively, of the Shamshi-Adad family and then Zimri-Lim. When Shamshi-Adad gained control of Mari and undertook a ceremonial march to the Mediterranean coast to mark his victory, he chose to follow the desert route through Tadmor to Qatna, with whose king he had contracted an alliance (again sealed with a marriage), because Yamhad was allied with the former royal family of Mari who lived in exile there. But when, on Shamshi-Adad's death, Zimri-Lim regained his ancestral throne with Yamhad's support, it was links with Yamhad that were favoured in Mari; Qatna, as a former ally of Shamshi-Adad, had to negotiate terms with Yamhad, with Mari acting as intermediary between the two rivals.

One of the factors in Mari's central importance was that, because of its strategic situation on important routes, it played a major role as an entrepot in international trade. The archives reveal that for states further west (including Crete, cf. Morris 1992: 102; now also M. Guichard, *NABU* 1993, n. 53) Mari was the main supplier of tin, essential in the manufacture of bronze, coming from further east (Dossin 1970). The value put on this metal, and Mari's central role in its distribution, is illustrated by a letter from the king of Qatna, addressed to Ishme-Dagan, ruler of Ekallate further east and Yasmah-Addu's brother. The text was found in the Mari archives, where Ishme-Dagan had presumably forwarded it for his brother to deal with, because of Mari's role in supplying the western states with this material:

> This matter is unspeakable, yet I must speak and relieve my feelings: you are a great king; you asked me for two horses, and I had them sent to you. And now you sent me (only) 20 minas (*c.* 10 kilos) of tin. Is it not the case that, without any quibbling and in full, you got (what you wanted) from me? And you dare to send me this paltry amount of tin! If you had sent nothing at all, by the god of my fathers, I could not have been so angry!
>
> (ARM 5.20; *ANET*: 628f.)

The diplomatic links maintained between the courts of different rulers is another aspect illuminated by the Mari texts. On the face of it the kings cultivated formal, friendly relations, sending valuable gifts to each other which tied recipient and donor together in the mutuality of gift-giving, and marrying each other's daughters to cement such relationships (Zaccagnini 1983). Yet at the same time there was an element of mistrust, and the ambassadors sent to neighbouring courts reported back to their lords what was really going on:

> To my lord speak thus: thus speaks Yarim-Addu, your servant. Tab-eli-matim and Sin-bel-aplim, the servants of Hammurabi (of Babylon), who have been for several days in Mashkan-Shapir (part of the rival kingdom of Larsa), have arrived in Babylon. From the 4 men riding donkeys, men of Larsa, who accompanied them, I learnt their message. They are bearers of the following message (to Hammurabi): 'Concerning the troops about which you are continuously writing to me, I have heard (that) the enemy is directing his efforts towards another country. That is why I have not sent you my troops; (but) my troops are ready. If the enemy should turn against you, my troops will come to your aid; [and] if the enemy should turn against me, may your troops come to my aid.' That is what Rim-Sin has written to Hammurabi about the people of Mutiabal.
>
> (ARM 2.72; Oppenheim 1967 [OI]: 46)

Here, then, the king of Mari was receiving intelligence of an alliance between two important neighbouring powers and rivals.

The kingdom of Mari

The large royal palace is one of the most important finds made at Mari. Until the discovery of the palace of Sinkashid at Uruk (*UVB* 22 (1966); see p. 80) and the Rimah excavations, this was the only palace of the Old Babylonian period more or less fully excavated; the palace at the small centre of Alalah VII (modern Tell Atchana, just inland from the Orontes mouth, see Woolley 1953) is about a century later and displays a number of different architectural features, perhaps more typical of the Levant. The Mari palace was certainly much the larger and more elaborate structure. Rooms were clustered around a series of courtyards, with indications in some places of a second storey: over 260 chambers, courtyards and corridors have been found, and make up a large part of the 2.5 ha (*c*. 6 acre) site it originally covered. The continuing French excavations are clarifying the layout and functioning of this magnificent palace year by year (al-Khalesi 1978; Margueron 1982; Gates 1984; Durand 1987). A great surprise, given the normally unfavourable conditions for the preservation of painted decoration, was the discovery of brilliantly coloured frescoes – in particular, a complex composition (now in the Louvre, see fig. 9) depicting in its centre the 'investiture of Zimri-Lim' by a warrior-goddess, very probably Ishtar. The iconography of the scene is directly comparable to that at the top of the Hammurabi stele (fig. 11) and shows that, while we must be careful not to assume automatically that the Mari evidence provides an insight into conditions in other states, there was a common culture in this period. These palaces were impressive showpieces, and the various kings were keenly interested to know what those of their neighbours looked like: a Mari official reported to his king how impressed he had been by the palace at Karana; another Mari letter is from the king of Yamhad forwarding a request from the king of Ugarit, who had heard of the wonders of the palace at Mari and wished to visit it himself.

The economic base for the Mari state, which made the construction of such an opulent building possible, remains unclear in many details, although the the Paris research team, working on the texts, archaeology and more refined interpretation of the mass of material, is casting ever more light on this and other problems. It is known that the kings of Mari, like kings elsewhere, undertook irrigation work to increase crop production, and that a major palace industry, run with the active participation of the queens, was the production of textiles. The Iltani archive from Rimah illustrates this especially well (Dalley *et al.* 1976; Dalley 1984; for royal women and women in cult, see Batto 1974). The fact that a lot of the texts come from the palace tends to give the impression of an exclusively palace-centred economy, but it is clear from various references that this was not the case: as in neighbouring states, there were wealthy landowners, merchants, small farmers and poor tenants and sharecroppers. A system of rations and gifts was in operation for remunerating royal officials – probably an income additional to their personal

Figure 11 Scene at top of Hammurabi stele (from Susa; Louvre)

103

resources. How taxation worked is not completely certain, but state income was certainly derived from revenues levied on the transit trade, crossing-dues, tolls, boat taxes and dues demanded in return for land grants. Given Mari's control of crucial commercial routes, royal income derived from trading ventures must have been considerable. Diplomatic gifts were another source of royal wealth (Zaccagnini 1983). Because they figure prominently in the royal correspondence from Mari, it has been argued that long-distance market exchange did not take place in this period at all: rather it was limited to tiny quantities of prestige articles exchanged between courts (K. Polanyi *et al.*, *Trade and Markets in Early Empires*, Glencoe, Ill., 1957: 257ff.). This thesis should be rejected (Silver 1985 [0N], ch. 5). With the advances made in the study of the Old Assyrian trade-mechanism (see chapter 2b), the evidence for private commercial ventures in the Ur III (Powell 1977), Isin-Larsa (Oppenheim 1954) and Old Babylonian (Leemans 1950; 1960; 1968) periods, it has become increasingly evident that, while the palace actively took part in trade, and at times may have played a dominant role, extensive private commercial networks also flourished – constituted, indeed, a substantial sector of the Mesopotamian economy (see generally Archi 1984 [0E]).[8]

The close interaction between the herders living on the fringes of the rich arable lands and the urban-based communities and central government was an important feature of socio-political life for all states at this time; but it is only known in any detail from the Mari documents. Different pastoralist groups inhabited particular regions, within which they normally moved with their herds to seasonal grazing-grounds. This is shown by the various clan-names that appear in the texts: e.g. 'Hanaeans', which indicates that the orientation of this particular group was the area of the old territory of Hana in Upper Mesopotamia. The terminology used for their social organisation appears generally to have been Amorite rather than Akkadian, which probably reflects their ethnicity. Some herders performed tasks such as acting as caravan-guides through the steppes. The state also employed them on a seasonal basis, recruited them for the army (Sasson 1969), regulated their access to water and supplied them with essential manufactured goods and occasionally land. The agreements made between the government and pastoral groups were formalised through ritual acts (such as 'killing a donkey'), quite unlike those current in inter-state relations (Munn-Rankin 1956; Luke 1965; Matthews 1978).

An old misconception, which can finally be laid to rest as a result of the rich documentation from Mari, is the idea that the two-wheeled, horse-drawn chariot was introduced into the Near East by Indo-European conquerors, who entered the area some time soon after 1600. The exact role of the two-wheeled chariot (much faster and more flexible than the four-wheeled donkey-drawn one) in war at this time is still not clear, but it is evident that both it and the horses trained to draw it were in use (Moorey 1986). The letters that refer to fine horses as special gifts exchanged between kings show plainly that they were available (cf. p. 101). A plea made to the king of Mari offers a glimpse into how use of the fast horse, as opposed to the more sedate mules and donkeys, was evaluated at this time:

> May my lord honour his position as king!
> As you are king of the Hanaeans and, secondly, king of the Akkadians, may my lord not ride with horses; may my lord ride (instead) in a cart with mules and thus honour his position as king!
>
> (ARM 6.76)

Although much remains to be clarified (and corrections of older views and new texts are published almost annually), the wealth of documentation from Mari on almost every conceivable aspect of life is truly astonishing. The evidence for the practice of revealed prophecy, comparable to that familiar to us from later Israel, has been one of the most startling discoveries. The seers, male and female, were not necessarily attached to cultic centres, which seems surprising at first sight. The divine will could be made manifest in a great variety of ways. One of the most important, at all times, in ancient Mesopotamia was liver divination, for which a sheep was ritually slaughtered and the different parts of its liver studied and interpreted, because the sun-god was thought to 'write' signs upon the liver. This was a highly developed science (Jeyes 1980; 1989), which demanded considerable training, and clay models of livers, possibly used for instruction, have been found at Mari (as well as at other sites in other periods). But natural phenomena were also watched and any unusual occurrences noted, because they, too, might be expressions of divine intent: freak weather conditions, strange births, animals turning up in unexpected places and movements of planets are just some examples. Reporting these events to the king was important, since they could affect the outcome of political events and the well-being and stability of the country. An important additional route through which divine messages might come was a dream, or the utterance of divinely inspired words. It is in the nature of such divine revelations that anything and anyone may be the channel for them, and so it is quite possible to miss them because the agents of revelation are unpredictable and hence not regularly consulted. It was very important, therefore, that any such occurrences be noted by officials as they came to their notice and that they be communicated to the king himself (cf. most recently, Durand 1988). The following text will give an idea of how such reports ran, although, in this instance, the 'divine messengers' were both connected with cults:

> Speak to my star (ie. my lord, the king): thus (speaks) Inib-shina. Earlier, Shelebum, the *assinnum*[9] had given me a message and I wrote it to you. Today a *qammatum*-woman[10] of Dagan of Terqa came to look for me and spoke with me.
> Here is her statement:
> 'The overtures for peace by the man (i.e. king) of Eshnunna are a trick.

Under the straw flows water, and with the net he is knotting I shall gather him up (i.e. catch him in a trap of his own making). I shall destroy his city and his treasure, which comes from days of yore, I shall have confiscated.'
This is what she told me. Now take care. Do not enter the city without an oracle. Herewith what I heard: 'He is constantly trying to make himself famous.' Do not strive to make yourself famous (i.e basic meaning: do not act without divine direction; do not trust in yourself).

(ARM 10.80; Durand 1988: no. 197)

One aspect of Mesopotamian life that has become much clearer as a result of the Mari material is the nature of the legal process known as the 'river-ordeal' (Bottéro 1981). This was a method used to establish guilt in cases where there was no evidence for what had happened apart from the word of the accuser against that of the accused (such as adultery, witchcraft, treason, and certain property disputes). The king was involved, at least to the extent of receiving a report of the ordeal; it also seems that it was often he who ordered the implementation of this solemn and risky procedure. The accused had to spend the night before the ordeal in a specified place, having washed his/her hands and feet, and at dawn had to recite certain words ordered by the king. This stressed the seriousness of the accusation. For Mari, the place for the ordeal seems to have been the Euphrates near Hit, where the local bitumen source perhaps made the river (conceptualised as a god) seem particularly powerful and mysterious. Hit lay at this time within the kingdom of Babylon, and this probably explains the reference in one text to 'Babylonian servants' being present at the ordeal (see below p. 107). The process was initiated by the two parties stating and rejecting the accusation:

Before Sin-iddinam married me, I said yes to the father and to the son (i.e. the accused, now the wife of Sin-iddinam, formerly worked as a prostitute). One time when Sin-iddinam was absent, he sent me news by his son Asqudum. The latter said to me: 'I want to wed you.' He kissed my lips, touched my genitals, (but) his penis did not penetrate my sex. I said to him: 'It is not possible that I should sin against Sin-iddinam!' In the house where I was, I did not do that which I should not do to my lord.

(Charpin *et al*. 1988: no. 488)

The dangerous ordeal was frequently undergone by a substitute for the accused: in the case of nobles, the inhabitants of their towns and villages acted for them, in that of the queen a lady-in-waiting underwent the ordeal on her behalf, a man could use his wife, and in one case, where a young girl was accused, her mother jumped into the river instead. One long text shows that the accused, or their substitutes, had to dive into the river and then swim a considerable distance below water before emerging in order to be vindicated.[11] This demanded some stamina and so, at times, whole teams of people would undergo the ordeal, with the strongest entering the water first and the weaker last:

> Speak to my lord: thus (speaks) Meptûm, your servant.
> As for the people who had to dive on behalf of Shubram and Haya-Sumu whom my lord had sent, I sent with that group men of integrity and trust. To start with, they made a woman dive and she emerged. After her, they made an old man dive. (By swimming) for a distance of 80 (measures) right in the middle of the god (i.e. the river), he succeeded and then got out. After him, a second woman was made to go down and she, too, came out. After her a third woman; the river 'married' (her: i.e. she drowned). Given the fact that the old man only tested the case over a distance of 80 (measures) and that the river 'married' the third woman, the people of Haya-Sumu refused to allow the remaining three women to undergo the diving. They acknowledged: 'Town and land are not ours.' The old man, falling at the feet of the people of Shubram, said: 'Don't make the remaining women dive (in the river) in case they die! We will be pleased to produce a tablet abandoning the claim to town and land so that there will be no claim forever and that the town and land belong to Shubram.' Then before the men of integrity, the Babylonian servants and the elders of the town, they were made to compose a no-claims tablet. I am now sending the people who had to dive to my lord so that he may interrogate them.
>
> (Bottéro, 1981; Durand, 1988: no. 249)

The evidence for the river-ordeal from Mari is very important, because other Mesopotamian law-codes, such as that of Hammurabi, refer to it as a method of resolving certain cases without specifying, naturally, what it involved. It seems to have been a traditional practice of long standing, as is shown by the fact that there are allusions to the river-ordeal from the third millennium down to the sixth century.

The information still to come from the Mari material promises as much again as is already known, and only a tiny proportion of the many aspects of life that it illuminates have been mentioned here (for a lively introduction to many more, see Dalley 1984). The immense wealth of detail the archives contain has revolutionised understanding of the Near East in this period. But what is perhaps most welcome is the direct insight the texts allow into some of the individual quirks of the major political figures of the day. The aggrieved and wheedling tone of Yasmah-Addu, frequently reprimanded by his father, Shamshi-Adad, for not being as vigorous as his brother, Ishme-Dagan of Ekallate, is particularly amusing:[12]

> Speak to Daddy: thus (speaks) Yasmah-Addu, your son. I listened to the tablet which Daddy sent me, which ran as follows: 'How much

longer do we have to keep you on a leading rein? You are a child, you are not a man, you have no beard on your chin! How much longer are you going to fail in running your household properly? Don't you realise that your brother is commanding enormous armies? So you (jolly well) command your palace and household properly!' That is what Daddy wrote to me. Now, how can I be a child and incapable of directing affairs when Daddy promoted me? How is it that, although I grew up with Daddy from when I was tiny, now some servant or other has succeeded in ousting me from Daddy's affections? So I am coming to Daddy right now, to have it out with Daddy about my unhappiness!

(ARM 1.108; Dalley 1984: 34)

2e Hammurabi and the First Dynasty of Babylon
(1894–1595)

The rise of Babylon

Babylon is yet another example of a city ruled by an Amorite dynasty, which became suddenly prominent: striving, on the one hand, to emulate the earlier great empires, and, on the other, struggling to survive by establishing an overall political hegemony and eliminating its competitors, such as Larsa, Eshnunna, Assyria and Mari.

There are some difficulties in tracing the rise of the First Dynasty of Babylon, beginning with Sumuabum in 1894 down to Hammurabi's father, Sin-muballit (1812–1793; see table 8). The site of Babylon poses a problem: it has produced very little indeed from the period preceding its most glorious phase as the capital of the Neo-Babylonian empire (626–539; see chapter 11d), because of the very high water-table. So the political centre of Hammurabi's realm has yielded virtually no material at all. For reconstructing its history we therefore depend on the surviving year-names and on archives from other sites. Some of these are large and very informative, especially with respect to economic affairs, but also social conditions and practices (cf., for example, Stone 1977; Yoffee 1977; Kraus 1979; Jeyes 1983; Charpin 1986). There are also occasional mentions of Babylon in the Mari archives, and a fair number of mostly rather laconic royal inscriptions of rulers of the dynasty (Kärki 1984; Frayne 1990). An important site that has provided quite a lot of material is Sippar not far from Babylon, which fell quite early on under the control of the kings of Babylon (Harris 1975). But expansion by the kings of the hitherto unimportant town of Babylon was fairly limited prior to Hammurabi: at Hammurabi's accession (1792) Babylon controlled Dilbat, Sippar, Kish and Borsippa – all of them located in its immediate vicinity.

One fact that is fairly certain is that the victories, after which Hammurabi's years 7–11 are named, were the result of wars waged by him not as an

108

independent ruler but as ally of the then more powerful kings, Shamshi-Adad I of Assyria and Rim-Sin of Larsa. In other words, Hammurabi himself was initially no more than one of the many kings who 'followed' another, stronger overlord, graphically described in the Itur-Asdu letter from Mari (p. 99). His political expansion cannot be dated earlier than his thirtieth regnal year (1763), but then his control spread very rapidly. A successful campaign to the east Tigris region was followed by the defeat of the great Rim-Sin of Larsa, which gave Hammurabi at one stroke control over Isin, Uruk, Ur and Nippur as well as the sizeable dominions of Larsa. Thus, within a short space of time, the main south Mesopotamian cities, important in terms of royal ideology and agricultural and commercial wealth, were within Hammurabi's grasp. In 1761, he added control over Eshnunna, which gave him direct access to the Diyala route, linking the Iranian plateau to the Mesopotamian plain and its rich trade; Assyria with its own important trade network and parts of the Zagros were also conquered. In 1760 these rapid and extensive conquests were crowned by the capture of Mari, whose walls were destroyed two years later. This spelled the end of Mari's role as a major political centre, and Hammurabi was able to extend his power westwards along the Euphrates, including the important overland route through the Jezira (see p. 100). He was now in direct contact, and shared a frontier, with the kingdom of Yamhad/Aleppo, which played such an important role in the Near East at this time (see pp. 98–100). In 1755 Eshnunna was totally destroyed by flood. Hammurabi was now undisputed, sole and direct ruler of a very large territory that easily bears comparison with the Ur III empire, and commanded the routes along which precious, as well as essential, items and materials (silver, gold, lapis lazuli, carnelian, exotic woods, tin, copper, horses) were traded.

King, country and subjects

The bulk of sources for understanding the political structure of Hammurabi's realm comes from Sippar (north of Babylon) and the Larsa area to the south. The latter is one-sided inasmuch as it represents the archives of royal officials in charge of land belonging to the crown. Hammurabi's style of exercising power, based on this material, has been characterised as representing a programme of deliberate 'secularisation' (Harris 1975) and the re-establishment of centralised royal control of production and trade (Yoffee 1977). Such views require modification, as they are based on misconceptions surrounding the role of the temple in earlier periods, on the one hand, and, as pointed out, on material emanating from the administration of royal land, on the other (Kraus 1979; Charpin 1987). Political control was, of course, to a considerable extent centred on Babylon as a result of Hammurabi's conquests, and large tracts of land that had belonged to defeated kings were now the property of the king of

Babylon. Such new crown estates were extended by land-reclamation and irrigation schemes, and this led, not surprisingly, to increased royal production of wool, textiles, fish, dates and cereals. As a result a comparably larger role was played by the crown in foreign trade; but, as Kraus (1979) has shown, this role, while large, was not a monopoly and amounted to only a half share – the remaining commercial capital for trading ventures was put up by private merchants. Similarly, the notion that cultic personnel were turned into royal dependants, as opposed to being dependent on supposedly 'autonomous' temples, is unconvincing: as cities, such as Sippar, came under the rule of Babylon, it fell to the king there to make cultic appointments in these centres and authorise their emoluments. To see in this a planned programme of secularisation is to beg the question of the relationship of such offices to the political fabric earlier, and where evidence exists (ED III Lagash, Agade, Ur III, Isin, Mari) everything points to the fact that appointments to high cultic office were always made by the king.

Material from the reign of Hammurabi, and to a lesser degree that of his successors, allows some insight into Mesopotamia's social structure and how people were tied to the king. Officials and royal servants were given subsistence fields as part of their emoluments, while various grades of soldier were given landholdings which carried with them the obligation to fulfil certain duties required by the government. *Ilkum* is the term for this complex of duties, and military service was certainly one of them, although not the only one – supplying labour for royal building-schemes and producing certain items for the palace were others. Land grants of this type were closely watched: there were strict regulations about willing them to descendants, and restrictions on their sale. Anyone who acquired such a land-parcel, but had not been the original grantee, was required to take over the duties incumbent on the land. It has been suggested that these restrictions on the disposal of land resulted in the leasing of plots becoming more extensive, and as lessees became more and more indebted as a result of poor harvests they were reduced to debt-slaves. Again, this pattern should not be seen as something peculiar to Hammurabi's reign and his dynasty; rather it was a perennial feature of Mesopotamian life that is simply rather better illuminated at this time. The promulgation of 'righteousness' (*mīšarum*) as a recurring royal act on accession, intended precisely to release people from debt obligations and bondage, is attested in earlier periods and other places (see p. 77) The best-preserved exemplar of such an act is the *mīšarum*-edict of Ammi-saduqa (1647–1626), the penultimate ruler of the First Dynasty of Babylon (Kraus 1958; 1984), but the practice and economic relations it implies existed much earlier. Royal land was cultivated by people who paid an annual tax (*biltum*), partly in agricultural products or goods and partly in silver. The palace, for its part, supplied the cultivators with oxen, agricultural implements and water for the ever essential irrigation. Similarly, the royal herds were looked after by private herdsmen, who contracted to graze them, saw to it that the flocks multiplied annually, and paid a sum of silver in return for the private profit that accrued to them from having the animals at their disposal. Accounts were kept of dead animals, whose carcasses were handed over to knackers; in return they handed over a stipulated quantity of materials per carcass, such as wool and skin, as well as some silver. In all cases, both the palace and those contracting to work for it derived profit and sustenance from the arrangement, which usually provided additional income to the contracting individuals (Charpin 1987).

Hammurabi is most celebrated for his law-code, inscribed on a large stone stele (2.25 m high) which was found early this century by the French excavators at Susa; it had been pillaged by the Elamite kings in the thirteenth century, probably from the temple of Sippar at Shamash (for translations cf. *ANET*: 163–180; *TUAT* I/1: 39–80). The text is partly effaced by a space made to carry an inscription of the Elamite king, but beyond that it is extremely well preserved. An enormous amount of ink has been spilt by scholars trying to understand its function, and this debate has by no means been resolved. The rounded top of the stele (just under a third of its height) shows a 'royal investiture' scene analogous to that on the painted fresco in the Mari palace (see fig. 9): Hammurabi stands in reverent pose before the throne of the god Shamash (sun-god and thus patron of justice, as the sun illuminates all), who sits with rays sprouting from his shoulders, wearing his tall, multi-horned crown and presenting the king with the measuring rod and coiled rope – symbols of his role as a just king and conqueror (fig. 11). Below this are the laws, beautifully inscribed, and framed by a lengthy prologue and epilogue written in a hymnic style: the literary form of these sections of the 'code' is reminiscent of the earlier royal hymns, and they stand among the finest examples of early literary Akkadian. The prologue and epilogue make it quite certain that the stele was set up very late in Hammurabi's reign, as they describe his realm as embracing regions and cities which he conquered only after his thirtieth regnal year. In fact, the earliest one could date the stele would be somewhere around the fortieth year (he reigned forty-two).

It is difficult to know what type of royal edict Hammurabi's code represents: it is not one of the promulgations dissolving debts, and although it contains a reference to an image of Hammurabi as 'the king of justice' this was probably set up in his twenty-first year and so cannot easily be identified with the stele itself. The collection of prescriptive laws which it contains is a rather eclectic sample, and the prices it recommends for various goods seem to be idealistic, and bear little relation to actual prices paid, which are fairly fully attested by subsequent business texts. Finally, it has been remarked that there are only very rare references in the extant legal documents that might be to the Hammurabi code. All of this

111

has led to the influential suggestion (Finkelstein 1961; 1965) that the code should be classified as an example of royal self-praise, whereby the king at the end of his reign gave an account to the gods of his achievements, among which an important place was held by his role as upholder of justice (Westbrook 1989). This view would then reduce the famous code to an elaborate piece of royal ideology, which did not affect the life of Hammurabi's subjects in any tangible way. While it certainly played this role, that does not necessarily exclude a more practical function. These observations, therefore, may need to be modified, and a partly transliterated letter suggests that the labour-wages fixed by Hammurabi in the stele *were* referred to on occasion:

> the (amount of) wages for a hired worker is written on the stele, (therefore) in accordance with what they told you, do not withhold their wages, be it barley or silver.
>
> (Chicago A 3529: 12; *CAD* N/1: 364–365)

If this is a reference to Hammurabi's laws, as seems very likely, then it clearly reflects the important role played by the king as a source of equity and legal authority, actively and effectively protecting his subjects against exploitation, in keeping with his own statement in the epilogue to the laws:

> I, the king who stands head and shoulders above kings – my words are choice, my diligence is unequalled. At the command of the sungod, the great judge of heaven and earth, may my justice become visible in the land; at the command of Marduk (patron-god of Babylon) may what I have written find no-one who removes it; in Esagila (Marduk's santuary in Babylon), which I love, may my name be pronounced with gratitude eternally.
>
> May a citizen who has sustained damage and is involved in a legal case come before my statue (called) 'king of justice', may he read my inscribed stele, may my stele elucidate the legal situation for him, may he see his legal decision, may he let his heart breathe easily (and say): 'Hammurabi, the lord, who exists for the people like a real father, has cared at the command of his lord Marduk, reached the wish of Marduk above and below, pleased the heart of his lord Marduk and determined well-being for the people for ever and helped the land obtain its justice' – may he say this and before my lord Marduk and my lady Sarpanitum (Marduk's consort) may he bless me with all his heart.
>
> (CH XLVII: 80–XLVIII: 47)

Whatever one thinks the code's function was supposed to be (an attempt to resolve conflicts between the crown and local bodies (Diakonoff 1971)? a collection of particular royal decisions on specific cases (Petschow 1984)?), there can be no doubt of the wealth of information which it provides on many aspects of Old Babylonian society. Despite continuing problems in under-

112

standing some of the terminology, in particular for various social groups (Diakonoff 1971), it illustrates the busy life of this period, and meshes with the vivid material found in the many small private archives containing family letters and business documents. In a text from Ur we find, for example, neighbours resolving a quarrel about their adjoining property:

> Length: 1½ perch 2 ells (c. 10 m); width: 1 ell 6 fingers (0.60 m): the party wall belonging to Lu-Nanna and Ela. Ela will repair it at his expense: for the expenses of the wall, for 6 m. Lu-Nanna will indemnify Ela. Ela must attach the bolt (of the door) of Lu-Nanna.
> (UET 5: 25; cf. Charpin 1986: 100–102)

While the river-ordeal (cf. pp. 106–107) was used to resolve accusations of some crimes (e.g. sorcery, CH §2), the solemn oath sworn on divine attributes was used in other cases (Ries 1989), as here in an Ur text:

> In the courtyard of the temple of Ningublaga, Uselli and Enamtisud were examined. They approached; the weapon of Ningublaga was brought out and Uselli declared on oath: 'I swear that I do not know, have not hidden, and do not possess the grain, silver, clothing and turban belonging to Enamtisud.' (Followed by list of seven witnesses)
> (UET 5 254: Charpin 1986: 88–89)

Many laws concern matrimony and inheritance. The complex rites associated with marriage have been reconstructed in detail from a document of this period (Greengus 1966). The wedding was a long-drawn-out affair. First, gifts (garments, silver and a ring) were sent by the bride's father to the bridegroom; then offerings were made in the temples of the bride's and groom's home towns; the marriage-gifts, consisting of food and other items, were delivered to the bride's house on a tray, to be returned by the bride's father by the hand of the groom's brother with more food, so that the groom's family would share in eating food prepared by the family to which they were allying themselves. Then the groom's relatives visited the bride's house to be feasted and a rite of some kind was performed, after which the groom's mother (in this instance she may have been acting for the deceased father) arrived and was also fed. She then performed a rite in the temple and stayed for the ritual bathing of the bride and the pouring of oil on her head. Afterwards she returned home, escorted by some of her relatives and taking more gifts of food with her. Then the groom finally entered the bride's house (Malul 1989) and lived for four months, together with four of his wedding-companions, in the bride's house, after which the bride was taken back to her new home to live with her husband and in-laws.

As in many patrilocal societies, wives could become the foci of hostility and scapegoats in family quarrels – they are the newcomers, with loyalties outside their husband's family. An interesting small group of texts (Walters 1970/1) shows a father and son locked in a quarrel in public before the village mayor. It is quite clear that the son had misbehaved in relation to a family field, but the father, interestingly, did not identify him as the real villain, but put the blame on to his daughter-in-law and her mother who, he maintained, had bewitched his son. The son responded in kind, saying that the father had been bewitched by 'his sorceress' – unfortunately her identity (and hence exact relationship to the family) is not known. But the important feature of the case is that the two male blood-relatives shift the responsibility for the conflict between the father and his son to the more vulnerable female outsiders.

Three social groups are distinguished in the Hammurabi laws in several instances: *awīlum* ('man'), *muškēnum* (?'dependant') and *wardum* (slave). The last category is uncontroversial, but the first two have proved extremely hard to define precisely. It is possible that by *awīlum*, a free citizen was meant, as opposed to *muškēnum*, 'royal retainer/palace dependant' (Diakonoff 1971), but the question remains open. The terms certainly indicated differences in juridical status, as penalties varied, depending on which group the wrongdoer and victim belonged to. But what is not at all clear is whether the three categories reflect a descending social hierarchy, so that it is not certain that a *muškēnum* was necessarily always placed lower down the social scale than the *awīlum* (Postgate 1992: 239–240). Chattel slaves, by contrast, pose no problem of definition: they were marked either by a special hairstyle or some kind of tattoo which it was a crime to change or remove. Many laws deal with the problem of runaway slaves and their return. Two laws concern the case where both a wife and a household slavegirl have borne children to the husband. The kind of emotional and social problems that could arise from this situation may be imagined. The ruling by Hammurabi is clear:

> §170: If the wife of a man bears him children and his slave-girl also bears him children, and if the father in his lifetime acknowledges as his children the children which his slavegirl has borne him, and places them on an equal footing with his wife's children, then, when the father has died, the children of the wife and the children of the slavegirl shall share the property of the father's house equally; the heir, the son of the wife, may choose his share and take it away first.

> §171: If, however, the father during his lifetime does not acknowledge as his children the children which the slavegirl has borne him, then, when the father has died, the children of the slavegirl may not share the property of the father's house equally; the slavegirl and her children shall be freed, and the children of the wife may not claim the children of the slavegirl as slaves.

(CH §§170–171)

Interestingly, a range of female cultic personnel also figure in the code, and their relationship to the rest of society is regulated. Some of them could be married, but were not allowed to bear children, in which case they supplied their husband with a slavegirl to bear a child on their behalf. One group (although not identical to the one appearing in the Hammurabi code), the *nadītu* of Sippar, are particularly well known from archives recovered from the cloister in which they lived (Jeyes 1983; Harris 1989). They were daughters of high-ranking families, including princesses from neighbouring states. The girls were dedicated to the god Shamash of Sippar as 'betrothed', and developed a particularly close bond with his consort, Aya. They brought their dowries with them to the cloister, and may have taken a new name on entry (Dalley 1984: 105). Then they lived with their servants in a house inside the cloister walls, secluded and unmarried. One of their main duties seems to have been to pray for the well-being of their families. They also engaged very actively in business, using outside agents, and, while the dowry thus augmented was returned to the *nadītum*'s family on her death, she could will some of her own property freely. She could also adopt, and leave property to her adopted daughter, although her family might contest the will. Although denied the domesticity of normal family life, the *nadītu* retained close relations and emotional bonds with their families, on whom they continued to depend. They were well aware of the lustre their position brought their parents, and used it to wheedle extras from them, as in this letter from Erishti-Aya, daughter of King Zimri-Lim of Mari:

> I am always, always praying, always! . . . When I wrote to you last year, you sent me two servant girls, but one of them died, and now they have brought me two more, and one of them has died too. I am the emblem of your father's house, so why am I not provided for?
>
> (ARM X 39; Dalley 1984: 105–106)

✳   ✳   ✳

These are merely samples of the wide range of day-to-day activities that appear in the code and are reflected in the personal documents of the period. While the political history may be hard to recover, the documentation covering details of daily life is a veritable treasure-trove of information.

The decline of Babylon

It is usual to maintain that Hammurabi's dominions crumbled almost immediately on his death, and that his achievements were as transitory as those of Shamshi-Adad. That is an exaggeration. It is true that his successors did not maintain control of all the areas he had conquered, and the area of Mari was lost to Babylon about twenty years after his death, with the development of the new kingdom of Hana (probably centred on Terqa), covering virtually the same territory as Mari had done in its heyday (G. and M. Buccellati in Weiss 1985 [0Gc]; Rouault 1984). Similarly, a series of political disturbances to the south of Babylon, including a revolt in Larsa, resulted eventually (about eighty years later) in the loss of direct control of the profitable Gulf trade and some of the rich areas in the extreme south, in particular date-groves and the important fishing areas of the marshes, with the successful establishment of the still poorly known 'Sealand Dynasty' here (*RLA* 8: 6–10). It is, then, certainly the case that the realm governed by Hammurabi's descendants shrank over a period of time, but this process was quite gradual, and the kingdom of Babylon remained a fairly important political entity, along with Yamhad and Hana, until the city was sacked in a raid by the Hittite king, Mursili I, in 1595 BC (see chapter 5c): i.e. for a period of just over 150 years. It is this relative success of the dynasty, rather than its problems and ultimate failure, that require more study.

Notes

1 In this chapter, I have picked out just five topics which illustrate salient aspects of this period of Mesopotamian history; the reader should be aware of the selectiveness of the material.

2 Rim-Sin and his father Warad-Sin (1834–1823) were members of the family of Kudurmabuk, who controlled the tribal territory of Emutbal; it lay to the east of the Tigris and probably embraced Larsa (Stol 1976).

3 The special place occupied by the king in relation to the community may also be expressed by another term, occasionally used in documents, i.e. *waklum* = 'overseer'; Larsen 1976.

4 It is probable that the colonies located in and near the north Syrian region would have referred themselves directly to Ashur and bypassed the *kārum* at Kanesh.

5 The source of the tin imported by Ashur into Anatolia has been discussed extensively, and there is no absolute certainty except that it comes from an area to the east of Ashur; for discussions see Muhly 1973; 1985; Muhly and Wertime 1973; Stech and Pigot 1986 (also *RLA* VIII, 131–132). Recently, an Anatolian source of tin (Cilician Gates) has been identified which, it is claimed, could have been used as a tin-source in the fourth and third millennium (K. Ashiham Yener and Hadi Özbal, *Antiquity* (1987), 220–226); but this has been argued against by Belli (1991). A large part of *AJA* 97/2 (1993) is devoted to discussions of the matter and contains full bibliographies of earlier material.

6 The famous Mari archives are contemporary with the reigns of Yasmah-Addu and Zimri-Lim.

7 Jezira (lit. 'island') is the name given to the zone between the Tigris and Euphrates (lying in modern north-west Iraq, north Syria and south Turkey). It is a barren area, but has great agricultural potential if irrigated.

8 Most of the volume edited by Archi contains contributions critical of Polanyi's thesis, except for a long essay by J. Renger on the Old Babylonian period. For an excellent full review, with extensive criticism of Renger's position, see P. Vargyas 'The problem of private economy in the Ancient Near East', *BiOr* 44 (1987): 376–385.

9 The *assinnum* seems to have been an effeminate homosexual who played the part of a sort of jester in certain rituals; it has been thought that he was a eunuch, but this is not certain (for discussion, see Durand 1988: 395).

10 The *qammatum*-woman, attached to the temple of Dagan at Terqa (another centre in Mari's kingdom), has been thought to be a sibyl-like prophetess, but it has been

argued recently that she was a female cultic actor, distinguished by her hairstyle, which gave her her particular title (Durand 1988: 396).

11 The Mesopotamian river ordeal is not like the European medieval one where the accused lost their life whether they sank or swam – in Mesopotamia, the guilty sank and drowned, the innocent swam and survived.

12 I have followed Dalley's (1984: 34) translation, particularly her felicitous suggestion of rendering the pet-form 'Addaya' of Shamshi-Adad's name by 'Daddy', which gives something of the flavour of the mode of address.

3

EGYPT FROM DYNASTY I TO DYNASTY XVII (*c.* 3100/3000–1552)

Country and environment

Herodotus' famous statement that 'Egypt is the gift of the Nile' (2.5) is not an exaggeration. The country is the largest and naturally most fertile oasis in north Africa, because the Nile has cut here a relatively broad flood-plain through the lime and sandstone. This is in sharp distinction to the region stretching southwards from just north of Aswan into the Sudan. Here the flood-plain is extremely narrow, the river channel is often disrupted by large rocks, which makes navigation impossible, and the land often very stony. This rock-strewn area is known as Nubia, often called (misleadingly) 'Ethiopia' in older books. The Nile valley also marks Egypt off from the deserts to east and west. The contrast is striking not just from the air, but even at ground level: as far as the irrigated and tilled soil reaches, the earth is dark brown; immediately adjacent to it, the yellow sands of the arid desert begin. It is possible to stand with one foot on the fine cultivated earth and the other on the hostile desert sands. Given the severely limited area available for agriculture, it was generally (although not always) the case that settlements and fields were located in this irrigable land, while burials were sited in the desert.

Aswan and the first cataract marked the traditional southern frontier of Egypt from early in dynasty I onwards. From here, northwards along the Nile to Memphis, stretched the area now conventionally referred to as 'Upper Egypt', divided in historical times into twenty 'canonical' administrative districts (see map 7). North of Memphis lies the Nile delta, where the river divides into a number of arms. Much of this region was very marshy. The land-area is large and potentially very rich, but its marshiness makes it harder to exploit. This northern section of Egypt is traditionally called 'Lower Egypt' and it, too, was divided into a series of administrative districts. Quite often, the region between Memphis and Abydos is termed 'Middle Egypt' by modern scholars. This defines the part of Egypt where the flood-plain is considerably more extensive than further south. But it was not regarded as a distinct region by the Egyptians themselves – when they refer in the historical period to the 'Two Lands', they inevitably mean Upper and Lower Egypt as defined above.

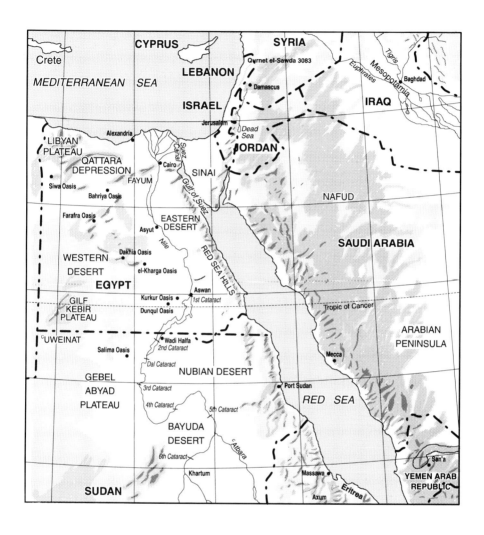

Map 5 Egypt: physical features

119

The Nile was Egypt's lifeline, linking the communities strung along its banks, and communications were primarily by riverboat. The centrality of the Nile in all Egyptian life is well illustrated by the Egyptian terms for directions: north was called 'downstream' and south 'upstream'. A most amusing (to us) description is preserved in a text of Tuthmosis III (fifteenth century) who, in describing the Euphrates river in north Syria (which flows from north to south) for the Egyptians, had to say that 'in flowing downstream it flows upstream'.

But Egypt did not just consist of the narrow strip of cultivated land lying either side of the river. The neighbouring deserts contained important resources. To the west lay the Libyan desert, inhabited by pastoralists, and dotted with a series of oases, of which the largest were Bahriya, Siwa, Farafra, Dakhla, and Kharga. During periods of political strength, Egypt attempted to control them, and people could be exiled there. When Egypt's power over them was less certain, they could serve as places of refuge. They were very fertile regions, lying along a route that linked them to each other and with Nubia further south. Routes also led from them to the Nile valley (Giddy 1987). What is less certain is whether the longer desert routes could have been traversed regularly before the use of the camel became common in Egypt (not before the sixth or fifth century). Also to the west of Egypt, but closer to the Nile valley, lay the Fayum depression with a lake fed by an arm of the Nile (Bahr-Yusuf), to the south-west of Memphis. To make the region usable for farming, the water feeding the lake had to be diverted. This was an immense task: in the Ptolemaic period (third to first century) a great effort was made and an enormous acreage of land put under production here. But earlier reclamation work was also done by the kings of the twelfth dynasty, who developed the region substantially. It has been thought that they made about 450 km^2 available for cultivation, but the exact area is uncertain. With careful management, two crops could be produced here per year. Another region away from the Nile in the west was the Wadi el-Natrun, close to the western delta, with its salt-lake, a source of natron used for cleaning, the manufacture of glass and in mummification.

To the east, the Sinai peninsula linked Egypt to western Asia. Control of its inland routes and the coastal road was important for Egyptian security and trade. Within Sinai itself were located important turquoise and copper mines (Serabit el-Khadim, Wadi Maghara). The turquoise was certainly exploited by the Egyptians from early in their history, but the evidence for copper-mining is not usually associated with Egyptian remains. In the later New Kingdom the rich copper source much further east at Timna, near modern Elat, was worked for Egyptian profit (Rothenberg 1972). Further south, directly to the east of the main Nile valley, the eastern desert was rich in mineral resources, in particular alabaster (Hatnub), quartzite (Gebel Ahmar), greywacke and gold (Wadi Hammamat). At a number of points routes led through the Red Sea hills to the coast, and there were a small number of Egyptian ports located here. From here, the seaborne expeditions set out to the wondrous land of Punt, a source of incense probably located in modern Eritrea.

One of the richest of Egypt's neighbours, and a constant focus for ambitious kings, was Nubia. Further south, in the region of the fifth and sixth cataracts, Nubia is potentially very fertile, and a number of important political entities with distinctive cultures flourished here at the same time as Egypt (Trigger 1976). The land of Nubia is conventionally also divided into two sections, 'Lower Nubia' designating the region from the first to the second cataract, with 'Upper Nubia' the region beyond reaching into the Sudan. Lower Nubia was at times called by the Egyptians 'Wawat', and Upper Nubia known frequently as 'Kush'. But Kush could also be used more vaguely of the whole of Nubia. Other terms also appear and probably reflect political changes in the area. Nubia is a region especially rich in copper deposits, gold, amethyst and diorite. But it also had a fairly substantial, albeit scattered, farming population, and from very early in Egypt's history there are records of raids for cattle and prisoners mounted by Egypt against her southern neighbour. It was one of Egypt's most important sources of manpower, particularly for the army; a kind of police regiment seems to have been constituted almost entirely of a particular Lower Nubian population group, the Medjay. Nubia also provided the Egyptians with access to rare and exotic items from sub-Saharan Africa – pygmies, ostrich eggs, ebony and many others – that were highly prized by the Egyptian rulers. Not for nothing has Nubia been dubbed the 'corridor to Africa' (Adams 1975 [0Gg]). Time and time again the Egyptians made efforts to control, or even incorporate, Nubia, at least the northern part, and conflict between the two regions was endemic.

Egypt's climate for most of its traceable history has always been very dry, so that it is absolutely dependent on irrigation from the Nile for its survival. It has been subject to long-term climate changes, such as the 'Neolithic Wet Phase' (Butzer 1976), extending from c. 10,000 to c. 5000, during which the deserts to east and west were probably more heavily populated. This was succeeded by a gradual desiccation, which seems to have become marked in the late fourth millennium and which led to increased settlement in the Nile valley. But, apart from such profound, slow changes, Egypt is subject to constant fluctuations in the level of the Nile floods on which it depends for growing its crops. The Ethiopian monsoons swell the Blue Nile; annual rainfalls and melting snow raise the level of the White Nile. These swollen tributaries used to cause the Nile to rise and flood the Sudan and Egypt regularly each year. The annual inundation is now controlled by a series of dams and sluices, begun in the last century (AD 1830) and completed in the 1960s by the great Aswan dam, which has flooded most of Lower Nubia permanently and formed Lake Nasser. But, before that, the annual flooding would begin in Egypt in July, climaxing in August and September and receding in October. It normally provided sufficient water for growing one crop. The floodwaters did not simply spill over the banks, but spread along a number of overflow channels to the lower land behind the levees along the river banks where settlements were sited. The main effort had to be directed towards controlling the floodwater and using it as efficiently as possible, a task that could be carried out at the level of the administrative districts into which Egypt was divided (Butzer 1976). Once the water had receded, leaving behind the rich black silt, the crops (emmer, barley, pulses, vegetables, sesame and flax for linen) were sown and harvested between January and March. After the harvest, the Nile was at its lowest. The rise and fall of the Nile created the seasonal pattern for Egyptians: not the four seasons we are accustomed to in temperate Europe, but three seasons marking a very different farming cycle: 'Inundation', 'Going down of the Inundation' (Cultivation) and 'Drought' (Harvest/Summer). Good (i.e. high) Niles were awaited anxiously each year, and men posted in the south to watch for the rising water sent messages north to let the central administration know whether it was likely to be a generous flood, and hence a good harvest, or not. Good Niles were hoped for by kings as a sign that their reign was blessed, as shown by this passage from a hymn celebrating the accession of Ramesses IV (dynasty XX, twelfth century):

> High Niles have come forth from their caverns, that they may refresh the hearts of the common people.
> (G. Maspero, *Recueil* ii (1880): 116–117; Erman 1927/1966 [OI]: 279;
> *ANET*: 378–379)

One other feature of Egypt's landscape needs to be noted. There were marginal areas of swampy land, which could not easily be utilised for regular farming. In part they could provide excellent grazing ground for large cattle, such as cows. But more extensive areas of marshland were overgrown with papyrus thickets, which served as cover for waterfowl. Fowling in the marshes is one of the most frequent scenes shown in tomb-paintings and was obviously an élite pastime. But the thickets also provided quite regularly an additional source of food, as did fishing. The papyrus was, of course, a very important plant in Egypt. It had a multiplicity of uses, ranging from small river boats to matting, but most importantly, for modern scholars, it was turned very early on into an excellent writing material. Given Egypt's dry climate, many papyrus documents have survived and provide a mass of information on Egypt's history. Papyrus no longer grows in Egypt – it seems to have died out in the Middle Ages. More recently, within the last three centuries, the hippopotamus and crocodile have also vanished; earlier they infested the banks of the river and swamps, endangering the life of all who lived along the Nile. Hippopotamus hunting in particular is frequently shown in tomb-scenes, and was almost certainly a necessary sport.

Dynastic history: sources and problems

Egyptian history before the hellenistic (Ptolemaic) period is divided into a number of 'dynasties', with the prehistoric period predictably called the 'predynastic' period. The convention of 'dynasties' and associated terminology is derived from Manetho, an Egyptian scholar who wrote a history of Egypt in Greek in the early third century, and divided it into dynasties. His work is only preserved in citations and summaries of later writers. His precise reason for grouping certain kings together is not always clear, because kings combined by him into one dynasty were not always members of the same family. What is important about Manetho's arrangement is that some similar groupings were used by an Egyptian document, not completely preserved, known variously as the 'Turin Canon', the 'Turin King List', or the 'Royal Canon of Turin' (Gardiner 1959). This text, which presents a list of Egyptian kings, was compiled in the course of the nineteenth dynasty (thirteenth century) and is now in the Museum of Turin. The fact that Manetho and the Turin Canon correspond in their structure suggests that Manetho is a potentially good and reliable source inasmuch as he reflects Egyptian historical traditions of the New Kingdom period (Málek 1982).

How exactly does Manetho's arrangement work? After listing periods of rule by gods (like the Turin papyrus), he described thirty dynasties of Egyptian kings, extending from the supposed first 'unifier' of Egypt, Menes (c. 3100/3000), down to a period just before the conquest of Egypt by Alexander (332). This very long time-span is subdivided into a sequence of periods by modern scholars (table 9). The first two dynasties can be distinguished to some extent from the subsequent period by the form and place of royal burials (mastaba tombs at Abydos). In the course of the third dynasty the first developments towards the pyramid, a classic form for royal tombs for the next thousand years, began. They were located in the north, and Abydos as a royal cemetery site ceased to function. From the fourth dynasty onwards the royal titulary and name expanded, and two of the king's names were henceforth always enclosed in a 'cartouche' (see fig. 12), whose oval shape perhaps symbolised that the king ruled over everything encircled by the sun. In the preceding period, the king's name was shorter and its most prominent element was set within a picture of a palace façade (serekh), normally surmounted by the falcon Horus, son of Osiris, with whom the reigning king was identified (Gardiner 1957, Exc. A). Because of these changes, the first two dynasties (sometimes the third as well) are regarded as a formative period and called the 'Early Dynastic' period. This is followed by the 'Old Kingdom', technically embracing dynasties IV (sometimes III) to VIII. A breakdown in state control, lasting perhaps no more than a hundred years, followed, known as the 'First Intermediate Period'. It ended with the re-emergence of a strong central authority. This is the Middle Kingdom (late dynasty XI to early dynasty XIII). Structural and institutional changes were not perhaps as profound as once thought between the Old and Middle Kingdom, and the two phases are sometimes treated together by Egyptologists (e.g. Kemp in Trigger *et al.* 1983 [0D]; 1989 [0Ga]). The Middle Kingdom was followed by quite a long period of fragmented rule, the 'Second Intermediate Period', lasting about two hundred years. For some of this period, a large part of Egypt was ruled by kings of foreign origin, the so-called 'Hyksos' dynasty. The next five hundred years form the New Kingdom (dynasties XVIII to XX), which in turn was succeeded by the 'Third Intermediate Period' (XXI to XXV) lasting almost four hundred years. Then begins the 'Late Period', with control established over all of Egypt by the rulers of dynasty XXVI (the 'Saites'). In 525 Egypt was conquered by the Persians and became a province of the Achaemenid empire until *c.* 400. Three short-lived, but ideologically important, dynasties of local Egyptian rulers succeeded until the Persians reconquered Egypt in 343. Manetho's history and arrangement of dynasties appears to have ended with this event. A 'dynasty XXXI', representing the second 'Persian domination' was added later to Manetho's work; it was brought to an end by Alexander of Macedon's conquest in 332.

Table 9 Egypt: general chronology

Predynastic		?–3100*
Early Dynastic/Archaic	(dynasties I–II)	*c.* 3100–2686
Old Kingdom	(dynasties III–VI)	*c.* 2686–2181
First Intermediate Period	(dynasties VII–X and early dynasty XI)	*c.* 2180–2040
Middle Kingdom	(late dynasty XI– early dynasty XIII)	*c.* 2040–1730
Second Intermediate Period (including 'Hyksos')	(late dynasty XIII– dynasty XVII	*c.* 1730–1550
New Kingdom	(dynasties XVIII–XX)	*c.* 1550–1080
Third Intermediate Period	(dynasties XXI–XXV)	*c.* 1080–664
Saite Period	(dynasty XXVI)	664–525
Late Period (including 1st and 2nd Persian domination)	(dynasties XXVII–XXXI)	525–332

* The transitional period from late Predynastic to Early Dynastic is sometimes called 'Protodynastic'.

The pattern presented by this rough classifying of Egyptian history is one of periods of strong unified state control alternating with 'intermediate periods', when Egyptian unity broke down. It also gives the impression of enormous continuity – of a constant struggle to return to an ideal, 'correct', political form. Continuity – institutional, cultural, artistic – there certainly was. Many of the basic forms of Egyptian life developed standard shapes very early in its history and deviated relatively little later. But it is important to realise that these norms represent idealised stereotypes that effectively mask the realities of often profound change. This can make it very hard to pinpoint substantial upheavals: the immobility of the outward, eternal form is stressed again and again, beneath which important transformations are hidden. This is not a feature unique to Egypt. But the fact that this potent ideology dominates the Egyptian historical record at many periods means that the historian faces particular difficulties in trying to challenge the official picture.

3a The formation of the Egyptian state

The tradition of unification

A dominant trait in Egyptian culture, which has created a normative picture of what constituted the land, is that Egypt was a country made up of two parts – Upper and Lower Egypt (see p. 118) – united by and under the Egyptian king. The powerful image presented by Egyptian kings at periods of political strength was that Egypt 'unified' was the only harmonious and correct way for Egypt to exist. This picture is strengthened by the Turin Canon and Manetho: both begin with Menes of dynasty I, as the first non-divine king who ruled over all of Egypt. It is also supported by the Abydos list of kings, which is inscribed on the walls of the temple of Sety I there (dynasty XIX, 1305–1290 (1294–1279)). The list gives as Sety I's predecessors only those kings who ruled over the whole of Egypt, entirely ignores kings of the two Intermediate Periods, and again begins with Menes.[1] More or less the same kind of pattern is found in the so-called 'Karnak list of kings', which again gives kings from Menes to Tuthmosis III (dynasty XVIII, 1490–1436 (1479–1425)), but omits the rulers of the Intermediate Periods. So the overwhelming impression, looking at these sources, is that, at the beginning of dynasty I, Menes united Egypt and instigated its development as a powerful and prosperous state. All subsequent kings attempted to maintain or, if necessary, re-create this unity, which was expressed most typically in the royal titulary and names, and a range of royal symbols (Frankfort 1948 [OL]). So the king was always ideally the 'king of Upper and Lower Egypt' (his *'nsw-bity'* name), symbolised by the sedge of Upper Egypt and the bee of Lower Egypt (see fig. 12). He was also 'the beloved of the two ladies'. This referred to two goddesses: one was the vulture Nekhabet, goddess of Nekhab (near Hierakonpolis), in Upper Egypt; the other was the cobra, Wadjet, of Buto in the Delta. The king also wore a double crown, the two elements of which were again linked to Upper and Lower Egypt: the white crown of Upper Egypt was a kind of tall, leather(?) helmet; the red crown of Lower Egypt appears to have been made, originally, of reeds (at least in part). The two crowns were traditionally shown being worn combined (see fig. 12) – again evoking, concretely, the union of the 'two lands', Upper and Lower Egypt.

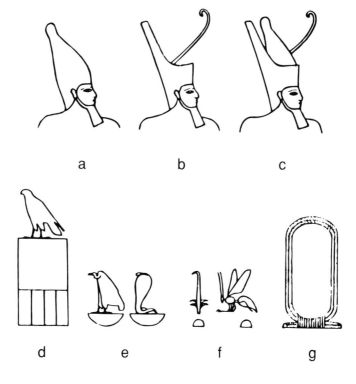

Figure 12 a: white crown; b: red crown; c: double crown; d: *serekh* (palace façade surmounted by Horus falcon); e: 'two ladies' (vulture and cobra); f: *nsw bìty* (sedge and bee); g: cartouche

This notion, that Egypt was made up of two lands which were united by, and in the person of, the king, was absolutely pervasive, and informed almost all aspects of royal imagery throughout the dynastic period.

This helps to illustrate the importance in the Egyptian view of history of the unification as a royal act: for ancient Egyptians the beginning of human history was marked by the emergence of Egypt as a state. But there are problems for modern scholars in accepting the tradition as it stands. Questions arise, such as what exactly is to be understood by 'unification' at this time? Was it something achieved by a single, powerful ruler or was it a long-drawn-out process? What precisely was unified at this early period? Was it the delta and Upper Egypt, or should we envisage quite different geo-political units in the predynastic period? Is there a clearly definable difference in the period before the 'unification' and the immediately succeeding 'early dynastic' phase, or was there a gradual, piecemeal development from the late predynastic into the Early Dynastic period?

The evidence

The answers to these questions depend on a variety of sources, and problems connected with their interpretation. It is plain that Manetho reproduced a tradition current in the New Kingdom (as shown by the Turin Canon, and the Abydos and Karnak lists), but what does this New Kingdom tradition reflect? Was it based on documentary material of some kind that went back to a yet earlier time? Or had it been constructed in accordance with notions prevailing in the New Kingdom in the absence of any evidence? Another problem with the lists is that they give usually only one of the names of the kings, normally his *nsw-bìty* name, but the king already had at least three different names in the Early Dynastic period, i.e. a *nsw-bìty* name, a 'two ladies' (*nbty*) name, and a Horus name (i.e. the name he bore in his incarnation as the divine falcon, associated with Re, the sun god). Unfortunately, many of the inscriptions on extant monuments of the earliest period give only the royal Horus name. The problems that can arise in trying to match a particular *nsw-bìty* name with a particular Horus name are obvious.

A very important source, much closer in date to the Early Dynastic period than these, is the Palermo stone. Originally this was a large stone slab, about 2m long by 0.60m high. The text was compiled in the fifth dynasty (2494–2345) and so is nearer in time to the first historical rulers than the New Kingdom documents, although it is still about six to seven hundred years removed from them. In form it is a kind of 'annals' text, giving some of the main events of the reign of each king by dated years. Unfortunately, only very small fragments of the stone survive (the largest piece is in the Palermo Museum – hence its name), and the names and events of most of the kings of dynasties I and II are lost. One interesting thing about the text is that it listed kings ruling before the 'unification'. In fact, the Palermo stone suggests that a unification had already taken place at a date well before Menes, which had then broken down again, so that Menes seems to have have been presented as reinstating an earlier political order. This evidence has resulted in divergent views: some have taken it more or less at face value (Scharff and Moortgat 1950); while others have argued (Baines and Málek 1980 [0A]; Trigger in Trigger *et al.* 1983 [0D]) that the pattern of unification–disintegration preceding the first dynasty is a projection back into time immemorial of a basic historical pattern, and is a later construct with no basis in reality – it reflects the idea that there could be no unification without a previous fragmentation, which in turn could not have existed if there had not been an earlier unity, and so on.

Another king-list, inscribed in the tomb of a nineteenth-dynasty scribe (1306–1185 (1295–1186)), is known as the 'Saqqara tablet'. It lists kings down to Ramesses II, but begins only with the sixth king of the first dynasty (Anedjib, see table 10). Does this mean that there was a tradition that did not recognise the rule of the preceding five kings? If so, why? Was there some

Table 10 Chronology of predynastic and Early Dynastic Egypt

	Upper Egypt	Lower Egypt
5000	Badarian	Merimde/Fayum A
4000	Amratian (Naqada I)	Omari A?
3500	Early Gerzean (Naqada II)	Omari B?
3300	Late Gerzean (Naqada II)	Late Gerzean/Ma'adi
3100	Protodynastic (Naqada III)	Protodynastic
c. 3100–c. 2890	*Dynasty I* Narmer Djer Djet Den (Udimu) Anedjib (Enezib) Semerkhet Qaa (Ka'a)	
c. 2890–c. 2686	*Dynasty II* Hetepsekhemwy Nynetjer Weneg (personal name) Sened (personal name) Sekhemib ⎱ same ruler? Peribsen ⎰ Khasekhem ⎱ same ruler? Khasekhemwy ⎰	

resistance to the rule of the earlier kings in this part of Lower Egypt (Emery 1961)?

A different category of evidence is constituted by the 'unification monuments'. This term is used to describe a variety of inscribed and pictorial material approximately datable to the crucial time around the beginning of the first dynasty (for a recent discussion, see Millet 1990). The major, and most striking, objects are some very fine commemorative slate palettes and maceheads, in particular the Scorpion mace, the Narmer palette and the Narmer (or 'wedding') mace (see fig. 13). They were found carefully deposited between much later walls in the temple at Hierakonpolis, and their chronology is problematic. The labels and sealings from grave-goods at Abydos, associated with some of the earliest kings, constitute another source, although here the problem of matching *nsw-bity* with Horus names arises.

The prime archaeological sites for the crucial period are tombs at Naqada, Abydos, Hierakonpolis (all in Upper Egypt, see map 6) and lower Egyptian tombs at Saqqara and Helwan. Important is that the Upper Egyptian sites

Figure 13 Narmer palette (Cairo Museum; drawing by D. Saxon)

provide material both from the predynastic and Early Dynastic periods, so that here there is a real possibility of tracing developments in material culture. This archaeological material gives the impression that the Upper Egyptian predynastic culture known as 'Late Gerzean' (or 'Naqada II', cf. table 10) went through a very rapid development and spread in its later stages over almost the whole of Egypt (*c.* 3300–3100). It reflects a wealthy, socially differentiated, society with access to considerable quantities of luxury material, whose élite members emphasised their pre-eminent status by large buildings, prominent tombs, and elaborately decorated objects. A number of items suggest that chiefs or kings stood at the apex of the political system, and some aspects, such as the form of burials, the royal activities presented visually, and the artistic styles, display close links with the succeeding Early Dynastic period.

Despite these apparent cultural continuities from the Late Gerzean period, certain differences in Early Dynastic civilisation need to be stressed. Thus the tomb-structures are vastly more elaborate and larger in the Early Dynastic period and writing appears suddenly, and apparently fully developed. Massive surpluses, in technological products, food and material resources, appear to be commanded by the kings of the Early Dynastic period on a quite unprecedented scale. Obviously, a very large political state had come into being with precisely defined frontiers, headed by a king with a highly developed and sophisticated divine ideology, imagery and ceremonial. So while we can see forerunners to this development in Late Gerzean Egypt, nothing prepares us for the sheer size and elaboration of the Early Dynastic phase. Why and how this development took place so suddenly and quickly is one of the most debated issues in Egyptian history. And it is, of course, fundamentally, unanswerable. Attempts at explanation range from foreign invasions (based mainly on linguistic considerations) and less direct stimuli, especially from Mesopotamia and Elam (based on artistic motifs), to population pressure and climate changes (reflected in increased settlement size and intensified land use). Probably, as has been well argued by Hoffman (1980), it is a mistake to look for a single factor as the chief stimulus in Egypt's astonishingly rapid development.[2]

Predynastic cultures

In order to define how these various factors might have played a role in Egypt's emergence as a state, it is important to understand something of its predynastic cultures (Baumgartel 1955/1960). Problems exist with the available evidence, such as the marginal nature of some of the excavated settlement sites (Fayum A), and the deliberate destruction by early excavators of seemingly unexciting material (Abydos). There is also debate about where the basic items for the development of agriculture (plants and animals) in Egypt came from (Hoffman 1980; Trigger in Trigger *et al* 1983 [0D]). Finally, there are uncertainties in cultural sequences and their dating. The brilliant pioneering attempt by Petrie to chart the latter on the basis of pottery (his famous system of 'sequence dating', abbreviated 'SD'; Petrie 1901; 1920/1921) set up a relative chronology that has remained fundamental and been largely vindicated by later work (Baumgartel 1970; Hoffman 1980; Adams 1988). In spite of uncertainties, the general picture of predynastic Egypt is clear: there was a distinct cultural divide between Lower and Upper Egypt.

In Upper Egypt, the type site for the earliest settled culture is Badari, and material has also been found at Deir Tasa and Hemamiya. Precise dating is not certain, but it *may* reach back as far as *c.* 5000 and seems to last to *c.* 4000; it also seems to overlap slightly with the succeeding Amratian culture (from the site of El Amrah). In the Badarian period, farming and herding were practised, but signs of social differentiation are slight. The Amratian (also known as Naqada I) culture (*c.* 4000 to *c.* 3500) is characterised by black-topped pottery and more sophisticated stone-working. In particular animal-shaped slate palettes (for grinding eye-paint) and disc-shaped mace-heads form part of the cultural assemblage, which suggests the emergence of an élite group who used these to define their status. The Gerzean (Naqada II–III, *c.* 3500–3100/3000) culture spread in its later phases throughout Egypt. It

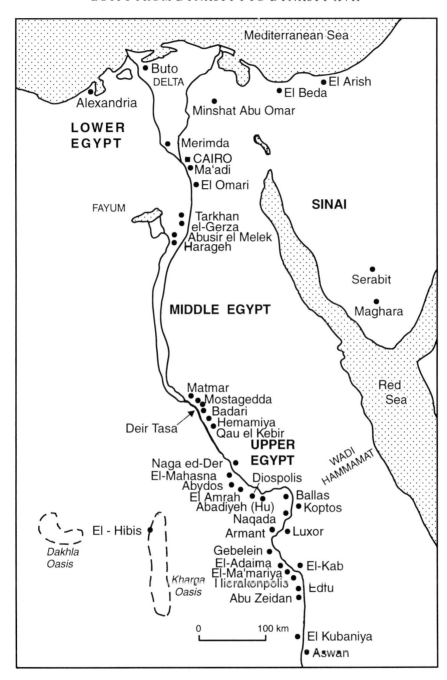

Map 6 Predynastic sites in Egypt

displays quite a number of links with the Amratian and represents perhaps a direct development. For example, typical Amratian items, such as palettes and maces, ever more elaborately decorated, were produced, although their shapes (rhomboid palettes and pear-shaped maces) differ. Copper was used increasingly and, late in the period, there is clear evidence, e.g. the use of lapis lazuli, carnelian, and certain artistic motifs, for contacts with places beyond Egypt. The Gerzean displays some similarities with cultures in Nubia to the south (as far as Khartoum). But the two areas diverged more and more sharply as Egypt began to coalesce into a large, powerful state. The recovered, scanty evidence of settlement patterns for this phase indicates that houses were grouped around a chief's house, that population density increased, and that the élite members of the society were buried with sumptuous funerary rites (Hoffman 1980).

By contrast, in Lower Egypt excavated sites do not display the kind of uniformity displayed in Upper Egypt. Merimde (c. 4300–3800), on the western edge of the delta, was a village settlement of small family units engaged in farming; while Fayum A (c. 4600–c. 4000) had a population pursuing primarily a hunting-gathering existence. El Omari (c. 3500 onwards), near Helwan, embraces several sites some of which continued to flourish into the Early Dynastic period with very little evidence of structural change: this was a simple farming community with virtually no evidence of social stratification. Ma'adi (c. 3300–3100), is located just 10 km to the north on the route leading to Sinai, where the Egyptians later sent mining expeditions. The site has links with southern Palestine, as shown by its partly subterranean dwellings and ledge-handled jars. Ma'adi has also produced the earliest evidence for smelted copper in Egypt. The assumption must be, therefore, that Ma'adi was in regular contact with the Sinai region and perhaps southern Palestine beyond. The picture in Lower Egypt that these sites present is one of a number of culturally distinct communities, displaying no close interconnections and no real signs of social stratification. But a word of caution is in order: the important site of Buto in the delta, conventionally thought to be the centre of the 'Lower Egyptian kingdom', is only now being investigated in the face of great physical difficulties. Evidence for a predynastic settlement has been found, which may lead to eventual modifications of our image of Lower Egypt in this period (Spencer 1993).

Reconsidering Egypt's unification

Constructing a picture of the process leading to state formation on this basis must remain hypothetical. A *possible* model, based on the evidence from Hierakonpolis, is that, as a result of the increasing aridity of the desert between c. 3300 and 3100 (Butzer 1976), the Nile valley became more densely inhabited with the main population concentrated in the areas most easily accessible from the desert. Such a pattern can be traced at Hierakonpolis, where settlement was originally strung out into the wadi to the west, but contracted *c.* 3100. This growth of population in the valley made it ever more important to make optimum use of the natural Nile inundation and protect communities against disastrous flooding. It probably also led to an extension of the amount of land usable for cultivation. But with the high-lying desert edges unusable, access to more land was only possible to the north and south. In fact, southward expansion was bound to be limited as tillable land is scanty beyond the first cataract. On the whole, then, expansion northwards along the valley was the most obvious move and this is what seems to have happened. This would have generated pressure which created conflicts with other settlements. An alternative, or sequel, to such clashes might have been alliances between neighbours in order to maximise military strength and maintain control of land won. The ultimate result would have been a marked growth in the size of political units.

Given the evidence from Upper Egypt for élite groups, or ruling families, it seems likely that they played an important role in this growth, and that their political pre-eminence grew. The surviving material suggests that this is exactly what happened: ruler-figures, depicted on the decorated palettes and mace-heads, are portrayed as enormously large, dwarfing their companions, and they are shown involved in significant political acts, such as initiating irrigation works, triumphing in battle and hunting (see fig. 13). The scale of the figures and the activities they engage in prefigure representations typical of the Egyptian king later. Cult-buildings (Hierakonpolis, possibly el-Gerza) and personal large tomb monuments (Naqada) imply that surpluses were produced to sustain and support the activities initiated by such rulers and intended to commemorate their achievements. The subsidiary burials surrounding the large, prominent tombs probably reflect the creation of groups of retainers.

The exotically decorated items, which are found sporadically in this period, using Mesopotamian and Elamite motifs, reflect the demands of a small wealthy ruling group, who used such prestige objects to emphasise their greater power and status (Hoffman 1980; Moorey 1987). These luxury items also suggest the existence of skilled artisans able to meet the requirements made by prominent members of the community. The use of rare materials implies the existence of a fairly extensive and complex exchange system, which would surely have been organised, and controlled to a significant degree, by the local rulers. As competition for rare resources intensified, the rulers who controlled access to them would have been in a position to strengthen their position *vis-à-vis* neighbouring rivals. Such a hypothesis would help to explain the importance, in this period, of places such as Hierakonpolis, Koptos/Naqada, and Abydos, which are all situated at the end of wadi-routes near gold, copper and hard stone sources in the eastern desert. The southerly location of these places would also have made it easier for them to establish trade contact with Nubia, from where ebony and, possibly, ivory were imported.

This model for state development in the late predynastic period suggests that the process was one of gradual transformation, which contradicts the Egyptian tradition of a single act of unification by one king, Menes. This need not present major problems for making sense of the available information. It is quite possible that the Menes of later tradition was simply one of the important figures in the long process of welding the country into a single whole. He was associated with the founding of Memphis, which suggests that establishing this city as one of the main royal centres was a crucial step in the process of expansion, intended to strengthen control of the delta. One thing that seems probable is that this first 'unification' was not that of Upper and Lower Egypt. There is no unequivocal evidence that there was ever a substantial Lower Egyptian kingdom. Everything points to the formation of an increasingly homogeneous Upper Egyptian kingdom with developing political institutions. It was this strong and distinctive entity that, shortly before and during dynasty I, gradually succeeded in incorporating the disparate smaller communities of Lower Egypt. The later traditional division between Upper and Lower Egypt may well be a much later creation of the historical period, and have nothing to do with Egypt's emergence as a state (Kemp 1989 [0Ga]: 44).

Early Dynastic Egypt

The relatively gradual process of Egypt's formation as a state means that the shift from the prehistoric to the historical period is hard to pinpoint precisely. The Early Dynastic period (c. 3100–2686) is perhaps best considered as one of transition and consolidation, which took a considerable time (250–400 years) to accomplish – a time during which Egypt developed those traits considered typical of later Egyptian civilisation. It is, unfortunately, impossible to reconstruct its history, beyond listing the names of kings, the order of which is fairly firm after the first four.

But the main features, which provide hints of the great socio-political changes taking place, can be defined. First, from early in dynasty I, one king was acknowledged to be in control of Egypt from the delta to the first cataract. Secondly, the cultural regionalism of the predynastic period disappeared totally, certainly at the top of the social structure; Egyptian culture acquired a homogeneity clearly separating it from neighbours to the west, south and north-east. As a result of this process of political and cultural self-definition, the peoples beyond Egypt's frontiers were classified as Egypt's enemies, eternally posing a threat to the coherence and security of the state (Valbelle 1990). The image of the king smiting these foes became one of the standard recurring images of royalty. Memphis emerged as an important seat of government, ideally located for dominating the more recently incorporated area of the delta, for exploiting its rich pastures and arable land, and close to routes leading to the rich copper and turquoise deposits of Sinai and beyond to Palestine. Seal-impressions and objects bearing the names of kings of dynasty I found in Palestine show that already in this very early period the Egyptian rulers and royal family operated a trade mechanism with their northern neighbour (Quark 1989; Ben-Tor 1992: 93–95). The massive tomb-fields, laid out at Saqqara and physically expressing the royal presence and control, emphasise the importance of Memphis – although it is probable that the kings themselves were buried at Abydos (Kemp 1966), where they received an elaborate cult.[3] The use of the complex hieroglyphic writing system (cf. Davies in Hooker 1991 [OH]) increased enormously in this period to celebrate royal exploits (J. Ray, *World Archaeology* 1986 [OH]; Baines 1989) and, more prosaically, to keep accounts of royal income and expenditure.[4] Taxes were levied on the basis of agricultural production, crops and animals. The level of tax was traditionally assessed at a biennial inspection, conducted by the king and his court. This regular royal tour of inspection was called the 'cattle-count' or, more grandly, the 'following of Horus' (Horus = king), and served as a system of counting the years of a king's reign. The taxes were collected in kind and stored in royal storehouses for distribution as required and ordered by the king. The regular noting of Nile-levels, which began in this period, suggests that there was a certain amount of economic forward planning; on the basis of the river levels a rough forecast of crop-yields could be made by the state. The king himself owned extensive tracts of land, including vineyards in the delta, but what proportion of arable land was in royal hands is not known. It seems likely that the administrative officials came initially from local élites, who themselves owned land. They were gradually transformed into royal functionaries, dependent on the king, and shifted around as the government required, although how total this change was is unknown. It is probable that the highest echelons of the administration were members of the royal family.

All these fundamental developments become visible in the first and second dynasties. By the end of the Early Dynastic period, Egypt was a large state united under one supreme and absolute ruler who had effectively con-centrated all wealth and political power in his hands. His position was underpinned by extremely complex and elaborate ceremonies and rituals, which stressed his divine nature. The huge and amazingly elaborate royal burials, in whose construction, maintenance, supplying and cult a significant proportion of the human and material resources of Egypt were involved, were another enduring expression of this.

3b Egypt in the Old Kingdom (dynasties III–VI: *c.* 2686–2181)

The Egyptian Old Kingdom is usually defined as beginning with the first ruler of dynasty III (of whom almost nothing is known) and coming to an end effectively with the reign of Pepy II of dynasty VI (2345–2181). Successors of Pepy II and two more dynasties (VII and VIII) from Memphis are known, but the reigns of the kings are so short, and their number so large, that it looks as though they experienced serious problems in maintaining control. So it is perhaps best to consider this phase together with the question of the breakup of the Old Kingdom (cf. chapter 3c). The time covered by the Old Kingdom is about five hundred years – a period during which Egypt held together as a strong, cohesive unit.

The chronology of the kings is established by using king-lists. The Palermo stone (see p. 127), which mentions some of the major events of individual reigns, gives Nile-levels and refers to the royal 'cattle-counts' (*ARE* I: §§ 146–148; Roccati 1982: §§ 6–33; cf. Barta 1981), is especially important. There is a slight problem as it is not certain whether the cattle-counts continued to be carried out biennially, or whether at some point they became an annual event. This can obviously affect the calculation of the lengths of reigns. But

Table 11 Chronology: Old Kingdom

Dynasty III (c. 2686–2613 or 2649–2575)	*Dynasty VI (c. 2345–2181 or 2323–2150)*
Sanakhte	Teti
Netjerirykhet (Djoser/Zoser)	Userkare
Sekhemkhet	Meryre Pepy I
Khaba	Merenre Antiemsaf
Huni (Nisuteh)	Neferkare Pepy II
	Netjerykare
	Queen Nitokris
Dynasty IV (c. 2613–2494 or 2575–2465)	
Snefru	*Dynasty VII (c. 2181–2173 or 2150–2142)*
Cheops (= Khufu)	*c.* nine kings
Redjedef (Djedefre)	
Chephren (= Khafre)	
Mycerinus (= Menkaure)	*Dynasty VIII (c. 2173–2160 or 2142–2129)*
Shepseskaf	*c.* six kings
Dynasty V (c. 2494–2345 or 2465–2323)	
Userkaf	
Sahure	
Neferirkare Kakaï	
Shepseskare Isi	
Neferefre	
Neuserre	
Menkauhor Akauhor	
Djedkare Isesi	
Unis	

the main difficulty with the valuable information on the Palermo stone is that it does not extend beyond dynasty V. The other source is the Turin Canon (see p. 123). It lists all the kings of dynasties III to VIII as being from Memphis (as does Manetho). In the papyrus the name of king Djoser (second king of dynasty III) has been picked out in red, which probably signals the fame he enjoyed in the New Kingdom as builder of the great step-pyramid at Saqqara, an associate of Imhotep, the revered sage and supposed architect of his tomb.

Contemporary evidence

The kinds of source that have survived make it impossible to write a connected, narrative history of the Old Kingdom. On the other hand they are, by comparison with the preceding period, quite full. But they suffer from a number of limitations. Contemporary sources consist, first, of royal texts, found, for example, on royal monuments. Inscribed royal monuments survive extensively, and consist of tombs, reliefs in funerary temples (especially from dynasty V on) and royal statues, invariably connected with the royal funerary cult. But the amount of historical information that can be gleaned from these texts is slight. The same is true of short inscriptions which record royal expeditions to, for example, Sinai where military campaigns and expeditions by a number of kings from dynasties III to VI are recorded (Gardiner and Peet 1952–5; Roccati 1982: §§224–239); others commemorate the royal presence at Aswan, the southern frontier (Pepy I and Merenre (dynasty VI): *Urk*. I 69, 9–10; Roccati 1982: §§56–57). One stele, from the reign of Sahure (dynasty V), records a series of campaigns (east, west, Nubia); it comes from the king's funerary temple, it gives a list of booty (animals) and mentions prisoners of war (*Urk*. I 167–169; Roccati 1982: §§37–39); but, again, it is very brief. The Palermo stone and some short texts from the region south of Aswan show that there were a number of royally led campaigns to Nubia, which sound like raids to acquire cattle and manpower.

A more fruitful source of longer royal documents is the tombs of officials. Because tombs were built for eternity, they were the perfect place for commemorating favours received by the tomb-owner from the king: special privileges granted, gifts bestowed, royal letters of commendation. As a result, some royal decrees are known from this source. Most famous are the so-called Koptos decrees, granting special exemptions and privileges for the funerary chapel of royal relatives by several very late Old Kingdom rulers (*Urk*. I 214; Goedicke 1967). But there are a number of others: the autobiography of Harkhuf, who conducted trading expeditions to the very south of Nubia on the king's behalf, preserves a particularly exuberant decree issued by Pepy II, probably still a child at the time, which Harkhuf had inscribed in his rock-cut tomb facing Aswan:

The king's own seal: year 2, third month of the first season, day 15. The king's decree to the sole companion, lector-priest, chief of scouts, Harkhuf. Notice has been taken of this dispatch of yours which you made for the king at the palace, to let one know that you have come down in safety from Yam (Kerma basin, Nubia) with the army that was with you. You have said in this dispatch of yours that you have brought all kinds of great and beautiful gifts, which Hathor (goddess), mistress of Imaau, has given to the *ka* (personal life-force) of King Neferkare (Pepy II), who lives forever. You have said in this dispatch of yours that you have brought a pygmy of the god's dances from the land of the horizon-dwellers (foreigners living east/south-east of Egypt), like the pygmy whom the god's seal-bearer Bawerded brought from Punt (probably in Eritrea) in the time of King Isesi (Dynasty V). You have said to my majesty that his like has never been brought by anyone who went to Yam previously.

Truly you know how to do what your lord loves, praises and commands. His majesty will provide your many worthy honours for the benefit of your son's son for all time, so that all people will say, when they hear what my majesty did for you: 'Does anything equal what was done for the sole companion Harkhuf when he came down from Yam, on account of the vigilance he showed in doing what his lord loved, praised, and commanded?'

Come north to the residence at once! Hurry and bring with you this pygmy whom you brought from the land of the horizon-dwellers live, hale, and healthy, for the dances of the god, to gladden the heart, to delight the heart of King Neferkare who lives forever! When he goes down with you into the ship, get worthy men to be around him on deck, lest he fall in the water! When he lies down at night, get worthy men to lie around his tent. Inspect ten times at night! My majesty desires to see this pygmy more than the gifts of the mineland (i.e. Sinai) and of Punt! When you arrive at the residence and this pygmy is with you live, hale, and hearty, my majesty will do great things for you, more than was done for the god's seal-bearer Bawerded in the time of King Isesi, in accordance with my majesty's wish to see this pygmy. Orders have been brought to the chief of the new towns and the companion overseer of priests to command that supplies be furnished from what is under the charge of each from every storage depot and every temple without making an exception among them.

(*Urk*. I 120–131; *ARE* I §§350–4; Lichtheim 1973–80 [OI] I: 26–7;
Roccati 1982 §196)

This is a splendidly vivid and revealing letter, but few are so full, and such texts are thinly scattered over the five hundred years of the Old Kingdom.

A larger body of written material is provided by the autobiographies of officials inscribed in tombs. The tomb autobiography, which continued as a typical Egyptian literary form right down into the Ptolemaic period (Lichtheim 1988), developed from two features associated with the burial: first, from the 'prayer for offerings' to be continued after death, in which the tomb-owner explained why he merited them; and, secondly, from the list of titles of the tomb-owner, which marked his rank and position and so gave the tomb its specific identity. By tracing how the titles were acquired, the owner composed his life-story, although he would naturally omit any setbacks and humiliations. These autobiographies – one of the most important sources for Egyptian history – come mainly from the great necropoleis near Memphis (Giza, Saqqara) during the Old Kingdom, and provide an unrivalled insight into the structure of officialdom, life on great estates, state-work and its organisation. The earliest preserved one is that of Metjen (early dynasty IV, *Urk*. I 1–5; *ARE* I §§170–175; Roccati 1982 §§59–64), which contains extracts from official documents listing the properties that were to supply his tomb. It provides important information on the disposition of a high official's landed holdings (scattered throughout Egypt) and the varieties of farming activities carried out on them (Gödecken 1976). Some of the longest and liveliest autobiographies, however, come from the later Old Kingdom, the most famous being the long and detailed account of the career of Weni (Lichthcim 1973–80 [OI] I: 18–23; Roccati 1982 §§177–188). They also provide important information on administrative personnel, such as their social background and their rise up the court ladder. A striking fact that emerges is the way in which officials accumulated honorific, as well as functional, titles (forty-eight in one instance). They showed the individual's rank and position within the state hierarchy and his entitlement to particular privileges. Only a few of the titles relate to what he actually did – rather they reflect an amazingly elaborate system of court ranking (Baer 1960).

One archive of administrative papyrus documents has been partly published and studied. They are the papyri from Abusir, representing a small fraction of the archives of the funerary temple of Neferirkare of dynasty V (Posener-Kriéger 1976). More papyri from the cult of Neferefre (also dynasty V) were discovered in the early 1980s (Posener-Kriéger 1983; Roth 1987), but have not yet been published. From the reign of Pepy II (dynasty VI) comes a sadly scattered and tattered archive found in a clandestine excavation at Elephantine, only bits of which (including two letters) have been published (Smithers 1942; Roccati 1968). The royal funerary endowments are a striking feature of this period, and the Abusir archive provides an unrivalled glimpse into their functioning. They reveal the organisation of 'priests' into groups, who worked as cult officials on a rota system for one month; the rest of the year, they carried out farming and other activities on the estate which supplied the funerary cult. The terminology for this organisation, as for most work-groups in Egypt, was derived from shipping, which shows how central boat-transport was in the country. The archive also illuminates details of cult-service, such as the daily dressing of the cult-statue, its feeding, washing and the make-up applied to it. The resources needed for this are mentioned, including the kinds of food prepared for the daily service and for the many festivals that were celebrated. The economic base of such a temple (one among many in Egypt) emerges clearly: its income was derived from land, the people working on it and from herds of animals. The personal names of the people attached to the temple-estate were made up from the names of temple-domains. This suggests that either the personnel remained attached to the endowment and became a hereditary group or they were recruited locally. An important question is how such funerary endowments interacted with the state. It seems likely that they remained a royal resource, which could be, and was, used by the king to generate revenue for himself and his officials. This is shown by the fact that, increasingly, officials obtained offices and titles related to functions connected with such estates; these entitled them to draw on their resources as income (Roth 1987).

Great royal tombs in the form of pyramids, set prominently on the desert-edge, are the best-known symbol of the Old Kingdom. The huge pyramids of dynasty IV were never again equalled in size and amazed people in antiquity as much as they do today – witness Herodotus (2.125), who was astounded by the details of construction, cost, length of time and manpower involved in Cheops' (Khufu's) pyramid, which he heard about in Egypt. Why the pyramids developed as a specific form of royal tomb is not known – it is possible that they developed from the idea of the primeval mound which symbolised one of the first acts of creation in Egyptian mythological thought, but that remains speculation. The first pyramid was the step-pyramid of Djoser (dynasty III) at Saqqara. It was built of stone, in contrast to the mud-brick tombs of the earlier kings. The funerary enclosure was laid out over an enormous terrain enclosed within palace-like walls and memorialised in stone some of Egypt's most significant royal rituals and ceremonies (Kemp 1989 [0Ga]: 58–63). In dynasty IV (2613–2494), the gigantic pyramids of Cheops (Khufu) and Chefren (Khafre) and the smaller one of Mycerinus (Menkaure), represent the acme of this architectural form: their cores were encased in stone so that the 'stepped' or 'tiered' look vanished. Queens, too, were occasionally buried in smaller pyramids at this time. In some instances, a ceremonial boat (some examples were huge) was buried near the tomb – presumably intended for use by the dead king, so that he could travel through the sky with the gods (fig. 14). An important element in the funerary complex was the valley-temple, where goods were brought and the funeral procession arrived; a ramp led from it up to the pyramid-temple and tomb.

Significant reflections of the Old Kingdom political system have some-times been read into the layout of the tombs surrounding the pyramids of dynasty IV. They are arranged in an orderly manner like houses fronting a street, and it has been argued that the largest and closest to the king's tomb reflect the importance of the tomb-owner within the political hierarchy. This is perhaps too simplistic an interpretation. It is plain that men involved in

Figure 14 Boat-grave of the queen's pyramid, Giza (courtesy of M.S. Drower)

royal works, such as the chief builders of the pyramids and their families and servants, and those who rendered direct personal services to the king, were also those favoured with burial close to the royal one. But many other officials, including quite important ones, cannot have been buried at the royal funerary sites as the number of tombs is too small. The exact places of burial of local governors is at present not certain, although in the later Old Kingdom some are known to have been buried in their provinces. The fact that one of the tombs at the kings' cemetery is that of a royal dog (Reisner 1936; Roccati 1982 § 75) shows that the necropolis did not mirror the political system realistically (Janssen 1978). Another way of using the pyramid-fields, in order to squeeze historical evidence from them, has been to see dynastic struggles reflected in the siting of individual pyramids: for example, the fact that Djedefre's pyramid (dynasty IV) was located at Abu Roash, away from Giza, has been interpreted in this way. Another suggestion is that the position of the royal pyramids was related to the sites of the royal palaces. But it is impossible to sustain these arguments very convincingly, since there are so many aspects of life in the Old Kingdom of which we are ignorant. One eminent scholar has taken an entirely different approach and suggested that the varying locations of the pyramids were simply the result of a search for suitably flat, firm, unencumbered sites for building (Kemp in Trigger *et al.* 1983 [0D]).

In view of this uncertainty, it is also not easy to read any sort of 'decline' into the fact that the pyramids become smaller after dynasty IV. In the case of the pyramids of dynasty V (2494–2345), this is connected with the fact that royal resources and building efforts were poured into the construction of large sun-temples, connected with the greatly increased emphasis on the cult of the sun-god, Re, in this period. The king's name also reflects the importance of the sun cult, with the element 'son of Re' being added at this time. In dynasty VI (2345–2181), the pyramids were small and built to a uniform size. Why this should be is unknown, but their construction does not show a decline in building standards, and it is possible that resources that had previously been ploughed into the royal tomb were being distributed differently. Connected with this question are problems of interpretation concerning the significance of the location, size and elaboration of the tombs of officials. A traditional argument has been that the breakdown of centralised control and the growing impoverishment of the crown can be read off from the shift of governors' tombs away from the royal burial and from their increasingly sophisticated construction and decoration at precisely the time that the royal pyramids decrease in size. But, as has already been pointed out, the reasons for these changes are often uncertain, and it is untrue to maintain that all officials were buried around the king even in dynasty IV. Moreover, inasmuch as there is evidence, there is no consistent linear development in the burials of officials. Clearly, matters were considerably more complex (Kanawati 1977; 1980).

The elaboration of the royal tomb was accompanied by the development of standard reliefs in royal funerary temples, which show the king smiting the traditional enemies of Egypt. The preserved reliefs of different kings make it plain that this was an idealised royal act and did not depict individual, historical, military exploits. By contrast, the private tombs, as with the autobiographies, provide the most astounding wealth of pictorial informa-tion, on agriculture, markets, cattle-rearing, wine-production, metal-work, textile-working, and domestic activities such as brewing and baking. Par-ticularly interesting are some of the bits of very colloquial dialogue placed in the mouths of various participants in the scenes. 'Go! go!' shouts a driver to a herd of donkeys, while his companion advises him: 'Prod him in the rear, my friend!' Or: a woman winnowing – an agricultural activity frequently performed by women – says to her fellow-worker: 'Put your hand in this barley – it is still full of chaff!' The scenes and the conversation of workers make life in the Old Kingdom vividly immediate (for stunning photographs, see Málek 1986). This is in striking contrast to the repetitive, formulaic scenes associated with royal burials.

Women were usually buried with their husbands, and the tomb-owner is often shown in a charming, idyllic family group, with the wife fondly embracing her husband. Although always subsidiary to the husband, the wife is usually separately labelled and named, as in this tomb stele from Naqada, dating to dynasty VI:

> An offering which the king gives and Anubis (jackal-headed god associated with cemeteries), who is upon his mountain and in the place of embalming, the lord of the necropolis. Buried be the royal seal-bearer, sole companion, chief scribe of boat crews, judge, chief scribe, Ni-hebsed-Pepi in his tomb which is in the good western desert. She has taken his hand, he has joined land, he has crossed the firmament. May the western desert give her hands to his in peace, in peace before the great god. An offering which the king gives and Anubis, so that funerary offerings be given to the royal seal-bearer, sole companion, honoured by Osiris, Ni-hebsed-Pepi.
> [Above the woman's head:] His wife, his beloved, the royal ornament, priestess of Hathor, Sepi.
> (H.G. Fischer, *Inscriptions from the Coptite Nome: dynasties VI–XI* (1964) no. 5; Lichtheim 1973–80 [OI] I: 17–18)

Apart from a small number of excavated funerary temples, sanctuaries are scarcely known from the Old Kingdom. It seems likely that, while local temples were economically and administratively important at the regional level, they were not of major importance in the state cult. The only ones that are known to have been significant in an area beyond their immediate vicinity were Heliopolis, the great centre of the sun-cult, Re (Horus in this period became an aspect of Re), and the Ptah temple in Memphis (Goedicke 1979). But archaeological remains of these undoubtedly splendid structures are almost non-existent, save for some relief fragments from Heliopolis.

Towns and settlements are only very scantily attested, and all the ones investigated so far lie in the south of Egypt (Hierakonpolis; Abydos; Elephantine; Edfu). None of them are large; they all represent fairly small provincial towns, but all were surrounded by a thick enclosure wall. In one instance (Elephantine), a small, unwalled, extramural settlement was attached to the main one. Each town had a shrine, which normally lay inside its own walled area. At Elephantine and Edfu the shrines contained the cults of important local dignitaries. As far as we can tell, the houses within the towns were packed closely together and the population density was high. Where continuity of settlement from the Early Dynastic period can be traced, as at Hierakonpolis, there was a marked increase in size from the earlier period.

Beyond the Nile valley

One area of Egyptian settlement that has been studied recently (Giddy 1987) is the great oases to the west of Egypt in the Libyan desert (Dakhla, Kharga, Bahriya, Farafra). They were linked to the Nile valley and with each other, and from Kharga an important route led down into Nubia. Control of the oases was of great importance in Egypt's defence of its western frontier. Dakhla, the most fully explored, was the site of a substantial town in the late Old Kingdom: traces of enclosure walls, pottery kilns, mud-brick structures and some cemetery sites have been identified (Fakhry 1972; Mills 1980).

Nubia has also provided important information on Egypt in the Old Kingdom. The construction of the great dam at Aswan was preceded by intensive survey and excavation work conducted by archaeologists from all over the world. The main focus of Egypt's interest in this region was its manpower and cattle resources, its hard stone quarries and mineral deposits (diorite, amethyst, copper and, later, gold). Nubia also provided access to exotic and highly prized materials from sub-Saharan Africa, such as ebony, panther-skins, ivory, and special fine oils. Definitely by dynasty IV, the Egyptians had established a colony at Buhen, in the second cataract region. The evidence shows that it was founded to exploit the local copper deposits and handle Egyptian trading interests (Emery 1965: 111–112; 127). Such activities are further illuminated by an inscribed stone block, perhaps indicating Egyptian quarrying of diorite at Toshka West (about 80 km west of Abu Simbel: Roccati 1982 §276), and the finds of graffiti in several places by leaders of Egyptian expeditions.

But at the end of dynasty V a change took place in Nubian society with the appearance of a new cultural group – the Nubian 'C group' – who appear, from about that time onwards, to have formed small princedoms. As a result, Egypt's relations with Nubia had to be restructured. This is signalled by the abandonment of the Buhen settlement, which suggests that Egypt's direct exploitation of Nubian resources was no longer feasible. The changes are also echoed in a number of autobiographies of royal officials and traders of dynasty VI, such as Weni (*Urk.* I 98–110; *ARE* I §§292–324; Gardiner 1961 [OD]: 95–96; *ANET*: 227–228; Lichtheim 1973–80 [OI] I: 18–23; Roccati 1982 §§177–188), Sabni (*Urk.* I 135–140; *ARE* I §§362–374; Roccati 1982 §§205–207), and Harkhuf (*Urk.* I 120–131; *ARE* I §§335–354; Lichtheim 1973–80 [OI] I: 23–27; Roccati 1982 §§189–196). From the accounts of their journeys to Nubia to obtain luxury goods and hard stone, it is evident that the expeditions were only made possible by enlisting the help of, and receiving permission from, the various local rulers.

Finally, there is quite a bit of evidence for Egyptian contacts with the Levant (Wright 1988), especially with the great harbour town of Byblos, from where the Egyptians imported timber for coffins, large boats and statues – all of which required for their manufacture wood of a type not available in Egypt. Relatively recent is the evidence from Ebla in North Syria (see chapter 1b) showing contacts between this area and Egypt in the fifth and sixth dynasties (Scandone-Matthiae 1979–80; 1982). Regular expeditions were mounted by the Egyptian rulers to mine turquoise in the Sinai desert; the main evidence for Old Kingdom activities here comes from the Wadi Maghara. It is very probable that, as in later times, the Egyptians needed the co-operation of the local communities of herders and their leaders in order to conduct these ventures successfully.

Literature and literary sources

Several literary genres developed in the course of the Old Kingdom, which illuminate rather different aspects of Egyptian culture. They help to provide some insight into a distinctive Egyptian worldview, although they must be used with care.

Most impressive (and most problematical) is the great 'Memphite Theology' (Junker 1941; *ANET*: 4–6; Lichtheim 1973–80 [OI] I: 51–57). It explains the relationship between Ptah, god of Memphis and creator, and his establishment of the falcon-god, Horus, embodied by the king and an aspect of the sun-god, Re, as overall lord. It was obviously intended to emphasise the primacy of Memphis and Ptah in the Egyptian order of things, and link all Egyptian gods to him. But there is a dispute about the date of composition of the treatise. The extant text (inscribed on stone) dates to the late eighth century, but purports to be a copy of an ancient worm-eaten papyrus. The language is archaic, and an early Middle Kingdom ritual text, the Ramesseum dramatic papyrus, hints that the concepts expressed by the 'Theology' were in existence by the beginning of the twelfth dynasty (cf. *LÄ* 4: 1177–1180). This makes it conceivable that the claim of the preserved text to be a genuine copy of an Old Kingdom original could be true. But a number of scholars are convinced that it should be regarded as pseudepigraphic, that its linguistic archaisms are phony and that it illuminates theological ideas current in the late period and not earlier (Junge 1973; Lichtheim 1973–80 [OI] III: 5; for its possible composition in the late New Kingdom, see Kitchen, *JAOS* 102 (1982): 389). Significantly, it was included in a British Museum exhibition of 'fakes' in 1990.

One genre that almost certainly developed in the Old Kingdom is that of 'instructions', although the surviving texts cannot be dated earlier than the Middle Kingdom. This became a very long-lived and endlessly varied category of literary composition, examples of which come from most periods of ancient Egyptian history. The 'instructions' consist of teachings and prudent maxims, usually cast in the form of a father addressing his son on how to conduct himself in order to gain success in public life. They relate, therefore, very much to the educated social élite. Three instruction texts were attributed to historical figures of the Old Kingdom: Hardjedef, a son of king Cheops (Khufu, Brunner-Traut 1940); Ptahhotep, a dynasty V vizier (Dévaud 1916); and Kagemni, vizier at the turn of the third to fourth dynasty (Gardiner 1946b); *ANET*: 412–414; for translations of all three, cf. Lichtheim 1973–80 [OI] I: 58–80; *TUAT* III: 195–221). The ideals set out for gaining advancement and an honoured position provide a lucid exposition of the pragmatic morality that underpinned and strengthend the political *status quo*. The date of the preserved texts precludes their use as a direct source for the Old Kingdom, but their ethics echo what we find in the tomb auto-biographies.

The famous 'pyramid texts', which were inscribed on the walls of the royal tombs from the late fifth dynasty onwards (Sethe 1907; Faulkner 1972; for selected examples, cf. Lichtheim 1973–80 [OI] I: 29–50; Roccati 1982 §§43–44), are another literary type developed at this time. Their function was magical – to aid the resurrection of the dead king and ensure his supremacy as a god in the afterlife. They are poetic in form and rich in mythological allusions. An interesting feature is that they do not reflect the existence of a single, orthodox text, monotonously inscribed over and over again, as one might have expected. Instead, the surviving texts are full of variations and novel theological speculations. This shows that different ideas concerning the divine nature of kingship were current and debated within contemporary Egyptian society (on the complexities of the king's position, see Goedicke 1960).

The later stories that were told in Egypt about some of the kings of the Old Kingdom belong to a very different category of evidence (Wildung 1969). Some of them are found only in very late sources, including Herodotus. It is clear that in the period of Achaemenid and Macedonian (Ptolemaic) rule Egyptians still told stories about the great Old Kingdom kings: Cheops (Khufu) and Chephren (Khafra), for example, were both seen as oppressive despots, while Mycerinus (Menkaure) was presented as much kinder, but unfortunate (Herodotus 2.124–132). A cycle of stories, probably composed during the Middle Kingdom (although the papyrus dates from the Hyksos period (*c.* 1650–1550)), uses the device, found at other periods of Egyptian history, too, of 'entertaining the bored monarch' (Westcar Papyrus, Erman

1890; cf. Erman 1927/1966 [OI]: 36–47; Lichtheim 1973–80 [OI] I: 215–221). The setting is Cheops' court, and one of his sons brings on a magician to divert him. After performing various miracles, the magician looks into the future and predicts that the wife of a priest will give birth to triplets, who will be the sons of Re, the sun-god, and they will rule Egypt in succession. The allusion is to the first three rulers of dynasty V, and is connected to the great prominence given to the Re-cult beginning with that dynasty (p. 142). Another story, composed either in the early New Kingdom or late Middle Kingdom but still circulating in the eighth to sixth centuries, concerns King Pepy II and one of his generals (Posener 1971; Parkinson 1991 no. 11). Unfortunately, it is very fragmentary, and only two episodes have been partially preserved; in one the king is creeping around secretly at night to visit the general with whom he is in love. It is impossible to reconstruct the story: it may have been a comic tale or one reflecting Egyptian disapproval of homosexuality. It is important to realise that humorous tales were quite regularly told about kings in Egypt, as were stories casting them in a bad light – the concept of the extraordinary, divine majesty of the king did not preclude him being perceived at one and the same time as fallibly human (cf. Lloyd 1983 in Trigger *et al.* [OD]: 295–297). None of these tales can be used to reconstruct the history of Egypt in the Old Kingdom, because they survive from later periods only. What they do show is how later Egyptians thought about some of the great kings of the Old Kingdom, and which royal figures were remembered in popular traditions of the distant past.

State and society

The sources, for all their richness, still leave many gaps when we try to reconstruct Old Kingdom society and many aspects remain unknown at present. But some things are plain. Broadly, the king and royal family stood at the apex of the state, while below them were royal advisers, officials and governors clearly distinguished from the peasants working the land. They are the least consistently represented in the archaeological and documentary records, but it was on their labour that the entire structure depended.

The king was the incarnation of sacred power. As such he guaranteed and defended the cosmic order, the earthly equivalent of which was 'law and order' according to the established *status quo*. This was encapsulated in the Egyptian concept of *ma'at*, a word embracing a complex of ideas such as 'truth', 'right behaviour', 'correct balance'. The king, as maintainer of *ma'at*, was simultaneously subject to it, inasmuch as he had to rule in accordance with it; although tenure of his office also brought him automatically into harmony with the cosmic order. In relation to his subjects, the king was omnipotent: 'If anything comes from the mouth of his majesty, it happens immediately' (*Urk.* I 39, 13–14). At the same time he was dependent on the gods and their goodwill. Although himself a god in some sense, he did not share in their omnipotence at all levels. This is illustrated by the auto-biography of the vizier, Washptah (dynasty V). Washptah fell ill during a royal inspection of the king's tomb, which was under construction. The king was very concerned, consulted doctors and had boxes with medical prescriptions brought to help his sick official. But in spite of royal efforts Washptah died, and the king ordered his burial. Washptah's important standing is evidenced by the fact that the story of the royal care lavished on him was inscribed in his tomb (*Urk.* I 40, 4–45, 9; *ARE* I §§241–9; Roccati 1982 §§78–81). Despite the fact that the king's power was limited in some spheres (as in this episode), his person was considered sacrosanct and dangerously potent. It was, there-fore, usual to kiss the ground before the king's feet only; it was a very special mark of royal favour to be permitted to kiss the royal feet themselves. From the tomb inscription of Rawer (dynasty V; *Urk.* I 232–234; Roccati 1982 §74) comes a revealing anecdote depicting the real danger inherent in fortuitous contact with the royal person. On one occasion, the king's sceptre accidentally struck Rawer on the leg; immediately the king said: 'Be not injured!' and, turning to the court as a whole, he added: 'My majesty wishes him to be unhurt, for I did not intend to strike him.'

The king is normally depicted wearing special royal robes which set him apart from his subjects. The most regular items of regalia were a special kind of kilt, a bull's tail hung from the king's waist, a ceremonial beard tied around his chin, the sceptre, flail and crook grasped in his hands, and on his head the great double crown. A cobra (the 'uraeus', associated with the goddess Wadjet, but also visualised as the 'eye' of the sun-god, Re) was depicted as rearing up aggressively on his forehead, ready to protect the king by destroying his enemies with its venomous spittle. The throne on which he sat was conceptualised as his divine mother, Isis, wife of Osiris, with whose son, Horus, the king was regularly identified, as shown by one of his names (see p. 123). He was normally accompanied by a fanbearer, and the office of 'royal fanbearer' was proudly claimed by many officials in their tombs.

The king acceded to the throne as soon as his predecessor died, but seems to have been formally 'crowned' only at a later point. Documents relating to the coronation survive only from later periods, but it is assumed (with reason) that the ceremony was very similar in the Old Kingdom. The coronation symbolised the creation of the world, and included a ritual uniting of the two lands and a formal pacing around the walls of Memphis. The official seals were renewed and functionaries were formally confirmed in their positions. The day of the coronation was commemorated annually and even re-enacted, in a slightly different form, when the king had been on the throne for a considerable period of time – ideally thirty years – at the Sed festival (*LÄ* 5: 782–9). This was the formal 'jubilee' of the king, repeated at more frequent intervals thereafter. The great jubilee courtyard, laid out within Djoser's step-pyramid complex, allows us to trace the elaborate nature of this festival in the Old Kingdom (Kemp 1989 [0Ga]: 59–62).

No royal palaces survive, but textual evidence indicates that they included temples to the 'two ladies', i.e. the vulture (Nekhabet) and cobra (Wadjet), so closely associated with the king (see p. 125). There were numerous other chapels, formal reception and state rooms, domestic quarters and workshops. There were also gardens with lakes where the monarch could relax and refresh himself. Although the Westcar Papyrus dates from a later period (see pp. 146–147), the picture it paints of the royal garden is probably not inappropriate for the Old Kingdom:

> [One day King Snefru wandered through all the rooms] of the palace in search of [relaxation and found none. Then he said]: 'Go, bring me the chief lector-priest, the scribe of the books, Djadja-em-ankh!' He was brought to him straightway. His majesty said to him: ['I have gone through all the rooms] of the palace in search of relaxation and found none.' Djadja-em-ankh said to him: 'May your majesty proceed to the lake of the palace. Fill a boat with all the beautiful girls of your palace. Your majesty's heart will be refreshed by seeing them row, a rowing up and down. As you observe the fine nesting places of your lake, as you observe the beautiful fields and shores, your heart will be refreshed by it.'
>
> (Westcar Papyrus: 4, 22–5, 7; Lichtheim 1973–80 [OI] I: 216)

The king usually married more than one wife, but there was no harem either in the Old or Middle Kingdom, although such an institution perhaps developed in the New Kingdom (Ward 1983). The customs governing royal marriages are not clear, but it is generally thought that endogamy within the royal family was frequent (i.e. the king married close female relatives). This may have been for a variety of dynastic considerations (of which we are ignorant), but was certainly not a rule, as shown by some of the kings of dynasty VI, who married several women from a family of provincial officials. There is nothing to substantiate the widespread idea that Egyptian kingship was matrilineal (Robins 1983). As elsewhere, it was the eldest son of the 'principal wife' (what exactly determined this status is unclear) who normally succeeded his father on the throne, but in fact the decision as to who should become crown prince lay entirely in the king's hands. The uncertainty surrounding the succession could result in the formation of court factions, who tried to procure the throne for different sons of the king. It is conceivable that the official Weni (dynasty VI) refers to a such a plot at court in his long autobiography, although this must remain speculative:

> When there was a secret charge in the royal apartments against the Queen Weret-yamtes, his majesty made me go to hear it alone. No chief judge and vizier, no official was there, only I alone; because I was worthy, because I was rooted in his majesty's heart; because his majesty had filled his heart with me. Only I put (it) in writing together with one

other senior warden of Nekhen, while my rank was (only) that of overseer of royal tenants. Never before had one like me heard a secret of the royal apartments.

(Urk. I 98–110; ARE §§292–4; Lichtheim 1973–80 [OI] I: 19;
Roccati 1982 §180)

How did the Egyptian masses live? We usually picture Egyptian peasants as serfs, no better than slaves except in name, groaning in appalling conditions of forced labour reminiscent of Nazi concentration camps. This image (popularised in Cecil B. de Mille's film *The Ten Commandments*) is probably greatly exaggerated. Undoubtedly their life was hard, they were to some extent tied to the land and subject to recruitment for public works, particularly royal building programmes. But it is unknown to what extent, and whether all, peasants were subsumed into work on royal estates and those of officials. It is also by no means certain that their legal status differed from that of other members of Egyptian society. To judge by a story popular in the Middle Kingdom, but set in the First Intermediate Period ('The Tale of the Eloquent Peasant', see Erman 1927/1966 [OI]: 116–131; Simpson 1973 [OI]: 31–49), the proclaimed ideal of Egyptian society was that all, however humble, had access to the same justice and, ultimately, the pharaoh as the fount of all legal wisdom. The existence of markets suggests further that not all peasant labour was consumed by state requirements. The market scenes occasionally illustrated in tombs show, not great emporia where luxury commodities were being traded, but simple local markets. Because the scenes come from private tombs, they sometimes have accompanying dialogue which help with making sense of the activities depicted in them. The illustrations show that the main items sold in such markets were food and drink, since they feature refreshment stalls. Simple manufactured goods, such as wooden headrests (widely used in ancient Egypt instead of pillows for sleeping), spindle-whorls, oils, cloth, fish hooks, simple jewellery and fans, are also shown being traded. In one scene, a man offers fish in a basket to a man holding a seal, which could imply that a barter system was used. Other similar scenes show people having a manicure and being shaved. These vignettes are often placed near lively river scenes. It has, therefore, been suggested (Eyre 1987) that they represent typical small-town markets set on the river bank, where trading between neighbours, simple craftwork, and personal services, such as hairdressing, were carried on and where refreshments could be purchased. Such markets would have drawn people together regularly from surrounding villages and provided an opportunity for them to sell surplus produce. The scale of economic transactions can hardly have been quantitatively significant in comparison to the overarching state economy, but it shows that possibilities and surpluses for private small-scale trading existed.

Another oversimplified view of Egypt's poorer social strata that needs modification is the idea that all work was state-directed, compulsory and rewarded with barely enough food to survive. Several times there are references that show the existence of independent craftsmen working for pay under contract. In one example, a tomb-owner states that he paid the craftsmen who made his tomb. Another one says more plainly:

> I have caused this statue of mine to be made by a sculptor who was satisfied over its payment which I made to him.
>
> (*Urk.* I 225, 8–10)

The evidence is not extensive and does not allow us to argue for a large corps of independent artisans; but it does show that the obligations of workers were much less automatic and rigid and much more subject to negotiation and mutual agreement than has been thought (see Eyre 1987).

The administration of the state developed out of the organisation of the royal house. Government activity and public office at all levels was in origin an expansion of the functions of royal service. At the head of the administration stood an official whose title is regularly, and with some justification, translated by the term 'vizier' (*tj3ty*). He controlled all departments of the state administration and was responsible directly and solely to the king (Kanawati 1977; Strudwick 1985; Pardey 1989). It is possible that in the earliest periods he was a royal relative, but later the office was certainly held by people from outside the royal family. Because the administration originated in personal royal service, many officials acquired titles, which reflected a rank at court and entitled them to certain benefits, although they did not literally occupy the position specified by the title. The title 'king's son' is one example of this; the frequent one of 'royal sandalbearer' another – both were simply important officials. This practice can make it hard to define the administrative structure clearly, although some offices, such as 'state granary official', 'state treasurer' and 'overseer of the great courts (of justice)', hint at the complexity of the bureaucracy.

More evidence is provided by the system of 'nomes' (the word is derived from the Greek *nomos* = 'district', 'province'), which was certainly in existence by the Old Kingdom period: villages, royal estates and small towns were all grouped together into regional administrative units (nomes) under the control of a local governor (nomarch). Egypt was separated into the 'two lands' (see p. 118): Upper Egypt, extending from Aswan to just south of Memphis, was divided into twenty-two nomes, traditionally numbered from the south northwards; Lower Egypt began at Memphis, the 'Balance of the Two Lands' and at the heart of its first nome, with the nineteen other names of lower Egypt lying in the delta. The system of nomes, in spite of changes and political vicissitudes, continued in existence right into the Roman period.

An important aspect of Egyptian officialdom was the theoretical possibility that anyone could attain high office – it was not limited to an exclusive, traditional aristocratic group. This opportunity for advancement provided

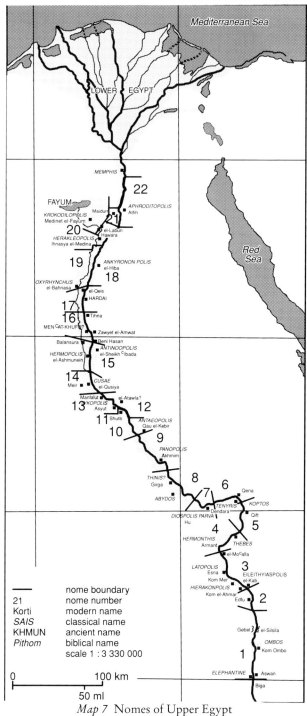

Map 7 Nomes of Upper Egypt

the impulse and motif of the 'instruction' literature (see p. 146), and explains the repeated exhortation to 'follow a man of worth and do not despise him for his former poverty, but respect him, because his wealth resulted from his merit and divine favour'. Long genealogies that indicate pride in one's family and noble origins are absent in the tomb inscriptions – instead individual service and the way it has been rewarded by the king are the themes. Although it is clear from careful analysis that family connections were extensively used to gain access to, and promotion up, the scale of officialdom, in principle there was no hereditary office, no entitlement to position by noble birth. The dominant ideology was that an official had only reached office because he had performed his public duties well for king and people, helping the poor and destitute, giving fair judgements, paying workmen satisfactorily, refraining from oppression. This high concept of duty and devotion to the state was the ideal, and theoretically the only reason why anyone obtained access to lucrative posts. The typical official virtues were at times stylised into symmetric phrases, as in this inscription from the tomb of Sheshi (dynasty VI) in Saqqara:

> I have come from my town,
> I have descended from my nome,
> I have done justice for its lord,
> I have satisfied him with what he loves.
> I spoke truly, I did right,
> I spoke fairly, I repeated fairly,
> I seized the right moment,
> So as to stand well with the people.
> I judged between two so as to content them,
> I rescued the weak from one stronger than he
> As much as was in my power.
> I gave bread to the hungry, clothes <to the naked>,
> I brought the boatless to land.
> I buried him who had no son,
> I made a boat for him who lacked one.
> I respected my father, I pleased my mother,
> I raised their children.
> So says he whose nickname is Sheshi.
>   (*Urk*. I: 198–200; Lichtheim 1973–80 [OI] I: 17)

         *   *   *

It is all too easy to see the Old Kingdom with its gigantic pyramids as a monolithic structure, with everything subordinated to state, i.e. the king's, demands. Closer analysis reveals that the political system was much more multi-faceted and vital. It is only unfortunate that the picture still remains obscure in many details.

3c Herakleopolis and the rise of Thebes (c. 2180–1991)

The 'First Intermediate Period', as it is conventionally known, stretches from the end of dynasty VI to the early part of dynasty XI (c. 2180–c. 2040; see table 12). Royal buildings and inscriptions – the signs of centralised control – are strikingly absent during this time. The end of dynasty XI (c. 2040–1991) constitutes the beginning of the Middle Kingdom. It is marked by the reappearance of a strong central power controlling all of Egypt. Although royal monuments and texts are sparse in this transitional period, the tombs of the nomarchs (provincial governors) in their local centres in Upper Egypt become more numerous and elaborate, and some contain quite long and informative autobiographies describing their activities and achievements. In sum, there is a correlation between declining royal control and growing provincial power. This feature has led a number of scholars to suggest that some provincial families attempted to shake off all constraints imposed by the crown from at least dynasty VI onwards: i.e. they aimed to establish themselves as independent rulers and so were directly responsible for the collapse of the Old Kingdom system (e.g. Stock 1949; Wilson 1951/1956, ch. 4; cf. Simpson in Hallo and Simpson 1971 [OC]: 235). In outline the picture of events is clear: there was an apparent economic decline; central control became weaker and eventually broke down altogether in dynasties VII and VIII; a period of intermittent civil war followed; a dynasty of kings (centred on Herakleopolis: dynasties IX and X) ruled only part of Egypt at this time; finally, a king (from dynasty XI), based at Thebes, emerged as the victorious reuniter of Egypt. What is debatable is how the nomarchs fit into this picture of disintegration and change. The uncertainty stems in part from the fact that the evidence for independent provincial governors comes from Upper Egypt only: in other words it is impossible to trace a development from centralised control to dispersed local power-holders in the region where royal power is strongly marked throughout the Old Kingdom period, i.e. Memphis. Conversely, there is very little evidence from Upper Egypt itself for how precisely the south was governed in the Old Kingdom (for discussion, see Pardey 1976; Kanawati 1980). Another problem is that it is difficult to know how nomarchs had been tied to the central government, and what the basis of their position was in the Old Kingdom: did they originate from the local communities they governed, or were they installed by the king from the ranks of his courtiers? These are the unknown factors that need to be considered when we try to explain what happened. It is also important to remember how very little, in detail, is really understood of the political events and problems of the Old Kingdom period itself, masked as they are by the uniform façade of an apparently unchanging majestic power.

How can we get a grip on this difficult and turbulent period of Egyptian history? A first step is to look at what sources survive from which an attempt can be made to reconstruct it. Then a return to dynasty VI may help us to visualise the process of transition from the seemingly strong Old Kingdom state through political fragmentation to the highly centralised structure of the Middle Kingdom. The procedure is difficult, and much will remain uncertain.

Chronology and sources

The chronology is beset by problems, but two things help to clarify it somewhat, although not entirely (table 12). First, the Turin Canon gives a total of kings at the end of dynasty VIII. The reign-lengths of kings are fairly well known almost down to the end of dynasty VI. Combining this information shows that there is a period of only 22½ years for the whole of Manetho's dynasties VII and VIII (ends c. 2160). Obviously, then, the rulers of these 'dynasties' were ephemeral figures. Despite this, they did exercise control throughout the whole of Egypt. This is shown by the Koptos decrees (Weill 1912; Goedicke 1967), according to which some of these short-lived kings confirmed and deputed powers and exemptions to the nomarchs of Koptos. In other words, even if the Koptos decrees reveal the weakness of the central power in relation to the provincial nobility (as can be argued), that nobility still based its claims to power and privilege on royally promulgated grants emanating from the court in Memphis. So, although the Koptos decrees may show a devolution of central power, local governors still acknowledged the authority of the Memphite kings to legitimise their position. Secondly, the relatively well fixed dates of dynasty XII yield a date of 1991 for its inception. Since the re-unification of Egypt was achieved by Mentuhotep II of dynasty XI c. 2040, we can calculate the approximate length of dynasty XI and date its beginning c. 2133. That has been the conventional chronology; but there are now attractive proposals to lower the starting date of dynasty XII to 1963, and consequently that of Mentuhotep's unification to 2023. The result of this is to lengthen the time of the First Intermediate

Table 12 Chronology: the First Intermediate Period

(*Dynasty* VII: *c.* 2181–2173)	
(*Dynasty* VIII: *c.* 2173–2160)	(total of 15+ kings for both 'dynasties')

| *Dynasties IX and X: c.* 2160–2040
  = 'per Khẹty'
(main kings): Meryibre Akhtoy I
           Nebkaure Akhtoy II
           Wahkare Akhtoy III
           Merikare | *Dynasty XI (pre-conquest):*
  c. 2133–2040 [or 2023] (Thebes)
     Inyotef, 'great chief'
     Mentuhotep I, 'ancestor'
     Inyotef I
     Wahankh Inyotef II (2119–2068)
     Nakhtnebtepnefer Inyotef III
     Nebhepetre Mentuhotep II (2060–2010) |
| *Dynasty XI (post-conquest): c.* 2040–1991
           (or: 2023–1963) | (= Smatowy: 'Uniter of 2 lands')
     Sankhkare Mentuhotep III
     Nebtowyre Mentuhotep IV |

155

Period. That is not too problematical, as there has been a dispute, for years, between those scholars who wish to compress the First Intermediate Period into a span of less than a hundred years (Beckerath 1962) and those who think it lasted almost a hundred and fifty years. The difference of opinion revolves around the question of whether the Theban rulers, who eventually formed the successful dynasty XI, were entirely contemporary with the Herakleo-politan kings (dynasties IX and X), or whether this is impossible because too many kings of Herakleopolis are attested to fit such a short time-span (*CAH* I, ch. 10).

The struggle between Herakleopolis and Thebes

Manetho and the Turin Canon are the only sources that list the Herakleo-politan rulers, and from Manetho comes the division into two dynasties (IX and X) of nineteen kings each. Scholars have generally rejected this separation, and prefer the Turin Canon which lists just one dynasty of eighteen kings. What do we know of this dynasty? The main evidence comes from the tombs of Middle Egyptian nomarchs (i.e. those located in northern 'Upper Egypt'), particularly those at Asyut (Brunner 1937; cf. Schenkel 1965). They attest the existence of seven Herakleopolitan kings definitely; but it is quite uncertain where exactly they fit into the chronology. The reason for this is because either the royal name is damaged or the king is simply called 'Khety' (i.e. Manetho's 'Achthoes'), which is a recurring name in the Herakleopolitan dynasty (at least three, possibly four, are known). One Khety must have been the founder of the dynasty, since it seems to have been referred to as *pr-Hty* = 'the House of Khety'. Their dynastic centre was Herakleopolis (not far from Memphis), as the Asyut nomarchs, who had very close links with the Herakleopolitans, as well as the Turin Canon, make clear.

It is only with the reign of the best-known figure of the dynasty, Merikare, that it becomes possible for us to get closer to the Herakleopolitans and the history of the time. A well-known literary composition, 'The Instructions for Merikare' by his father (Volten 1945: 3–82; Erman 1927/1966 [0I]: 75–84; *ANET*: 414–418; Lichtheim 1973–80 [0I] I: 97–109), is asssociated with his name. The text is modelled on the instruction genre (see p. 146), but used rather differently. Its form is that of a political testament, which outlines policy and describes past achievements, including inglorious episodes. Al-though only eighteenth-dynasty copies of the text survive, several scholars nevertheless think that it was composed some time in the reign of Merikare as a statement on direction of policy (Lichtheim 1973–80 [0I] I: 97). Such scholars argue that the historical information in it is fairly reliable. But others have expressed reservations (Kemp in Trigger *et al.* 1983 [0D]), and the text can only be used with caution. One episode in the 'Instructions' that can be harmonised with other material is the war waged by Merikare's father against people pressing into the eastern delta. This frontier needed permanent defence, and there is some evidence which supports a Herakleopolitan presence in this region (Beckerath 1966). The 'Instructions' and the evidence of the Middle Egyptian nomarchs suggest that the Herakleopolitan kings wielded fairly extensive control, which stretched northwards into the delta and included taking some military action along Egypt's frontiers. They quarried stone at Hatnub (nome 14), and were acknowledged as kings by the nomarchs of Asyut (nome 13), of the Cerastes Mountain (nome 12) and, probably, the Hare nome (nome 15) (see map 7). But further south their power was challenged by Thebes (nome 4), and one passage in the 'Instructions for Merikare' seems to refer to this long-drawn-out conflict:

> Troops will fight troops
> As the ancestors foretold;
> Egypt fought in the graveyard,
> Destroying tombs in vengeful destruction.
> As I did it, so it happened,
> As is done to one who strays from the god's path.
> Do not deal evilly with the Southland,
> You know what the Residence foretold about it;
> As this happened so that may happen.
> Before they had trespassed . . . —
> I attacked This (Abydos) straight to its souther border at Taut,
> I engulfed it like a flood.
> (further on the theme is taken up again:)
> The nome of This was ravaged;
> Though it happened through my doing,
> I learned it after it was done.
>   (Helck 1977; Lichtheim 1973–80 [OI] I: 102; 105)

Despite its obscurity, the passage indicates that a bitter struggle took place in the area of Abydos between Herakleopolis and Thebes. Can we reconstruct anything of this clash? Until the end of the Old Kingdom, Thebes was an unimportant provincial temple centre. Tombs and stelae in any number appear only after dynasty VIII (Schenkel 1965). Similarly, it is only after the end of dynasty VI that a certain Inyotef, 'Great Chief of the Sceptre Nome (i.e. nome 4 = Thebes), Great Chief of Upper Egypt', began to claim more grandiose titles. He appears as an ancestor of the royal line in the Karnak king-list (p. 125) without a cartouche or royal titles. He was succeeded by a Mentuhotep, who was also regarded later as an ancestor of the Theban line, although again he himself claimed no royal titles. Mentuhotep's second successor, Inyotef II (2119–2068), succeeded in expanding Thebes' control during his fifty-year reign. The evidence for this growth in Theban power is the stele from his tomb (Winlock 1943: 257–259), in which he describes his capture of the Thinite nome (nome 8 = Abydos) and the extension of Theban power north to Qaw el-Kebir (nome 10) . Simultaneously, he expanded successfully southwards. This is attested, first, by his dedication of a statue in, and repair of, the Old Kingdom temple of Hekayeb in Elephantine, and, second, by the stele of Djary, one of his officials, who refers to the time when Inyotef II 'had fought with the house of Khety to the north of This' and then describes his area of control as extending 'from Elephantine to Qaw el-Kebir' (Winlock 1943: 257; cf. also the stele of the treasurer Tjetji, Schenkel 1965: no. 75; Lichtheim 1973–80 [OI] I: 90–93).

The autobiography of Ankhtify of Mo'alla (Hierakonpolis = nome 3), one of the most famous nomarchs' inscriptions of the period (Vandier 1950), may also refer to the reign of Inyotef II and his aggressive expansion of Theban power. Ankhtify himself had taken over the adjoining nome of Edfu (nome 2) to the south, so that he controlled nomes 2 and 3, to which he later added Elephantine. When Thebes (nome 4), with the help of Koptos (nome 5), attacked Armant (in the Theban nome), Ankhtify led his forces against them. He was ultimately unsuccessful, as not much later Thebes was in control of all the southern nomes from Elephantine (nome 1) to Hu (nome 7). The Theban capture of This followed, during which perhaps the ravaging of graves referred to by Merikare's father (see p. 157) occurred. This was perhaps the first time that the Herakleopolitans and Thebans came into direct conflict. The devastation in the Abydos area seems to have been succeeded by a period of relative peace. But not for long: in the fourteenth year of Nebhepetre Mentuhotep II (2060–2010) a 'rebellion of Abydos' led to the final defeat of Herakleopolis and its allies by Thebes. Mentuhotep II signalled this victory by adopting the name *Smatowy* = 'Uniter of the Two Lands', by which he laid claim to have re-established Egypt as a harmonious whole under one king.

Egypt in turmoil and the nomarchs

This is an approximate, possible outline of events based on problematical sources and brief, uncertain references in inscriptions. The most important and useful evidence for conditions in this period comes from the tombs of the nomarchs. Most people in Upper and Middle Egypt must have depended in this period primarily on the good offices of the nomarchs, and their texts provide an insight into the economic and political situation. The nomarchs acted as guarantors of safety, defending their nomes and protecting local inhabitants during the devastating civil wars from the depredations of soldiers.

Another responsibility shouldered by the nomarchs was the food supply, endangered by the military conflict between rival leaders. Most revealing of the kind of action (and advantage) taken by nomarchs to deal with this political chaos, is the inscription of Ankhtify of Hierakonpolis (see above), from his tomb:

The Prince, Count, Royal Seal-bearer, Sole Companion, Lector-priest,

General, Chief of Scouts, Chief of Foreign Regions, Great Chief of the Nomes of Edfu and Hierakonpolis, Ankhtify, says:

'Horus brought me to the nome of Edfu for life, prosperity, health, to reestablish it, and I did (it). For Horus wished it to be reestablished because he brought me to it to reestablish it.

I found the House of Khuu (Edfu) inundated like a marsh, abandoned by him who belonged to it, in the grip of a rebel, under the control of a wretch. I made a man embrace the slayer of his father, the slayer of his brother, so as to reestablish the nome of Edfu. How happy was the day on which I found well-being in this nome! No power in whom there is the heat of strife will be accepted, now that all forms of evil which people hate have been suppressed.'

(Vandier 1950; Schenkel 1965: no. 37; Lichtheim 1973–80 [OI] I: 85–86)

Here Ankhtify describes himself as saving Edfu from a terrible civil war, which had resulted in disastrous flooding. This had been caused by the flight, or deposition, of its nomarch. The vaunted restitution of order and peace serves to conceal his seizure of control over the province, which was probably not as peaceful, or welcome, as he would have the reader believe. Another text, from Edfu itself, refers to a drought, which caused famine – perhaps the factor that precipitated the destabilisation of the local government (Merer of Edfu, see Schenkel 1965: no. 42; Lichtheim 1973–80 [OI] I: 87–88). But the end result was that Ankhtify built up his personal power-base by gaining control of Edfu (and also eventually Elephantine, see p. 158). Other nomarchs almost certainly did the same, before being swallowed up by the victorious Thebans (Kemp in Trigger *et al.* 1983 [OD]).

The end of the Old Kingdom

The discussion above concerned the situation in dynasties IX–XI. Is it possible to determine what happened in the time between late dynasty VI and the emergence of a dynasty at Herakleopolis? The sparse evidence indicates that by the late sixth dynasty considerable instability in royal control had developed. The reasons for this are entirely unknown and unknowable. It has been posited that climate changes led to protracted drought, which made it impossible for the king to maintain his supreme position (Bell 1971); another suggestion is that pressure on the frontiers increased, especially in the north-east (Gardiner 1909). These are possible factors, but should perhaps be seen more as exacerbating an existing state of crisis rather than causing one. The argument that the provincial families eroded royal power by seizing privileges for themselves (e.g. Schenkel 1964), is also hard to maintain. The evidence suggests that, while some families may have become more powerful in the late Old Kingdom, they nevertheless continued to acknowledge the Memphite rulers (see p. 155): only when the Memphite kings disappeared and they were thrown on their own resources did they act completely independently. In other words, their increasing independence seems to be a result of, rather than the cause of, the fading of central control. Moreover, it is difficult to trace the background and rise of the local families that emerge as powerful in this period. None of them are attested before late in dynasty VI and some even later. This raises the possibility that, only as the situation became catastrophic, did local power struggles arise and new people seize the position of nomarch within particular provinces. This was certainly the situation in Edfu and in the Theban nome. Further north (nomes 9, 12, 13, 15, 16), where the nomarchs were closely linked to the Herakleopolitans, their rise in prominence may be directly related to their support of the kings. The background of the Herakleopolitan kings themselves is totally obscure, but their accession to royal power may have been a response to the disintegration of the Memphite royal line. Herakleopolis itself lies relatively close to Memphis and it is possible that they stepped in to take political and military defensive action as the Old Kingdom system broke down.

One piece of 'evidence' that has no place in studies of the First Intermediate Period is a literary text published in 1909 by Alan Gardiner, the 'Admonitions of Ipuwer'. The preserved papyrus dates from dynasty XIX (1306 (1295)–1187), but has, on the basis of style and language, generally been dated to dynasty XII (1991 (1963)–1786). It is cast in the form of warnings by a sage who describes a time of terrible disaster and social upheaval in Egypt: everything was turned upside down – the poor were rich, servants were masters, Egypt's nobles worked in the fields, murders and robberies were everyday occurrences, the timber-trade with Byblos had stopped, the country was overrun by foreigners and the Nile was low. Gardiner interpreted the text, influentially, as 'a direct and natural response to national calamity' which must, therefore, refer to the chaos which Egypt experienced in dynasties IX/X. This view becomes extremely unlikely (Lichtheim 1973–80 [OI] I: 149–150) if we compare it with other Middle Kingdom texts. A recurring *topos* of a number of Middle Kingdom literary compositions is the 'time of national disaster' followed by the appearance of a saviour who puts everything to right again (restoring *ma'at*). The development of this literary genre has been linked to the usurpation of the throne by Ammenemes I, the founder of dynasty XII, and served as a legitimising support for his dynasty (Posener 1956). The end of 'Ipuwer' is not preserved, but Luria (1929) argued plausibly that, after the very standardised description of chaos (the opposite of *ma'at*), the announcement of a saviour to put everything right would have followed, in accordance with the pattern found in comparable texts.

Egypt reunited

Just as the signs of political disintegration and economic problems are little or no royal buildings, no mining and quarrying expeditions or trading journeys, few royal inscriptions and relatively crude, provincial art-forms, so the reversal of all this indicates that a firmly established, central authority is back in action. The classic signs are all there from Mentuhotep II down to the end of his dynasty (only twenty years later). There is evidence for more intensive contacts with Nubia, the Wadi Hammamat route to the Red Sea was reopened and it is possible that mining in Sinai was resumed. Strong military action was taken against Libyan groups in the western desert and against the pastoral people of the eastern delta.

Royal patronage resulted in the emergence of a more elegant, courtly art recalling the fine, sophisticated forms of the Memphite court. The process of reviving the older art-forms is partially illustrated by the stele of Intefnakht (Barta 1970: 128–129). He describes how he first served the Herakleopolitan kings and was then brought to Thebes where he served Mentuhotep II as overseer of sculptors, craftsmen and casters of metal. The text encapsulates how someone trained in the northern court-art tradition could have influenced profoundly the formulation and execution of the visual programme at the command of a new king based in the provincial south. Large building projects were initiated, almost exclusively in Upper Egypt. One of the most impressive is the extraordinary mortuary temple and tomb of Mentuhotep II at Deir el-Bahri, which combines northern and southern traditions of funerary architecture (Arnold 1974). The stelae of Theban officials show that the administration was centred on Thebes, and that Thebans filled the most important government positions. At the same time, the nomarchs of Middle Egypt who had supported the Herakleopolitans, were largely left in place (Gestermann 1987). Perhaps the Theban kings had had to lean heavily on their help in their final successful push to establish control of the whole country; alternatively (or perhaps as a result) they may have been too powerful to shift. Although dynasty XI did not long survive Mentuhotep II's death, his significance in Egypt's vision of its past is shown by the fact that he continued to be venerated later as the reuniter of the country.[5]

3d Egypt in the Middle Kingdom
(c. 2040–c. 1730 (2023–1720))

Chronology and sources

The Middle Kingdom represents, in a number of respects, the 'classical' phase of Egyptian civilisation. The impression is of a period of great political strength and unity, especially in the time of dynasty XII ('the heart of the Middle Kingdom'), when Egypt was ruled, seemingly very smoothly, by one family. The dates of dynasty XII are generally accepted as being 1991–1785, based on an astronomical date derived from one of the el-Lahun (Fayum) papyri (Parker 1950: 63; cf. Parkinson 1991 no. 28b). According to a recent argument (Krauss 1985: 194–195; Kitchen in Aström 1987–9 [OO]: 43–4),

Sesostris III may only have ruled nineteen years, instead of the thirty-six he is traditionally assigned, and Sesostris II only six instead of eighteen. This shortens the span of time during which dynasty XII wielded power, and the possibility needs to be remembered (table 13). Dynasty XIII stands in complete contrast to the apparent solidity of dynasty XII: it consists of a large number of relatively short-lived kings, very few of whom are related to each other. Yet for the first fifty years or so of dynasty XIII the political framework *seems* very little affected by the turmoil which surely accompanied the disappearance of the preceding régime. It is, therefore, usual (though perhaps questionable) to include the earlier phase of dynasty XIII as an integral part of the Middle Kingdom.

Table 13 Chronology of dynasty XII

	standard	revised
(*Dynasty XI*	2040–1991	2023–1963)
Dynasty XII		
Ammenemes I (= Amenemhat/Imn-m-h3.t)	1991–1962	1963–1934
Sesostris I (= Senwosret/Senusert/S-n-wsr.t)	*1971–1926	*1943–1899
Ammenemes II	*1929–1892	*1901–1867
Sesostris II	*1897–1878	*1869–1862
Sesostris III	1878–1841	1862–1844
Ammenemes III	*1844–1797	1843–1798
Ammenemes IV	*1799–1787	1797–1790
Queen Sobeknefru	1787–1783	1789–1787
(*Dynasty XIII*	1783–1650?	1786–1650?)
	*Co-regencies	

There is a great wealth of documentary material, especially papyri from the Fayum, an area intensively developed by the dynasty XII kings. The papyri come from three separate archives, including a temple library and a collection of administrative records (Griffith 1898; for a brief discussion and selection with bibliography, cf. Parkinson 1991; Luft 1992). The recently discovered detailed annual records of Ammenemes II inscribed on a temple-wall at Memphis show that day-by-day records of some events were kept in this period. They provide a link between the Old Kingdom Palermo stone (see p. 127) and the annals of Tuthmosis III (dynasty XVIII, see p. 321): systematic record-keeping was probably a much more regular part of Egyptian political life than had previously been suspected. Full study of this important text is now in progress and promises to expand our understanding of Middle Kingdom Egypt substantially (Málek 1992). There are also a number of remarkable painted provincial tombs, stunning examples of royal sculpture and some very fine jewellery (Bourriau 1988). The remains of monumental architecture in Egypt proper are disappointing. Yet they must have been splendid, as shown by the description of the Heliopolis temple on the great Berlin leather roll, which preserves (in copy) a decree of Sesostris I ordering the building of a temple of Atum (Stern 1874; Lichtheim 1973–80 [OI] I: 115–118; Parkinson 1991 no. 5): all that remains of it now is a single obelisk. This dearth of building remains is partly attributable to the massive constructions undertaken by the New Kingdom kings, which have obliterated many Middle Kingdom structures, and partly to early haphazard excavations and lack of proper publication of sites. But this lack is offset, to some extent, by the large and impressive fortresses built in this period in Nubia (Emery 1965; Trigger 1976).

The founding of dynasty XII

The reign of Mentuhotep IV (at the end of dynasty XI) ended in turmoil, during which Ammenemes I seized the throne. He was, very probably, identical with the vizier of the last two kings of dynasty XI. His anxiety to justify his violent assumption of royal power emerges in several ways. First, he assumed the epithet 'Repeater of Births', to signify that his reign marked a new era – the renaissance of a strong united Egypt with himself at the head. Second, an *ex eventu* prophecy was composed, probably at his behest. It is set in the court of Snefru (dynasty IV), where a wise man, Neferty, prophesies that, after a period of dreadful disorder, a man, clearly identifiable as Ammenemes I, will appear to save Egypt:

> I show you the land in turmoil:
> The weak-armed is strong-armed,
> One salutes him who saluted.
> I show you the undermost uppermost,
> What was turned on the back turns the belly.
> Men will live in the graveyard,
> The beggar will gain riches,
> The great [will rob] to live.
> The poor will eat bread,
> The slaves will be exalted.
> Gone from the earth is the name of On (Heliopolis),
> The birthplace of every god.
>
> Then a king will come from the South,
> Ameny, the justified, by name,
> Son of a woman of Ta-Sety, child of Upper Egypt.

He will take the white crown,
He will wear the red crown;
He will join the Two Mighty Ones (i.e. the Two Ladies = the two lands),
He will please the Two Lords (i.e. Horus and Seth = the two lands) with
    what they wish,
With field-circler in his fist, oar in his grasp (implements used by the
    king during ritual dances).
Rejoice, O people of his time,
The son of man will make his name for all eternity!
The evil-minded, the treason-plotters,
They suppress their speech in fear of him;
Asiatics will fall to his sword,
Libyans will fall to his flame,
Rebels to his wrath, traitors to his might,
As the serpent on his brow subdues the rebels for him.
(Goedicke 1977; Lichtheim 1973–80 [OI] I: 139–145)

'Propaganda' of this type, designed to rally support for the new dynasty, informs the content of much literature in this period (Posener 1956) and, combined with competent rule, it seems to have been effective. The new king also returned the seat of government to the north of Egypt: this, together with a revival of the pyramid form for royal burials, declared visibly and tangibly the restoration of traditional order. Military expansion, trade, increasing prosperity and an efficient administration resulted in a period of well over one hundred years of relative political stability.

Several elements were of central importance in the success of dynasty XII. First, Ammenemes created a new administrative centre near Memphis (at Lisht, 65km south of Cairo) which helped to consolidate the Theban grip on Egypt. The full name of his new city was *Imn-m-h3.t it(w)-t3wy* ('Ammenemes-seizes-the-two-lands'), more regularly abbreviated to 'Itj-towy' and often called just 'the residence'. It was almost certainly fortified, perhaps in case of attacks from Libya or even to deal with local rebellion. Its position suggests that it was intended to control access to the Fayum. The royal tombs, and hence those of many officials, were relocated to this northern region (Lisht, Hawara *et al.*) and so officials connected with the mortuary cults also moved up here. Itj-towy was probably the principal centre of government, as shown by directions to send grain to the vizier there, and it contained a royal palace (Simpson 1963). The second feature, unique (in this form) to this phase of Egyptian history, was the institution of co-regency. The device allowed the designated successor to be associated in the exercise of royal power as co-ruler. This was obviously politically expedient, but, it has been argued, must have been difficult to institute in practice because of the religious basis of Egyptian kingship (Simpson 1956). Whatever the problems, they were overcome. How extensively the practice was implemented is less clear. The first, longest and best-attested co-regency is that of Ammenemes I and Sesostris I (ten years), but from Sesostris II onwards it seems to have fallen into disuse. Did the dynasty feel strong enough not to need this prop any longer? Or had it caused political problems?

The royal image

The political chaos of the First Intermediate Period is often thought to have led to profound changes in the vision of kingship. This is almost certainly wrong, since the royal ideology was very complex and multi-layered at all times, and subject to speculation and debate (see pp. 146–147). However, there does seem to have been a shift in the particular aspects of kingship that were emphasised in literary texts and sculpture. Royal statues of the Middle Kingdom, for example, are much larger than previously, well over life-size, and give an impression of great physical power, in contrast to the serene beauty of the Old Kingdom statues. The heroic, warrior-like image of the king is also echoed in a contemporary royal hymn, possibly sung by the local population at a ceremonial reception of the king on a visit to Upper Egypt. The text is preserved (together with five other hymns) on a large twelfth-dynasty papyrus from the Fayum:

> Horus: Divine of Form; the Two Ladies: Divine of Birth; Gold Horus:
> Being; the King of Upper and Lower Egypt: Khakaure; the Son of Re:
> Sesostris – he has seized the Two Lands in triumph.
> Hail to you, Khakaure, our Horus, Divine of Form!
> Land's protector who widens its borders,
> Who smites foreign countries with his crown.
> Who holds the Two Lands in his arms' embrace,
> [Who subdues foreign] lands by a motion of his hands.
> Who slays Bowmen without a blow of the club,
> Shoots the arrow without drawing the string.
> Whose terror strikes the Bowmen in their land,
> Fear of whom smites the Nine Bows (all Egypt's traditional foes along
>   its frontiers).
> Whose slaughter brought death to thousands of Bowmen,
> [Who had come] to invade his borders,
> Who shoots the arrow as does Sakhmet,
> When he felled thousands who ignored his might.
> His majesty's tongue restrains Nubia,
> His utterance makes Asiatics flee.
> Unique youth who fights for his frontiers,
> Not letting his subjects weary themselves.
> Who lets the people sleep till daylight,
> The youths may slumber, his heart protects them.

Whose commands made his borders,
Whose words joined the Two Shores!
                    (Grapow 1953; Lichtheim 1973–80 [OI] I: 198–199)

Another feature of the royal statues from this period is that many of the kings are portrayed with worried frowns on their faces. It has been thought that the wrinkled foreheads reflect the 'burden of kingship', although artistic conventions of this type can be difficult to interpret (Aldred 1950). Certainly, the impression some of these fine heads make on us today is that of a weary, disillusioned ruler. Whether that understanding of the sculptures is right or wrong, this aspect of kingship does appear in a most interesting text of the 'instructions' genre: the 'Instructions of King Ammenemes I to King Sesostris I'. Here, uniquely, the dead king recounts how he was assassinated while sleeping in his palace and warns his son and successor to trust no man:

Risen as god, hear what I tell you,
That you may rule the land, govern the shores,
Increase well-being!
Beware of subjects who are nobodies,
Of whose plotting one is not aware.
Trust not the brother, know not a friend,
Make no intimates, it is worthless.
When you lie down, guard your heart yourself,
For no man has adherents on the day of woe.
I gave to the beggar, I raised the orphan,
I gave success to the poor as to the wealthy;
But he who ate my food raised opposition,
He to whom I gave my trust used it to plot.
Wearers of my fine linen looked at me as if they were needy,
Those perfumed with my myrrh poured (or: passed) water while
    wearing it (meaning uncertain).
You my living peers, my partners among men,
Make for me mourning such as has not been heard,
For so great a combat had not yet been seen!
If one fights in the arena forgetful of the past,
Success will elude him who ignores what he should know.
It was after supper, night had come. I was taking an hour of rest, lying
on my bed, for I was weary. As my heart began to follow sleep, weapons
for my protection were turned against me, while I was like a snake of
the desert. I awoke at the fighting, alert, and found it was a combat
of the guard. Had I quickly seized weapons in my hand, I would have
made the cowards retreat in haste. But no one is strong at night; no one
can fight alone; no success is achieved without a helper.
Thus bloodshed occurred while I was without you; before the courtiers
had heard I would hand over to you; before I had sat with you so as to

advise you. For I had not prepared for it, had not expected it, had not foreseen the failing of the servants.

(Griffith 1896; *ARE* I §§474–483; *ANET*: 418–419; Lichtheim 1973–80
[OI] I: 135–139; Parkinson 1991 no. 9)

The bitterness and disillusionment of the murdered king are plain, as is the isolation that is the inevitable concomitant of absolute monarchy. What the occasion might have been for which the text was composed is not known, but other texts (e.g. 'The Story of Sinuhe', Lichtheim 1973–80 [OI] I: 222–235) show that retribution was swift and the conspirators relentlessly persecuted. It also bears witness to the persistent opposition that the founder of the new dynasty (himself a usurper) had to contend with.

The government of Egypt

Government and administration in the Middle Kingdom are illuminated by finds of papyri from Upper Egypt, as well as from the site of el-Lahun at the mouth of the Fayum, where the rulers of dynasty XII began a major project of land-drainage, which greatly increased the area of land available for agriculture (Butzer 1976: 92). The evidence from the nomes in Middle Egypt shows that for a considerable period, up to the reign of Sesostris III, the kings permitted some nomarchs to maintain substantial power-bases and even increase them. This was probably a legacy of the complex of alliances struck during the process of the Theban reunification (see chapter 3c). The tombs of the local hereditary nobles at Beni Hasan (nome 16) and el-Bersheh (nome 15) are the most impressive examples. Long autobiographical inscriptions illustrate their wealth and position, strengthened by intermarriage with neighbouring nomarchs' families and supported by their connections with powerful people at court. The painted reliefs mirror the information in the texts: the most spectacular scene shows the transport of a colossal seated statue of the nomarch Djehutihotep II (el-Bersheh) from the alabaster quarries at Hatnub. He obviously commanded great resources of manpower and income to fund such an undertaking. How and why these local power-centres were eventually, and effectively, curtailed is unclear, but the process was completed in Sesostris III's reign (Franke 1991; Lloyd 1992).

Although Itj-towy was developed into the chief seat of government, Thebes as a dynastic centre continued to be of great importance. It was referred to as the 'southern city' to distinguish it from the northern 'residence'. Evidence for building is very fragmentary, but the surviving traces show that significant constructions were certainly undertaken, as one would expect (see fig 15). Amun, originally just a local god of Thebes, became prominent in the Egyptian pantheon now and was increasingly amalgamated with Re. Papyrus Boulaq 18 (early dynasty XIII; Scharff 1920) contains fragments of a court journal, showing that king and court frequently visited Thebes: the king's presence is attested on the occasion of major festivals, to put down local unrest and execute the chief trouble-makers, and to negotiate with some of the people living in the surrounding desert. A list of the king's entourage is preserved in one instance: he was accompanied by one of his wives, a prince, three royal daughters, nine royal sisters, a group of nurses tending small children, and a large number of court officials. The royal retinue's needs were met, in part, by the government department responsible for administering Upper Egypt, in part by the central state treasury, and partly by goods provided from the estates of the local Amun-temple.

As in the Old Kingdom, the vizier continued to be the most important and powerful executive next to the king; whether there was more than one, in charge of separate 'departments' (*waret*) of the country is a moot point. The government's chief concern was the regular collection of all types of resources in order to support the court and its projects. Royally owned land, estates attached to funerary endowments, and privately owned land subject to tax provided the bulk of the crown's income. Private land is more clearly definable in this period than earlier, as is its complex interlocking with income from public offices (Théodoridés 1971; Kemp in Trigger *et al.* 1983 [OD]: 106). But this does not reflect a fundamental change in the Egyptian system of landholding, as it had existed in the Old Kingdom too. The tight control exercised in the collection of taxes and dues is sharply defined by the Brooklyn papyrus (early dynasty XIII; Hayes 1955): it contains extracts from a 'prison register', which lists Egyptians who were assigned to government farms and 'labour camps' because they had failed to meet the labour obligations required from them by the central authority. The level of policing and its efficiency must have been considerable to carry out such control effectively.

Egypt abroad

For Egypt's relations with Nubia there is a mass of material from this period (Säve-Söderbergh 1941; Trigger 1976). Most impressive are the string of massive fortresses with their double fortifications, glacis, and watchtowers at the corners of the walls enclosing the settlement, which was laid out on a grid-plan and contained the Egyptian commander's house. These great forts were erected at a number of points between the first and second cataracts, and were royal foundations. They were more heavily concentrated in the second cataract area, where their massed presence and a number of inscriptions indicate that this now constituted the southern border of Egypt, fortified and garrisoned against an enemy even further south – very probably a kingdom centred on Kerma (south of the third cataract; Reisner 1923; Hintze 1964). The twin boundary inscriptions of Sesostris III from there make this clear:

> The living Horus: Divine of Form; the Two Ladies: Divine of Birth; the King of Upper and Lower Egypt: Khakaure, given life; the living

Figure 15 Kiosk of Sesostris I from Karnak, Thebes (courtesy of M.S. Drower)

169

Gold-Horus: Being; the Son of Re's body, his beloved, the Lord of the Two Lands: Sesostris, given life-stability-health forever. Year 16, third month of winter: the king made his southern boundary at Heh (modern Semna):

I have made my boundary further south than my fathers,
I have added to what was bequeathed me.
I am a king who speaks and acts,
What my heart plans is done by my arm.
One who attacks to conquer, who is swift to succeed,
In whose heart a plan does not slumber.
Considerate to clients, steady in mercy,
Merciless to the foe who attacks him.
One who attacks him who would attack,
Who stops when one stops,
Who replies to a matter as befits it.
To stop when attacked is to make bold the foe's heart,
Attack is valour, retreat is cowardice,
A coward is he who is driven from his border.
Since the Nubian listens to the word of mouth,
To answer him is to make him retreat.
Attack him, he will turn his back,
Retreat, he will start attacking.
They are not people one respects,
They are wretches, craven-hearted.
My majesty has seen it, it is not an untruth.
I have captured their women,
I have carried off their dependants,
Gone to their wells, killed their cattle,
Cut down their grain, set fire to it.
As my father lives for me, I speak the truth!
It is no boast that comes from my mouth.

As for any son of mine who shall maintain this border which my majesty has made, he is my son, born to my majesty. The true son is he who champions his father, who guards the border of his begetter. But he who abandons it, who fails to fight for it, he is not my son, he was not born to me.

Now my majesty has had an image made of my majesty, at this border, which my majesty has made, in order that you maintain it, in order that you fight for it.

(*Ägyptische Inschriften* I: 257–258; *ARE* I §§653–660;
Lichtheim 1973–80 [OI] I: 118–120; Parkinson 1991 no. 6)

The archaeological material confirms the impression that Nubia, from the first to the second cataract, was effectively occupied by Egypt, and the local

Nubian population subjected. They probably provided much of the labour needs for the Egyptian mining and quarrying enterprises mounted in this mineral-rich region: gold, copper, amethyst, diorite. Some Nubians were recruited directly into Egyptian royal service to man garrisons, serve in the army and undertake policing activities. Nubia's role as a reservoir of manpower for Egypt was at least as important as its mineral resources. The Nubian 'C-group', which had emerged late in dynasty V in lower Nubia and formed small princedoms (see pp. 144–145), must have been defeated by the twelfth-dynasty kings. An important spin-off from the excavation of the Middle Kingdom fortresses in Nubia is that it has made it possible to visualise more clearly how fortified sites in Egypt itself, such as Itj-towy and the forts in the eastern delta, must have looked (see p. 164).

Egypt's links with the Levant and Sinai are known from a variety of sources. A provincial tomb-painting from Beni Hasan in Middle Egypt (nome 16 of Upper Egypt; p. 167) shows the arrival of a chief and retinue from Sinai bringing goods to the local governor (Newberry 1893, pls. XXX and XXXI). Such interchange was probably quite frequent and would have helped to lubricate any requests by these groups of herders to pass Egyptian frontier-posts in order to find grazing-grounds when necessary. Co-operation between the Egyptian authorities and the local communities in Sinai, probably based on a series of formal agreements, lies behind Egypt's successful exploitation of turquoise in the region. Egyptian mining in the Sinai peninsula was intensive in the Middle Kingdom, and a temple to the goddess Hathor and the desert-god Soped was begun early in dynasty XII at Serabit el-Khadim (Gardiner and Peet 1952–5). The official Egyptian presentation of all contact with local inhabitants as 'enemies' and 'barbarians', to be persecuted relentlessly (most clearly reflected in the so-called 'execration texts', cf. Posener 1940), was the obligatory rhetoric which hides this pattern of positive interaction.

There is some evidence for occasional hostility with parts of Palestine (cf. stele of Khu-Sobek, *ARE* I §676; Farag *RdE* 32 (1980): 79–82; Posener *SSEA Journal* 12 (1982): 7–8), but this seems to have been the exception. The predominant impression, revealed by the 'Story of Sinuhe' (Blackman 1932; Lichtheim 1973–80 [OI] I: 222–235), is of Egypt's interest in fostering close diplomatic relations. This involved the sending of Egyptian envoys to the courts of local rulers as far north as Kadesh and Byblos. Egypt was able, by these means, to participate in the extensive trading networks of the Levantine and Mesopotamian states (see chapter 2d), and items found in Egypt, such as the Tod treasure (cf. Porada 1982), show by their material and style that Egypt was in contact with them.

Middle Kingdom literature

The Middle Kingdom is perhaps most famous for the great flowering of Egyptian literature. The category of 'loyalist literature' (first defined by

Posener (1956)), which was part and parcel of the efforts of the twelfth-dynasty rulers to assert and propagate an image of themselves as 'legitimate' rulers (pp. 163–164), is the most striking. Even the 'Story of Sinuhe', one of the liveliest and most popular of all Egyptian stories, has been thought to be related to this genre, although that is improbable (Baines 1982). The story recounts, in autobiographical form, the adventures of a courtier of Ammenemes I, who felt threatened by the assassination of the king, fled to Palestine in fear of his life and found fame and fortune with a local chieftain living off the beaten track; eventually he was pardoned by Sesostris I and returned to die and be buried in Egypt. More broadly, the Middle Kingdom is regarded as providing the classical models in language and literature. The form and spacing of hieroglyphs of the Middle Kingdom was admired and imitated for as long as the script remained in use, and taught in schools later (Quirke in Bourriau 1988: 76). A very emotive type of literary text, first attested in this period, is the 'harper's song'. It turns on the fleeting nature of life and the impossibility of taking one's worldly goods into the after-life. The songs show, in spite of all appearances to the contrary for which Egypt is so famous, the uncertainty the Egyptians felt about their fate after death:

> The song which is in the tomb-chapel of King Intef, justified, in front
> of the singer with the harp:
> He is happy this good prince:
> Death is a kindly fate.
> A generation passes,
> Another stays,
> Since the time of the ancestors.
> The gods who were before rest in their tombs,
> Blessed nobles too are buried in their tombs.
> (Yet) those who built tombs,
> Their places are gone,
> What has become of them?
> I have heard the words of Imhotep and Hardedef,
> Whose sayings are recited whole.
> What of their places?
> Their walls have crumbled,
> Their places are gone,
> As though they had never been!
> None comes from there,
> To tell of their needs,
> To calm our hearts,
> Until we go where they have gone!
>
> Hence rejoice in your heart!
> Forgetfulness profits you,

Follow your heart as long as you live!
Put myrrh on your head,
Dress in fine linen,
Anoint yourself with oils fit for a god.
Heap up your joys,
Let your heart not sink!
Follow your heart and your happiness,
Do your things on earth as your heart commands!
When there comes to you that day of mourning,
The Weary-hearted (i.e. Osiris) hears not their mourning,
Wailing saves no man from the pit!

Refrain
Make holiday,
Do not weary of it!
Lo, none is allowed to take his goods with him,
Lo, none who departs comes back again!
(P. Harris 500; Erman 1927/1966 [OI]: 133–134; *ANET*: 467–468;
Lichtheim 1973–80 [OI] I: 194–7; Parkinson 1991 no. 56)

3e The Second Intermediate Period and Hyksos rule in Egypt (*c.* 1720–*c.* 1550)

About two hundred years separate the Middle Kingdom from the beginning of the New Kingdom (dynasty XVIII (1552/1550)). This is another phase of Egyptian history when the central authority lost control of the whole country and parts of Egypt formed independent units: an 'intermediate' period. But whereas the First Intermediate Period was relatively limited in time (about a hundred years), and was marked by intermittent civil war for most of that time between local groups contending for control of the country, the Second Intermediate Period lasted much longer, and the larger part of Egypt was dominated by foreign rulers, the so-called 'Hyksos', for at least the last hundred years or so. Evidence for fighting by Egyptians against their rule is limited to the very end of the period, and suggests some accommodation, perhaps even co-operation, with them. The eventual Egyptian success against them, which led to the emergence of the New Kingdom, was commemorated by a triumphalist rhetoric that reviled the rule of the Hyksos as irreligious and destructive. A later folk-story echoes this negative image (Redford 1970). Serious problems, created by chronological uncertainties and a dearth of contemporary, less emotive sources, beset attempts to gain a more balanced picture of the period. This section considers some of these difficulties, so that the problems in understanding this time will become clear.

Chronology

General points and dynasty XV

Manetho, the main chronographic source, is very confused and almost certainly suffers from manuscript corruption. He lists, after dynasty XII, the following:

dynasty XIII: 60 Diospolites (i.e. Thebans)	= 453 years
dynasty XIV: 76 Xoites	= 184 years
dynasty XV: 6 shepherds	= 260 years
dynasty XVI: 32 shepherds ⎫ dynasty XVII: 5 Thebans ⎭	= 251 years
	————
Period totalling in all:	1148 years
	————

Most scholars consider the figure '453' for the 60 Thebans of dynasty XIII to be corrupt and usually adjust it to 153 years; but that still leaves a total of 848 years for the whole period, which is impossible

Can we obtain any more reliable information from the Turin Canon? Unfortunately, the papyrus is very fragmentary at this point, which means that reconstruction of a plausible sequence of kings remains somewhat hypothetical. The most widely accepted arrangement of the kings in the Canon runs thus:

VI.5–VII.26	= 50 kings	(Thebes: probably dynasty XIII)	Total: lost
VII.28–X.13	= 76 kings	(Delta: probably dynasty XIV)	Total: lost
X.15–20	= 6 'Hyksos' (dynasty XV)		*Total = 108 years*
	(*ḥq3w ḥ3swt* = 'chieftains of foreign countries')		
X.22–29	= 8 kings	(dynasty XVI?)	Total: lost
X.31–XI.14	= 15 kings	(probably dynasty XVII)	Total: lost
XI.16–35(?)	= 20(?) kings	(dynasty XVI?)	

(Roman numerals indicate columns; Arabic numerals indicate lines in columns)

On this reconstruction it is possible to equate some of the Turin Canon entries with the material in Manetho (as indicated above: dynasties XIII, XIV, XV); where the two lists diverge, the evidence of the Canon should be preferred. Unfortunately, no totals for dynasties are preserved apart from one (dynasty XV = 108 years). Although the Canon introduces some chronological improvements, it, too, lists an enormous number of kings which need to be fitted into the period between the end of dynasty XII and the beginning of dynasty XVIII – a period which, on the basis of fairly firm dates, can be no longer than about 230 years. One striking parallel between the two lists is the '6 shepherds' of Manetho and the '6 chieftains of foreign countries (*ḥq3w ḥ3swt*)' in the Turin Canon. These are the 'Hyksos'. Josephus, the Jewish

Table 14 Chronology of the Second Intermediate Period

Upper Egypt	Middle Egypt	Lower Egypt
	Dynasty XIII (1785/1783–c. 1648)	
		Dynasty XIV (c. 1720–c. 1648)
Dynasty XVII (c. 1648–1552)	Dynasty XV ('Hyksos') (c. 1648–1540)	
Kamose	and 'dynasty XVI' (c. 1648–1540?)	
	Dynasty XVIII	
	Amose 1552–1527 (or: 1550–1525)	

(Reconstruction after Beckerath 1984)

historian of the first century AD, preserves a story in his tract *Against Apio*, purporting to come from Manetho, which relates to the 'Hyksos':

Tutimaios. In his reign, for what cause I know not, a blast of god smote us; and unexpectedly from the regions of the east invaders of obscure race marched in confidence of victory against our land. By main force they easily seized it without striking a blow; and having overpowered the rulers of the land, they then burned our cities ruthlessly, razed to the ground the temples of the gods, and treated all the natives with a cruel hostility, massacring some and leading into slavery the wives and children of others. Finally, they appointed as king one of their number whose name was Salitis. He had his seat at Memphis, levying tribute from Upper and Lower Egypt, and always leaving garrisons behind in the most advantageous places ... In the Sethroite nome he found a city very favourably situated on the east of the Bubastite branch of the Nile, and called Avaris after an ancient religious tradition. This place he rebuilt and fortified with massive walls ... After reigning for 19 years, Salitis died; and a second king, Bnon, succeeded and reigned for 44 years. Next to him came Apachnan, who ruled for 36 years and 7 months; then Apophis for 61, and Iannas for 50 years and 1 month; then finally Assis for 49 years and 2 months. These six kings, their first rulers, were ever more and more eager to extirpate the Egyptian stock. Their race as a whole was called Hyksos, that is 'king-shepherds'; for *hyk* in the sacred language means 'king' and *sos* in common speech is 'shepherd'.

(Manetho Fr. 42)

This confirms the suspected equation between Manetho's 'shepherds' and the Turin Canon's '*ḥq3w h3swt*'; the Egyptian term had obviously been garbled as 'Hyksos' and was misinterpreted by Josephus, on the basis of phonetic similarities. We can, therefore, say with certainty that dynasty XV consisted of 'rulers of foreign countries', six in number, whose total reign amounted to 108 years.[6]

Several New Kingdom texts refer to the Hyksos dynasty: first, and most important, are the two stelae of Kamose and the Carnarvon tablet, which is a copy of the first stele dating from dynasty XVIII (Smith and Smith 1976). Kamose was, in fact, the last ruler of the Theban dynasty XVII; he recorded on the stelae (and the text was copied later in Egyptian schools) an important push northwards by the Theban king and an attack on Avaris, the Hyksos capital in the eastern delta and seat of power of king Apophis. Second, there is the tomb autobiography of Amose, son of Ebana, a soldier and naval captain in the army of Amose (the identically named first king of dynasty XVIII), who accompanied his king in numerous wars. The first campaign he describes is the battle for Avaris, followed by an extension of the war against the Hyksos into southern Palestine (*Urk.* IV 1–11; *ARE* II §§1–16, 38–39, 78–82; *ANET*: 233–234; Lichtheim 1973–80 [OI] II: 12–15). Third, an inscription of Queen Hatshepsut, from the façade of a temple near Beni Hasan (Speos Artemidos) in Middle Egypt (nome 16), refers more generally to the Hyksos as offensive to *ma'at* and to their expulsion (Gardiner 1946a; *ANET*: 230). Finally, Papyrus Sallier I (dynasty XIX) contains a folk-tale in which the Hyksos king Apophis and Seqenenre, the predecessor of Kamose, are shown locked in a battle of wits and insults – with the Hyksos ruler, predictably, coming off worst (Erman 1927/1966 [OI]: 165–167; Gardiner 1932: 85–89; *ANET*: 231–232; Simpson 1972 [OI]: 77–80). This material shows that dynasty XV was eventually brought to an end by the last king of dynasty XVII and the first one of dynasty XVIII. The expulsion of the Hyksos seems to have been more or less completed by about 1540 (Vandersleyen 1971). By using the 108-year total for dynasty XV and calculating backwards, we obtain a start for the 'Hyksos' dynasty of 1648. But this still leaves a chronological space between the end of dynasty XII (1786) and the beginning of dynasty XV, a span of 138 years in which, even with the lower numbers of the Turin Canon, about a hundred and fifty kings have to be accommodated. Many of these kings must have ruled simultaneously with each other, but the problem is defining when and where.

Dynasties XIII and XVII

Dynasties XIII and XVII are both described as 'Theban'. The reason for the separation of the one from the other seems to be the fact that, while the kings of dynasty XIII regarded themselves (and largely were) kings of the whole of Egypt with their capital at Itj-towy (Lisht; see p. 164), the rulers of dynasty XVII were restricted in their control to the area of the 'head of the south', perhaps no larger than from Koptos to Aswan, with their capital at Thebes. Since the Kamose stelae, Carnarvon tablet and Papyrus Sallier I make both Kamose and Seqenenre, the last two kings of dynasty XVII, contemporaries of Apophis of dynasty XV, and since all kings of dynasty XVII seem to have been restricted in their power to southern Egypt, the fifteen Theban kings were perhaps entirely contemporary with the Hyksos dynasty XV. More kings may need to be included in dynasty XVII on the basis of tomb evidence from Thebes (Winlock 1924; Beckerath 1984). Their lengths of reign must, on average, have been rather short – a problem not really soluble at present.

Dynasty XIII presents even more difficulties. Manetho preserves no royal names, the Turin Canon some, and a few additional sources (the Karnak table of kings and the Memphite genealogy of a priest from dynasty XXII (Beckerath 1984)) provide more names, which may be identical with some listed in the Turin Canon or need to be added. Many regnal years are lost, as is the summation, and Manetho's 453-year total is thought to be corrupt. Correcting his number to 153 helps, but it is basically a rationalising manoeuvre – there is no real indication from a historiographic source how long the dynasty lasted. Many of the dynasty XIII rulers were from Thebes and, for the first fifty years or so, Egypt functioned much as it had done during dynasty XII and controlled just as much territory. As far as we can tell, what separates them from dynasty XII is the lack of family relationships within the dynasty, which contrasts sharply with the tightly knit family group of the dynasty XII kings. It is possible that dynasty XII died out, as its last ruler was a queen, Sobeknefru, suggesting a crisis in the royal succession. As the Hyksos dynasty began in 1648, and as later evidence shows it to have been in control of Egypt perhaps down to the Koptos area, thus including the area of Itj-towy, we should probably consider dynasty XIII as ending in 1648 when its kings lost control of this important capital (cf. the stele of Horemkhauf, Hayes 1947; Lichtheim 1973–80 [OI] I: 129–130). This rather mechanical solution means that the number of kings ruling between 1786 and 1648 is immense. That is not impossible. The evidence for lengths of reign (where preserved) shows that some kings ruled only for very short periods (less than a year). Another feature is that their backgrounds were extremely varied: some seem to have been from military families, some of foreign origin, many, apparently, were not from royal or even courtly circles (Van Seters 1966). The impression is of extraordinary instability in the crucial office of kingship, and no one has yet been able to explain this situation satisfactorily. But against this we must set considerable continuity within the highest echelons of the bureaucracy. This seems to have offset the rapid changes in holders of the throne and helped to maintain a certain political stability.

Dynasties XIV and XVI

Dynasty XIV is described by Manetho as consisting of seventy-six kings of Xois, ruling 184 years. Xois is a place that seems to have been utterly unimportant throughout the Pharaonic period and was not particularly important later. It was, however, close to Sebennytos in the western delta, which was Manetho's home town. Scholars have, therefore, suggested that an element of local pride may have inspired Manetho's description, and that the kings were in fact scattered throughout the delta area (Beckerath 1984). The names of the equivalent rulers in the Turin Canon are very odd: about one-third of them consist of 'nick-names' which should perhaps be deleted as spurious. This leaves us with about fifty kings, whom we should visualise as making up a series of small, local dynasties ruling contemporary with each other in the delta. But where, chronologically, should we place this phase of kinglet rule? The evidence is very complex, and a number of different interpretations is possible. The most plausible arguments (in my view) are those put forward by Beckerath (1984) in his meticulous analysis of the period. One of the early delta dynasts (Nehesy/dynasty XIV) dedicated monuments to the god Seth of Avaris; a much later text (the '400 Year Stele' of Rameses II; Montet 1933; *ARE* III §§538–542; *ANET*: 252–253) com-memorates the four hundredth year since the foundation of a temple of Seth at Avaris in *c.* 1320; the date of the foundation must, therefore, have been *c.* 1720. It looks as though the two pieces of evidence may refer to the same event: i.e. Nehesy of dynasty XIV was involved in the foundation of a temple to Seth at Avaris in *c.* 1720. This, in turn, suggests that control of Lower Egypt had been lost by *c.*1720 by the kings of dynasty XIII. Manetho's statement that Sobekhotep IV (dynasty XIII) only reigned from Memphis southwards and the fact that no monuments of this king have been found in the delta (in contrast to his predecessor, Neferhotep) confirm this. The foundation of the Seth temple may, then, have signified the establishment of independent principalities in the delta. This means that dynasty XIV began in 1720. The development marked the beginning of a serious erosion of central royal power. The delta kinglets are unlikely to have survived much beyond the establishment of Hyksos control, since one of the important royal centres for the powerful Hyksos kings (dynasty XV) was Avaris. So the end of dynasty XIV fell somewhere around 1648.

Manetho's dynasty XVI consists of 'thirty-two shepherds' – so they are associated with the Hyksos in some sense, but are separate from the main Hyksos dynasty. We should perhaps equate them with the two groups of eight and twenty(?) kings respectively of the Turin Canon. The names of the kings are lost, and they probably did not form a coherent dynasty. They may perhaps be thought of as rulers subject to, and hence contemporary with, dynasty XV. Some of the many scarab-seals that have been found bearing royal names, but which cannot be assigned to known kings, probably reflect princes included in this dynasty. Quite a number of such scarabs have been found in southern and inland Palestine, which suggests that at least some Hyksos principalities lay in this area (Weinstein 1981: 8–10).

The Hyksos and Egypt

This chronological rearrangement (see table 14) paints a picture of progressive and extensive fragmentation of political power in Egypt, and the eventual formation of an overarching royal power, non-Egyptian in origin, controlling the greater part of Egypt and dominating a number of local leaders, including some in Palestine. How this situation developed and where the 'foreign rulers' came from remains uncertain (Bietak 1987). A variety of archaeological material suggests that interaction between Egypt and Palestine was very intensive in this period, but this does not, by itself, help with defining the origins of the Hyksos (Van Seters 1966; Dever 1985). The Hyksos royal names have also resisted satisfactory philological analysis, so this avenue of research has rather run into the sand. The description of Apophis in the Kamose stelae as an 'Asiatic' and 'a man of Retenu (general term for the Levant)' points to a perception of the Hyksos as linked with the Levant, but is otherwise unspecific. The work that is now being carried out on the site of Tell ed-Dab'a in the eastern delta (Bietak 1975; 1981/1986) is the most hopeful development. Tell ed-Dab'a shows a growing presence, within a basically Egyptian town, of a non-Egyptian population group, with strong Levantine links and distinctive, non-Egyptian styles of burial. The site expanded enormously in the late seventeenth century, which coincides approximately with the time when the Hyksos dynasty XV assumed control over Egypt. A startling find, first made in the 1991–2 season, was the discovery of fragments of painted frescoes, quite incontrovertibly linked, by style, technique and motif, with the famous Minoan wall-paintings known from Crete and Thera (Bietak 1992; Hankey 1993). Still more Minoan-style paintings were discovered in 1992–3. The interpretation of their significance is uncertain at present: was a princess from the Aegean married to one of the Hyksos rulers? Was the tradition of such wall-paintings and motifs perhaps more widespread in the eastern Mediterranean than has been suspected (Niemeier 1991)? These questions will be debated for years to come and easy solutions are not possible.

One thing that is pretty certain, and accepted by practically everybody, is that Tell ed-Dab'a was part of the site of Avaris, the centre most intimately associated with the Hyksos. A careful study of the environment (Bietak 1975) and the descriptions in the Kamose stelae show that the city was protected by water on two sides (that is, by branches of the Nile; see Smith and Smith 1976); vineyards were close by, it had dwelling houses and was dominated by a well-fortified citadel. Kamose in his stelae evokes the heavy fortress graphically:

I caught sight of his women on the top of his palace looking out of their embrasures at the river bank, their bodies not stirring when they saw me – as they peeped out of the loopholes on their walls like the young of lizards from within their holes . . .

(Smith and Smith 1976: 60)

Avaris also had a harbour, which served as a staging post for riverborne traffic, particularly trade goods waiting to be shipped southwards. In his attack on the city, Kamose found 300 ships of Retenu moored in the harbour, filled with 'lapis lazuli, silver, turquoise, bronze axes, *ben*-oil, incense, fat, honey' and various types of timber. The list indicates that the Hyksos were in full control of Egypt's traditional commercial links (the Levant, Sinai, Byblos, the Red Sea), which normally moved through the eastern delta. The Egyptian kings at Thebes probably had no access to such goods except through fostering relations with the Hyksos.

How far Hyksos control extended in Egypt is still not completely certain (Bourriau, in press). Opinions have wavered between positing an at least temporary Hyksos rule right down to Aswan, with the Theban kings in the position of subjects (Helck 1968 [OD]: 134; Habachi 1972), and assuming that Hyksos control never really extended much beyond Middle Egypt (Beckerath 1984: 148). The evidence suggests a quite gradual northward extension only of Theban control, with the dynasty XVII kings eventually able to establish garrisons at Koptos and Abydos (Franke 1985). The Theban kings also set up, at some point, a royal residence (or military headquarters) at Deir el-Ballas, 32 km north of Thebes (Lacovara 1990). But this does not necessarily imply that Thebes had previously been under direct Hyksos rule. All that the Theban expansion shows is the increasing territorial ambitions of the kings, which climaxed in the more spectacular campaigns of Kamose and Amose. The pottery evidence, too, argues against Hyksos control over all of Egypt (Bourriau, in press).

One area the Hyksos certainly did not control was Nubia. Large numbers of Hyksos sealings have been found at Kerma, which was probably one of the political centres of the kingdom of Kush (Kemp in Trigger *et al.* 1983 [OD]: 160–173). The material prosperity of this kingdom developed remarkably during the Second Intermediate Period (Trigger 1976: 82–102), and it probably extended north to at least the region of the second cataract. The Hyksos sealings and the finds of Palestinian pottery (Tell el-Yahudiyeh ware) at Kerma are evidence of flourishing trade-relations between Nubia and the rulers in Lower Egypt. The close relations between the two are borne out by the Kamose text, which provides evidence for an alliance between the two powers who regarded each other as of equal political rank (Smith and Smith 1976). The Kamose stelae make it clear that, in spite of the advances made by his predecessors, the Thebans were still confined to the region south of Cusae (near Hermopolis in Middle Egypt) late in dynasty XVII. But south of

Thebes the situation had changed definitively by Kamose's third year: Kamose had attacked the Nubian ruler and gained control of Buhen at the second cataract. This gave Thebes access to additional manpower and possibly to Nubia's rich mineral resources. So, by the end of Kamose's reign, the Thebans had pushed forward to the region around Hermopolis, established their supremacy in Lower Nubia, and demonstrated their growing strength by attacking Avaris and ravaging its environs.

How far Hyksos control reached north beyond Egypt is also obscure. Two bits of evidence are suggestive, but vague. First, Kamose calls the Hyksos king, Apophis, 'great man of Retenu', which could imply that he ruled over parts of the Levant. Second, Amose, son of Ebana (see p. 176), describes King Amose following up the fall of Avaris with the siege of a Hyksos stronghold, Sharuhen (Tell el-Ajjul?), south-east of Gaza. The finds of scarabs with Hyksos royal names in south and central Palestine also testify to their presence in this region (see pp. 178–179). The very close relationship between Egypt and Palestine may mean that some of the towns here were in a tributary relationship to the 'Great Hyksos' rulers of dynasty XV; the Hyksos may have employed a similar political pattern in Egypt, too ('dynasty XVI'). The Kamose stelae certainly refer to local dynasts in Egypt, who were subjects of the Hyksos king in Avaris, but perhaps enjoyed a certain level of autonomy.

It is very difficult to get an impression of Hyksos rule in Egypt beyond these bare bones. Their place of origin, linguistic affiliations, and the process leading to their seizure of power remain obscure (although many accept that they were 'Canaanite' in some sense). One idea, propagated by the later New Kingdom rulers who came to power as a result of their successful war against the Hyksos, should be rejected, i.e. that the Hyksos deliberately trampled on Egyptian religious and political institutions and were hated by the Egyptian population. Surviving contemporary inscriptions make it clear that the Hyksos kings adopted the standard titulary of Egyptian kings, and were regularly designated 'son of Re' in keeping with Egyptian royal protocol. Egyptians served as high officials (e.g. treasurer) at the Hyksos court; the local dynast of Hermopolis, Pepy, was certainly an Egyptian and a loyal Hyksos subject; and King Amose had to deal with rebellions against his rule by an Egyptian, who may have been another Hyksos supporter. The later genealogy of the Memphite priest of dynasty XXII (see p. 177) lists several of his ancestors as serving the Hyksos kings, which suggests that the Theban-generated tradition about the Hyksos was not shared wholeheartedly by the inhabitants of northern Egypt. The great Rhind mathematical papyrus (Robins and Shute 1990), one of our major sources for knowledge of Egyptian mathematics, was copied in the reign of Apophis, as was Papyrus Westcar with its collection of stories set at Khufu's court (see pp. 146–147). Earlier Middle Kingdom archives had obviously been preserved, scribes were trained in standard Egyptian traditions and continued to practise their skills in the service of the new rulers. The Turin Canon, too, included the Hyksos kings as recognised, albeit foreign, rulers. The evidence is thin and biased, but enough traces survive hinting that, despite its foreignness, Hyksos rule was widely accepted, and the rulers were reasonably integrated into the Egyptian cultural and political framework.[7]

Notes

1 The Abydos list also omits the ideologically unacceptable episodes of Hatshepsut's reign and the Amarna pharaohs (see chapters 4b; 4c).

2 The continuing excavations at Hierakonpolis and Abydos are now adding more flesh to the skeleton of events, and the picture of Egypt's development is filling out (Dreyer 1993); for a general, up-to-date discussion, see Spencer 1993.

3 There has been considerable disagreement about this question with Emery, the excavator of the magnificent and elaborate mastaba tombs at Saqqara, arguing strongly for these as the 'true' burial-places of the early dynastic rulers (Emery 1961). However, Kemp, in an important and carefully argued article (Kemp 1966), has convinced many scholars that the kings of the first two dynasties were buried at Abydos, despite the apparently smaller size of the tombs.

4 Recent evidence from Abydos may show that Egyptian writing began to develop before c. 3100. The conciseness of the earliest surviving inscriptions and the evidence for the use of abbreviations makes it likely that rules for writing are likely to have been established earlier (Spencer 1993: 61–62).

5 One group of documents that dates to the eve of Egypt's reunification is worth mentioning here. It includes two (fragmentary) letters that seem to have been discarded after being read; they were found in western Thebes. Enough remains to show that they were part of the correspondence of an Upper Egyptian farmer, Hekanakhte, who was absent in the north, but continued to issue a stream of instructions about the management of his household and land to his eldest son. It provides one of the most vivid insights into a relatively modest farm, patterns of domestic life and family structure, including hints of strains and tensions between family members. So lively are the letters, indeed, that Agatha Christie used them as the basis for a murder story (*Death Comes as the End*) set in the Egypt of this period. For publication and full discussion, see James 1962.

6 Beckerath 1984 has confirmed the total of 108 years for the rulers of dynasty XV.

7 In the New Kingdom (chapter 4), several items appear in Egypt which are not attested earlier, such as the two-wheeled, horse-drawn chariot and the composite bow. Bronze-working, too, is a novelty in the Egyptian New Kingdom. It is possible that the innovations were introduced by the Hyksos rulers, but the details remain obscure.

Part II

THE
GREAT POWERS
(*c.* 1600–*c.* 1050)

4

IMPERIAL EGYPT: THE NEW KINGDOM (1552/1550–1069)

The Egyptian New Kingdom (dynasties XVIII–XX) is the time when Egypt was at its most spectacular, wealthy and powerful. Although there were political shifts, dynastic crises and occasional setbacks in imperial power, they never lasted long enough to shake fundamentally Egypt's power over an immense area, embracing northern Sudan in the south and stretching into southern Syria and the Lebanon in the north. Institutionally, militarily and economically Egypt proved enormously resilient, and the factors that eventually did lead to its decline as a great power are very hard to pinpoint. It is a time rich in sources of all kinds: there are many very long royal inscriptions and autobiographies of officials; some of the fullest documentation illustrating important aspects of social history, such as land tenure, grain prices, and court proceedings, comes from dynasty XX. Several of Egypt's best-known monuments date from this period, such as the great temples of Abu Simbel (Nubia), Karnak (Thebes), Abydos and Medinet Habu (western Thebes). Finds that have made news headlines date from the New Kingdom: the town-site of el-Amarna (ancient Akhetaten), where the beautiful head of Nefertiti was found in a sculptor's workshop; the rich treasures of the tomb of Tutankhamun (Reeves 1992b); and, more recently, the private tomb of Horemheb at Saqqara. Some of Egypt's best-known monarchs ruled at this time: Queen Hatshepsut, Tuthmosis III, Akhenaten, Ramesses II. It was a phase of Egyptian history unrivalled in wealth and pomp.

4a Chronology and sources

New Kingdom chronology depends primarily on two astronomical dates: one for the reign of Tuthmosis III and one for Ramesses II. There are, nevertheless, disagreements about the exact chronology and individual lengths of reign (Krauss 1985; Helck and Kitchen in Aström 1987–9 [OO]). The main differences concern the accession dates of Tuthmosis III (either 1490 or 1479) and Ramesses II (either 1290 or 1279). There is no way of resolving this at present; the prevailing convention is to accept the earlier dates, although a number of scholars now favour the later ones (see tables 15–17). I prefer the lower dates, but in view of the very real uncertainties I have merely indicated the alternatives throughout, especially as the slightly higher ones have generally been used in textbooks. The much higher dates used by the revised edition of *CAH* (Tuthmosis III's accession: 1504; Ramesses II's accession: 1304) have been abandoned by most scholars. One proposal with chronological implications, now rejected by virtually everyone, is the idea that co-regency was a fairly continuous practice throughout early dynasty XVIII (Aldred 1968). The only co-regencies that are widely accepted are: a) the one between Hatshepsut and Tuthmosis III, which represents an atypical situation (see pp. 191–193); b) the one between Smenkhare and Akhenaten. There is a divergence, with respect to the latter, between those who think that all of Smenkhkare's reign was included in that of Akhenaten (Aldred 1968; Kitchen in Aström 1987–9 [OO]) and those who allow him an independent reign of one year after Akhenaten's death (Helck 1968 [OD]). The exact length of Horemheb's reign is another important area of debate, with opinions ranging from as low as sixteen years (Helck in Aström 1987–9 [OO]) to as high as thirty years (Kitchen in Aström 1987–9 [OO]).

Table 15 Early Dynasty XVIII: chronology

	CAH	*conventional*	*low*
Amose	1570–1546	1552–1527	1550–1525
Amenophis I	1546–1526	1527–1507	1525–1504
Tuthmosis I	1525–c. 1512	1507–1494	1504–1491
Tuthmosis II	c. 1512–1504	1494–1490	1491–1479
Tuthmosis III	1504–1450	1490–1436	1479–1425
Hatshepsut	1503–1482	1490–1469	1479–1458
Amenophis II	1450–1425	1438–1412	1425–1398
Tuthmosis IV	1425–1417	1412–1403	1398–1390

The sources are very full. Documents which allow us to reconstruct the political history are, as often, unsatisfactory. The only 'historiographic text', worthy of the name, is the 'Annals of Tuthmosis III' (*Urk.* IV 645–667) inscribed on the walls of the temple at Karnak. It was based on day-to-day records kept during campaigns. Royal texts are, more usually, edicts affirming tax exemptions (e.g. Nauri decrees of Sety I (Griffith 1927)), righting wrongs related to revenue collection (e.g. Horemheb's edict (Kruchten 1981)), or restating ideals of royal policy (e.g. Tutankhamun's restoration stele (Bennett 1939)). Some royal inscriptions commemorate cult-foundations (e.g. Tuthmosis IV's dream stele (*Urk.* IV 1539–1543)), praise royal military and hunting prowess (e.g. Amenophis II's sphinx stele (*Urk.* IV 1276–1283)), or relate to building activities (e.g. Amenophis III's stele (*Urk*. IV 1646–1657; Akhenaten's boundary stelae (*Urk*. IV 1981–1990)). Others celebrate (sometimes in epic poetic form) military triumphs (e.g. Ramesses II's Battle of Kadesh (Kitchen 1968–: II 2–124); Merneptah's Libyan victory (Kitchen 1968–: IV 12–19); Ramesses III's defeat of the 'sea-peoples' (Edgerton and Wilson 1936)). The many splendid tomb biographies of officials and soldiers (e.g. Rekhmire (*Urk*, IV 1986–1093), Amose son of Ebana (*Urk*. IV 1–11), Amenemhab (*Urk*. IV 889 ff.), Senenmut (Theban Tombs nos. 71 and 353, Meyer 1982)) amplify many details of political history and administrative structures. One documented political scandal was the attempt to murder the aged king Ramesses III, and install one of his sons on the throne; the royally ordered hearings and punishments (execution, compulsory suicide, facial mutilation), which involved a large number of officials, a royal wife and son, were recorded on two large papyrus scrolls (de Buck 1927). The 'Report of Wenamun' (Gardiner 1937: 61–76), which dates to the very end of the period, is an interesting text but difficult to classify. It is cast in the form of an official report by a man, Wenamun, sent from Thebes to Byblos to buy timber for the sacred barque of Amun – a mission on which he encountered any number of vicissitudes and disastrous setbacks. The picture it presents of Egypt is of a country divided in all but name, whose political prestige has vanished to the point where Egypt's emissaries are treated with contempt and publicly insulted. Was it really based on an actual report of Wenamun's mission, perhaps embroidered by him once safely home? Or is the text a purely literary creation, revelling in exaggeration to create comic scenarios? It is hard to know, yet the view taken obviously affects how we visualise the historical situation. The fragmentary state of the text (its end is lost) makes the question even more difficult. The treaty drawn up in 1269 (1258) between Ramesses II and Hattusili III of Hatti (see chapters 4d, 5d), which ended almost two centuries of intermittent conflict between the two powers, is one of the best-known texts concerning Egypt's foreign relations. Most unusually, both the Hittite version of the treaty, as well as the Egyptian one, have been found. We also know much more about the appearance of palaces and the villas of dignitaries in this period than earlier, largely the result of the intensive royal building programmes at Thebes and the excavations of the famous, though short-lived, royal centre of el-Amarna (Akhetaten) in Middle Egypt.

The 'Amarna letters' are the main source for understanding Egypt's control of the southern Levant (EA, Moran 1987/1992). They are a collection of clay tablets containing the correspondence, mainly in Akkadian, between Egypt and the neighbouring powers of the day (Hittites (chapter 5d), Cyprus, Babylonia (chapter 7a), Mitanni (chapter 6a), Assyria (chapter 7b)) and – by far the largest number – letters exchanged with subject princes and cities in the Levant (chapter 6d). The archive dates from later dynasty XVIII, to the reigns of Amenophis III, Akhenaten and Tutankhamun (1403–1335 (1390–1327)). Topographical lists, naming the towns and regions over which the Egyptian king claimed control, which were carved in the great temple at Karnak, give some additional information on the Egyptian Levant, but are not easy to use (Redford 1992: 143 and n. 61). The journal of a frontier official late in dynasty XIX (Papyrus Anastasi III, Gardiner 1937: 31–2) lists movements of messengers and soldiers between Egypt and the Levant and fills in some of the day-to-day detail of Egyptian control in the region. Archaeological finds from Palestine and south Lebanon (Hachmann 1983; Gonen 1992) supplement this material. Quite a number of royal inscriptions have been found in Nubia, which demonstrate how tightly this region was controlled by Egypt. The many magnificent royal temples constructed here (e.g. Abu Simbel, north of the second cataract) are the most renowned Egyptian buildings marking Egypt's power. But one of the most interesting is the small temple of Amenophis III at Soleb (between Dal and third cataracts; Trigger 1976: 126–127), which shows the king worshipping a cult-statue of himself.

Documents reflecting day-to-day administration and life are numerous. A set of palace accounts from Memphis (Sety I (dynasty XIX), Helck 1961–70 IV: 633–641)), the tomb-robber trials held late in dynasty XX (Peet 1930), the indictment of a minor cult-official of the Khnum temple on Elephantine (dynasty XX; Peet 1924) and the Turin strike papyrus (dynasty XX; Edgerton 1951) are among the most significant. A number of model letters (Gardiner 1937: 99–116), used in the training of scribes, contain some additional information on administrative practice. The Wilbour papyrus (Gardiner and Faulkner 1941–52) and the Great Papyrus Harris (*ARE* IV §§151–412) tell us about land-tenure and temple-estates and incomes, respectively. The rich finds from the site of Deir el-Medina have revealed a microcosm of Egyptian life. This was a settlement, founded in dynasty XVIII, in western Thebes where the artisans, involved in constructing and decorating the royal tombs, lived with their families. It shows us the layout of a small town or village, with its closely packed family houses, small shrines, and an occasional more substantial dwelling. A mass of written material on ostraca and papyrus has been found at Deir el-Medina (almost all date to dynasty XX), which gives vivid insights into family structure, inheritance, neighbourhood quarrels, buying and selling, strategies for coping with food shortages, religious behaviour and levels of education and literacy (Bierbrier 1982). It has also provided important evidence on grain prices and their fluctuations (Janssen 1975).

4b The foundation of imperial Egypt: from Amose to Tuthmosis IV (dynasty XVIII: 1550–1403 (1390))

At the inception of dynasty XVIII stands Amose, brother of Kamose of Thebes, who made such great strides in pushing back Hyksos power with his attack on Avaris (chapter 3e). The king-lists separated Amose from Kamose because he represented a new period of Egyptian unity, as it was he who finally and successfully drove the Hyksos out of Egypt and pursued them into southern Palestine, as his namesake, the soldier Amose, son of Ebana (see p. 176), described in his tomb:

> Now when I had established a household (i.e. married), I was taken to the ship 'Northern', because I was brave. I followed the sovereign on foot when he rode about on his chariot. When the town of Avaris was besieged, I fought bravely on foot in his majesty's presence. Thereupon I was appointed to the ship 'Rising in Memphis'. Then there was fighting on the water in 'Pjedku' of Avaris. I made a seizure and carried off a hand (i.e. proof of killing an enemy soldier). When it was reported to the royal herald the gold of valour was given to me.
>
> Then they fought again in this place; I again made a seizure there and carried off a hand. Then I was given the gold of valour once again. Then there was fighting in Egypt to the south of this town, and I carried off a man as a living captive. I went down into the water – for he was captured on the city-side – and crossed the water carrying him. When it was reported to the royal herald I was rewarded with gold once more. Then Avaris was despoiled and I brought spoil from there: one man, three women; total, four persons. His majesty gave them to me as slaves. Then Sharuhen (southern Palestine) was besieged for three years. His majesty despoiled it and I brought spoil from it, two women and a hand. Then the gold of valour was given me, and my captives were given to me as slaves.
>
> (Urk. IV 1–11; ARE II §§1–82; Lichtheim 1973–80 [OI] II: 12–15)

The pursuit of the Hyksos beyond Egypt's north-eastern frontier led to the first tentative moves towards control, by military force, of areas in southern Palestine. It climaxed eventually in Egyptian control of a substantial area, and brought the Egyptians into conflict, first with the powerful state of Mitanni (fifteenth century; chapters 6a, 6d) and later the Hittites (fourteenth and thirteenth centuries; p. 207; chapter 5d).

The aggressive militarism that went hand in hand with these expansionist ambitions had a profound effect on Egypt's internal development. The king's role, as mighty warrior and defender of Egypt from its enemies, had always been an important aspect of Egyptian monarchy, and is found in the earliest royal images (e.g. Narmer palette, cf. p. 133; fig. 13). Raids into Sinai, Palestine and Nubia and civil wars had been frequent, and the Middle Kingdom forts in Nubia provide ample evidence of the efficiency of Egyptian defensive architecture and the posting of long-term garrisons. But the military, as an important, high-ranking profession among officials, was largely absent in earlier periods. Right from the beginning of the New Kingdom (possibly already in dynasty XVII; Baines 1986) this changed, and people claiming military ranks of all sorts become prominent, and are found occupying significant positions close to the king. The sheer scale of military operations must, in part, be responsible: the regular and continuous campaigning abroad and hence the need for permanent forces. Amose son of Ebana is just one example of this new trend. Other evidence shows that a professional army was established, that soldiers were trained in camps from their youth (Kemp 1989 [0Ga]: 227ff.) and that new weapons were developed: it is possible that one of the tangible legacies of Hyksos rule was the introduction of the fast, two-wheeled, horse-drawn chariot into Egypt, which now became the most important weapon of the Egyptian army. The new militaristic emphasis, it has been argued, is reflected by a new item of royal headgear. This is the blue crown (see fig. 16), which has been thought to represent a war-helmet (Aldred 1968). But that is a mistake (Davies 1982): the blue crown developed (although the details remain obscure) as a symbol of coronation at this time (Bell 1985).

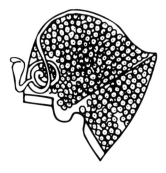

Figure 16 Blue crown (after Davies 1982)

Amose's next move, crucial in providing economic support for Egypt and royal enterprises, was to campaign in Nubia. He consolidated Egyptian control as far as the second cataract and seems to have set the boundary south of Buhen. His predecessor, Kamose, had already fought against the ruler of Kush (see p. 181), ally of the Hyksos king, so Amose's campaign was probably intended to follow up Kamose's initiative and discourage Kushite attempts to control earlier Egyptian-held territory. Egypt's expansion, early in the New Kingdom, into the Levant and into Nubia can be seen to originate in attempts to strengthen the boundaries of the burgeoning new realm against powerful and threatening rulers in the north and the south. Amose's successor, Amenophis I (1527–1507 (1525–1504)), strengthened Egypt's hold in Nubia, extending the boundary as far as Semna and installing an official in the newly created office of 'King's son of Kush and Overseer of the southern foreign lands' to administer the region. It is also probable that he undertook some campaigning in Syria, although the evidence is not unequivocal (Redford 1992: 149). Amenophis I's reign is scantily documented; he was revered for centuries by the workmen at Deir el-Medina (Bierbrier 1982), which shows he made a deep impression – but, unfortunately, we do not know how or why.

Tuthmosis I (1507–1494 (1504–1491)), Amose's second successor, was the real architect of the dynastic programme, who introduced major innovations that had a profound and lasting effect on the shape of the New Kingdom state (Redford 1967). In his reign the main centre for the court was moved from Thebes north to Memphis. A royal palace was constructed there that continued in use for the next hundred and fifty years. Memphis became the place where the great military campaigns mounted by the rulers were planned, and where the soldiers were 'armed before pharaoh'. At Thebes, the entire Middle Kingdom city was gradually destroyed by a series of massive building programmes (Kemp 1989 [0Ga]: 201ff.). The provincial shrine of Amun was turned into a state-temple (Karnak) of ever grander proportions for the important imperial cult of Amun-Re and the king. In the reign of Tuthmosis I it was first enclosed by a fortification wall (the fortress-like appearance of temples is a feature of the New Kingdom), the first pylon was built to create an imposing façade and obelisks were erected; colossal statues of the king flanked the approach to the temple. The Amun temple became the starting-point for annual festival processions and royal rituals, such as the 'Festival of the Valley' and the great Opet festival performed at New Year. They eventually moved around the whole circuit of the greatly enlarged city of Thebes including crossing over to the west bank of the Nile. Tuthmosis I also introduced a new style of royal tomb, which became standard for centuries. He abandoned the practice of burying kings in pyramids near Memphis, and Tuthmosis I was laid to rest in a rock-cut tomb located in a deserted wadi opposite the city of Thebes where there were no previous burials. The royal funerary temple was sited a considerable distance away from the king's tomb. This rocky wadi is the famous 'Valley of the Kings' where all subsequent rulers down to the end of dynasty XX were buried (Reeves 1992a). Queens, some courtiers and nobles were buried fairly close by in another wadi, now known as the 'Valley of the Queens' (fig. 17). Tuthmosis I's other achievements were new in terms of scale rather than aim. His wars in the Levant reached as far as the Euphrates in the north, setting a new goal for successors to emulate. What sort of arrangements for control he tried to make for this large area (if indeed any) remains unknown (*CAH* II ch. 10; Weinstein 1981).

His successor, Tuthmosis II, did not reign for very long; estimates vary betweeen four (Helck 1968 [0D]: 1494–1490) and twelve years (Kitchen 1982: 1491–1479). His widow, Hatshepsut, who for twenty-one years acted, certainly on occasion, as a male sovereign, is better known. She employed pharaonic titles, wore male royal dress, such as the ceremonial beard, used her daughter, Neferure, to act ritually as queen and was acknowledged as 'king' by her officials. She mounted successful campaigns into Nubia and probably south Palestine (Redford 1967), and organised a ship-borne expedition to Punt (in the region of modern Eritrea), which brought back great quantities of luxury goods (gold, baboons, ebony, incense-trees) in return for gifts presented by the Egyptian expedition to the local leaders. Her celebrated

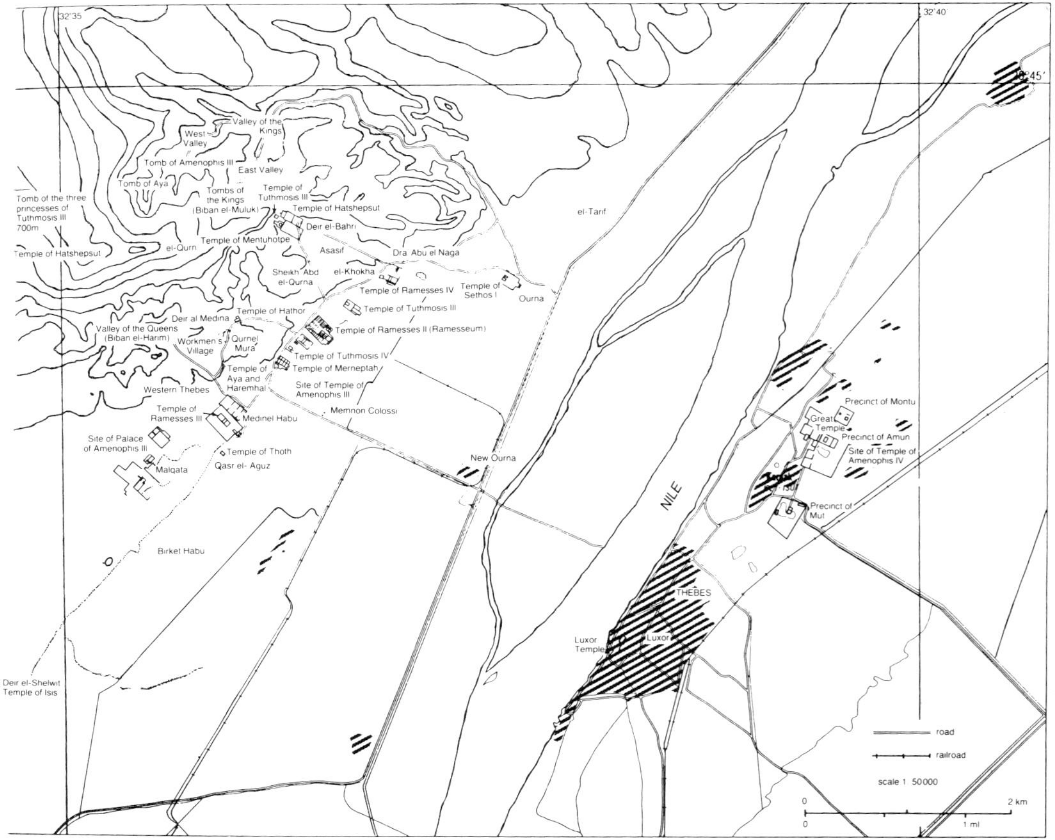

Figure 17 Plan of Thebes
(after Baines and Málek
1980 [OA])

funerary temple at Deir el-Bahri in western Thebes[1] was decorated with elaborate scenes depicting the Punt voyage, as well as her divine birth and the story of her selection to the kingship by her father, Tuthmosis I.

Many of the details of this curious episode in Egyptian history, when a woman occupied the throne, are obscure. It is fairly certain that Hatshepsut gained her position of power as a consequence of acting as regent for Tuthmosis III, the young son of Tuthmosis II. We should probably understand her action as a dynastic defence mechanism:[2] i.e. in a situation where the kingship was in crisis, with the successor to the throne a tiny child, she was able to protect the dynasty's hold on power by assuming the role of pharaoh in certain ceremonies herself. If this interpretation is correct, then she was extremely successful. Tuthmosis III entered smoothly on his sole rule at her death (1469 (1458)), apparently encountering no opposition; the fledgling Egyptian empire and its dominions in Nubia and the Levant had been maintained and even consolidated. Tuthmosis III was, therefore, able to launch his series of large-scale campaigns into the Levant immediately in his first year of sole rule (*CAH* II, ch. 10). The throne remained in the hands of the same family for another hundred and fifty years. Later official Egyptian historical records ignored Hatshepsut's reign, and some of her monuments were defaced by Tuthmosis III. This suggests that, once the politically delicate situation had been weathered successfully, the Egyptian establishment felt that Hatshepsut's position had been incompatible with *ma'at*, perhaps even that it was disgusting; therefore, they tried to erase it from the public record. We should firmly reject one approach to her reign: that is the idea that Hatshepsut's rule and Tuthmosis III's later hostile reaction to it shows that originally royal power in Egypt was always passed on in the female line – an insidious situation finally scotched by Tuthmosis III (Redford 1967). There is no evidence whatever to sustain such an interpretation (Robins 1983).

Tuthmosis III mounted seventeen campaigns into the Levant during the remaining thirty-three years of his reign. He penetrated deep into northern Syria, invaded the western part of Mitanni and was able to erect a stele next to that of his grandfather, Tuthmosis I, on the bank of the Euphrates. But Egypt was not able to subjugate all this immense territory. At the end of his reign, and probably later, the frontier was near Ullaza on the coast (near Hellenistic Orthosia, at the mouth of the Nahr el-Barid) and included Kumidi (Kamid el-Loz) in south Syria inland (see chapter 6d). Mitanni, Egypt, and the Hittites fought over the small states beyond this line for some time; but Egypt ultimately made no further lasting gains.

Amenophis II, Tuthmosis III's successor, certainly campaigned in north Syria and compelled Kadesh to acknowledge Egyptian sovereignty, but not for very long (chapter 6d). Egypt's hold in the Levant was still relatively precarious after Tuthmosis III's conquests, as demonstrated by a serious rebellion in Palestine in Amenophis II's ninth year. This was brutally crushed and the corpses of seven local dynasts involved were publicly exhibited: six were hung upside down on the walls of Thebes and one on the walls of Napata beyond the third cataract. The situation in the Levant appears to have stabilised after this, and Mitanni, Babylonia and the Hittites sent embassies to congratulate the Egyptian king on his successes. The Egyptians seem to have concluded fairly quickly that their imperial interests in the southern Levant would be best served by reaching an accommodation with their closest large neighbour, Mitanni. The decision was probably inspired by the threat of an expanding Hittite empire (see chapter 5d), which threatened both Mitannian and Egyptian power. A considerable portion of Tuthmosis IV's eight-year reign was taken up with negotiations between the Egyptian and Mitannian kings. The success of this rapprochement was crowned by the marriage of the Egyptian ruler and the daughter of King Artatama of Mitanni. This was no mean achievement, considering the earlier history of repeated and bloody wars between the two states. The Mitanni–Egypt agreement ushered in a period of co-operation and active interchanges (including several more royal marriages in the reigns of Amenophis III and Akhenaten), which lasted almost fifty years, before Mitanni was dismembered by the Hittites and Assyrians, and so ceased to be a player in the great power game (cf. chapters 6a; 7b; for a reassessment of Tuthmosis IV's reign, see Bryan 1991). As a result, the momentum of Egyptian campaigning declined: the nearly forty-year-long reign of Amenophis III was by and large a time of peace and prosperity for Egypt, reflected in the opulence of royal enterprises (*Aménophis III* 1993).

4c The Amarna period: late dynasty XVIII (1403–1306 (1390–1295))

The 'Amarna period' is one of the most famous in Egyptian history. King Akhenaten is the enigmatic figure at its centre: he has been the subject of operas, plays and novels, and has been regarded variously as an idealist, individualist, monotheist, internationalist and pacifist. The material for studying this historical phase is ample, but difficult to understand, and has sparked many differences of opinion.

Table 16 Late dynasty XVIII: chronology

	CAH	*conventional*	*low*
Amenophis III	1417–1379	1403–1364	1390–1352
Amenophis IV (= Akhenaten)	1379–1362	1364–1347	1352–1336
Smenkhare	1364–1361	1348–1345	1338–1336
Tutankhamun	1361–1352	1345–1335	1336–1327
Ay	1352–1348	1335–1332	1327–1323
Horemheb	1348–1320	1332–1306	1323–1295

The sequence of events is roughly as follows (see table 16): Amenophis III (1403–1364 (1390–1352)) was succeeded by his son, Amenophis IV (1364–1347 (1352–1336)), who, at some point, renamed himself Akhenaten. Fairly early in his reign he began work on a new royal centre in Middle Egypt, near Hermopolis, called Akhtetaten. He was married to Nefertiti and they had at least six daughters. Some time after his fourteenth year, Nefertiti seems to have died, and he probably married one of his daughters. Smenkhkare, probably his brother, became co-regent, and may have reigned on his own for a year or two after Akhenaten's death, before dying himself. He was succeeded by Tutankhaten (possibly another brother), who renamed himself Tutankhamun, and reigned for about nine years (1345–1335 (1336–1327)); he was married to one of Akhenaten's daughters, Ankhes-en-pa-aten, whose name was changed to Ankhes-en-amun. Akhetaten was probably abandoned as a residential centre for the court during his reign. No male members of the royal family survived Tutankhamun's death and so Ay, an elderly, high-ranking official, possibly related to Akhenaten's family, seized the throne. He almost certainly married Tutankhamun's widow. His reign lasted only four years, possibly because of his advanced age (1335–1332 (1327–1323)). Horemheb, a former general of Tutankhamun, then seized the kingship (1332–1306 (1323–1295)). He appears to have tried to separate himself definitively, in terms of policy, from the previous four kings. Scholars disagree considerably about who was related to whom and how, and differ on some chronological problems (Aldred 1968; Redford 1984).[3]

The site of el-Amarna in Middle Egypt first focused attention on this period. The first discoveries were made in the 1870s, when some rock tombs and stelae were found. But it was the find of a large number of clay tablets, mainly written in Akkadian and representing the Egyptian imperial correspondence (the 'Amarna letters'), that aroused real excitement. Intensive exploration of the site by British and German archaeologists followed and they unearthed the city's extensive remains: wealthy houses, palaces, temples and an artisans' quarter (Petrie 1984; Davies 1903–8; Peet *et al.* 1923–51). The royal court used the site only briefly, and the later king, Ramesses II (dynasty XIX: 1290–1224 (1279–1213)), reused blocks from Amarna in his buildings at Hermopolis on the opposite side of the Nile (Cooney 1965; Spencer and Bailey 1983–92).[4] The finds at Amarna brought to light two unusual features of Akhenaten's reign: first, the human figure, especially the king himself, was represented in a very curious way; secondly, a new cult of the 'Aten' (the sun-disc) had come into existence and other Egyptian gods were apparently not worshipped. What were scholars to make of this?

One approach was to look more closely at the period following Akhenaten's reign. It became rapidly clear that the king was not accepted into the later list of Egypt's kings, his name and those associated with him were excluded from monuments, and the years of his reign were counted together with those of Horemheb, the former general, who became king at the very end of the dynasty. So the period was blocked out from the official record; when it was impossible to avoid a mention of Akhenaten (e.g. for dating purposes) he was simply called 'the enemy'. This would only happen if something particularly appalling had happened. What could that have been? One possibility is to see whether the inscriptions of Akhenaten's immediate successors contain any hints. The stele of Tutankhamun from Karnak (Bennett 1939) does, indeed, make some veiled allusions: sanctuaries throughout the land were destitute; the land was in chaos; Egypt had suffered military defeats; the gods were so enfeebled that they could not answer prayers. While due allowance must be made for the exaggeration inherent in the language of royal texts, it is clear that the previous reign was already being regarded with some horror. The situation had to be rectified and Tutankhamun says he did so, by re-habilitating the sanctuaries, giving them properties and staffs as of old and remaking divine images. Although the statements are vague and generalised, something of Akhenaten's reign does emerge: he had turned the established Egyptian order effectively on its head.

But how and in what way? One of Akhenaten's policies, that used to be thought quite incontrovertible, was that he neglected Egypt's imperial holdings; some even argued that military action was against his religious principles. The argument was based on some of the Amarna letters. Several contain dire warnings to the Pharaoh against the treacherous activities of neighbouring rulers, and some repeatedly bewail the Egyptian king's failure to send troops. But we should note two features of the letters: first, Egyptian control in the Levant relied to some extent on the principle of 'divide and rule', which encouraged local princes to shop each other to the Egyptian court (Liverani 1979; 1990); secondly, Byblos and Tyre, the cities that report apparently serious problems, lay near the Egyptian imperial frontier and were the ones most likely to be affected by contemporary Hittite military aggression in the area (see chapters 5d; 6d). In fact, neither Byblos nor Tyre were ever lost to Egyptian control, so it is perfectly possible that the essential aid *was* sent. The apparent absence of any publicly proclaimed military action by Akhenaten in the region, is not to do with his beliefs, but rather with the fact that Egyptian control was so solid that major campaigns were not necessary. In Amenophis III's reign the same was true: after the peace with Mitanni and the marriages with Mitanni's royal house (see p. 194), the two great powers could easily control the smaller states without mounting huge military expeditions. Moreover, later evidence makes it quite clear that none of the solidly held core of Egypt's Levantine empire was ever lost at this time, nor was it substantially diminished. If anything, it was around this time that the Egyptian grip on the region was considerably tightened, judging by the archaeological evidence, which shows that a number of Canaanite cities were re-sited along well-controlled Egyptian routes, while others were destroyed or reduced in size (Gonen 1984). The recent find of re-used blocks from Amarna at Hermopolis, showing the king in the traditional pose of smiting the enemy, proves that Akhenaten was certainly not opposed to war. His wife, the famous Nefertiti, too, is depicted in some remarkably violent poses (Samson 1977; Morkot 1986). Moreover, there is growing evidence that Akhenaten did campaign in the Levant (Schulman in Redford 1988; see chapter 6d). He also deported people from Damascus to Nubia, where he had ordered his viceroy to conduct an important campaign in the south, at the close of which some of the defeated were impaled on stakes. The conclusion on this aspect of Akhenaten's activity, then, must be that he behaved in a very traditional, pharaonic manner with respect to Egypt's empire and war.

A key to what Akhenaten did may, then, lie in the city that he created for his new cult of the Aten, now the desert plain of el-Amarna, and the main site on which our impressions of Egyptian cities are based (Kemp 1977). Akhetaten ('Aten-on-the-horizon') was a newly created royal city and built very rapidly. Akhenaten founded it in his fourth year specifically to provide a centre for the cult of the Aten. This was not because the Aten cult was limited to this area, but because all Egyptian gods were, in origin, associated with a particular place. The promotion of the Aten cult, which was the elevation of a particular physical manifestation of the sun-god, i.e. the sun-disc, as an object of worship, had, by its very nature, not been associated with a particular locality. The foundation of Akhetaten aimed to rectify this. It was stated on the great boundary stelae from Amarna, which marked the extent of the city, and also avowed that the king, too, would live there and that the royal burials would henceforth be near the new city (Murnane and van Siclen 1993). Akhenaten had built an earlier temple to the Aten at Karnak (reconstructed only recently, cf. Smith and Redford 1977; Gohary 1992), but the massive weight of tradition there must have made it difficult to force through a major religious re-orientation satisfactorily. Possibly around year eight the king, who had rejected his name of Amenophis (IV) and renamed himself 'He-who-is-beneficial-to-Aten' (Akhenaten), moved the court up to his new city, which must still have been in the process of construction.

Akhetaten was laid out on a grandiose scale (with an estimated population of 30,000; see fig. 18). An area in the centre was linked to the northern city by a royal road, which may have provided a place for the king's chariot-rides. The northern city contained a substantial riverside palace surrounded by a massive fortification wall, which may have been the principal royal residence. A large administrative building, containing storage-rooms, lay beyond. There was also a self-contained, isolated building, probably intended for Meritaten, one of Akhenaten's daughters, which included a palace with columned reception-halls, an open-air temple, gardens and courtyards decorated with painted frescoes showing scenes from nature. The northern suburb was packed with closely built private houses, larger houses jostling tiny hovels. The more prosperous houses contained, in addition to a central reception room with wooden columns, a well, a garden, a tiny solar shrine, and storage facilities. A similar suburban area lay to the south. It was here that a sculptor had his house with adjoining studio, in which were found the many well-known, fine 'Amarna heads', including the world-famous one of Nefertiti now in Berlin. The central city was laid out around the terminus of the royal road. To the west, covering the stretch down to the river, lay the Great Palace equipped with a brightly painted court and halls. At its core lay a huge courtyard surrounded by colossal stone sculpted figures of Akhenaten and more halls and smaller courts. This may have been used for receiving embassies and rewarding officers – a scene frequently depicted in the Amarna tombs. At its southern end was a hall, decorated with 544 brick columns and its walls encrusted with glazed tiles. A brick-built bridge connected the Great

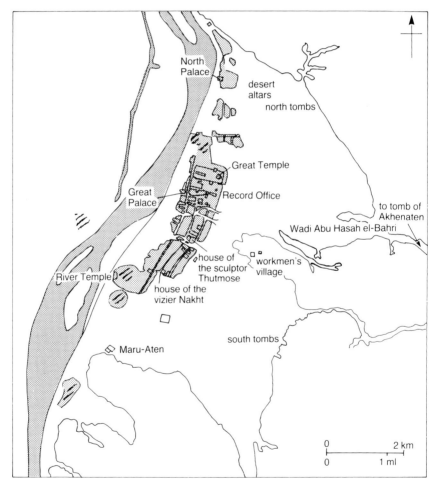

Figure 18 Plan of Amarna (after Baines and Málek [1980 [0A])

Palace with the king's house on the opposite side of the royal road. The royal residence was set in spacious, formal gardens and contained the 'window of appearances' (*maru*; Kemp 1976), where the king appeared on formal occasions to hand out public honours to his officers.

The city also contained, of course, several temples to the Aten. As his physical form was the sun, his worship had to take place in the open. The Great Temple, a huge structure of 229 × 731m, catered for this. The worshipper, after entering through the formal gateway, passed through a columned hall and came into an open court filled with offering tables, at the back of which lay a separate area called 'The Aten is found' (Gem-Aten). The 'Mansion of the Aten' had a similar layout, although it was not as spacious. Another site devoted to Aten-worship lay at the eastern end of the city, where two areas were enclosed by walls. Inside the walls lay lakes surrounded by gardens, within which were set pavilions and shrines, and altars to the sun stood on small islands. This was Maru-Aten and, in the words of one scholar, it exemplified 'the spirit of sun worship, providing an idyllic landscape of greenery and water presided over by the sun' (Kemp in Smith and Hall 1983 [0Ga]: 68).

Close to the rock-tombs lay the village of the people who prepared the tombs. The tomb workmen may have stayed on for some time after the site was abandoned as a royal and cult centre. Although not many of the tombs were ever completed or used, given the short life of the city, they do provide important evidence for how the new cult was observed and for Akhenaten's officials. They also provide rich evidence of the 'Amarna style' – a radical departure from the traditional Egyptian depiction of the human form, using an entirely different canon of proportions (Robins 1986 [0M]). Everyone was now shown with a flowing, rounded outline, protruding belly and rounded shoulders. The shape of the head, too, was different, with an overhanging chin and a projecting back to the head. In the finest examples of Amarna sculpture this can look extraordinarily elegant, in others it strikes the modern viewer as grotesque.

The tombs reveal, importantly, that there was considerable continuity in the families from whom the highest officers of state and court were drawn. It was thought at one time that Akhenaten, in his reforming zeal, cut himself off from the earlier establishment and promoted entirely new groups to serve under him. But it is now clear that, as far as we can tell, the king recruited his retinue from exactly the same set of people. The officials imitated and followed the king's lead – they did not form an indignant opposition to him. One other significant aspect revealed by the Amarna tombs is a change in the repertoire of decorative scenes. The scenes from the tomb-owner's private life (fowling in the marshes, overseeing his estates, etc.) were largely replaced by depictions of officials abasing themselves before the king and the royal family (the latter often shown in unusually intimate settings with king and queen fondling each other or their tiny daughters: fig. 19), or awaiting the arrival of the royal family on formal occasions. The central focus of the tomb

Figure 19 Akhenaten and family (drawing by D. Saxon after Aldred 1973)

decoration was always the king, sometimes with his family, worshipping the Aten. The king and his god, as the centre of all activity that mattered in life and death, overrode all other representations in importance.

Amarna obviously provides us with important clues to the cult of the Aten. But how is this cult to be understood? How did it come into being? How did it differ from other Egyptian cults, in a country rich in the variety and number of its deities and even receptive to gods from beyond its frontiers? And what effects did this theological change bring in its wake? These questions are interlinked and very difficult to answer. It is possible to argue, as has been done (e.g. Aldred 1968), that the Aten cult stands at the culmination of a process that had been going on already for some time in dynasty XVIII. The sun-god, Re, had effectively absorbed many of the features of other deities, so that a kind of syncretistic monotheism developed, with other gods regarded as Re's various bodies (e.g. Amun-Re; Re-Harakhty). Re, in many of his aspects, was particularly closely associated with the king and kingship. So the strong emphasis on Re was really a way of stressing the king's all-powerful and divine nature. The physical form of the sun, the sun-disc (Aten), emerged within this process as a separate, and increasingly important, aspect of Amun-Re, which emphasised its relationship to the king: e.g. the king is called 'the disc in the horizon'; the palace is called 'the mansion of the disc'. This development came to a head with Akhenaten: in his reign the form of the Aten was defined in abstract form as a sun-disc with royal attributes, that is, it was equipped with a uraeus (see chapter 3b); its name was enclosed in cartouches; it celebrated jubilees. The effect was to present the Aten as sole heavenly king with Akhenaten as his earthly incarnation. The very close association, indeed virtual identity, between the two was affirmed by the rays emanating from the Aten disc, each ending in a tiny hand holding the Egyptian symbol of life, the *ankh*, to the nostrils of the king and members of his immediate family (wife and children) when present, but not to anyone else. The non-anthropomorphic image of the Aten allowed the god to be presented simply as a disc hovering directly above the king and blessing him, thus both enhancing the king's position and shifting him to the centre of all scenes – king and royal family effectively replaced the conventional divine family triads. The merging of king and god had reached its peak (Redford 1984). It is possible that the curiously androgynous representations of the king should be understood in the context of this new, powerful identification of the monarch; that, rather than reflecting the king's real appearance (perhaps a sufferer from Fröhlich's syndrome? see Aldred 1968), it was deliberately intended to present him as a non-gendered being, who could be regarded as 'the father and mother' of the Egyptian state (Yoyotte in Bottéro *et al.* 1966 [OB]: 250).

This theological reinterpretation resulted in the exclusion of other gods in cult – the only potent deity was the king's god, so the resources of temples dedicated to the traditional gods were re-channelled to supply the Aten cult and the names of other gods, particularly that of Amun, were erased, physically and in personal names (at least among the royal family): the king formally renamed himself, all the known names of Akhenaten's daughters have 'Aten' as their theophoric element, and Tutankhamun, possibly Akhenaten's brother, started his life as Tutankhaten. How thoroughgoing this reorientation of religious life was on the wider social level is difficult to assess. A little evidence exists to suggest that many people of less elevated rank did not adopt the new cult; but they must have been affected by the change in functioning, or effective closures, of such major cult-centres as the great Amun temple at Thebes. It is undoubtedly to this state of affairs that Tutankhamun refers in his 'Restoration Stele' when he says:

> If one prayed to a god to ask things of him, he did not come. If one supplicated a goddess, likewise she did not come. Their hearts were enfeebled because what had been made was destroyed.
>
> (Bennett 1939: ll. 9–10)

It is very hard to determine how all the religious and cultic changes worked in detail. Particularly difficult is the question of how the temple-staffs of the traditional temples were affected. It is possible to imagine that they simply shifted to administering the Aten cult on behalf of the king, given the manner in which the 'priesthood' worked in Egypt (Kemp 1989 [0Ga]: 184–197; 229–230; see pp. 221–222). There is certainly no clear indication that the Amun (or any other) priesthood actively opposed Akhenaten's changes, nor that they were responsible for his later vilification.

Why and how did the cultic reforms collapse, as they eventually did? Given the king's supremacy and overall control, it is difficult to see why this should have happened. There was, moreover, no immediate hostile reaction to Akhenaten's relatives and close associates: Tutankhamun may have been his brother and was certainly married to one of Akhenaten's daughters, yet he became his successor; Ay, the next king, may have been the father of Nefertiti, and definitely married one of Akhenaten's daughters; Horemheb, last ruler of the dynasty, held a very high position in Tutankhamun's court and was married to a daughter of Ay, who may thus have been a sister of Nefertiti. So it looks very much as though members of Akhenaten's family continued to be at the hub of power, even while they emphasised a progressive and definitive distancing from his religious changes. This makes it all the harder to see what considerations dictated the swift rejection of the Aten cult. One possibility, no more than a hypothesis, is perhaps worth considering. There was an enormous number of deaths within Akhenaten's family during his seventeen-year rule: his wives and four of his six little daughters died; Smenkhkare, his co-regent and probable brother, and Tutankhamun both died at a young age. Hittite evidence shows that around this time a devastating plague was raging in the Levant (see p. 254), which also decimated the Hittite royal family and population. It is, therefore, conceivable that the same plague was responsible for the multiple deaths at the Egyptian court (Helck 1971: 187–188; Redford 1984: 186–187). If that is right, then it is possible that the Aten cult was abandoned in the wake of these disasters. A connection may have been made between the horrors of the plague and the abandonment of Egypt's conventional pantheon and modes of worship, and later rulers therefore interpreted the many royal deaths from plague as a divine punishment for neglect of the old gods.

One can hardly leave a discussion of the Amarna period, however brief, without quoting a short extract from the magnificent hymn to the Aten, one of the finest examples of hymns to the sun to have survived from ancient Egypt. Although it has now been shown that it was not as novel in all its tenets as once thought, it illustrates brilliantly how the cult of the sun in this period was infused with a concept of universality, and it provides us with a flavour of the revolutionary Aten cult. It was inscribed in the Amarna tomb of Ay and its composition attributed to Akhenaten himself:

> Earth brightens when you dawn in lightland,
> When you shine as Aten of daytime;
> As you dispel the dark,
> As you cast your rays,

The Two Lands are in festivity.
Awake they stand on their feet,
You have roused them;
Bodies cleansed, clothed,
Their arms adore your appearance.
The entire lands set out to work,
All beasts browse on their herbs;
Trees, herbs are sprouting,
Birds fly from their nests,
Their wings greeting your *ka* (life-force).
All flocks frisk on their feet,
All that fly up and alight,
They live when you dawn for them.
Ships fare north, fare south as well,
Roads lie open when you rise;
The fish in the river dart before you,
Your rays are in the midst of the sea.

Who makes seed grow in women,
Who creates people from sperm;
Who feeds the son in his mother's womb,
Who soothes him to still his tears.
Nurse in the womb,
Giver of breath,
To nourish all that he made.
When he comes from the womb to breathe,
On the day of his birth,
You open wide his mouth,
You supply his needs.
When the chick in the egg speaks in the shell,
You give him breath within to sustain him;
When you have made him complete,
To break out from the egg,
He comes out from the egg,
To announce his completion,
Walking on his legs he comes from it.

How many are your deeds,
Though hidden from sight,
O Sole God beside whom there is none!
You made the earth as you wished, you alone,
All people, herds, and flocks;
All upon earth that walk on legs,
All on high that fly on wings,

The lands of Khor (Syria) and Kush,
The land of Egypt.
You set every man in his place,
You supply their needs;
Everyone has his food,
His lifetime is counted.
Their tongues differ in speech,
Their characters likewise;
Their skins are distinct,
For you distinguished the peoples.
(Davies 1903–8: VI 29–31; *ANET*, 369–371;
Simpson 1972 [01]: 289–295;
Lichtheim 1973–80 [OI] II: 96–98)

4d The Late New Kingdom: dynasties XIX and XX (1306 (1295)–1069)

A lot of inscribed material and building remains survive from the late New Kingdom. Ramesses II, the longest-reigning and best-known ruler of this period (1290–1224 (1279–1213), either put up, or substantially added to, many buildings throughout Egypt and Nubia. But all the great kings of this period are well represented: Sety I (1305–1290/1294–1279), Merneptah (1224–1204?/1213–1204), and Ramesses III (1184–1152). There were some political problems. Dynasty XIX ended in struggles about the succession, perhaps ultimately due to Ramesses II's enormously long reign, and the large number of children he produced in the course of it: we know of fifty-nine daughters and seventy-nine sons, and the kind of in-fighting for the throne this could have caused is not hard to imagine. Yet Ramesses II's immediate heir (Merneptah) seems to have acceded quite smoothly. The precise relationship between Setnakht, the supposed founder of dynasty XX, and the kings of dynasty XIX is not known. His son, Ramesses III, presented him as re-establishing order after chaos (presumably a reference to the dynastic troubles at the end of dynasty XIX), although it is probably Ramesses III himself who deserves the credit. He and his eight successors all bore the name 'Ramesses', perhaps a symbolic linkage with the famous and long-lived Ramesses II. Dynastic troubles flared up again in the years following the reign of Ramesses III, and only two kings at the very end of the dynasty reigned for a reasonable length of time (Ramesses IX and XI, with 19 and 29 years respectively). A number of problems had developed in Egypt by that time. Their exact nature is not always easy to determine; but it is clear that during the reign of the last Ramesses (XI: 1098–1069) the country was effectively divided into a northern and southern sphere, run from separate centres (Thebes and Tanis; see table 17). This state of affairs, with sporadic attempts at unification and ever greater fragmentation, continued for about four hundred years after the end of dynasty XX. This long period of political divisions, which succeeds the New Kingdom, is the Third Intermediate Period (chapter 12a).

Table 17 Chronology: dynasties XIX, XX and XXI

	CAH	conventional	low
Dynasty XIX			
Ramesses I	1320–1318	1306–1305	1295–1294
Sety I	1318–1304	1305–1290	1294–1279
Ramesses II	1304–1237	1290–1224	1279–1213
Merneptah	1236–1223	1224–1204(?)	1213–204
Amenmesse	1222–1217?	1204–1200	1204–1200
Sety II	1216–1210?	1200–1194	1200–1194
Siptah	} 1209–1200	1194–1188	1194–1188
Tawosret		1188–1187	1188–1187
(wife of Sety II, mother of Siptah)			

Dynasty XX		*South*: High Priests
Setnakht	1186–1184	
Ramesses III	1184–1152	Ramesses-nakht (son of Merybast)
Ramesses IV	1152–1146	
Ramesses V	1146–1142	
Ramesses VI	1142–1134	
Ramesses VII	1134–1133	
Ramesses VIII	1133–1126	
Ramesses IX	1126–1107	Nesamun
Ramesses X	1107–1098	
Ramesses XI	1098–1069	Amenhotep

1080 beginning of 'renaissance era' (*whm mswt*)	Herihor 1080–1074

Lower Egypt		
Smendes	1080–1069	Piankh 1074–1070
Dynasty XXI		
Smendes	1069–1043	Pinudjem I 1070–1055
Pinudjem	1054–1032	
Amenemnisu	1043–1039?	Masaharta 1054–1046
Psusennes I	1040–993	Menkheperre 1045–1992
Amenemope	993–984	Smendes 992–990
Osorkon	984–978	
Siamun	978–959	Pinudjem II 990–969
Psusennes II	959–945	Psusennes 969–945

War and peace

Ramesses I, who reigned barely a year (1306–1305/1295–1294), was the founder of dynasty XIX. He had been a vizier of Horemheb, who seems to have had no sons. Horemheb, therefore, appointed Ramesses I quite deliberately as his successor in order to maintain Egypt's stability, which had been threatened so recently (see chapter 4c). Horemheb took this step, it is argued, precisely because Ramesses I had a son and was thus in a position to found a dynasty (Kitchen 1982). These peculiar circumstances may explain the strong emphasis of the dynasty XIX rulers on the continuity of the line of Egyptian kings from Menes onwards and on their vigorous defence of Egypt's territory and socio-political order. One expression of this is the list of acknowledged legitimate kings, beautifully carved on the walls of one of ancient Egypt's architectural jewels, Sety I's funerary temple at Abydos. It traces the rulers right back to Menes, the first king to rule a united Egypt (see chapter 3a); it largely excludes rulers of intermediate periods; and it collapses the whole period from Akhenaten to Ay into the reign of Horemheb. Sety I (1305–1290 (1294–1279)) presents the royal predecessors as his ancestors; he is depicted adoring them together with his young son, the future Ramesses II, who had obviously already been selected as crown-prince. Ramesses II set up a duplicate to this list in his own temple at Abydos. This focusing by the dynasty XIX kings on Abydos (Merneptah also did some work here) may be linked with the image which these kings projected of themselves as embodying the oldest and most enduring aspects of Egyptian kingship. Abydos was the place where some of the very earliest Egyptian kings were buried (see chapter 3a). It was also closely associated with Osiris, king of the dead and father of Horus, who had been killed, cut to pieces, and, according to legend, buried at Abydos. The dynasty XIX kings now built the fine mortuary temples here and so associated their own cult as dead kings with Osiris, the legendary ruler of the dead, who symbolised victory over the dangers constantly threatening Egypt.

The kings themselves continued to be buried in the Valley of the Kings as before, and the great funerary temples near Thebes (Gurna, Ramesseum, Medinet Habu) show that the city of Amun had fully regained its earlier significance. The rulers of dynasties XIX and XX endowed Thebes lavishly, the Amun cult was supplied with substantial estates and incomes, any remnants of Aten worship were removed and Amun's name re-engraved where it had been erased. Reports of the king's victories were set up here and war-booty dedicated. Most of the surviving material from the workmen's village at Deir el-Medina, on the west bank of Thebes, dates from dynasty XX, which shows how active life in and around Thebes was once more. The refounding in the eastern delta of the old centre of Avaris as a royal and dynastic capital, Per-Ramses ('The House of Ramesses'; Uphill 1968/1969; 1984; Bietak 1975; 1981/1986), was a new departure. The royal family probably had its home in this region. Significantly, the god Seth (a frontier-god, who had, with the development of the empire, come to be identified with a number of Canaanite deities, Beckerath 1984), traditionally associated with this area, forms the theophoric element of some of the royal names in this period. The royal family's connection with the eastern delta may also explain why Ramesses II commemorated the four hundredth year of the temple era of Seth of Avaris (see chapter 3e). Some hymns written in praise of Per-Ramses and its beautiful buildings have survived (Erman 1927/1968 [OI]: 206–207; 270–271; Caminos 1954: 73–82; 153–155; *ANET* 470). They describe the city as situated at the 'balance-point' between Egypt and its imperial territories to the north. The term illustrates how fully the Canaanite region had been incorporated into Egypt

All the great kings of this period acted vigorously to protect Egypt's boundaries, particularly against nomadic and landless groups in Libya and the Levant, some of whom were enrolled in the army (see chapter 8a). Sety I and Ramesses II also tried to expand Egypt's boundaries in Syria; the battle of Kadesh, fought against the Hittites in Ramesses II's fifth year, is the best-documented of these wars. Despite the triumphant language used to describe the battle, it cannot be counted an Egyptian success. But neither was it a disaster: ultimately the boundaries between the Hittite and Egyptian spheres did not change substantially. Both Egypt and Hatti had to cope with some serious difficulties around this time: Hattusili III lost the territory of Mitanni to the rising power of Assyria (see chapters 5d; 7b), and the Libyan attacks on Egypt's western borders became a chronic problem for Egyptian rulers from Sety I onwards (Kitchen 1973/1986). A great chain of fortresses was established in the reign of Ramesses II, stretching from the western delta to el-Alamein, which shows that the situation was serious enough to require permanent policing. The new problems besetting the two neighbouring empires perhaps moved them to sign a peace treaty in 1269 (1258) (see pp. 214–215). A friendly correspondence between the two courts ensued: the two kings and their queens, as well as Ramesses II's mother and one of his sons, exchanged letters (*CTH* 155–170). The friendship betwen the two states, who had been so long at loggerheads, was sealed, once and for all, in 1256 (1245) by the marriage of Hattusili III's daughter to the Egyptian king. Egyptian royal ideology demanded that this event be cast in the form of a totally unexpected plea for surrender by the Hittites, which was graciously granted by Ramesses II. The text begins with a description of Ramesses II's victories, which so depressed the Hittite king that he thought the only way out was to present his daughter together with tribute to the Egyptian ruler as gifts signifying subordination.

[Then one] came to make communication to his majesty, saying: 'Behold, even the Great Prince of Hatti! His eldest daughter is being brought, carrying abundant tribute of everything. They cover the [valleys with?] their [numbers?], the daughter of the Prince of Hatti and the [daughter of the?] great princess of Hatti among them. They have passed difficult mountains and wicked ravines. They have reached the frontier of his majesty. Let our [army?] and the officials [come] to receive them.' Then his majesty received [great] joy, and the palace was in happiness, when he heard of these mysterious matters, which were completely unknown in Egypt. So he despatched the army and the officials hastily, in order to make the reception before them.

Then his majesty took deliberate council with his heart, saying: 'How will it be with those whom I have sent, going on a mission to Djahy (Syria), in these days of rain and snow which come in winter?' Then he offered a great oblation to his father Seth, appealing to him about [it?] with the words: 'Heaven is in your hands, and earth is under your feet. What happens is what you command. May you [delay] to make the rain, the cold wind, and the snow, until the marvels which you have bestowed upon me shall reach me'.

Then his father Seth heard all that he had said. So the skies were peaceful, and days of summer fell to [hi]m, while his army went, being happy, their bodies free-striding, their hearts in joy. So the daughter of the Great Prince of Hatti marched to Egypt, while the infantry, chariotry, and officials of his majesty accompanied her, mingling with the infantry and chariotry of Hatti, for they were chariot-warriors like the troops of Ramesses II and like his chariotry, all the people of the land of Hatti being mingled with those of Egypt. They ate and drank together, being of one heart like brothers, without shunning one another, for peace and brotherhood were between them after the manner of the god himself, Ramesses II.

(All other foreign rulers were amazed at Egypt's extraordinary power; then:)

Now after [many days they] reached (the city) of Ramses Meri-Amun . . . and we celebrated the great marvels of valour and victory in the year 34, 3rd month of the second season (January). Then they ushered the daughter of the Great Prince of Hatti, who had come marching to Egypt, into the presence of his majesty, with very great tribute following her, without limit . . . Then [his] majesty saw that she was fair of face [like] a goddess. Now (it was) a great, mysterious, marvellous, and fortunate affair. It was unknown, unheard of from mouth to mouth, not mentioned in the writings of the ancestors . . . So she was beautiful in the heart of his majesty and he loved her more than anything, as a good fortune for him through [the command of] his father Ptah-tenen. Then his majesty caused that her name be made to be: the King's wife Maat-nefru-Re, the daughter of the Great Prince of Hatti and the daughter of the Great Princess of Hatti . . .

And so it was that, if a man or a woman proceeded on their mission to Djahy, they could reach the land of Hatti without fear around their hearts, because of the greatness of the victories of his [ma]jesty.

(*ARE* III §§415–424; Kuentz *ASAE* 25 (1925): 181–238;
ANET: 256–258)

This political event was recorded on stelae that have been found in Nubia (Abu Simbel and Amarah) and Upper Egypt (Karnak, Elephantine), which shows its great importance. The peace and goodwill between the two countries was a reality: when the Hittites suffered from famine in Merneptah's reign, he helped them by sending a consignment of grain. The wars fought by Egypt's later kings (Merneptah and Ramesses III) were directed almost exclusively against the Libyan frontier, pirates and landless peoples (see chapter 8a); no more wars were fought against the Hittites.

The decline of the New Kingdom

States further east, such as Assyria and Babylonia (see chapters 7b and 7d), also experienced perennial problems with similar groups at approximately the same time; by the middle of the eleventh century, both they and Egypt had lost considerable territory and their political power had shrunk. But the earliest of the four great powers to suffer were the Hittites. They were, moreover, not simply affected adversely for a while, like the others: between c. 1200 and 1150 (precise dates uncertain, see chapter 5d) the Hittite state vanished completely. The effect of this on the balance of power, on commercial interconnections and communications is difficult to gauge, but the repercussions from the disaster probably adversely affected the Hittites' political partners, such as Egypt (Liverani 1987). Certainly after the reign of Ramesses VI (1142–1134) Egypt's control of its Canaanite territories was lost. A series of dynastic crises, difficulties with maintaining security on the western frontier, famines, fluctuating grain prices and civil war exacerbated the situation and, conversely, made it harder to cope with problems that, in themselves, need not have been disastrous. By year 19 of Ramesses XI's reign (1080), the effective power in Upper and Middle Egypt was in the hands of a certain Herihor, who combined for the first time military powers with the economically important office of high priest of Amun. This implies a major political crisis, probably connected with a civil war involving the previous high priest of Amun (Amenhotep). Whatever the precise background, Herihor proclaimed a new 'renaissance era' to signal the end of the preceding confusions and the restoration of peace. Normally only kings proclaimed such eras. But in this case the king appears to have been so helpless that he had no choice but to accept this overriding of his authority: henceforth many texts used double-dates, dating by Ramesses XI's regnal years and the new renaissance era. Herihor's power extended north as far as Herakleopolis, at the entrance to the Fayum. Egypt's military security, from here down to Aswan in the south, was in his hands, and he used the Amun priesthood to shore up his power-base. Egypt probably lost Nubia at this point, although the details are obscure. At the same time, Lower Egypt was administered by Smendes (Nesbenebded), Ramesses XI's vizier, who may have been related to Herihor and was perhaps married to a daughter of the king (Kitchen

1973/1986). The 'Report of Wenamun' (Erman 1927/1966 [OI]: 174–185; Gardiner 1937: 61–76; *ANET* 25–29; Simpson 1973 [OI]: 142–155; Lichtheim 1973–80 [OI] II: 224–230; see p. 187) is set in this period: Wenamun was an emissary of Herihor, who made a voyage to Byblos to buy timber. He dates the journey in the renaissance era, and describes how he travelled down the Nile and called formally upon Smendes and his wife, Tentamun, in Tanis. They examined his letters of commendation and provided him with a ship and supplies so that he could carry out his mission. When he was in pecuniary difficulties later, he was able to send a message back to Smendes, who furnished the resources for Wenamun to make the necessary payments. The role of Ramesses XI in all this is not clear. But we should note that his reign continued to be acknowledged, that the renaissance era never completely replaced his regnal years, and, when Herihor died in 1074, the new dating system was abolished and the old regnal years used exclusively. So at no point was the king actually deprived of his official position. Only at his death, perhaps with no sons surviving, did Smendes formally take the throne for himself (dynasty XXI: 1069–945).

With Ramesses XI's death, the division of Egypt, which had come into being with Herihor, was perpetuated. The court of the new kings (dynasty XXI) was in Tanis (*c.* 25 km north of Per-Ramses, but on a different Nile branch; *Tanis* 1987; Brissaud *et al.* 1987), built with blocks pillaged from the former great capital of Per-Ramses (Uphill 1984). Thebes was abandoned as a royal burial-ground; the new rulers now had their tombs in Tanis (Montet 1952; von Känel 1984). The village of the workmen at Deir el-Medina, with its *raison d'être* removed, ceased to function. Henceforth, although the kings in Tanis claimed to be kings of all of Egypt, they actually divided rule of Egypt with the Amun establishment in Thebes. The hows and whys of this situation are extremely hard to understand (Beckerath 1951). The decline of Egypt from its position as an enormously rich imperial power, a position it seemed to hold securely only seventy years earlier, is startlingly clear. On the other hand, it is possible to exaggerate the reversal in Egypt's fortunes and position by comparison with the earlier 'age of opulence' (Aldred 1968). The 'broken obelisk' of Ashur-bel-kala of Assyria (see p. 361), dating to *c.* 1070, records a gift of exotic animals made to the Assyrian ruler, on campaign in the Lebanon, from the Egyptian king, probably none other than the shadowy Ramesses XI (1098–1069). It is also possible that an Assyrian inscribed lapis lazuli bead from this period formed part of a diplomatic counter-gift made on this occasion. This implies that Egypt's status, as an important state with a recognised influence in the Levant, continued to be asserted and acknowledged. Egypt's role in subsequent periods, as a ready haven for political exiles and refugees from states in the Levant, and a power to be called upon for support against Assyrian expansion, bears this out.

4e The New Kingdom state

The broad framework of Egypt's state and society in the New Kingdom appears unchanged in many essentials. But Egypt's acquisition of an empire, its aggressive territorial expansion and the Theban 'war of liberation', which laid the foundation of the New Kingdom, brought profound political, socio-economic and cultural transformations in its wake. One change, for example, was the increased size and wealth of the royal household as a result of the much greater power and resources at the disposition of the king that came with the creation of an empire. It became common in this period to refer to the Egyptian ruler simply as the 'great house' (*per'ao*) from which the term 'Pharaoh' comes.

King and kingship

The most emphasised aspect of kingship in the New Kingdom is that of the king as warrior, excelling in his mastery of the important weapons of war, in particular the light, two-wheeled chariot drawn by teams of horses – a novelty in New Kingdom Egypt (fig. 20). This is obviously related to the militaristic tone of the period. The young Amenophis II's detailed description of his great

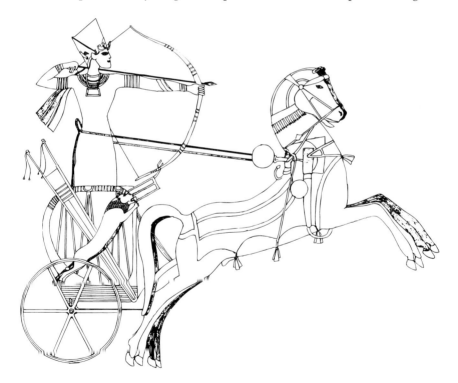

Figure 20 Egyptian king in chariot (Ramesses II, Luxor Temple)
(drawing by D. Saxon)

211

prowess in these (and other) pursuits evokes this perfectly; it was his expertise in handling horses, which demonstrated to his father that he was the son most suited to succeed to the throne, as he tells us in his 'sphinx stele':

Now then his majesty appeared as king, as a beautiful youth who was well developed and had completed eighteen years upon his thighs in strength. He was one who knew all the works of Mont (war-god); he had no equal on the field of battle. He was one who knew horses; there was not his like in this numerous army. Not one among them could draw his bow; he could not be approached in running.

Strong of arms, untiring when he took the oar, he rowed at the stern of his falcon-boat as the stroke-oar for two hundred men. Pausing after they had rowed half a mile, they were weak, limp in body, and breathless, while his majesty was strong under his oar of twenty cubits (c. 10m) in length. He stopped and landed his falcon-boat only after he had done three miles of rowing without interrupting his stroke. Faces shone as they saw him. He drew three hundred strong bows, comparing the workmanship of the men who had crafted them, so as to tell the unskilled from the skilled. He also came to do the following which is brought to your attention. Entering his northern garden, he found erected for him four targets of Asiatic copper, of one palm in thickness, with a distance of twenty cubits between one post and the next. Then his majesty appeared on the chariot like Mont in his might. He drew his bow while holding four arrows together in his fist. Thus he rode northward shooting at them, like Mont in his panoply, each arrow coming out at the back of its target while he attacked the next post. It was a deed never yet done, never yet heard reported: shooting an arrow at a target of copper so that it came out of it and dropped to the ground – (done) only by the King rich in glory, whom Amun made strong, the King of Upper and Lower Egypt, Aakheprure, a fighter like Mont.

Now when he was still a youth, he loved his horses and rejoiced in them. He was stout-hearted in working them, learning their natures, skilled in training them, understanding their ways. When it was heard in the palace by his father, the Horus, Strong-Bull, Arisen-in-Thebes, his majesty's heart was glad to hear it. Rejoicing at what was said of his eldest son he said in his heart: 'He will make a ruler of the whole land whom no-one can attack. He is eager to excel and rejoices in strength while as yet a charming youth without wisdom. Though not yet at the age to do the work of Mont, he ignores the thirst of the body and loves strength. It is the god who inspires him to act, so as to become the protector of Egypt, the ruler of the land.'

His majesty said to those at his side: 'Let him be given the very best horses from my majesty's stable in Memphis and tell him: "Look after them, master them, trot them, and manage them if they resist you."'

Then the king's son was told to look after some horses of the king's stable. He did what he was told, and Reshef and Astarte (Syrian deities included in the Egyptian pantheon as a result of the Levantine conquests) rejoiced over him as he did all that his heart desired.

He raised horses that were unequalled. They did not tire when he held the reins; they did not drip sweat in the gallop. He would yoke (them) with the harness at Memphis and would stop at the resting place of Harmakhis (i.e. Horus-on-the-horizon). He would spend time there leading them around and observing the excellence of the resting place of Kings Khufu (Cheops) and Khafra (Chephren), the justified. His heart desired to make their names live. But he kept it to himself until there would occur what his father Re had ordained for him.

(*Urk.* IV 1276–1283; *ANET*: 244–245; Lichtheim 1973–80 [OI] II: 39–43;
Cumming 1982–4, I: no. 372)

Amenophis II had this text carved on a stele after he became king and set it up in a small temple built by him for the cult of the great sphinx at Giza.[5] Several New Kingdom rulers used the area to exercise their horses, practise chariot-driving or hunt desert game, and a small palace, perhaps a hunting lodge, was maintained here (Kemp 1989 [OGa]: 219). On one such hunting expedition, Amenophis II's son and eventual successor, prince Tuthmosis (IV) fell asleep at mid-day and the sphinx, in its new aspect of Horus-on-the-Horizon, appeared to him in a dream and foretold his future kingship. He had the account of this divine experience engraved on a stele set up between the paws of the sculpture. Military campaigns could also provide the occasion for great royal hunting exploits – the two activities were closely connected, both demonstrating the king's power in overcoming threatening and untamed forces. Two of Amenophis III's beautiful commemorative scarabs (issued in his second and possibly his tenth year) recorded his catching of wild cattle and hunting of lions, respectively.

The age-old image of the king punishing Egypt's enemies was restated firmly in every conceivable context: the 'window of appearances' (*maru*), a part of the palace through which the king could look out, and down, upon his officials prostrating themselves before him and hand out rewards (Kemp 1976; 1989 [OGa]: 212–213), was flanked by scenes of the king smiting Egypt's traditional foes and leading them captive. Directly beneath the sill, heads of foreign captives were depicted. In the court of the palace at Amarna, Petrie (1894) found a painted pavement leading through the palace; the painting was of bound foreign captives and bows, which symbolised Egypts' enemies in general (Valbelle 1990). Every time the king moved through the main part of the palace he was thus literally trampling his enemies underfoot. The same imagery appears over and over again on all kinds of royal equipment, most strikingly perhaps on the baton from Tutankhamun's tomb (Desroches-Noblecourt 1963: pl. 82): the handle was carved in the form of a bound

'Syrian' and a Nubian, their feet touching; as the king wielded the cane he crushed the two subject peoples in his hand, which reinforced the image of his total supremacy over these regions.[6] The king's military might was further impressed upon his subjects by the public execution of prisoners-of-war in the course of a temple ceremony, symbolising his defeat of all 'rebels' (Schulman 1988).

Royal rhetoric, too, stressed this triumphalist stance. A famous example is the account by Ramesses II of the battle of Kadesh (1296/1275), celebrated in prose, in an epic poem, and in detailed reliefs. No one could doubt but that the Egyptian king had won a magnificent victory and the opposing Hittite army was crushed to smithereens. The sober reality, which Hittite and Ugaritic documents make quite clear, is that neither side made much in the way of territorial gains. The language in which the introduction to the Egyptian version of the later treaty with the Hittites (1269/1258; carved on stelae set up at Karnak and in the Ramesseum) is couched is very revealing. The Hittite version and the content show that it was a parity treaty, between two powers recognising each other as equal (the only one to have survived from the ancient Near East). But Egyptian royal ideology has transformed the circumstances, so that Ramesses II is presented as graciously acceding to pleas for peace from an inferior:

(Date, names and titles of Ramesses II)
On this day, while his majesty was in the town of Per-Ramses Meri-Amun, doing the pleasure of his father, Amun-Re; Harakhti; Atum, Lord of the two lands, the Heliopolitan; Amun of Ramses Meri-Amun; Ptah of Ramses Meri-Amun; and [Seth], the Great of Strength, the son of Nut, according as they give him an eternity of jubilees and an infinity of years of peace, while all lands and all foreign countries are prostrate under his sandals forever – there came the royal envoy, the deputy of the chariot-corps, Anti-h[etep], the royal envoy [. . . the royal envoy . . . the messen]ger [of the] land [Kheta . . . Tili]teshub, the sec[ond m]ess[enger] of Kheta, Ra[mose], (and) [the messeng]er of [Carch]emish, Piyassili(?), with the silver tablet, [which] the great prince of Kheta, Hattusili, had brought to Pharaoh – life, prosperity, health! – in order to beg for [pea]ce [from the majesty of the king of Upper and Lower Egypt User-maat-Re] Setep-en-Re, the son of Re, Ramse[s] Meri-Amun, given life for ever and ever, like his father Re every day.

(Kitchen 1968– : II 225ff.; *ARE* III: §§367–391; *ANET*: 199–201; *TUAT* I/2: 143–153)

Contrast this with the sober beginning of the Akkadian text of the Hittite version:

[The treaty, which] Reamas[esa Mai-]Amana, the great king, the king [of the land of Egypt, drew up on a silver tablet] with Hattusili, [the

214

grea]t [king], king of the land of Hatti, his brother, for [the land of Egypt and the land of Hatti], in order to create [great] peac[e] and great [brother]hood between them for e[ver].

(*CTH* 91; *ANET*: 201ff.; *TUAT* I/2: 136–143)

Alongside this warlike and triumphant tone, the king's divine nature was reaffirmed repeatedly, through the cult of the immortal part of his nature, the royal *ka*, for which a special temple was built at Luxor so that it was included in the annual Opet festival (see p. 191). Many more temples to the royal *ka* were erected throughout Egypt. The king was simultaneously linked with the god Amun-Re, as demonstrated by his conceptualisation as the 'listening ear' in the great Karnak temple of Amun. In this form he could be invoked to act as intermediary with the great gods on behalf of the worshipper (Kemp 1989 [0Ga]: 202; Morkot 1986). The cult of the sun, associated with the image of empire, is something else that became increasingly prominent in this period, with which the king, as the divine son of Amun-Re, was closely connected.

The jubilees (Sed festivals, see p. 148), celebrated by Amenophis III in his thirtieth, thirty-fourth and thirty-seventh years, show how traditional rituals were reworked and thus infused with a previously unknown splendour and opulence (*Aménophis III* 1993: 31–33). The details of the ancient Sed festival can only be reconstructed in part and many uncertainties remain (*LÄ* 5: 782–789), although its function as a ritual re-enactment of the coronation seems plain. It began with traditional royal acts such as building inspections and a cattle-count, followed by a procession when the king appeared in the distinctive Sed-costume for the first time. A ceremony, probably intended to aid the king's rejuvenation, was performed away from public view inside a building. Then the king, his strength ritually renewed, appeared seated in the special jubilee kiosk to receive homage from his subjects. This was followed by the king and his retinue visiting the various gods in their chapels and inviting them to join him in a procession. After changing his garments, the king ran a ritual race, presenting gifts to the gods at its successful completion. He then mounted a sedan chair and, wearing the double crown symbolising his rule over a unified Egypt, was carried ceremonially in another procession accompanied by divine standards. At the culminating point of the ceremonies, the king was presented with a bow and shot arrows to the north, south, west and east, which signalled his claim to hold sway over the whole world.

For his great jubilee celebrations Amenophis III created an immense festival site (Malkata), equipped with an artificial lake for water ceremonies (a new element in the festival), a temple and palaces. The tomb of the courtier, Kheruef, contains a summary of some episodes of the splendid festivities. At one point the king was revealed, standing within the double doors of the palace. Then the courtiers and officials were presented to him in distinct groups: officials, king's friends, chamberlains, 'men of the gateway', 'king's acquaintances', the royal barge-crew, castellans, king's dignitaries. Then came a formal presentation of royal rewards in the form of gold, 'gold of praise' (great necklaces of gold), gold ducks, gold fish, and green linen ribbons, with the highest in rank receiving the honours first. The feeding of the group thus decorated followed: this seems to have been a symbolic partaking of food of which the king too had eaten ('They were fed with food as part of the king's breakfast'). Strengthened by the repast, they had to row the royal barge about on the new festival lake, finally bringing it to rest at the steps leading to the royal throne. Kheruef's final words emphasise both the antiquity and novelty of the festival:

> It was his Majesty who did this in accordance with the writings of old. [Yet] past generations of people since the time of the ancestors had never celebrated such jubilee-rites.
>
> (Epigraphic Survey, *The Tomb of Kheruef*, Chicago (1980), pl. 28, p. 43)

Royal wives

As the figure of the king was decked out ever more with symbols of potency and divinity, an analogous development, not too well understood at present, seems to have occurred in the position of the queen. She was closely associated with female divinities, particularly Hathor. She held a number of 'priestly' offices, including at times the important one of 'god's wife of Amun', which was ritually and economically prestigious (Troy 1986). She also came to play a role in the Sed festival in the New Kingdom, although not a central one (*LÄ* 5: 785). The queen could also function, on occasion, as another avenue of approach to the king and, via him, the gods (Morkot 1986); the cult of her *ka* seems to have been very important at times; and, most strikingly, she is sometimes presented in late dynasty XVIII acting with the king in trampling foreign enemies underfoot. In this aggressive aspect she can be depicted as a female sphinx and is associated with violent goddesses, such as the lion-goddess, Sakhmet (Morkot 1986).

The New Kingdom king always had a principal wife, and a substantial number of subsidiary wives, although exactly how the ranking of royal wives worked is not clear. Where evidence exists, the king's principal wives were Egyptian. In the case of Tiye, principal wife of Amenophis III, the queen's parents were high-ranking members of the court élite: her father was a master of the king's horse, lieutenant of the chariotry, owned extensive estates in Upper Egypt and *may* have been related to Amenophis III's mother (Aldred 1968: 71–72). Among the (apparently) 'lesser' wives were princesses from the courts of neighbouring kings (a Hittite, three Mitannian, and two Babylonian princesses are definitely attested; Schulman 1979). They arrived at the Egyptian court with enormous trains, bearing gifts and dowry, and a huge retinue of maids and ladies-in-waiting, as shown by the Amarna letters (see p. 187), Ramesses II's marriage to Hattusili III's daughter (pp. 207–208), and one of Amenophis III's commemorative scarabs:

> Marvels brought to his majesty: Gilukhepa, the daughter of Shuttarna, the prince of Naharin (i.e. king of Mitanni), with the chief part of her retinue, consisting of three hundred and seventeen women.
>
> ('Marriage scarab' from Year 10: *Urk.* IV 1737–1741)

How the many royal wives and attendants were organised is not altogether certain. Specific establishments for royal women are, however, attested. One was sited near the entrance to the Fayum (Medinet el-Ghurab), where senior royal women were housed with a staff of officials, personal servants and weavers (Kemp 1978). Members of the royal family were assigned tracts of land throughout Egypt and the dominions, which provided them with revenues. Amenophis III had a large lake, possibly for irrigation purposes, excavated for his wife, Tiye, in her home town of Djarukha, presumably to increase the potential income from her domains there (Blankenberg-van Delden 1969: no. E8; Aldred 1968: 45; Morkot 1986; *Aménophis III* 1993: 56–57).

The army

The new chariot contingents, which came into use in Egypt after the Second Intermediate Period, formed the most valuable and glamorous section of the army. The chariot drivers constituted a new élite. Some of the tomb autobiographies suggest that it was considered a special honour to grow up in the 'stable of the king', i.e. the royal chariotry. The special status accorded the drivers is reflected by the fact that they were sometimes used as royal emissaries on diplomatic missions. The evidence implies that, in dynasty XVIII, it was soldiers, and particularly members of the chariot corps, who received some of the most influential court appointments. The result was that the personnel surrounding the king included a significant number of high-ranking army officers among the throng of traditional civil servants (Aldred 1968). A picture of the main groups of Egyptian officials of the New Kingdom can be gleaned from a decree found inscribed at Nauri in Nubia (Edgerton 1947). In this, Sety I addressed all responsible officers, ordering them to protect the exempt status of lands donated to his new funerary temple at Abydos; those connected with the royal horse are prominent among them:

> Decree addressed in the majesty of the royal court on this day (i.e. year 4, 5th month, 1st day) to (the) vizier, (the) magistrates, (the) courtiers, (the) councils of hearers, (the) viceroy of Kush, the commandants, (the) superintendents of gold, (the) mayors (of towns and) controllers of camps/tribes of Upper and Lower Egypt, (the) chariot-eers, (the) stable-chiefs, (the) standard-bearers, every agent belonging to the king's estate, (and) all persons sent on mission to Kush.
>
> (Edgerton 1947: 220–221, ll. 29–30)

Military officers received grants of land, in addition to being honoured with gold and allowed to keep some prisoners-of-war as slaves (see p. 189). They administered local areas, carried out mining and trading expeditions for the king, organised local commercial networks using their agricultural surplus, and acted as recruitment officers for both the army and the workforce. Following the expulsion of the Hyksos and the battles against Kush, Egypt had to be on a permanent war-footing in order to protect its newly created and enlarged boundaries and defend against attacks and renewed invasions. This resulted in the creation of a permanent military administration, headed by a 'great army general' – a position at times held by the crown-prince (Helck 1939). Another effect was the establishment and maintenance of standing garrisons abroad and within Egypt. A continuous levying and training programme was initiated to create a large and experienced military reserve which could be mobilised quickly. The state's interest and direct investment in all this is indicated by the fact that the soldiers were 'armed before Pharaoh', i.e. equipped with their fighting implements by the state. The organisation of the army was professional, divided into special units of infantry and chariotry, as well as specialised intelligence and supply troops (Schulman 1964). The Egyptian navy, essential for the transport of soldiers and supplies long distances north of Egypt, also developed in the New Kingdom (Säve-Söderbergh 1946). When Tuthmosis III planned to cross the Euphrates and attack Mitanni, the army was brought up to the north Syrian coast on ships; timber for boat-construction, which had been felled in the Lebanon, was then loaded on to carts, driven to the Euphrates, and fitted together on its banks; then king and army sailed victoriously along a stretch of the river (*Urk*. IV 889 ff.; *CAH* II, ch. 10).

This state of constant military preparedness had repercussions on the system of land tenure and land exploitation. Many veterans, for example, were given land-parcels for settlement in Egypt. These were modest plots, sufficient to support a family, which could be inherited by descendants probably with an implied obligation that a soldier be available for military training and service (Katawy 1989). Butzer (1976) has noted that Egypt was more densely settled in the New Kingdom than earlier, particularly the potentially rich Middle Egyptian area with its comparatively wide flood-plain. The shaduf, a device for lifting water used in the Middle East up to modern times, was introduced, which allowed land lying away from the river to be irrigated, especially slightly higher-lying gardens (Butzer 1976). This intensification in land-use and the bringing of extra land into cultivation must, in part, be connected to the practice of rewarding with land the many veterans (including Libyans and peoples from the Levant), who had fought in royal wars.

Egyptian soldiers did not only serve abroad, but were also stationed within Egypt to ensure peace and provide on-the-spot forces as needed. One particular service they performed was to supply the king with a regular bodyguard changed every ten days; the relief in guard-duty was marked by special provisions for the soldiers. It is impossible to quantify numbers precisely, but the impression is that most Egyptian families had at least one member in the armed services of the state. In contrast to the glories of war extolled by paeans to kings and commemorated proudly in the tombs of the upper ranks, a dynasty XX school text (Papyrus Lansing) paints a picture of the awfulness of a common soldier's life. The description is deliberately grim and exaggerates the ghastliness of such an existence, since its aim was to encourage the student to be diligent in his studies in order that he may become a scribe and avoid this dreadful fate. But the experience of many Egyptian soldiers from the poorer strata of society cannot have been too dissimilar:

> Come, <let me tell> you the woes of the soldier, and how many are his superiors: the general, the troop-commander, the officer who leads, the standard-bearer, the lieutenant, the scribe, the commander of fifty, and the garrison-captain. They go in and out in the halls of the palace, saying: 'Get labourers!' He is awakened at any hour. One is after him as (after) a donkey. He toils until the Aten (the sun-disc) sets in his darkness of night. He is hungry, his belly hurts; he is dead while yet alive. When he receives a grain-ration, having been released from duty, it is no good for grinding.
>
> He is called up for Syria. He may not rest. There are no clothes, no sandals. The weapons of war are assembled at the fortress of Sile (starting-point for the campaigns into the Levant). His march is uphill through mountains. He drinks water every third day; it is smelly and tastes of salt. His body is ravaged by illness. The enemy comes, surrounds him with missiles, and life recedes from him. He is told: 'Quick, forward, valiant soldier! Win for yourself a good name!' He does not know what he is about. His body is weak, his legs fail him. When victory is won, the captives are handed over to his majesty, to be taken to Egypt. The foreign woman faints on the march; she hangs herself <on> the soldier's neck. His knapsack drops, another grabs it while he is burdened with the woman. His wife and children are in the village; he dies and does not reach it. If he comes out alive, he is worn out from marching. Be he at large, be he detained, the soldier suffers. If he leaps and joins the deserters, all his people are imprisoned. He dies on the edge of the desert, and there is none to perpetuate his name. He suffers in death as in life. A big sack is brought for him; he does not know his resting place.
>
> (Gardiner 1937: 99–116; Caminos 1954: 373–428;
> Lichtheim 1973–80 [OI] II: 168–175)

Central administration and economy

Side by side with these new socio-political developments, there were also important institutional continuities from the earlier periods. Thus the main administrative office in the state was still that of vizier, although there were now definitely two – one responsible for the north of the country, one for the south. The all-embracing duties of the vizier are described in detail in the Theban tomb of Rekhmire, vizier of Tuthmosis III (Davies 1943). The formal installation of the vizier by the king and the instructions he received were probably part of the long tradition that had built up around this office (Kemp in Trigger *et al.* 1983 [0D]: 84–85). The vizier was, within his extensive area of power, responsible for civil order, the assessment and collection of taxes, and the maintenance of government archives and retrieval of information from them. He was also in charge of appointing and supervising officials serving under him and examined claims to land and property. He had to inspect and generally keep surveillance over local government. As part of these concerns, and crucial to the state's stability and annual budget, he received reports on the climate, in particular weather conditions that might affect agricultural production and the harvest. The expected level of the inundation was, therefore, regularly reported to the vizier, i.e. whether high or low Niles were expected, which could be gauged near Aswan by the Nilometer (see pp. 122; 135). The condition of the river affected the likely income that the state could expect, as is well illustrated by the Old Testament story of Joseph (*Genesis* 41). Finally, he also received reports from people observing the stars, which had a bearing on fixing the calendar (generally James 1984: 51–72).

The grain taxes and the grain harvest of royal estates were funnelled into the royal granary, where they was stored to be distributed as payment to palace staff and others entitled to such income, often in the form of bread (Memphis palace accounts, Helck 1961–70 IV 633–641; Kemp 1989 [0Ga]: 222–223). A proportion of the grain was also stored in the many provincial palaces, which marked the places where the king would stop on journeys up and down the Nile ('the mooring-places of Pharaoh') in order to provide official parties with supplies. The royal treasury received all other types of revenue and resource, and administered and financed royal projects, which underpinned the pre-eminent position of the rulers. Their enormous building works were the most prominent among them. Additional demands to supply the king, his retinue and other members of the royal family could also be made on the population, as required. Such demands were normally made through the local mayors (*ḥꜣty*).

This, in broad outline, is the picture of the state economy that has survived. As in earlier periods, it is not complete. The material found in the workmen's village at Deir el-Medina (see p. 188) shows that private property and production, buying and selling (grain, houses, slaves, oil, sandals, beds, clothing, animals) were a regular component of Egypt's economic life (see generally Bierbrier 1982). Values were expressed either as weights (*deben*) of silver or copper, or measures of grain or oil, and usually termed 'silver' (i.e. money); this is similar to practices in Mesopotamia (see chapter 1d) and elsewhere. A small hoard of scrap silver, simply made gold bars and rings, found at Amarna, probably represents a private person's cash wealth (Peet *et al.* 1923–51: II 59–61 and pl. XLIII). It is impossible to quantify the volume of this private economic activity in relation to the state's share of the economy, but the realities of the Deir el-Medina documentation cannot be denied: certainly the state collected and commanded great wealth and distributed some of it to officials, courtiers, members of the royal family, workmen. But this is not the whole picture: most people had access to other resources as well and engaged in numerous, quite complex economic and commercial transactions for profit. It is a mistake, as Kemp (1989 [0Ga]: 233) has cogently pointed out, to assume that any of the great pre-industrial states, including Egypt, could have succeeded in creating total state economic control where a modern industrial polity, like the Soviet Union, has failed.

State temples and popular piety

The king could, and did, as earlier, exempt many temples from taxation and from having to supply people for public labour service. The coffers of the great cult-centres were swelled by the grants of estates dotted throughout Egypt and its imperial territories. Some temple-land was worked by war-captives, but most of it was leased out to a great variety of tenants (from high officials down to simple soldiers and women), in return for a part of the revenue. The king could, in addition, dedicate booty from wars (captives, treasures, animals) directly to the temples. The temples, therefore, present another large section of the economy. It has sometimes been thought that, as a result of the many donations to temples and accompanying grants of tax-exemption, the state impoverished itself as it gradually lost this potential source of income, which fell under the control of priests. But this is a misunderstanding of the system: Egyptian 'priests' (an inappropriate word if understood in Christian terms) consisted of administrators, appointed by the king from among his officials, and of a great variety of cultic functionaries supplied by local citizens, who performed their temple duties on a rota. The temple and its property did not thus stand apart from the state – it was integral to it, providing prestige and income for many. We must also remember that the king, as a divine being in special favour with the gods, had a duty to supply the temples, which he did by bestowing material wealth directly, rather than laboriously collecting taxes only in order to hand them out again. Many of the temples, in any case, included statues and a palace of the king, or were dedicated to the royal cult (e.g. the royal *ka*, the great funerary temples), so that royal and other divine interests were closely intertwined. So the ruler protected the temple exemptions sedulously, since any depredations affected directly his own projects. The great decree of Sety I, found at Nauri in Nubia (Edgerton 1947), illustrates this well. It is wrong to see the royal protection of exempted temple incomes as the king succumbing to pressure exercised by a sinister 'priesthood' with potentially opposed interests – an anachronistic and inappropriate concept.

The Deir el-Medina finds have revealed some interesting aspects of popular piety. A number of votive stelae were dedicated in the small local shrines of the town, in the hope that the dedicators would be cured from illness, which they thought was a punishment for their sins. The stele of the draughtsman Neferabu, who was struck blind because he swore a false oath (but see Robins 1993 [0Ga]: 160) and then repented in hope of a cure, is a fine example of this:

> I am a man who swore a false oath by Ptah, Lord of Ma'at,
> And he made me see darkness by day.
> I will declare his might to the fool and the wise,
> To the small and the great:
> Beware of Ptah, Lord of Ma'at!
> Behold, he does not overlook anyone's deed!
> Refrain from uttering Ptah's name falsely,
> Lo, he who utters it falsely, lo he falls!
>
> He caused me to be as a dog in the street,
> I being in his hand;
> He made men and gods observe me,
> I being as a man who has sinned against his Lord.
> Righteous was Ptah, Lord of Ma'at, toward me,
> When he taught a lesson to me!
> Be merciful to me, look on me in mercy!
>
> > (Gunn *JEA* 3 (1916): 88–89; Bierbrier 1982: 98;
> > Lichtheim 1973–80 [0I] II: 109–110)

The people of Deir el-Medina also appealed to divine statues for decisions on matters of daily life. It was an established tenet in Egypt that, during the great processions, when the divine images sitting in their sacred boats were carried on the shoulders of priests, it was possible for the god to perform a miracle. An example of this, on the royal plane, was the way Tuthmosis III claimed to have been picked for the kingship during a procession of Amun; other grand instances concern appointments to priesthoods. In Deir el-Medina, some gods were consulted for decisions in the same way quite regularly. The early dynasty XVIII king (and god), Amenophis I, was a particular favourite with the community. The god was asked to answer specific questions or indicate which version of a petition he favoured. He indicated this by swaying towards one side or another or moving up and down, a feat not difficult to achieve given the weight of the boats with their statues bearing down on the shoulders of the carriers; the direction of movement was the decisive factor (Bierbrier 1982: 98–99).

The collapse of the New Kingdom: problems of evidence

A large proportion of the evidence for the economy and society of Egypt in the New Kingdom dates from dynasty XX, much of it from the site of Deir el-Medina. So it is chronologically and spatially limited. This raises two problems. First, it is tempting, with hindsight, to take the evidence of, for example, tomb robberies in the Valley of the Kings, or corruption among officials, as signifying the decline of the Egyptian state at this time. In other words, rather than seeing in it the random survival of evidence, which provides information on typical situations and recurring problems, it is possible to argue that the material dates from this period precisely because Egypt was in crisis and it thus signals a significant failure of the central authority to control crime. On the other hand, we must remember that modern scholars only know these events from records of trials, which show that the courts took action and the perpetrators were brought to book. There are also hints that tomb robbery was a chronic problem in a country where lavish burials were a public, advertised activity. Corruption among officials at all levels, again, is something that can hardly have occurred only at this time. So it is equally possible to argue that the material represents chance survivals illustrating typical situations. In the absence of comparable quantities of documentation from other periods, it must remain difficult to decide which interpretation is the correct one. But it is important to beware of giving the evidence a specific significance that it may not have had.

The second problem relates to the fact that so much of Egyptian daily life is reconstructed on the basis of the craftsmen's village in western Thebes. Yet these people were not typical of Egyptian peasants at all: many of them were highly trained, relatively prosperous specialists, in receipt of all kinds of extra pay and supplies from the court because of the particular work that they did (building and decorating royal tombs). When, therefore, we hear of strikes by the workmen, which could suggest widespread problems experienced by the state in meeting its obligations, and which has been taken by scholars to reflect the progressive bankruptcy of the central authority in the course of dynasty XX, caution is appropriate (see also Gentet and Maucourant 1991). What the workmen appear to be have been striking about was, in fact, lateness in providing extra rations and bonus payments, which they were entitled to as a result of the specialised work they were engaged in. Moreover, these payments seem eventually to have been made. So while the strikes certainly indicate problems of supply, closer examination shows that this was connected with disruptions caused by raids, perhaps by Libyans; further it was a technical problem of who exactly would make the extra payments, not an inability to make the provisions. The strikes and disturbances may have been a localised problem and reflect temporary difficulties only. It would, therefore, be wrong to read into this either a general failure of the state apparatus as a whole, or extensive hardship suffered by peasants throughout Egypt. The fact that we know that Egypt was experiencing problems and that it was losing control of its imperial holdings at this time must not tempt us to invest this material with a significance it may not have.

Notes

1 In the words of Alan Gardiner, 'even now there is no nobler architectural achievement to be seen in the whole of Egypt' (Gardiner 1961 [OD]: 185).
2 This view is suggested to me by J. Goody (ed.), *Succession to High Office* (Cambridge Papers in Social Anthropology), Cambridge, 1966: 10–12, who demonstrates how 'outsiders' and 'neutrals' (including women) can act as stakeholders to protect political interests in transitional periods.
3 For some unusual proposals on family relationships see Samson 1977.
4 Further survey and excavation is currently being carried out by B. Kemp and G.T. Martin (el-Amarna) and J. Spencer (Hermopolis).
5 The sphinx was an Old Kingdom sculpture representing, in the form of a sitting human-headed lion, King Chephren (Khafra, dynasty IV). During the New Kingdom, the sphinx was worshipped as a manifestation of the god Harmakhis = 'Horus-on-the-horizon'.
6 Desroches-Noblecourt (1963) argues that the bound figures were located at the bottom end of the baton, i.e. she wishes to turn the implement on its head. This is somewhat difficult to imagine and I have followed the more usual interpretation of seeing it as an example of a 'human-headed walkingstick'.

5

THE HITTITES

5a Anatolia from the Old Assyrian period to the emergence of the Hittite kingdom (*c.* 1800–*c.* 1650)

From *c.* 1650 until *c.* 1200 central Anatolia (and areas further afield) was dominated by the kings of 'Hatti-land', based at their great fortified capital of Hattusa (Boğazköy) north of the Halys river; but the dynasty appears to have originated in Kussara (location disputed: Divriği? Elbistan? Alishar? see *RLA* 6: 381–382). A problem in the history of the ancient Near East is trying to explain how the Hittite kingdom came into being, since there is no written evidence from the end of the period of the Assyrian trading settlements (cf. chapter 2c) until the appearance of this fully fledged and powerful state. The archaeological sequences, too, are difficult to relate to historical events.

The picture of central Anatolia that emerges from the texts of the merchants of Ashur is one of small independent kingdoms, each centred on a fortified city containing a citadel with a palace, and including private houses. Several principalities appear to have dominated other city-states. The largest were Kanesh (modern Kültepe), Wahshushana and Purushhattum (Hittite: Purushanda, probably modern Karahüyük-Konya), each of which is called 'country' (*mātum*) in the Old Assyrian texts. All the states were ruled by prInces (*rubā'u* – except two states near north Syria ruled by 'kings' (*šarru*)), and the palace was the dominant political institution. Apart from the princes, the Old Assyrian texts sometimes mention (using Akkadian terminology) crown-princes (*rabi similtim*, 'great one of the staircase', Garelli 1963: 61–62; Orlin 1970: 80–81), princesses and palace officials. It is possible that the bigger Assyrian commercial settlements, the *kārum*s, were attached to the larger Anatolian political centres, while the smaller ones, the *wabartum*s, were connected with smaller Anatolian cities. But this may well be much too simplified and schematic a way of understanding the situation, since certain rather important cities, such as Nenassa, appear to have had no Assyrian merchant settlement at all, while other seemingly important centres, such as Zalpa on the Black Sea,[1] had only a small *wabartum*-settlement. So other considerations probably played a part – geographical location, specific resources, networks of established interests – that affect this pattern, of which we only receive a partial, and perhaps distorted, impression from the Assyrian material.

The city-states must have maintained fairly stable and peaceful relations with each other for the Assyrians to profit from the trade in Anatolia to the extent they obviously did. But several problems of interpretation relating to political history are raised by the remains and texts, primarily from *kārum* Kanesh II and Ib. First, the city of Purushhattum appears to have played a significant role in the system of central Anatolian states. How are we to understand this? Secondly, there is the question of whether there was any shift in the political balance in the transition from period II (*c.* 1900–*c.* 1830) to Ib (*c.* 1800–1780?/*c.* 1820–*c.* 1750?, see p. 90). Finally, why were the trading settlements of *kārum* II and Ib destroyed?

In the time of *kārum* Kanesh II, Purushhattum was the only Anatolian state at whose head stood a 'great prince' (*rubā'um rabi'um*). This implies that Purushhattum held a superior position acknowledged by the other Anatolian city-states. The title by itself cannot provide enough evidence to sustain such a view; it is quite possible, for example, that it reflected an old tradition, which had lost any real significance by the nineteenth century. But another piece of evidence indicates that Purushhattum did indeed hold a sovereign position in Anatolia. This is the 'Anitta text', a remarkable document (in Hittite and Akkadian) cast in the form of a literary autobiography. Three exemplars of it have been found at Boğazköy, including a copy dating between *c.* 1650 and 1500.[2] It recounts the capture of the city Nesa (the Hittite form of Kanesh)[3] by Anitta's father, Pithana, who was king of Kussara, and then Anitta's other achievements:

> Anitta, son of Pithana, king of the city Kussara, speaks thus:
> He was beloved by the storm-god of heaven, and as he was beloved by the storm-god, [. . .] of the king of Nesa the king of Kussara [. . .]
>
> The king of Kussara [came] down from the city with great force, and took the city of Nesa in the night by force. The king of Nesa he seized, but to the inhabitants of Nesa he did no evil to anyone, [but] made [them] into mothers (and) fathers.
>
> After my father Pithana I put down in the same year a revolt. Whatever country rebelled, I defeated them all with (the help of) Siu (god).
> (ll. 13–32 are rather fragmentary; they report the capture of several cities)
>
> These words on a tablet at my gate [. . .] In future no-one shall destroy th[is tablet]! Whosoever destr[oys] it, sh[all] be the enemy of [Nes]a! For a second time there c[ame] Piyusti, king of Hatti, and those of his helpers that he had brought with him, [I . . .] them near Salam[pa]. All the lands of Zalpuwa in the midst of the sea [. . .]. Long ago Uhna, the king of Zalpuwa, had taken away (the statue) of our god Siu from Nesa

to Zalpuwa; but [aft]erwards I, Anitta, the great king, took [the statue] of our god Siu from Zalpuwa back to Nesa. But Huzziya, the king of Zalpuwa, I brought al[ive] to Nesa. But the city of Hattusa [. . . . .] I departed. But, afterwards, when it (sc. the city) suffered famine, my god Siu delivered it to the goddess of the throne, Halmasuit, and at night I took it by force; in its place I so[wed] cress.

Whosoever becomes king after me and settles Hattusa again, may the stormgod of heaven strike him (down)!

I turned my face towards the city Salatiwara. But the city Salatiwara led its troops out of the city [. . .] against (me), and I brought them to Nesa.

And in Nesa I fortified the city. After the (fortification of) the city, I built a temple for the storm-god of heaven and a temple for our god Siu.

A temple for Halmasuit, a temple for the weathergod, my lord, and a temple for our god Siu I built. Whatever property I brought back from my campaigns, with that I adorned [them].

And I spoke a vow and spoke a curse. On the same day I brought 2 lions, 70 (wild) pigs, 9 pigs who live in reed thickets, 120 wild animals(?), be they leopards, be they lions, be they stags, be they bulls, be they [. . .] to Nesa into my city.

Still in the same year I campaigned against [. . . Salatiwa]ra. The man of Salatiwara arose together with his sons and went against [. . .]; he left his land and his city, and occupied the river Hulanna.

Of Ne[sa . . .] avoided [him] and set fire to his city, and [. . .] it i[n], the troops surrounding(?) the city (were) 1400 infantry and 40 teams of horses, si[lver] (and) gold he had brought (with) him, and he had left. When I [. . .] went into battle, the man of Purushanda [brought] me gifts, and he brought me a throne of iron and a sceptre of iron as a gift. But when I came back to Nesa, I brought the man of Purushanda with me. As soon as he enters the (throne)chamber, he shall sit before me at the right.

(Neu 1974; cf. Güterbock in Tadmor and Weinfeld [OK]: 23–24)

Pithana and Anitta are said by the text to have established themselves as king and crown-prince of Nesa while still controlling Kussara, and thence conquered a number of Anatolian city-states within the bend of the Halys river, in particular Hattusa and Zalpa. Towards the end of the text, Anitta states that the ruler of Purushanda (Akkadian: Purushhattum) gave him a gift of a throne and sceptre made of iron. Anitta took the ruler of Purushanda captive and declared that henceforth he would sit at his right hand. The implications of this surrender, together with the title given to the rulers of Purushanda in the level II texts, and the fact that Anitta refers to himself in this text as 'great king/prince', have been taken to argue in favour of the view that Purushanda wielded some kind of hegemony in central Anatolia. Anitta challenged its leadership successfully, and the gift of the throne and sceptre (perhaps insignia of political power) established his right to take the title 'great prince', and replace Purushanda with Nesa-Kussara as the foremost power among the central Anatolian principalities. If this is correct, then the central Anatolian states were not only culturally homogeneous (shared language, similar political structure, common technological and artistic traditions), but were also bound together politically, as they all accepted that one state wielded superior power. But this interpretation rests, in large part, on a text of about two hundred years later, which bears all the hallmarks of extensive literary reshaping. So although Pithana and Anitta (and Anitta's son and heir, Peruwa) appear in texts contemporary with *kārum* Kanesh Ib, showing that they were historical personages, it is not at all clear that the course of events described by the Anitta-text is historically trustworthy.

If we do accept it as in essence reliable, then we can observe a shift of political power in Anatolia from the time of level II to Ib. In this view, the various Anatolian states acknowledged Purushhattum/Purushanda as supreme in the nineteenth century (i.e. *kārum* Kanesh level II). The destruction of level II and the brief period of Ic could relate to an outbreak of hostilities among the Anatolian states, which may be referred to in the letter of Anum-hirbi of Mama (Ib; Balkan 1957). The old order was re-established for a while (in Ib), but it was not very stable, and eventually Pithana of Kussara was able to capture Kanesh/Nesa. He took advantage of its central position to fortify it as a base for himself and his son, Anitta; the latter went on to reduce a number of other Anatolian cities especially in the north, such as Zalpa, Salatuwar and Hattusa, which was totally destroyed and cursed. Anitta's crowning achievement was the surrender of Purushhattum/Purushanda, which left him the most powerful ruler. Anitta's continued occupation of Kanesh/Nesa may be attested by the find of a dagger on the citadel mound at Kültepe, inscribed with the words 'Palace of Anitta the Prince', although this is ambiguous evidence, as it could be argued that it was brought there from somewhere else.

If we take the activities of Pithana and Anitta as symptomatic of the political situation in Anatolia from the end of level II onwards, then we could envisage this time as one during which various central Anatolian states vied with each other to claim hegemony of the area for themselves. The Pithana/ Anitta material could be interpreted as showing that the Kussara dynasty was temporarily triumphant within this struggle; and the destruction of level Ib was perhaps the result of renewed inter-Anatolian struggles for the 'great princeship', with cities challenging the domination of the Kussara kings. If we accept this pattern of 'warring states' as characteristic of the time from *c.* 1830 onwards, then it provides a plausible context in which eventually a ruler from Kussara triumphed, seized and built up the old ruined city of

Hattusa, and emerged as the most powerful sovereign in central Anatolia, able to impose tight control on the previously independent cities.

Most of this is speculation; it is no more than an attempt to try to visualise how the Hittite kings might have gained supreme power and could have forged a realm, given the preceding clear pattern of independent principalities. The suggestive, but admittedly very sparse, shreds of evidence only reveal a) that the dynasty of Kussara, to which the early Hittite kings also belonged, somehow gained control of Kanesh/Nesa during the early eighteenth century; b) that the language of the Hittites was later called 'Nesite', i.e. 'the language of the city of Kanesh'; and c) that the grand achievements of Anitta were preserved and recopied in the later Hittite archives.

5b Problems of chronology, sources and geography

Historical phases and chronology of rulers

It is only from *c.* 1650 on that we can begin to reconstruct Hittite history – although problems of chronology and sources still loom large, with occasional totally blank periods. For example, the period between *c.* 1590 and 1500 is only known in the barest outline, although we can place a number of kings here. Similarly, although one of the most important texts for Hittite institutional and early history dates to *c.* 1500 (the 'Edict of Telepinu', see pp. 244–248), very little is known about Telepinu himself. Again, the period from his reign down to *c.* 1430 (1420) when, with Tudhaliya I, the Hittite 'empire' phase begins, is veiled in total obscurity, not helped by intense scholarly disagreement as to which and how many of a number of Hittite royal names might be assigned to this time-span (Gurney 1974; 1979; see table 18).

The very approximate chronology of the Hittite kings depends entirely on correlations with material outside Anatolia, and yields only unsatisfactory results. No precise regnal years are preserved for any Hittite king, and there is no Hittite 'king-list' of the type preserved in Babylonia, Assyria and Egypt.[4] The later Hittite kings, beginning with Suppiluliuma I, can be roughly dated by establishing links with datable Egyptian, Assyrian and Babylonian rulers. This yields a date for Suppiluliuma I of *c.* 1370–1330 (or 1344–1322, cf. both Kitchen, and Wilhelm and Boese in Aström 1987–9 [OO]; followed by Gurney 1990). After Suppiluliuma I the Hittite kings usually introduce texts by tracing their genealogy back to him, which helps to establish at least the succession of the kings and their relationship to each other. This gives us a generation count which effectively imposes some chronological limits. On the latest, most generally accepted, view (Gurney 1979), it is probable that four rather short generations separate Tudhaliya I (*c.* 1430 (1420)) from Suppiluliuma I. Recent finds of seal-impressions at Hattusa have now established the order of the kings in this phase, and it is known that a Tudhaliya was Suppiluliuma's father (Neve 1992: 57 Abb.147). Preceding

Table 18 Chronology of Hittite kings
(All reign lengths are approximate.)

Pithana (of Kussara)	
Anitta (of Kussara)	*c.* 1750
Old Kingdom	
[Labarna ?	before *c.* 1650]
Hattusili I	1650–1620
Mursili I	1620–1590
Hantili I	1590–1560
Zidanta I	1560–1550
Ammuna	1550–1530
Huzziya I	1530–1525
Telepinu	1525–1500
Tahurwaili (?)	
Alluwamna	
Hantili II	
Zidanta II	1500–1430 (or 1420)
Huzziya II	
Muwatalli I	
Empire	
Tudhaliya I (?)	1430–1410 / 1420–1400
Hattusili II (?)	1410–1400 / 1400–1390
Tudhaliya II	1400–1390 / 1390–1370
Arnuwanda I	1390–1380 / 1370–1355
Tudhaliya III	1380–1370 / 1355–1344
Suppiluliuma I	1370–1330 / 1344–1322
Arnuwanda II	1330 / 1322–1321
Mursili II	1330–1295 / 1321–1295
Muwatalli (II)	1295–1282 / 1295–1271
Urhi-Teshub (= Mursili III)	1282–1275 / 1271–1264
Hattusili III	1275–1245 / 1264–1239
Tudhaliya IV	1245–1215 / 1239–1209
Arnuwanda III	1215–1210 / 1209–1205
Suppiluliuma II	1210– / 1205–

Tudhaliya I, a fixed point is provided by an event in the reign of Mursili I. Mursili I is known from a Hittite text to have campaigned against Babylon, a statement confirmed by the later Babylonian *Chronicle of Early Kings* (*ABC* no. 20, B rev. 11); according to this text, a Hittite raid occurred in the reign of the last king of the first Babylonian dynasty, Samsuditana. The dynasty of Babylon cannot have survived much beyond this destruction, and on the conservative middle chronology its end is placed in 1595 (short chronology: 1531). As the Babylonian conquest appears to have been Mursili's final achievement, it is usual to end his reign shortly after this, around 1590. As Mursili I was a successful king who fought many wars, scholars credit him with a reign of some thirty years. His predecessor was Hattusili I, who built up Hattusa as the capital of the emerging kingdom and campaigned very widely. His reign, too, is therefore regarded as lasting about thirty years. On the basis of these rough estimates, Hattusili I ruled from 1650 to 1620 and Mursili I, 1620–1590 – the unsatisfactory and hypothetical nature of these dates is obvious (short chronology: Hattusili I – *c.* 1560; Mursili I – *c.* 1530). For the period from Mursili I to Telepinu, the 'Edict' (see pp. 244–248) provides a thread of interrelationships, which means that Telepinu is dated to *c.* 1525–1500. In the period between 1500 and Tudhaliya I, things are very uncertain, although recent finds (Otten 1986) have confirmed the suspicion that quite a number of kings should be placed here (particularly Hantili II, Zidanta II and Huzziya II, all now attested by seal-impressions; Neve 1992: 60 Abb. 163). The kind of surprises that the Hittite sources have in store for us is shown by the fact that, in the 1970s, the seal of a previously entirely unknown 'Great King', Tahurwaili, was discovered (Carruba 1974). Where he should be fitted in, and whether he ruled for any significant length of time, is unknown, although he, too, would need to be placed within the period between Telepinu and Tudhaliya I; into the same period must now be fitted a hitherto unknown, Muwatalli (Neve 1992: 61 Abb.166). In 1986, scholars were astonished to find evidence for yet another 'Great King', Kurunta, in the thirteenth century who, perhaps for a brief time only, seized control (Otten 1988).[5]

The convention is to divide Hittite history into three phases: 'Old Kingdom' (*c.* 1650–1500), 'Middle Kingdom' (*c.* 1500–1430/1420), and 'Empire' (1430/1420–1200). The period between 1430/20 to 1360 is usually dubbed the 'Early Empire' phase, indicating that it was the time when the Hittites gradually emerged from an inglorious period of weakness as an imperial power. More recently there has been a tendency to deny the existence of a definable 'Middle Kingdom' period as a meaningful historical phase, since it implies an abrupt break and changes in political structure, language and culture for which there is little evidence. Taking the chronologial uncertainties together with the fact that the Old Hittite conventions of handwriting, orthography and grammar seem to continue smoothly, with only very gradual and steady modifications into the early Empire period, the term 'Middle Kingdom' seems inept. Further, as a result of refinements in understanding language development and writing styles from study of the well-dated and dense Boğazköy archives, it is now widely accepted that a number of texts, which were for a long time dated to some of the latest kings of Hittite history (Tudhaliya IV and Arnuwanda III), need to be redated to Tudhaliya I and Arnuwanda I. These kings now appear to have been extremely active, already campaigning very far afield, and laying the foundations on which Suppiluliuma I was able to construct a solid and lasting realm stretching from western Turkey to north Syria (Houwink ten Cate 1970).

The sources

The main body of texts, on which our understanding of the Hittite state and its history depends, has been found at the site of the Hittite capital, Hattusa (modern Boğazköy), well to the north of the Halys river (see map 8). When Laroche put together his catalogue of Hittite texts in 1971, he estimated that about 25,000 tablets had been recovered from the archives, representing perhaps one-seventh of the original total. Since then, the regular annual German excavations have continued to find inscriptions and texts – some of them quite startling, such as the large, well-preserved bronze tablet of a treaty between Tudhaliya IV and his cousin, the powerful dynast Kurunta of Tarhuntassa (Otten 1988). The bulk of the archives date from the Empire period, but they include texts, and copies of texts, composed much earlier, and dating back to the reign of Hattusili I. The majority were found in the sanctuaries at Hattusa, in particular in the 'Great Temple', but also on the royal citadel where many documents had been carefully deposited. One problem with the Hattusa texts is that they include virtually no economic, legal or business documents that help to highlight day-to-day life, government, administration and social conditions.

Until 1975, no comparable finds, except single tablets (often quite important, such as the Inandık and Tarsus land donations (cf. Balkan 1973; Riemschneider 1958; Easton 1981)), had been made at other Anatolian sites. Fortunately, the excavations by Özgüç at the site of Maşat Hüyük (southwest of Zile), between 1973 and 1979, revealed a Hittite citadel and palace (*RLA* 7: 444–446; Özgüç 1978; 1982); in two rooms of the palace were found a total of ninety-six letters, as well as seventeen inventories, an oracle text and a small fragment of a religious text. The correspondence includes letters from the king to the local commander and letters exchanged between administrative officials. Their date is not completely certain, but they probably belong to the reign of Tudhaliya III, the father of Suppiluliuma I. What the ancient name of Maşat was is also doubtful, but the suggestion that it is Hittite 'Tappiga' is very plausible (Alp 1980; cf. *RLA* 7: 442–444). Recently, 1867 tablets and fragments were found in excavations at Ortaköy (between Boğazköy and Maşat); they include religious texts and letters (some very similar to the Maşat letters); some are in Hurrian (see chapter 6a). The findspot could be an administrative building, but neither the excavations nor the texts are yet published (for a preliminary report, cf. Süel 1992). So the material for studying Hittite society and government is growing very gratifyingly.

The complexities of the large Hattusa archives are aggravated by the presence of a multitude of different languages. Practically all ancient Near Eastern text collections include material in more than one language, but the Hattusa archives are exceptional in their range: seven different languages are attested. First, there is material in the language now commonly called 'Hittite', which was in fact known as 'Nesite' (i.e. the language of Kanesh) to

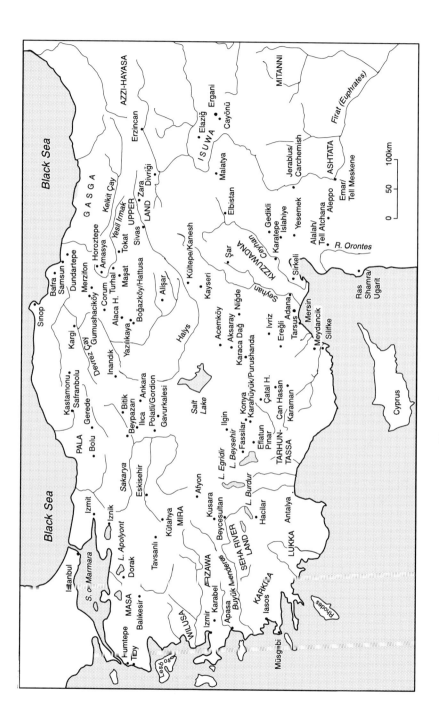

Map 8 Sites in Hittite Anatolia

the Hittites themselves. It, and two other languages in the collection, belong to the Indo-European language family (like Greek and English), and are the earliest surviving forms of this language group. The other two are Luwian, probably spoken more widely in the south and west of Turkey, and Palaic, associated with the area to the north-west and only scantily represented. There is also literature in 'Hattian', the Anatolian language probably widely spoken in central Turkey during the Old Assyrian period (see p. 93). Further texts are in Hurrian (see chapter 6a), in Akkadian, which was used for international correspondence and many treaties, and in Sumerian, which was closely associated (culturally) with Akkadian. All the texts are preserved on clay tablets written in an adapted form of the Mesopotamian cuneiform system. But some texts, mainly late-Empire royal rock inscriptions and, more regularly, royal seal legends, use a script called 'Hittite Hieroglyphs'. This writing-system is unrelated to Egyptian hieroglyphs – it operates quite differently and does not resemble it in appearance. Post-Empire texts, which employ this script, show that it was used to write Luwian (cf. chapter 8c(ii)). So far, it has only been found in monumental and formal contexts in the Hittite period; it is possible that it was written more regularly on materials other than clay, such as hide and wood. Some support for this suggestion comes from the chance find of a set of lead strips in the vicinity of Kültepe (ancient Kanesh, near modern Kayseri) dating to the early Iron Age; another set from the same period has been found at Ashur (cf. chapter 8c(ii)). They are inscribed with Hittite hieroglyphs, and the Kültepe set contains lists of items and a 'census' (Hawkins 1987). There are also occasional references in the Empire period to 'scribes on wooden tablets' (e.g. Otten 1988: 26 and 27, IV 37; for the use of wooden boards, cf. Symington *AnSt* 41 (1991)). It is thus possible that we need to reckon with documents written in Hittite hieroglyphs that have not survived, and which need, mentally, to be added to estimates of the original number of Hittite texts.

The most spectacular archaeological remains have also come from Hattusa, which a German archaeological expedition has been excavating continuously since 1906 (Neve 1992). The Hittite remains recovered so far date mainly from the later period of the Empire, when the fruits of imperial conquest and control were used to extend and rebuild major royal and sacred structures. As a result, the great palace on its rocky outcrop (see fig. 21) at Büyükkale, towering over the lower city to the north, the two bridges spanning the narrow gorge to link the growing city to the steep hill of Büyükkaya, the huge fortification walls with their cyclopean masonry and postern gates, the magnificent portals decorated with monumental sculptures, now cover the older remains, and make it difficult to determine the layout of buildings in earlier phases (Bittel 1970). The great outdoor, rock-cut shrine of Yazılıkaya (probably related to the cult of the dead king Tudhaliya IV), which was linked to Hattusa by a processional way and decorated with reliefs depicting all the

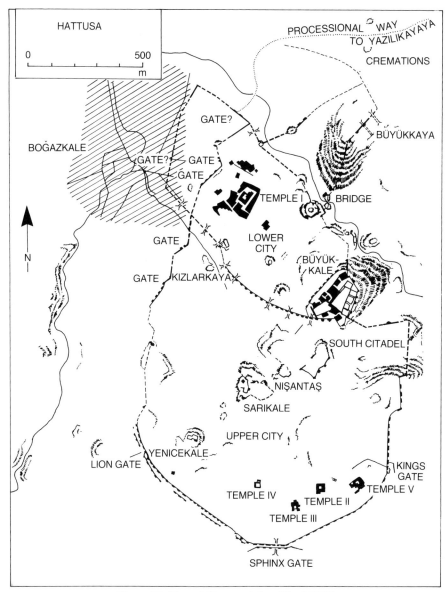

Figure 21 Plan of Hattusa (after Bittel 1970)

gods, is also a late structure (fig. 22); precise understanding of Yazılıkaya remains debated (Haas and Wäfler 1974; Bittel 1975; Güterbock 1975; 1982).

Other sites have been rather less intensively investigated: important finds have been made at Inandık (a temple of the Old Hittite period and an extraordinary 82-cm-high vase decorated in relief; Özgüç 1988), Bitik (a similar vase; Özgüç 1957), Tarsus (Goldman 1956) and Mersin in Cilicia

Figure 22 View of part of rock-shrine of Yazılıkaya (courtesy of M.S. Drower)

(fortresses in both cases; *RLA* 8: 70–72), Kültepe (Old Hittite period remains, unpublished), Maşat (*RLA* 7: 444–446) and Ortaköy (see p. 232). Alaca Hüyük (Koşay and Akok 1966) was fortified on a massive scale, comparable to Hattusa, with the gates decorated (and guarded) by carved stone figures; within, some handsome dwelling houses have been found and a couple of structures interpreted as shops. It also had some fine lively reliefs showing the Hittite king and queen engaged in a ritual, hunting scenes (lions and stags) and possibly entertainers, including a musician (with performing animal?), acrobats and a sword-swallower. Gordion, famous as the seat of the later Phrygian king, Midas (see chapter 10b), was closely linked to Hattusa throughout the Hittite period, as a number of Hittite hieroglyphic stamp-seal impressions, and the pottery, show. It lay on a major route, and may well have been the important Hittite cult-centre of Sallapa (Gunter 1990: 104–105). On the Black Sea coast, at the mouth of the Halys, the site of Ikiztepe may have been either part of the kingdom of Zalpa, or even Zalpa itself (Alkım *et al.* 1988; and note 1 below); exploration here should help to illuminate a poorly known region of great importance in the Old Hittite and earlier periods. To these sites we can add the remains of open-air shrines near springs, like the one at Eflatun Pinar, and a number of royal rock monuments located along routes, sometimes outside the boundaries of the kingdom (e.g. Karabel). The close interconnections within the territory stretching from northern central Turkey to the region east of the Euphrates are illustrated by the homogeneity of the pottery. On the western edges of the Hittite realm lay polities whose political allegiance fluctuated between the kingdoms of Ahhiya(wa), Arzawa and Hatti. Several late Bronze Age sites with Mycenaean remains are located here (e.g. Miletus, Iasos, Müsgebi), but the most striking remains are those at Beycesultan (shops, streets, stables and a palace: Lloyd and Mellaart 1955; 1956) and the imposing citadel of Troy (Blegen *et al.* 1953/1958).

Historical geography

One of the most rebarbative problems of Hittite history concerns the geography of a number of important places, especially in western Anatolia. Innumerable, obviously important, cultic and administrative centres and small countries are listed in the Hittite texts, but where they are to be located on the ground is disputed. The pioneering, and still very important, study of the political geography of Hittite Turkey was published by Garstang and Gurney in 1959. It was based (like all subsequent work) on tracing the direction of individual campaigns and plotting the places mentioned; on establishing which places occur together in similar contexts; and on the possible preservation of older Hittite place names in later classical ones (e.g. Lukka = Lycia, Karkisa = Caria, Masa = Mysia etc.). A particular focus of the study was the location of two quite powerful neighbours (and occasional enemies) of the Hittites: Arzawa and Ahhiya(wa). The latter was particularly tricky: Forrer had argued, years before (1924a; 1924b), that Ahhiya(wa) was no less than Mycenaean Greece (i.e. 'Ahhiyawa' = 'Achaeans') or some part of it, such as Rhodes, which attracted a good deal of attention from Homeric scholars. If a Mycenaean connection for Ahhiya(wa) was accepted, then it followed that a number of associated places would have to be placed in the same general direction. Although there was not (and still is not) any agreement where precisely Ahhiya(wa) was, it was generally accepted that it lay somewhere along the south-western coast or adjacent islands where Mycenaean settlement is attested. In 1968, the scholars McQueen and Mellaart challenged this on the basis of both archaeological and textual evidence: they placed Arzawa around Smyrna and Ephesus (i.e. further west than usual) and clustered associated countries from here in a northerly direction, so that the Lukka lands and the Seha River Land were placed along the Sea of Marmara, with Karkisa and Masa nearby. As Ahhiya(wa) was closely connected with Lukka and the Seha River Land, it follows that it should also be placed in this northern region, and in a neat turning around of the earlier approach they placed Ahhiya(wa) in the area of Troy. The theory was taken even further in the 1970s, when it was suggested that Ahhiya(wa) might be placed in Thrace. This geographical reconstruction is the one that has, naturally, been adopted by McQueen in his general textbook on Hittite Anatolia (McQueen 1986 [0Ge]). But throughout the 1980s more and more scholars have been arguing in favour of the traditional placing of Ahhiya(wa), Arzawa and hence associated places, such as Lukka (Singer 1983; Güterbock 1983; Bryce 1989). So, at the moment the map of Hittite Anatolia as set up by Garstang and Gurney (1959), with some refinements, is once again the one with which most scholars are operating (for an excellent, balanced assessment of the Ahhiya(wa) problem, cf. Gurney 1990: 38–47). The debate helps to illustrate the extreme uncertainties that exist about this fundamental question; until it is fully clarified (and that is a real possibility given the constant finding and publication of new texts), Hittite policy in the western area of Turkey and relations with the Mycenaean states cannot be defined.[6]

5c The Hittite Old Kingdom (c. 1650–c. 1500)

Some very interesting historical texts exist for reconstructing the period between c. 1650 and c. 1500. Where they are not fragmentary, they have a distinctive, sophisticated and lively form. There are historical epics, one of which concerns the siege of Urshu in north Syria (Güterbock 1938), and legends, such as the tale of 'The Queen of Kanesh' (Otten 1973), treaties, collections of anecdotes, a very detailed annalistic account of the campaigns of Hattusili I (Imparati and Saporetti 1965) and an edict known as the 'political testament of Hattusili I'.

Hattusili I's political testament[7]

The Great King Tabarna spoke to the warriors of the assembly (*panku*) and to the diginitaries: 'Behold I have fallen ill. The young Labarna I had proclaimed to you: "He shall sit (upon the throne)." I, the king, called him my son, embraced(?) him, exalted him and cared for him continually. But he showed himself to be a young man not fit to be seen(?)! He shed no tears, he showed no sympathy; he is cold and heartless. I, the king, have summoned him and made him come to my couch (and said): "How now? No-one will (in future) bring up the child of his sister as his foster-son. The word of the king he has not laid to heart; but the word of his mother, that snake, that he has laid to heart. And his brothers and sisters continually addressed to him unfriendly words and to their words he has hearkened. And I, the king have heard it. I will set feud against feud. Enough! He is my son no more!" Then his mother bellowed like a cow: "They have torn asunder(?) the womb in my living body – me the strong cow! They have ruined him, and you will kill him." – Have I, the king, done any evil? Have I not made him priest? I have always promoted him for his good. But to the wishes(?) of the king he has not shown consideration; how can he show consideration to the wishes of the subjects of the king(?) in(?) Hattusa? His mother is a snake!

(Hattusili contemplates the treachery, disloyalty and civil war which his nephew's appointment will surely bring about. These considerations have led him to choose another successor; so:)

Behold Mursili is now my son! Him you must recognise, him you must set (upon the throne). . . . And in the hour when a call to arms goes (forth) or perchance a serious rebellion(?) occurs, you, my servants and chieftains, must be at hand to help my son. . . .

(The king exhorts his officers to be loyal to Mursili, to protect him and go on campaign with him. Examples of rebellions by members of the royal family are recounted. Hattusili identifies a female relative ('the daughter') as a particular trouble-maker, whom he banished. These episodes are warnings to Mursili that he must heed Hattusili's words:)

Till now no-one of my family has obeyed my will; but you are my son, oh Mursili, you must obey it! Keep your father's word. If you keep your father's word, you shall eat bread and drink water. When maturity is in you, then eat two or three times a day and care for yourself well! And when old age is in your heart, then drink as much as you want! and (then) you may set aside your father's word!

(More warning examples of what happens to officials who do not obey the king's ordinances are recounted. In view of these, says Hattusili:)

But you must keep my – the great king Labarna's – words! So long as you keep them, Hattusa will stand high and your land will remain in peace. You will eat bread and drink water. But if you do not keep them, your land will pass (under foreign domination). And you must show respect to the affairs of the gods: their daily food and drink and their [bread-crum]bs(?) (and) their porridge must be set forth. And you (Mursili) shall not delay nor relax! If you delay, (it will mean) the same old mischief. So be it!' Great king Labarna spoke to Mursili, his son: 'My words I have given you; and this tablet they shall read out before you continually month by month. So you shall impress my words and my wisdom on your heart, and shall always rule over my servants and the chief citizens. If you see anyone to be guilty of an offence, whether anyone sins before the god, or utters any (unseemly) word, always consult the assembly (panku). (Any such) utterance must be stopped for the sake of the assembly. What, my son, (has been laid) in (your) heart, act upon it always.' Great king Labarna says to (the lady) Hastayar (his queen): 'You shall not obstruct me! – Let not the king nor the courtiers speak thus of her: "This person is continuously consulting the old women (sorceresses)!" – nor may the king say thus of her: "Is she still consulting the old women? I will know nothing of it!" – So, do not obstruct me! No! Always consult me alone, and I will reveal my words to you (i.e. through consulting the dead king's spirit?)!

Wash my body, as is seemly, hold me in your bosom, and in your bosom protect me from the earth!'

Tablet of Tabarna: when great king Tabarna fell ill in Kussar and called the young Mursili to the kingship.

(*CTH* no. 6; Sommer and Falkenstein *ABAW* 16 (1938))

This extraordinary document (bilingual: Akkadian and Hittite) projects the reader into the midst of a formal gathering at the Hittite court, assembled around the deathbed of the king to hear his final decisions, which he himself orders are to be written down and regularly read to his successor for his instruction. Difficulties had beset the country: the nephew, whom Hattusili had designated as his successor, had plotted against him together with his mother. Both are banished and assigned resources to keep body and soul together – the king stresses that he is refraining from taking vengeance although he could have done so. Mursili, Hattusili's grandson, possibly still quite young, is presented to the assembled dignitaries as the new successor, and all are given advice for the future conduct of affairs in Hatti. Even the ill king's wife is enjoined to stick to his arrangements, to consult his spirit only (not sorceresses) and, finally and touchingly, to see him properly buried (at least, that seems to be the meaning). Although Hattusili I is the first properly attested Hittite ruler, there is already a defined political structure in place with developed institutions such as an assembly (*panku*), elders of cities, priests and military commanders.

The preamble to the later Telepinu Edict (*c.* 1500; see pp. 244–248) refers to a king and queen who preceded Hattusili I, called Labarna (and its variant 'Tabarna') and Tawananna. It is possible that these were the names of the first Hittite ruler and his wife. But the testament of Hattusili I shows that he was himself more generally called L/Tabarna, and it is clear that later 'labarna' and 'tawananna' were titles of the Hittite king and queen. It is thus possible that the notion that Labarna was the name of the first Hittite ruler is the result of a later confusion; perhaps the royal title was attached to a supposed predecessor of Hattusili, who was no more than a conflation of earlier kings, representing an idealised form of Hittite monarchy and meaning basically 'his majesty'. What is certain is that Hattusili I had predecessors, since he himself refers to them. But where these kings ruled is unknown, since the Hattusa archives contain nothing earlier than Hattusili I, and his name suggests that he was perhaps the first to make Hattusa the capital. It is possible that the base of his predecessors was Kussara, which was obviously still an important royal centre since it was here that Hattusili called his court together for the important decree demoting the previously appointed successor and proclaiming the new one.

The wars of Hattusili I and Mursili I

Hattusili I fought many wars and extended Hatti's control substantially. His 'annals', extant in Akkadian and Hittite versions, and almost certainly

240

composed in his lifetime, contain valuable information about his conquests. The 'annals' may originally have been engraved on a statue, made from gold acquired as booty and dedicated by the king to his patroness, the sun-goddess of Arinna:

Thus speaks Tabarna Hattusili, the Great King, king of the land of Hatti, the man of Kussara: He reigned as king in the land of Hatti, (he) the Tawananna's brother's son. He campaigned against Sanahuitta (to the south-east) and did not destroy it, (but) destroyed the surrounding regions.

I left troops behind to occupy it in two places and the sheep-pens (that were there) I gave to the occupation force.

After that I campaigned against Zalpa (several places have this name: one is located in north Syria, another on the Black Sea coast at the mouth of the Halys) and destroyed it, and took away its gods and three two-wheeled *MADNANU*(-wagons) I gave to the sun-goddess of Arinna (most important female deity of Hittite pantheon).

A bull/cow of silver, a fist of silver I gave to the temple of the weathergod (chief male deity of Hittite pantheon), those (gods) who were left I gave to the temple of Mezzulla (daughter of the weathergod and the sungoddess of Arinna).

In the following year I campaigned to Alalha (Alalah, North Syria) and destroyed it. After that, however, I went to Warsuwa. But from Warsuwa I went to Ikakala, but from Ikakala I went to Tashiniya, and these lands I destroyed. But (their) goods I took away from them, and I filled my house to the top with the goods.

In the following year, however, I went to Arzawa (west/southwest Turkey), and I robbed them of cattle (and) sheep. But behind my back the enemy came from Hurri-land into my country. (Then) all the lands became hostile to me and the city of Hattusa alone remained. The Great King Tabarna, beloved of the sungoddess of Arinna (am I), and the sun-goddess of Arinna set me upon her lap and she took me by the hand and went before me in the battle. I went to do battle in Nenassa (west of Kanesh on route to Purushanda) and when the people of Nenassa beheld me they again opened (their city-gates).

But after that I went to do battle in the country of Ulma, and the people of Ulma opposed me twice in battle and twice I fought against them, and I destroyed Ulma and in its place I sowed cress and (its) seven gods I brought to the temple of the sun-goddess of Arinna, a bull/cow of silver, the goddess Salkatiti, the mountain(god) Aranhapilanni (I brought there). Those gods, however, that were left I gave them to the temple of Mezzulla.

(Hattusili recounts his other successes in subjecting cities; then:)

241

In the following year I went to the country of Zaruna and destroyed Zaruna. To Hassuwa (on route to Commagene) I went, and the people of Hassuwa opposed me in battle. Troops from the land of Halap (Aleppo) were with them to help, they attacked me in battle and I fought against them. In a few days I crossed the river Puruna (Euphrates) and with my feet I trampled the country of Hassuwa like a lion and like a lion I slew (it) and I brought dust (down) upon them and I took all their possessions with me and filled Hattusa (with it).

(Hattusili lists the booty he took and the dedications he made to various shrines; he also mentions the execution of a local ruler and a night-attack on Zippasna. Then:)

I went to Hahha (Elbistan/Taurus passes) and three times I brought battle into the city gates of Hahha. I destroyed Hahha, but its goods I took away and brought them to Hattusa, my city. Two complete (four-wheeled) carts were loaded with silver.

One (two-wheeled) *MADNANU*(-wagon), a stag of silver, a table of gold, a table of silver, these gods of Hahha, a bull of silver, a ship whose bows were covered with silver. The Great King Tabarna, the hands of slave-women I removed from the millstones and the hands of slaves I took away from (forced) labour and freed them from forced labour and corvée, loosened their hips, and bestowed them on the sun-goddess of Arinna, my lady. This statue of gold I made, and set it up before the sun-goddess of Arinna, my lady. Also the wall I covered with silver (from) the bottom (to) the top. Two statues of alabaster I brought her.

A (two-wheeled) wagon of silver the king of Timana had sent to the Great King (as a gift), but I brought it to the sun-goddess of Arinna. The Mala-river (Hittite name for Euphrates) no-one had crossed. I, the Great King Tabarna, crossed it with my (own) feet and also my army crossed it behind me with its (own) feet. Only Sharrukin (i.e. Sargon of Agade) had crossed it before me, against the troops of Hahha he had fought, but he had not done anything to the city of Hahha, had not burnt it down with fire and had not shown its smoke to the weathergod of heaven.

(I,) the Great King Tabarna, destroyed Hassuwa and Hahha and gave them over to fire totally, but their smoke I showed to the weathergod of heaven, and (the king) of Hassuwa and the king of Hahha I yoked to the (four-wheeled) cart.

(Subscript) Tablet . . . the manly deeds of Hattusili.

(*CTH* no. 4; Imparati and Saporetti 1965; *TUAT* I: 455–463)

The text provides invaluable evidence on the conduct of war in Anatolia in this period, and the methods by which the Hittite kings attempted to impose control and maintain it over conquered regions (Houwink ten Cate 1983/4).

The first campaign was aimed at areas to the north, where Hattusili installed permanent garrisons and allotted sheep to the troops for their sustenance. In the second campaign, he ravaged and destroyed towns and cities in north Syria, which implies that the Hittites wielded some kind of control over Cilicia, although this is not supported by any archaeological evidence. In the third 'year', Hattusili suffered a setback: while he was engaged on a cattle-raid in Arzawa far to the west, the Hurrians attacked the eastern territory of Hatti. This suggests that the new state of Mitanni was growing in power and reacted to the threat posed by Hittite expansion into north Syria (cf. chapter 6a). The Hurrian attack seems to have been disastrous and shows the fragility of Hittite political control at the time – all the conquered areas revolted, and only Hattusa and its immediate environs, the heartland of Hatti, remained loyal to the king. But the king renewed and intensified his wars of conquest after this setback, having turned to the gods for help in the hour of defeat. His subsequent successes, greater than the earlier ones, were all due to his protectress, the sun-goddess of Arinna, who personally comforted him, guided him by the hand, and walked alongside him in battle. Immediately, the king's fortunes improved: places opened their gates at his approach (Nenassa); attempts at resistance by direct confrontation in battle were fruitless, and punished with destruction (Ullama); places 'that had revolted' were besieged, destroyed and the population deported and dedicated to the sun-goddess of Arinna. A renewed attack on Hassuwa (one of the wealthy north Syrian centres) was so successful that the local population expelled their king; another city was attacked successfully under cover of night. The great centre of Hahhum was taken after three battles and burned. The kings of Hahhum and Hassuwa were yoked to the wagons on which the booty from their countries was piled, and ignominiously forced to draw the loaded carts back to Hattusa. The cult-centres of the principal deities of Hatti were enormously enriched by the massive plunder, especially from the north Syrian cities. The regular income of the Hittite gods and their cults was increased by settling deported people on their estates. This is, interestingly, represented as a 'freeing' of these people from earlier oppression – a way in which later Hittite kings, too, sometimes represent their acts of deportation. As a result of Hattusili's resounding victories, a neighbouring king hurried to send a gift of a silver wagon to the Hittite ruler, which he presented reverently to the sun-goddess of Arinna, without whose help his successes could not have been achieved. Looking back on his achievements, he compares himself to the great, now legendary, conqueror, Sargon of Agade (chapter 1c), whose exploits were obviously well known in Hatti, and decides that he has managed to outdo him by his destruction of Hahhum. His stature thus implicitly rivals, even outstrips, that of the greatest hero and empire-founder of the past.

The reign of Mursili I is less well documented, although his main exploits are clear. His overall aim seems to have been to consolidate his grandfather's achievements. Thus Mursili was able to destroy Aleppo, the powerful kingdom which had dominated north Syria for centuries (see chapter 2d) and had supported neighbouring cities against Hattusili's attacks. Another campaign was Mursili's raid on Babylon, perhaps allied with Aleppo, and obviously still considered a powerful state despite its shrinking territory (cf. chapter 2e). The reasons for the sudden Hittite expansion, and how the kings had the resources to mount their frequent campaigns and raids, some of them far distant from Hatti and involving long sieges, are unclear. The acquisition of land, manpower, control of routes and access to valuable ore-deposits (copper and lead) must have been a motive. Conflict and rivalry with Zalpa on the Black Sea; protecting Hittite interests in the east against the newly emerging power of Mitanni; defending the north-eastern frontiers against the Gasga people, who figure prominently later as exceptionally troublesome neighbours in the Pontic Alps; concern about the development of important centres in the west forging links with the Aegean and beyond – all these are possible factors in understanding Hittite policy, but remain speculative.

The Edict of Telepinu

Sudden and rapid territorial expansion often creates internal problems: the prizes to be gained from wielding power are that much greater, the consequences of not sharing in the profits that much more devastating. This may be what lies at the heart of the recital of bloody murders and usurpations which dominate Hittite history for the next seventy years: from the assassination of Mursili I (*c.* 1590) by his brother-in-law and cupbearer, Hantili, aided and abetted by Zidanta, until the accession of Telepinu (*c.* 1525). The long chronicle of dark deeds is contained in the 'Edict' of Telepinu, the king who stands at the end of this time of political chaos. He presents himself as resolving, once and for all, the terrible internal conflicts which brought Hatti's fortunes to a very low ebb. The text (like the preceding ones, preserved in a Hittite and an Akkadian version) is also the chief source for the history of this period. It is one of the most important sources for Hittite political institutions, and, therefore, worth quoting in full:

> Thus (speaks) Tabarna Telepinu, the Great King: Once Labarna was Great King, and his sons, his brothers, his in-laws, the people of his clan/family and his soldiers were collected around him (in harmony). The land was small. Wherever he campaigned, he held the lands of the enemies conquered with (his strong) arm.
>
> He constantly destroyed the (enemy-)lands and conquered the lands in their entirety and made them into the frontiers of the sea (i.e. he extended his realm as far as the sea). When he came back from campaign, each of his sons went somewhere in a (particular) land: Hupisna (Kybistra, modern Eregli), Tuwanuwa (Tyana, modern Bor), Nenassa,

Landa, Zallara, Parsuhanda (Purushanda, probably modern Karahüyük-Konya), Lusna; and they administered the (individual) countries, and the individual big towns were added to it.

After that Hattusili reigned as king and his sons, too, his brothers, his in-laws, the people of his family/clan and his soldiers were gathered (around him in harmony). Wherever he campaigned, he too held the lands of the enemy conquered with (his strong) arm.

He constantly destroyed the (enemy-)lands and subjected the lands entirely, and he made them into the frontiers of the sea. As soon as he returned from campaigning, each of his sons went somewhere in a (particular) country, and in his (sc. Hattusili's) hand the individual great cities were nourished.

But as finally the subjects of the royal sons became disloyal and began to consume their houses and to become powerful against their lords, they started to shed their blood.

But, as Mursili reigned as king in Hattusa, his sons, his brothers, his in-laws, the people of his clan/family and his soldiers were gathered (around him in harmony), and he held the land of the enemy conquered with (his strong) arm. He conquered the lands in their entirety and made them into the frontiers of the sea.

He went to Halpa (Aleppo) and destroyed Halpa, and the captive population of Halpa and their possessions he brought here to Hattusa. But after that he went (on) to Babylon and destroyed Babylon. He fought against the Hurrians and the captive population and their possessions he displayed in Hattusa.

Hantili was cup-bearer (at that time) and had Har[apsili] the sister of Mursili as his wife. Zidanta led Hantili [. . .] on, and [they planned] an evil deed. They murdered Mursili and shed (lit. 'made') blood.

And Hantili was afraid [. . .]

[And] Hantili too reached Tegaramma (and began) to [spea]k (thus): 'This (is), what I have done. I listened [. . . to the bad words of] Zidanta'. [As soon as] he [ru]led [as king] (however), the gods sought the blood [of Mursili].

(Very damaged at this point; an invasion of the Hurrians is mentioned; then)

As soon as Hantili [wa]s old and about to become a god (i.e. die), Zidanta murdered [Piseni] the son of Hantili, together with his sons [and also] the nobl[est] of his servants he murdered

And Zidanta also ruled as king and the gods sought the blood of [Pi]seni and made Ammuna, his own son, into his enemy and he murdered his father Zidanta.

And Ammuna also ruled as king and the gods sought the blood of his father Zidanta, and grain, wine, cattle, sheep to him, into his hand, they did not [. . .]

But the land became hostile against him: Ha[rt]agga, [. . .]la, Galmiya, the land Adaniya (Adana region), the land Arzawiya (Western Asia Minor), Sallapa (Gordion?), Parduwata, Ahhulassa. Wherever (his) soldiers campaigned, they did not return victorious. As Ammuna became a god, Zuru, the commander of the body-guard, sent secretly at that time a son of his family, Tahurwaili, the golden lance man, and he murdered the family of Tittiya together with his sons.

He (sc. Zuru) also sent Taruhsu, the courier, and he murdered Hantili together with [his] sons. Huzziya ruled as king. Telepinu had Istapariya, his (sc. Huzziya's) first-rank sister (as wife). Huzziya would have killed them, (but) the matter became known (before its time), and Telepinu chased them away.

To his five brothers he assigned houses (property) (saying): 'May they go (and) stay (there)! May they eat (and) drink, but noone shall do evil to them! I say: These have done evil to me, but I [shall not do] evil to them.'

As soon as I, Telepinu, seated myself on the throne of my father, I campaigned in Hassuwa (on route to Commagene) and destroyed Hassuwa. My troops were also in Zizzilippa, and there was a battle in Zizzilippa.

As soon as I, the king, came to Lawazzantiya (eastern Cilicia), Lahha [was hostile to me] and made Lawazzantiya rebellious to me. [The gods] gave him into my hand. The noblest was [. . .], the chief of the 'inspectors over a thousand', Karruwa, chief of the chamberlains, Inara, chief of the cupbearers, Kil[. . ., chief of the . . .], Tarhumimma, chief of the heralds, Zinwaseli and Lelli, many, and they sent secretly to Tanuwa.

I, the [kin]g, did not k[no]w (it). Huzziya and his brothers they killed there. As soon as I, the king, heard it, Tanuwa, Tahurwaili [and] Taruhsu were brought to me and the assembly (*panku*) sentenced them to death. But I, the king, spoke: 'Why should they die? One should hide them from (the public) eye(?)' And I, the king, made them into clear peasants, took their weapons from their shoulders and gave them the yoke. The blood(-deeds within) the 'Great Family (i.e. royal clan)' became great: Istapariya, the queen, died. After that it happened (that) Ammuna, the crown-prince, died. Then 'the men of the gods' spoke also: 'Behold, the blood(-deed) has waxed great in Hattusa.' Then I, Telepinu, called the assembly (*panku*) together in Hattusa (and spoke to it thus:) 'From now on no-one shall do evil to a son from the (royal) family in Hattusa and draw a knife on him.

Only a king's son of the first rank, a son, shall be king. If there should be no king's son of the first rank, whosoever (is there) as a son of the second rank, he shall (then) become king; if there is no male royal child, whatever daughter of the first rank (is there), a man who will marry into her house shall be taken for her and he shall become king.

He who shall become king after me (about him) his brothers, his sons, his in-laws, the people of his clan and his soldiers shall gather (in harmony). And if you come and hold the land of the enemy conquered with (your strong) arm, you shall not say: '(With this act) I make it pure!' You do not make it pure (in this way), (rather) you are really oppressing. Of the (royal) family kill no-one, it is not good!

Further, he who becomes king and plans evil against (his) brother (or his) sister, you (are) the assembly (*panku*) for him. Simply say to him: 'That matter is a blood-deed. Consult the tablet! Earlier the blood-deed was great in Hattusa, and the gods have imposed (it) on the "Great Family".'

Whoever does evil among (his) brothers (or his) sisters and (in doing that) looks at the head of the king (i.e. maintains that it is the king's responsibility), call together an assembly (*panku*, for him). If he is found guilty, then he shall be beheaded. But (he) shall not be killed secretly as with Zuru, Danuwa, Tahurwaili and Taruhsu. Evil shall not be done to his house, his wife (and) his children. If a royal son acts criminally, he shall also pay with his head, but no evil shall be done to his house and his children. For whatever reason royal sons may be executed, (it has) no (meaning) for their houses, their fields, their vineyards, their slaves, their slave-girls, their cattle (and) their sheep.

Now, if any royal son commits a crime, he shall pay with his head, but you shall not harm his house and his son. It is not justice to give (away) a person or a tool of a royal son. But those who do these evil things, the [. . .], the house-administrators, the chief chamberlains, the chief of the body-guard and chief of the wine, [by] desiring to take the houses of the royal sons and speaking thus: 'If only this town were mine!', they are harming the lord of the town.

Now, from this day on in Hattusa, remember in your own interest this matter, you chamberlains, body-guards, 'gold-servants', cup-bearers, table-attendants, cooks, heralds, stable-lads, (and) inspectors of a th[ousand]. As for Tanuwa, Tahurwaili and Taruhsu they shall be a warning to you. Henceforth if someone does something evil, be it a house-administrator or a chief chamberlain, chief of wine, chief of bodyguard, chief of the inspectors of a thousand, whether (it be) the last (or) the first in rank, d[eal] with it as an assembly (*panku*) and consume him with your teeth.

(Several very broken sections of text impossible to understand; they include a long list of 'seal-houses' in Anatolian towns (see p. 272). This is followed by:)

The matter of blood(-deeds is) as follows: He who sheds blood, what the 'Lord of the blood(-deed)' then says, if he says: 'He shall die!' then he shall die. But if he says: 'He shall pay the penalty!' then he shall pay the penalty, but for the king (it is) nothing. (In the case) of witchcraft in Hattusa, purify the matter! Whoever knows the witchcraft within a family, take him out of the family and bring him up to the gate of the palace; [wh]oever does not bring him forward, it will come (to pass, that) that person will suffer evil in his (own) house.
Colophon): Tablet 1 of Telepinu, completed.
(*CTH* no. 19; Sturtevant and Bechtel 1935: 175–200; Hoffmann 1984;
TUAT I/5: 464–470)

This is a fundamental text; partly, of course, because of the help it gives in reconstructing the history of this period, which would otherwise be practically blank. But even more important is the information it provides for the structure of the Hittite state, especially the rules laid down to regulate the royal succession. Rather like the Hattusili I testament, it places the reader inside the Hittite court, with the king rehearsing this time the history of Hatti, in abbreviated form, from its beginning, in order to show how the country has declined from its former glory. This decline is directly attributable to the sin committed, beginning with Hantili, in trying to seize power through murder. Murder inevitably breeds murder and the country collapses ever more, suffering enemy invasions, defeats in battle, and falling prey to chronic court intrigues.

The presentation of past history in the edict was intended to be a powerful indictment of Telepinu's predecessors, which justified his own seizure of the throne, since he himself had no especial claim to it (see the absence of any genealogy at the beginning). The righteous conduct of the first three kings is set within a golden age of perfect harmony, with a note of discord creeping in during the transition to Mursili's reign; but that disturbance was rapidly dealt with by the king, and success followed with the grand triumphs over Aleppo and Babylon. The complex pattern of murders, parricides and usurpations that then ensues is not always clear in detail, and the precise family relationships between the various actors are at times very obscure. But the overwhelming message is driven home by means of a significant contrast: Hantili, the brother-in-law of Mursili, to whom Mursili had done no wrong, put an end to the golden age by his foul murder of the king; conversely, Telepinu, the brother-in-law of Huzziya and threatened with murder by him, put an end to the years of horror by the bloodless deposition of Huzziya, whom he exiled together with his brothers, sparing their life, although he might easily have had them executed ('I say: "These have done evil to me, but I shall not do evil to them!"'). Instantly, the campaigns of the Hittite king were once more blessed by success, underscoring the rightness of his act, which had restored political health to Hatti: the golden age had been ended by unjustifiable bloodshed, bringing disaster at home in the form of crop-failures, and abroad in the form of defeats for the Hittite armies; but now, through the exercise of mercy, the golden age has been restored (Hoffner 1975).

There follow legal regulations on which the newly restored state is to rest: a universally recognised order of succession, which will eliminate ambiguities and the high-handed behaviour of kings. As a result, the king's actions are circumscribed, and he becomes accountable to the gods and the assembly (*panku*), although the assembly's power to punish is limited to the individual king or prince – their families are excluded from sentence. This royal ordering, whereby the king himself is placed under the legal power of an assembly, is remarkable. The term translated as 'assembly', *panku*, means in essence 'all', and it has been variously regarded as a council of all nobles or a council of fighting men. The edict itself suggests that it included all the high military commanders and court-officials, but no one else (Beckman 1982). Because of the powers devolved on it by the decree, it has been argued that the *panku* originally had the power to elect the king. But this is not supported by other evidence – if anything, the opposite seems to be true (see Hattusili's testament, pp. 238–240): the king alone appointed his successor and presented him to the *panku*. There is, moreover, no subsequent evidence that the *panku* played a signficant political role – in fact, it seems to fade out of the picture altogether. There is not a single attested instance of the *panku* ever exercising independent power: all the indications are that it was assembled at the command of the king, and served to suggest possible action which the king could modify, perhaps even override (cf. the Telepinu Edict itself). Telepinu's regulations appear to make this assembly of dignitaries (from which irregular attempts on the throne were most likely to come) itself responsible for upholding the royally ordered rules of succession: i.e. it may have been a way of setting the nobles to police themselves, report on each other to the king and so compete for political advantages *vis-à-vis* the monarch.

As far as we can tell, the rules for succession enunciated by Telepinu were respected. This is not to say that irregular accession and usurpation were now at an end, but the appalling sequence of events described by Telepinu seems never to have recurred. When, much later, Hattusili III (1275–1245/1264–1239) deposed his nephew, Urhi-Teshub, and took the kingship himself (see pp. 258–259), he was at pains to stress his initial, scrupulous action in ensuring that Urhi-Teshub acceded, despite not being the son of a wife of the first rank; Urhi-Teshub, maintains Hattusili, repaid his avuncular care by trying to undermine Hattusili's own position and bringing unfounded charges of treason against him; only then, when his very life was at risk, did Hattusili act, with support from other nobles, to depose and exile Urhi-Teshub. Similarly, right at the very end of the Hittite empire, a situation arose when there were no royal offspring, and the only candidate for the throne was the brother of the deceased monarch. The king carefully explained how this had come about:

> Because there was no progeny for him (i.e. the dead king), I asked about a pregnant woman: a pregnant woman did also not exist.
>
> (E. Laroche, *RA* 47 (1953): 70ff.)

Although these texts do not refer to Telepinu's Edict, it is likely that the decree did introduce some effective brakes on the arbitrary seizure of royal power.

How much the territory under Hittite control shrank during the period of anarchy, and before the recovery began under the early Empire is hard to define. Telepinu presents a picture of total collapse until he personally reversed the process and regained a wider territory. This is probably an exaggeration, both with respect to the totality of loss and the scope of subsequent recovery. Land-donations and parity-treaties with Kizzuwadna (in the eastern Cilician plain; Beal 1986) suggest that, while control of the north Syrian and Cilician territory was gradually lost and recovered only slowly by the immediate predecessors of Suppiluliuma I (1370–1330 (1344–1322)), Hittite domination of central Anatolia was not too seriously shaken. The northern and eastern frontiers appear to have been successfully defended at least from Telepinu's reign on, while the south-western territory, where Hattusili I had campaigned, remained beyond the Hittite realm until the reign of Tudhaliya I.

5d The Hittite Empire (*c.* 1430 (1420)–*c.* 1200)

The early Empire

The great period of expansion, which led to Hittite power at its height being acknowledged from points on the Aegean coast to the Khabur and down to Damascus, began in the reign of Tudhaliya I (1430–1410/1420–1400). He may have been the founder of a new royal line, since the kings' names, apart from very old and glorious ones such as Hattusili and Mursili, are henceforth quite different.[8] The obscurity that shrouds the period between *c.* 1500 and *c.* 1430 (1420) gives us no hint of how this change came about. His achievements are a little better known now, thanks to the re-dating of some texts to his reign and to that of his later successor, Arnuwanda I (1390–1380 (1370–1355), see table 18). The kings of this period made vigorous attempts, sporadically successful, to assert Hittite dominance over Kizzuwadna and north Syria, especially Aleppo, against the power of Mitanni (Talmi-Sharruma treaty, Weidner 1923: 80–89; chapter 6a). In this struggle, the early Empire rulers tried, as far as possible, to take advantage of setbacks suffered by Mitanni at the hands of the great Egyptian king, Tuthmosis III (see chapters 4b; 6d). But success was temporary, as Mitanni and Egypt drew together to exclude the

Hittites from the area by forming an alliance, cemented by a series of royal marriages, which lasted for about sixty years. An important Hittite achievement, which helped to persuade Mitanni that it was more advantageous to close ranks with Egypt, was Tudhaliya's expansion eastwards into the area of Isuwa with its very rich copper deposits. Isuwa lay directly north of Mitanni and the Mitanni kings claimed suzerainty over it.

The serious threat that the Hittites presented at this period to the interests of the other great powers of western Asia is illustrated by some events on the western edge of the Hittite realm and beyond. This was another area where Tudhaliya I was successful. Answering an appeal from a certain Madduwatta, who fled to the Hittite court when driven from his country by Attarissiya of Ahhiya(wa), Tudhaliya exploited the situation to Hittite advantage by installing Madduwatta as dependent king of Zippasla along the Hittite frontier. When subsequently, in the reign of Arnuwanda I, Madduwatta made common cause with Ahhiya(wa) against Hittite interests, the Egyptian king saw an opportunity to pen in the burgeoning power of the Hittites. He set up and welcomed contacts with the powerful west Anatolian kingdom of Arzawa. He must have hoped to build up the political strength of this western neighbour against the Hittite kingdom at a time of trouble, as had happened with Mitanni on the eastern flank of the Hittite kingdom. A letter, sent by Amenophis III of Egypt (1403–1364 (1390–1352)) to Tarhundaradu of Arzawa, provides a glimpse into these machinations (see chapters 4c; 6d):

Nimuwareya (i.e. Amenophis III), great king, king of Egypt, (speaks) as follows: Say to Tarhundaradu, the king of Arzawa: With me all is well. My houses, my wives, my children, my nobles, my troops, my chariot-fighters, everything that belongs to me, in all my lands, is well. May everything be well with you (also). May your houses, your wives, your children, your nobles, your troops, your chariot-fighters, all that belongs to you, in all your lands, all be very well.

Now, I have sent you Irshappa, my messenger (with the instruction): 'Let us see the daughter whom they are offering in marriage to my majesty.' And he shall pour oil on her head (first ritual of betrothal). Now, I have sent you a sack of gold; it is excellent.

As for the things that you wrote to me to do (as follows): 'Send it to me here!' – yes, I am going to send it, but later. (Before that) send back quickly your messenger and the messenger from me; they must come. Then they will come (back) to you (and) bring the bride-price for the daughter. My messenger and your messenger who came, who . . . . And send me also the . . . people from the Gashga-land. I have heard that everything is finished and the land of Hattusa has been paralysed (lit. 'frozen').

And now, I have sent you as a greeting gift a consignment in the charge of my messenger Irshappa: a sack of gold, weighing 20 minas of gold; 3 light garments of linen; 3 light coats of linen; 3 linen *huzzi*; 8 linen *kušitti*; 100 linen *šawalga*; 100 *happa* ... of linen; 100 linen *mutalliyašša*; 4 large *kukkubu*-containers of sweet oil; 6 [small] *kukkubu*-containers of sweet oil; 3 ebony chairs sheathed in fine *šarpa* [and gol]d; 10 ebony chairs inlaid with ivory; 100 (beams of) ebony as a greeting gift.

(EA 31)

Unfortunately, the reply of the Arzawan ruler is only preserved in part (EA 32). But enough survives to show that he welcomed the proposed marriage-link with Egypt. A nice touch is a note by the scribe who wrote the letter, requesting his colleague in Egypt to conduct future correspondence in Hittite (EA 32: 14–25). Serious problems were obviously being experienced by Arnuwanda I at this point, of which his enemies were taking full advantage. The Gasga people of the Pontic Alps (p. 244) appear to have been raiding with disastrous consequences: Hattusa may have been destroyed by them, as was to happen later too (see below, p. 258); indeed, Hittite contact with the Black Sea was never re-established. Arzawa was setting up close and friendly links with Egypt, and being accepted into the circle of great powers allied with each other. Meanwhile, Madduwatta, the former Hittite client-king, was making common cause with Ahhiya(wa) to raid Cyprus, over which the Hittite king claimed some kind of ill-defined control.

But these proved to be temporary setbacks only. From the later 'Deeds of Suppiluliuma' (*CTH* 40 (in fact, wrongly numbered)) it appears that, already under Arnuwanda I's successor, Tudhaliya III (1380–60 (1355–1344)), the area immediately east of Hatti-land, the 'Upper Land' and Azzi-Hayasa, were retaken by his son and eventual heir, Suppiluliuma. These countries abutted on Gasga territory and their capture was probably linked directly with the attempts to regain the capital, Hattusa. Its reconquest by Suppiluliuma probably happened early in his own reign, and a phase of major fortifications and rebuilding there is generally associated with this.

The conquests of Suppiluliuma I

A reasonable outline of the Syrian conquests of Suppiluliuma I (1370–1330 (1344–1322)) can be reconstructed on the basis of several later documents. They are: 'The Deeds of Suppiluliuma' (*CTH* 40, cf. Güterbock 1956), a reference in the Amarna letters (EA 17), and several treaties with small states in the Levant (e.g. Ugarit (quoted p. 307), Nuhashshe (Weidner 1923: no. 3), Amurru (Weidner 1923: nos. 5, 10), Aleppo (Weidner 1923: no. 6), and especially the first Shattiwaza treaty (Weidner 1923: no. 1)). The Hittite king's first attempt was to move directly south through the Taurus passes. This, as well as some surviving treaties between Hittite and Kizzuwadnian kings, implies that the region was under the control of the Hittites – another achievement attributable to the early-Empire kings, although the order and progress of events is exceptionally obscure (Wilhelm 1982: 43–44; Beal 1986). What is certain is that *a* king called Tudhaliya moved the cult of the 'Black Goddess' from Kizzuwadna to Samuha in Hatti-land. The assumption is that such a move can only have followed a conquest (cf. the deportation of deities referred to in the Hattusili I annals, pp. 241–242). It also seems that Suppiluliuma's father resided in Samuha for a while (perhaps because of the destruction of Hattusa). So it is possible that he was the one responsible for this conquest (Wilhelm 1982: 44), which allowed his son to use this most obvious route for gaining access to the Levant. Eventually, Suppiluliuma incorporated Kizzuwadna totally into the Hittite realm and put an end to the line of its local dynasts.

Suppiluliuma's first Syrian campaign, however, was not victorious. It was probably from the spoils of Suppiluliama's unsuccessful encounter with Mitanni that Tushratta (the ruler of Mitanni; see chapter 6a) was able to select some items to send to his ally and brother-in-law, Amenophis III of Egypt (EA 17). The failed campaign may date from fairly early in Suppiluliuma's reign, and his second, spectacularly successful one was probably fought considerably later. This time, Suppiluliuma moved eastwards, crossing the Euphrates near Malatya (into Isuwa), and thence into Mitanni. The success of this manoeuvre was crowned by the sack of Washshukanni, the capital of Mitanni. This was a disaster for Mitanni, which probably unleashed the internal conflicts that led to the murder of Tushratta and the eventual flight to the Hittite court of his son, Shattiwaza, where he sought asylum with his father's enemy (cf. chapter 6a). This turn of events allowed Suppiluliuma to control the western part of Mitanni by installing the Mitannian prince there as a Hittite client-king, and so turning it into a buffer-state against the expanding power of Assyria (see chapter 7b). The exact sequence of events, after the devastating Hittite attack on Mitanni, is not completely certain, but it seems likely that Suppiluliuma moved on towards Aleppo, Alalah, Nuhash-she and Amurru (see map 4), detaching them from their allegiance to Mitanni and setting up sworn agreements stipulating their future obligations to the Hittite throne. One of his own sons, Telepinu, was left as delegated ruler in Aleppo with responsibility for defending the Hittite gains. The important city of Carchemish, which dominated a major crossing-point of the Euphrates, seems to have been finally reduced at a yet later point after an eight day siege. Again one of Suppiluliuma's sons, Piyasslll (with the throne-name 'Sharri-kushuh'), was installed as regional ruler to whom the other local dynasts were accountable; Carchemish eventually became the main seat of Hittite authority in the area.

At this point, when Suppiluliuma controlled western Mitanni and all its former dependencies in Syria ('as far as Lebanon and Abina (Damascus region)'), friendly relations with Egypt were established for a while (the identity of the Egyptian king – whether Akhenaten or Tutankhamun – is uncertain). The Egyptian king acknowledged the Hittite king as a ruler of 'equal rank' (EA 41), although one (unfortunately very fragmentary) letter (EA 42) suggests that there may have been an initial wrangle about equality and precedence. Most surprising is the evidence that Tutankhamun's young widow, during the time of political turmoil in Egypt (cf. chapter 4c), requested a son of the Hittite king as husband – an amazing gift of political power and influence offered on a plate to the Hittites:

> My husband has died and I have no son. They say about you that you have many sons. You might give me one of your sons, and he might become my husband. I will not take one of my servants and (will not) make him my husband.
>
> (KBo V 6; Güterbock 1956: 94–8; 107–108)

Despite Suppiluliuma's wariness and careful investigations, the son he sent off to Egypt was murdered. The powerful group of royal relatives and military commanders, in whose hands the fate of the young widowed queen lay (Murnane 1985; Bryce 1990), probably engineered his death. Relations with Babylonia seem to have been more successful and lasting: a Babylonian princess was married to Suppiluliuma, although in the reign of his son, Mursili II, she was accused of causing the king's wife's death by witchcraft (CTH 70). Such a serious accusation must have had political repercussions.

The reign of Mursili II

Suppiluliuma's extraordinary achievements were cut short by a virulent plague, which ravaged the Levant and was brought back by the Hittite soldiers from the wars. The epidemic probably also carried off Arnuwanda II (1330 (1322–21)), Suppiluliuma's son and successor, who ruled for no longer than a year. He was succeeded by another son of Suppiluliuma, Mursili II (1330 (1321)–1295), whose vigorous efforts to consolidate his father's conquests were highly successful. With the possible exception of the temporary loss of Carchemish, Syria remained loyal to the Hittites. The recurrently trouble-some eastern area of Azzi-Hayasa had to be subdued again, when it refused to honour the terms of its earlier treaty with Suppiluliuma ('Ten Year Annals of Mursili' III 93 – IV 23 (CTH 61/I); Goetze 1933). But Mursili's most outstanding success was against Arzawa in the west, a region entirely ignored by Suppiluliuma:

> Then I marched in the same year to the land Arzawa. But to Uhhaziti I sent a messenger and wrote to him: 'Those of my subjects who have come to your country – although I have repeatedly asked back for them, you have not returned them to me and you have insulted me and treated me with contempt. So up! We will fight with each other! And the weather-god, my lord, shall judge our case!'
> As I marched, when I arrived in the mountains Lawasa, the mighty

weather-god, my lord, showed his divine favour. He cast the thunder-bolt(?), and both my army saw the thunderbolt as well as Arzawa. The thunderbolt went and struck Arzawa, the city of Uhhaziti, Apasa (possibly Ephesus), it struck. It caused Uhhaziti to sink to his knees and he became ill. And as Uhhaziti became ill, he subsequently did not oppose me in battle; he sent his son Piyamaradu with infantry and chariot-fighters against me, he advanced on me for battle at the Astarpa river near the locality Walma (possibly upper course of Maeander), and I, my sun (i.e. 'my majesty'), fought against him. And the sun-goddess of Arinna, my lady, the mighty weather-god, my lord, Mezzulla and all gods ran before me. I overcame that Piyamaradu, the son of Uhhaziti, with his infantry and chariot-fighters and defeated him. Then I pursued him, to the land of Arzawa I moved. Into Apasa, the city of Uhhaziti, I entered and Uhhaziti did not stay before me, but fled before me and went . . . and beyond the sea. And there he stayed.

The whole of Arzawa fled, some of the inhabitants went to the hill-country of Arinnanda and occupied the hill-country of Arinnanda, but the other inhabitants went on to the place Puranda and occupied Puranda. Other inhabitants went with Uhhaziti beyond the sea. I, my sun, followed the population to the hill-country Arinnanda and fought against the hill-country Arinnanda. And the sun-goddess of Arinna, my lady, the mighty weather-god, my lord, Mezzulla and the other gods ran before me in battle. I conquered the hill-country Arinnanda. And what I, my sun, brought into my palace of the captured population was 15,500 people. But what the generals of Hattusa, the infantry and chariot-fighters brought home of the captured population, about that there was no counting (i.e. the numbers were countless). After this I sent the captured population ahead to Hattusa, and they were taken there.

After I had conquered the hill-country Arinnanda, I then marched to the river Astarpa and had a fortified camp struck on the river Astarpa, and there I celebrated the New Year feast. All this I did in one year. As soon as spring arrived – because Uhhaziti was ill and stayed in the sea, his sons also were at his side. Then Uhhaziti died in the sea, but his sons separated one from the other. One stayed on in the sea, but the other, Tapalazunauli, came out of the sea, and because the whole of Arzawa . . . had gone up to the place Puranda, Tapalazunauli went up to Puranda – as soon as I had celebrated the New Year feast, I went to do battle in Puranda. Tapalazunauli came down from Puranda with his infantry and chariot-fighters and came to oppose me in battle, and on his own field he faced me in battle and I, my sun, fought against him. And the sun goddess of Arinna, my lady, the mighty weather-god, my lord, Mezzulla and all gods ran before me. I overcame Tapalazunauli with his infantry and chariot-fighters and defeated him. Then I pursued him. I went and shut up the place Puranda [and] harassed [it] and took away his water.

255

When I attacked Puranda, Tapalazunauli, the son of Uhhaziti, who was up in Puranda, was afraid and escaped down from Puranda in the night. [Also his wife, his children and the in]habitants he caused to run ahead down from their castle of refuge, and brought them down from Puranda. But as soon as I, [my sun], heard: 'Tapalazunauli escaped do[wn] in the night, even his wife, his children and the inhabitants he caused to run down before him and brought them down,' then I, [my sun], sent [infantry] (and) chariot-fighters after him, [and they] harassed Tapalazunauli on the way from behind, and they took his wife, his children and the inhabitants away and le[d] them back again. Tapalazunauli, however, was the only one who escaped.

(A very broken section describes the fall of Puranda and its booty, a victorious campaign to Ahhiyawa and the capture of a son of Uhhaziti; then:)

[As soon as I] returned [from the Seha River Land], I should have fought against [Manapatarhunda] who was lord in the Seha River; (but) as soon as [Manapatarhunda he]ard about me: 'The king of Hatti-land is coming!' he was [afraid] and did [not come] against me, (but) sent me his mother, old men and women. They came to me, [fell] before (my) feet. And because women were falling before my feet, I gave in because of [the women]. So I did [not] go to the Seha River. The people of Hatti-land, who were in Seha River, they handed over to me. And what they gave me of population were 4000 people; these I sent ahead to Hattusa and they were taken away. Manapatarhunda and the Seha River Land I accepted as subjects. Then I went to Mira and gave Mira to Mashuiluwa. But the Seha River Land I gave to Manapatarhunda, but the land Hapalla I gave to Targasnalli, and these lands I made subject on the spot, and I imposed on them by treaty (the provision of) troops, and from then on they always provided me with troops. And as far as my spending the winter in Arzawa is concerned, in the second year the sun-goddess of Arinna, my lady, the mighty weather-god, my lord, Mezzulla and all gods ran before me. I conquered Arzawa, and in part I led (it) home to Hattusa, and in part I made it subject on the spot and imposed the provision of troops on them by treaty, and from then on they provided me with troops.

(Ten Year Annals of Mursili II 8-III 32 (*CTH* 61/I);
Goetze 1933; *TUAT* I: 474–477)

Mursili was able to inflict a severe setback on the once powerful Arzawa: he reduced parts of it totally, deported inhabitants, entered the royal capital, drove its king and princes of the royal family to seek refuge on islands in the Aegean, won a victory over Arzawa's ally, Ahhiyawa, and eventually reduced Arzawa to the status of a subject-state of the Hittite empire (or, perhaps, broke it up into its constituent parts; see Heinhold-Krahmer 1977). A direct result of these triumphs was the surrender and subjection of the smaller countries neighbouring on Arzawa and Hatti, whose allegiance tended to fluctuate between the two; fragments of the treaties imposed on them by Mursili II have survived (Friedrich 1926/1930 no. 2 (Hapalla), no. 6 (Seha River Land), no. 3 (Mira), cf. *CTH* 67–69). Where enough of the text survives, it is clear that the kings on whom the obligations were imposed were all members of the local ruling families, who had at one time sought refuge at the Hittite court.

Mursili's other massive effort was a series of repeated, strenuous campaigns in the north against the Gasga people, so dangerously close to Hattusa and several important Hittite cult-centres. The repeated raids by Gasga into Hittite territory is now illustrated a little more by some of the Maşat letters:

> Thus his majesty: Speak to Kassu and Pulli! As for the matter about which you wrote to me as follows: 'See, the grain is already ripe. In the Gasga(-region) locusts have eaten the grain. So they attack your grain from Gasipura. Here there are no soldiers and chariot-troops. His majesty has ordered Kallu, commander of the chariot corps thus: "Lead out the chariot corps." (Until) now no chariot-troops have arrived.' Now behold, I, his majesty, have seized Kallu and he spoke thus: 'I have already sent out twenty teams of horses.' See, I am sending Pahinakka after. He is coming.
>
> (Alp 1980 Mşt 75/15)

With their restricted arable base in the high Pontic Alps, the Gasga appear to have attempted to make up any shortfalls caused by adverse weather or plagues (including locusts) by raiding into the richer grain-growing regions of Hatti. This cannot have been the only motive for Gasga raids – it would scarcely explain the sack of Hattusa, for example – and some moves of Gasga groups were more in the nature of attempts to expand territorially (see Hattusili III Apology, pp. 260–261). Very little is known of these peoples. Hittite references tend to be collective and undifferentiated; yet the four surviving treaties (not precisely datable) drawn up between Hittite kings and Gasga people suggest that they were divided into several distinct groups: some were ready to co-operate with the Hittite state at times and even supplied soldiers (*CTH* 236), while others remained hostile (von Schuler 1965). The treaties were always drawn up with a community of Gasga people, which implies that their political structure was not one in which kings or chiefs wielded effective power. A temporary institutional change was foisted upon the Gasga by a neighbouring dynast, who seems to have been successful in adding part of Gasga territory to his territorial control, as Mursili remarks in his annals:

> In the following year I went to the country Tipiya (possibly to be located between the Upper Land and Azzi-Hayasa). While my father was in Mitanni, Pihhuniya, a man of Tipiya, had arisen and had

257

continuously attacked the Upper Land; and he had reached further to Zazissa and had taken the Upper Land with him and taken it away down into the Gasga-land. The whole of the land of Istitna he had taken and had made it into a place of pasture.

Also, Pihhuniya did not rule according to the manner of the Gasga: Quite suddenly, while in a Gasga-settlement the rule of one is not (the custom), now this Pihhaniya ruled in the manner of kingship.

(Ten Year Annals of Mursili III 67–75 (*CTH* 61/I);
Goetze 1933; *TUAT* I: 479)

Mursili's continuous campaigns against the Gasga were perhaps ultimately not effective, since it was probably further devastation by the Gasga that led Mursili's successor, Muwatalli, to move the gods of Hatti and the court to Tarhuntassa in the Lower Land (see Hattusili III Apology, p. 260).

Muwatalli, Urhi-Teshub and Hattusili III

The abandonment of Hattusa probably explains the relative lack of documents for Muwatalli (1295–1282 (1271)). But a treaty, agreed between him and Alaksandu of Wilusa (tentatively located in the Troad), implies the maintenance, even a tightening, of the Hittite hold in the west. The Hittite presence in north Syria, too, continued to be strong, as shown by the fact that Muwatalli rewrote the agreement drawn up between his father and Aleppo, which had been stolen (Weidner 1923 no. 6 obv. 3–4). Hittite power was, above all, strengthened in the Levant by Egyptian attempts to expand once again beyond the region of Kadesh – an attempt brought to nought by the resounding defeat inflicted on Ramesses II by Muwatalli at the battle of Kadesh (1286 (1275); see chapter 4d)). The defeat left the Hittites in definitive control of the Damascus area, which had been one of the frontier regions of the Egyptian empire. Muwatalli tried also to reassert Hittite control in the northern area against the Gasga, by organising a new principality at Hakpis under the rule of his brother Hattusili. Repeated, wearisome campaigns were mounted from this base in order to wrest back territories lost to the Gasga and other peoples, especially, of course, the devastated city of Hattusa itself. In this massive effort, Hattusili was eventually successful. His crowning achievement (aside from the reconquest of Hattusa) was the recovery and rebuilding of the great cult-centre of the Hittite storm-god, Nerik, which had been lost to the Gasga during the Old Kingdom (reign of Hantili: 1590–1560, Haas 1970; but Hantili II is also possible).

The prestige and power that Hattusili gained by these successes made his nephew, Urhi-Teshub, who had acceded with the throne-name Mursili (III, 1282–1275 (1271–1264)), highly (and probably rightly) suspicious of him. Once Hattusili had won back the territories, Urhi-Teshub attempted to reduce the area under his uncle's control. Hattusili reacted to this with a well-planned revolt (Archi 1971; Ünal 1974), which ended in Urhi-Teshub's deposition and exile to Nuhashshe by his uncle: Hattusili became the third king of that name (1275–1245 (1264–1239)). This contravened the carefully regulated rules of succession and, in spite of Hattusili's fairly extensive support, he obviously needed to justify his usurpation of the throne, especially as Urhi-Teshub made at least one attempt to stage a comeback. This justification of Hattusili's kingship is contained in one of the best-known Hittite texts – the 'Apology of Hattusili III' (preserved in multiple contemporary copies, all found in the eastern storeroom of the Great Temple at Hattusa). It may have been composed to accompany the foundation of part of a sanctuary dedicated to Shaushga (the Hurrian form of Ishtar) of Samuha, Hattusili's especial patron-deity. The text is very long, but it is worth quoting substantial extracts:

> Thus Tabarna Hattusili, the great king, king of the land of Hatti, son of Mursili, the great king, king of the land of Hatti, grandson of Suppuluiuma, the great king, king of the land of Hatti, descendant of Hattusili, king of Kussar.
>
> Of the preferment of the goddess Shaushga I shall tell, and everyone shall hear it! And in the future the son of my sun (i.e. 'my majesty'), his grandson (and the further) descendants of my sun shall be (particularly) respectful towards Shaushga among the gods. My father Mursili begot us four children: Halpasulupi, Muwatalli, Hattusili, and Massanauzzi, a daughter. Of all these I was the youngest child. And as long as I was a boy, I was a 'reinholder' (important court function). Then Shaushga, my lady, sent to Mursili, my father, in a dream, Muwatalli, my brother (with the following words): 'For Hattusili the years are (now only) short, he will not live (long). So give him to me, he shall be my priest, and he shall survive.' Then my father took me, (as) a boy, and gave me to the deity in service. And as a priest I brought (drink-)offerings to the deity. And I saw well-being in the hand of Shaushga, my lady. And Shaushga, my lady, took me by the hand and led me along the right paths.
>
> But when my father Mursili became a god (i.e. died), my brother Muwatalli sat upon the throne of his father; but I became army-commander before my brother. And my brother gave me the dignified position of chief of the guard, he also gave me the Upper Land to administer and I reigned over the Upper Land. Before me Armatarhunda, the son of Zida, had administered it for a long time. Now because Shaushga, my lady, was favourable towards me, my brother Muwatalli also maintained his kindliness to me. When the people saw the kindness of Shaushga, my lady, to me and the favour of my brother, then they were envious. And Armatarhunda, the son of Zida, and then other people, too, began to make difficulties for me and they worked

against me. For me things were very unfavourable, and my brother Muwatalli ordered me to the 'wheel' (this appears to have been the place where the king heard accusations of treason; precise meaning not clear). But Shaushga, my lady, appeared to me in a dream and said to me in the dream these words: 'I am entrusting you to a deity, so fear not!' and thanks to the deity I was cleansed. Because the deity, my lady, held me by the hand she never let me (become the victim of) an unfavourable deity, an unfavourable court. Nor did she ever let the weapon of an enemy circle about me (?). Shaushga, my lady, took myself to her in all these matters. If at any time an illness befell me, then precisely because I was a sick man I saw in this the deity's preferment. The deity, my lady, held me by the hand in every situation. But because I was a preferred man and because I walked before the gods in righteousness, I never did a bad deed (in the way usual) of people. You deity, my lady, took me out of everything and all, was it not so? The deity, my lady, never passed me over in a critical period; she never surrendered me to an enemy and also to my accusers (and) those who envied me, she never surrendered me. Whether it was the word of an enemy, or the (word of) an accuser (or) whether it was the word of the palace: in everything Shaushga, my lady, held over me (her protective) garment. From all and everything she took me (away). Enemies and envious persons Shaushga, my lady, gave into my hand and I completely finished them off.

But when Muwatalli, my brother, examined the matter not a single bad matter concerning me remained. And he received me back and placed the whole army and the chariot-fighters of Hatti-land in my hand. (Thus) I commanded the entire army (and) the chariot-fighters of the land of Hatti. And my brother Muwatalli used to send me out (to battle). Now as Shaushga, my lady, was favourable to me – whenever I directed my gaze against an enemy-land, then no enemy returned my gaze, and I defeated the enemy-lands one after the other. But the favour of Shaushga, my lady, rested upon me. Thus I drove out every enemy from the Hatti-lands, who had settled himself in the Hatti-lands. Now the enemy-lands I defeated one after the other, while I was young, about that I shall prepare a separate tablet and place it before the deity.

(Hattusili describes the terrible devastation of central Anatolia as a result of the invasions by Gasga and others; he wins a battle in north Syria and some victories in central Anatolia; Muwatalli moves the Hittite government to Tarhuntassa and Hattusili is put in charge of the fight for the northern territories, based at Hakpis; he fights with his brother at Kadesh. Hattusili's successes re-excite the opposition of Armatarhunda and his family.):

Now as I returned from the land of Egypt, I went to the city Lawazantiya (east Cilicia) in order to offer to the deity and I performed (the cult of) the deity. Then I took the daughter of Pentipsarri, the priest, Puduhepa at the command of the deity in marriage. And we united, and the deity gave us the love of husband (and) of wife. And we had sons and daughters. Further the deity, my lady, appeared to me in a dream (and spoke): 'Together with the house enter my service!' So I went together with my house into the service of the deity. And into the house that we had made for ourselves, the deity entered for us. And our house made (good) progress (?); that was the honour (bestowed on us) of Shaushga, my lady. And I went forth and built the places Hawarkina and Delmuna. The city Hakpissa, however, was seized by enmity, [. . .] the Gasga I drove out, and the (city) I brought by myself back to order. Thus I became king of the land Hakpis, you, woman, became [the queen of] Hakpis.

(Hattusili's old enemy, Armatarhunda, is finally worsted; Muwatalli dies and leaves Hattusili in charge of reconquered Hattusa):

Thus when for my brother there was no legitimate son, I took Urhi-Teshub, the son of the palace-woman and [installed] him in the land of Hatti for the rulership. The whole of [Hattusa] I placed in his hand, and he was [Great King] in the land of H[atti]. But I was king of Hakpissa.

(Hattusili develops and strengthens his principality.):

But when Urhi-Teshub saw the extent of the benevolence of the deity (towards) me, then he became envious and sought to harm(?) me. So he took all my subjects away from me. Also the empty lands which I had resettled, he took all of them away from me and made me small. The city Hakpissa, however, he did not remove from me in accordance with a divine command. Because I was priest of the weathergod of Nerik, he therefore did not take the (town) away from me. And because of the esteem for my brother I did nothing and accepted this for seven years. But he tried, at divine command and on human advice, to destroy me and also took Hakpissa and Nerik away. Now I did not accept it any longer, but revolted against him. But when I became his enemy, I did not do it in the sense of a crime by rebelling against him on the chariot or in the midst of his house. (Rather) I told him in manly fashion: 'You started the quarrel with me. Now you are Great King, but I am the king of the one solitary fortress which you have left (me). Come here! And Shaushga of Samuha and the weathergod of Nerikka will decide the case for us!'

Now as I was writing thus to Urhi-Teshub – now if somebody says as follows: 'Why did you formerly place him in the kingship, why do you now write to him (about) enmity?' – (then I would reply:) 'If he had not started the quarrel with me, would (the gods) then really have allowed the Great King to be defeated by a petty king?' But because he has now begun the quarrel with me, the gods through their legal decision have allowed him to be defeated by me.

(The war between nephew and uncle begins):

But because Shaushga, my lady, had already announced my kingship earlier, at that very moment Shaushga, my lady, appeared to my wife in a dream (and spoke:) 'I shall go before your husband (as helper) and all of Hattusa will come over to the side of your husband! Because I have made him great I have never left him to the mercy of an evil court, an evil deity. Now I shall take him up and install him in the priesthood of the sun-goddess of Arinna (position always held by Hittite Great King). You, however, should celebrate me as Shaushga *parassi* (unknown Hurrian epithet)!' Shaushga, my lady, stepped behind me. And as she had foretold me, so (it) happened). Shaushga, my lady, showed very much just in this case (her) preferment. And to the lords, whom Urhi-Teshub had somehow driven out, Shaushga appeared in a dream, powerless as they were(?), (with the words:) 'The lands of Hatti in their entirety I, Shaushga, have turned over to Hattusili.'

Then I experienced the preferment of Shaushga on this occasion also in full measure; as she did not allow Urhi-Teshub to stay anywhere whatsoever, she shut him up in Samuha like a pig in a sty. The Gasga, who had been hostile against me, they came behind me; also the whole of Hattusa was behind me. In accordance with the respect I had for my brother I did nothing at all (that was evil). But I marched back down against Urhi-Teshub and led him away like a prisoner. I gave him fortified towns in the country Nuhashshe and there he stayed. He would have plotted another plot, and he would have driven to the land of Karduniash (i.e. Babylonia). Now as I heard of this matter, I seized him and sent him aside to the sea. Sipa-ziti (son of Armatarhunda) I also allowed to cross the frontier. I took away his house and gave it to Shaushga, my lady. I gave that to Shaushga, my lady; but Shaushga, my lady, step by step furthered me.

I was a prince and became chief of the guard. (As) chief of the guard, however, I became king of Hakpissa. (As) king of Hakpissa, however, I became Great King. Further Shaushga, my lady, gave me the envious people, opponents and enemies in court into my hand. And some died by means of the weapon, but others died from days (i.e. of old age). All together I defeated them; and Shaushga, my lady, gave me the kingship over the land of Hatti.

And I became great king; (because) she took me, the prince, and Shaushga, my lady, let me reach the kingship. And the kings who were older in relation to me (i.e. who had had their thrones longer than me) and who had good relations with me, they remained in the same good relationship to me; and they began to send ambassadors to me. They began to send gifts to me. But the presents which they sent they had never sent to my fathers and forefathers. He who was a king who had to show respect to me, he showed me respect; but (those lands) which were hostile to me, I defeated; to the lands of Hatti I added region upon region. Those (kings) which had been enemies at the time of my fathers and forefathers, made peace with me.

Now because the deity, my lady, remained favourable to me in this way, I out of respect for my brother never did anything (evil). I took up my [nephew] Kurunta and in the place which my brother Muwatalli had developed into the city of Tarhuntassa I installed him in the kingship.

(An account of the land, offerings and buildings presented to Shaushga; Hattusili dedicates his son, Tudhaliya, to her service:)

And whosover may arise (as) his son, his grandson (or) descendant in the future from Hattusili and Puduhepa, he shall be (particularly) respectful towards Shaushga of Samuha among the gods.

(CTH 81; Goetze 1925; Otten 1981; TUAT I: 481–492)

The text must have been composed a few years after Hattusili III's accession (1275 (1264)), as he refers to the acceptance of his position by neighbouring states, which presumably included Egypt and Babylonia. Yet it is clear that Egyptian attempts to nibble away at Hittite territory in north Syria continued; Ramesses II corresponded with the Hittite western frontier dependency of Mira; and Babylonia and Egypt, for a while at least, toyed with the idea of supporting Urhi-Teshub against his uncle. All of this, as well as the treachery of certain Hittite nobles, such as Armatarhunda, had obviously been dealt with reasonably effectively by the time Hattusili presented the detailed justification for his usurpation. His fairly rapid success in combating a tricky and dangerous political situation (with the exception of Mira, where control appears to have been lost) is shown by the great peace treaty finally signed between himself and Ramesses II in 1269 (1258), of which both the Egyptian and Hittite version (actually in Akkadian) have been preserved (CTH 91; Weidner 1923: no. 8; ANET: 201ff; TUAT I: 135ff.; chapter 4e). The treaty ushered in a period of peace and stability within the Levant, with the kings, their wives and even their children corresponding regularly with each other (CTH 155–165; 167–169); a royal visit to Egypt was planned, and a marriage between a Hittite princess and the Egyptian king was concluded (see chapter 4d). The drawing together of the two great powers was undoubtedly, in part, motivated by the ever-increasing threat of Assyria (see chapter 7b). Mitanni had already been effectively detached in the reign of Muwatalli, and the rich copper-bearing region of Isuwa was lost in Hattusili's reign. In spite of Hattusili's attempts to strengthen Hittite ties with Babylonia (CTH 174; 172) against Assyria, Babylonia seems to have been unable to respond effectively, given the very severe pressure of its northern neighbour. Muwatalli's earlier, rude response to the Assyrian king, when the latter sought to be included among the great powers (CTH 171; see chapter 7b), can hardly have helped to create an atmosphere in which a rapprochement could be countenanced; Babylonia was more and more cut off from its old allies by the territorial expansion of Assyria.

The last Hittite kings

In Hattusili III's apology he refers to the installation of his nephew, Kurunta, brother of Urhi-Teshub, at Tarhuntassa, which Muwatalli had developed as a royal centre at the time of the destruction of Hattusa and loss of much of the northern territories. Several texts demonstrate that Hattusili gathered a group of powerful supporters in his rebellious bid for the throne, and that they had to be, and were, well rewarded once Hattusili became king (Archi 1971). Kurunta was one of them: his relationship to the deposed king gave him a potential claim to the throne and made him a particularly serious threat that had to be neutralised. The most exciting find in recent years at Hattusa has been the discovery of a bronze tablet with a complete (not one break!) text of the treaty made between Hattusili's son and successor, Tudhaliya IV (1245–1215 (1239–1209)), and Kurunta of Tarhuntassa engraved on it (Otten 1988; cf. Houwink ten Cate 1992). It reaffirmed, in essence, the agreement originally made between Hattusili and Kurunta, but it also shows that Kurunta's importance (or threat) was such that Tudhaliya made extra-ordinary further concessions to his cousin: he granted him more territory, reduced his liability to supply troops for the Hittite army, exempted him from a number of taxes relating to cult supplies, and gave him a freer hand in appointing his successor. Most interesting is the statement that:

> With respect to the 'great throne' (i.e. the Hittite Great King) the same agreement/treaty (that exists for) the king of Carchemish shall exist for him: greater than the king of Tarhuntassa shall be the crown-prince alone, otherwise no other shall be greater than he! And whatever regulation with respect to royal position is right for the king of Carchemish, that shall also obtain for the king of Tarhuntassa!
>
> (Otten 1988 II §18; Lebrun 1992 §12)

The text spells out that Kurunta's position at Tarhuntassa (in the Konya plain) shall be like that of the king of Carchemish, who functioned as Hittite viceroy for the Syrian client-states (see p. 253). His rank will equal that of the privileged Carchemish ruler, second only to the designated successor to the throne. It also perhaps implies that Kurunta was being entrusted with a similar overarching authority over regions in the west. Throughout there is an emphasis on the closeness of Tudhaliya and Kurunta – they were 'sworn brothers', they had loved and honoured each other from early on, Kurunta had always been loyal to Tudhaliya. A hint of why this bond between the cousins was now being strengthened and Kurunta tangibly rewarded is the reference, in the treaty, to the fact that Hattusili had originally designated another son as his successor, but later deposed him and appointed Tudhaliya instead. It is possible that this brief mention (Otten 1988 II 43–44) reflects intrigues and struggles for the throne in which Tudhaliya triumphed, and that Kurunta was one of his chief supporters. This may explain why he is being so strongly favoured. At the same time, Tudhaliya IV tried to tie Kurunta, with oaths of loyalty, to the new pattern of succession established by Hattusili's usurpation:

> Now if you, Kurunta, do not keep the words of this tablet, and my sun (i.e. 'my majesty'), but later you do not protect the descendants of my sun in the lordship, or if you should strive for the kingship of Hatti – or somebody makes difficulties for my sun or the descendants of my sun with respect to the kingship of Hatti, but you favour him and do not fight against him, then these gods of the oath shall destroy you together with your descendants.
>
> (Otten 1988 IV 5–11; Lebrun 1992 §18)

A rider to the story is the find of some seal-impressions (from two different seals) at Hattusa with the legend 'Great King, Labarna, Kurunta' (Otten 1988: 4–5; cf. Neve 1992: 21 Abb. 40–42). They imply that precisely what Tudhaliya feared had happened, and that Kurunta did for a time seize the Hittite kingship. When exactly this happened is not known: it could have been at Tudhaliya's death, and explain the short reign of his immediate successor Arnuwanda III (1215–1210 (1209–1205)). But that is speculation.

Although Tudhaliya's massive rebuilding programme in and around Hattusa is plentifully attested, there can be no doubt that Hatti suffered setbacks in his reign. In the east and in north Syria, Tukulti-Ninurta I of Assyria's attacks on Hittite strongholds and deportations of Hittite subjects were serious encroachments on Tudhaliya's territory (see chapter 7b). We get a taste of the fear besetting the Hittite king from the treaty made with Amurru at this time, in which the king of Amurru is forbidden to trade with Assyria (*CTH* 105). At the same time, Hittite dependencies in the west were being lost and not recovered. One curious episode, still puzzled over, is the conquest by Tudhaliya (apparently followed up by his son, Suppiluliuma II) of part of Cyprus, and his imposition of tribute (particularly in copper) on it (*CTH* 121). Whether, as has been suggested, this was a deliberate attempt to offset the loss of the coppermines of Isuwa (McQueen 1986 [OGe]: 50), or whether it was linked to problems created by piratical raids, for which Cyprus provided a base (Singer 1985; Gurney 1990: 32), is unknown. Events are extremely obscure in the reigns of Tudhaliya's successors, and it is impossible to gain even a rough idea of how long the last one, Suppiluliuma II (acceded c. 1210 (1205)), reigned. Some Hittite sites, such as Gordion, show a gradual transformation only, with no burning or major destruction level (Gunter 1990: 105). But Hattusa bears all the signs of a massive destruction by fire and the Hittite records fall silent. To what invading force it fell, why it was not recovered by the Hittites (as earlier, pp. 252; 258), remains unknown. Nothing in the written record hints at such an impending disaster, which only reports Suppiluliuma II's victory in a sea-battle off Cyprus and his construction of a rock-sanctuary (probably the small chamber at Yazılıkaya) for his father's cult. The powerful Hittite empire, the cohesive political unit that had dominated Anatolia for over four hundred years, ceased to exist soon after.

5e The Hittite state

What kind of political entity was the Hittite state? A question sometimes raised is whether one is really justified in referring to it as an 'empire' in the period from *c.* 1400 to *c.* 1200. Was it not rather a motley collection of disparate units added on, step by step, which was never more than a rather ill-assorted patchwork? Given the linguistic complexity, it must surely have been a loose federation at best? While, undoubtedly, different regions and groups maintained their own local traditions, cultural, legal and linguistic, this fact does not by itself deny the imperial character of the Hittite realm. In so far as the term 'empire' is used to describe a situation where a) one central power encompasses a large territory and a number of societies, dominating them through military conquest and force and using the surpluses of the subjected countries, and b) some kind of overarching administrative framework exists, then the Hittite state was certainly an empire, at least in the period from *c.* 1400 onwards if not earlier. There is no real problem of definition, although there are difficulties with understanding exactly how it worked.

The Great King and subject rulers

The most immediately striking aspect of the Hittites is the great number of so-called 'vassal-treaties' that survive, which define relations between the Hittite king and other subject dynasts, also termed 'king'. But the king in Hattusa is invariably referred to as the 'Great King', a title not bestowed on any of the subject-rulers, however powerful they might appear to be. It is quite clear from the treaties that the power of the subordinate kings was limited territorially to a very precisely specified land-stretch; for example, in the new treaty with Kurunta of Tarhuntassa (p. 264), 102 lines are devoted solely to defining the frontiers and territorial rights of the kingdom of Tarhuntassa (Otten 1988). At the same time, it is clear, from the agreements drawn up with Ugarit (see chapter 6b) and the 'Apology of Hattusili' (p. 261), that a territory granted initially could also be reduced at the will of the Great King. It is further quite plain that, while certain close royal relatives, such as the king of Carchemish and, later, probably the king of Tarhuntassa, were given wider political powers in the regions where their power-centres lay (as shown, for example, by the Shattiwaza treaty (CTH 51; Weidner 1923 no. 1)), those powers were always circumscribed and the ultimate authority remained the Hittite Great King. Thus the final decisions in the long-drawn-out divorce of the Ugarit ruler were all made, or validated, by the Great King himself (see chapter 6b); in the treaty with Kurunta of Tarhuntassa it is specified that he and the king of Carchemish shall be next in rank to the Hittite crown-prince; and, finally, subjects could petition the Great King directly to have an action of the local authority reversed, as shown by a royal letter found at Emar on the Euphrates (modern Tell Meskene, see chapter 6c):

> Thus (speaks) my sun (i.e. 'my majesty'): to Alziyamuwa say (as follows): 'Now this Zu-Ba'al, a diviner, a man of Astata, prostrated himself before me (with this plea): "The house of my relative, AN-damali, and the vineyard, Alziyamuwa is taking it away from me and giving it to Palluwa. As for the dues, earlier I did not have to pay them at all. But now I have been subjected to dues and labour-duties." Now, his estate and his vineyard must not be taken away from him. If they have already been taken away from him, let them be given back! As for the dues which he never paid, now why have you imposed dues (and) labour-duties on him? So, what he did before, let him continue to do now. But he should not do anything else. And no-one is to bother him!'
>
> (Msk. 73.1097; Laroche 1982 no. 1)

So, while there was autonomy within the subject kingdoms, the delegation of political power was by no means total. Royal authority remained in the hands of the Great King and was only partially devolved, with limits carefully set.

The dependent position of the subject-ruler was always stressed in the treaties that established his position. Thus in the treaty with Shattiwaza (Weidner 1923 no. 2; *CTH* 52; see chapter 6a), the total destitution of the Mitannian prince, arriving empty-handed before Suppiluliuma I, was made plain; when Mursili II installed Kupantaradu as king of Mira and Kuwaliya (Friedrich 1926 no. 3; *CTH* 68) he repeated three times that, because Kupantaradu's father had revolted three times, the Great King had the right to execute him, but in his mercy was setting him up as king; Manapatarhunda of the Seha River Land (Friedrich 1930 no. 4; *CTH* 69) was formally told in his treaty that he owed his life and position only to the pleas made on his behalf by the old men and women who had entreated the Great King with tears on his behalf (see Mursili Annals, p. 256). So in every instance the total dependence on the Hittite Great King was emphasised, and the history of revolts and betrayals that could have justified summary execution rehearsed. Their fortunes lay entirely in the hands of the Great King, and their duty was to support him loyally in return, as clearly expressed in one instance:

> But if you, Kurunta, take the words of this tablet to heart (and) always strive (to maintain) the lordship of my sun (i.e. 'my majesty'), later the descendants of my sun, then these gods shall keep you in well-being, and may you become old in the hand of my sun!
>
> (Otten 1988 IV 12–14; Lebrun 1992 §18)

An important way of strengthening the relationship between subject-ruler and Great King was the frequent practice of marrying the subject-ruler to a female relative of the king. Depending on the dynast's importance and rank, this could be a sister or daughter of the Great King or a more distant blood relative. It was not an unvarying practice (indeed the individual, *ad hominem* nature of the treaties needs to be stressed), but where it occurred it represented a high mark of royal favour (cf. treaty with Amurru, *CTH* 105). The woman chosen for the marriage was sometimes selected by the queen herself and presented to the new dynast – perhaps as part of the formal ceremonies that accompanied the swearing of the treaty and his installation. The new appointee was ordered to rule his kingdom together with his wife, whose relationship to the royal family served as a further check on his ambitions. It also seems to have allowed the Great King to make very definite arrangements about the succession in the subject territory, as shown by the new Tarhuntassa treaty:

> Whatever woman the queen may give you as a wife, her son he will take for the kingship of Tarhuntassa.
>
> (Otten 1988 II 85–86; Lebrun 1992 §13)

As a result, many of the dynasts installed by the Hittite Great King, where they were not themselves already royal kin, certainly became so through marriage to a woman from the royal family; their children were the offspring of a minor Hittite princess or noblewoman, whose family loyalties and roots lay in the Hittite heartland. The Great King was at pains to protect the well-being of his female relatives, who might be married to the ruler of a country where customs about relations with women differed. The treaty with Hukkana of wild and mountainous Azzi-Hayasa, clearly considered an uncivilised place, illustrates this:

> My sister whom I, the sun, have given you as wife, has many sisters of (royal) family (i.e. full sisters) and (royal) seed (i.e. half-sisters) . . . As for the fact that you have (married) their sister, for Hatti there is a law: 'a brother may not have sexual intercourse with his own sister nor his female cousin; that is not right. Whoever does such a thing, he does not live in Hattusa, he is killed.' Because your country is barbarous, it is usual(??) that a brother takes his sister or female cousin (sexually). But that is not right in Hattusa. If ever a sister of your wife, or a half-sister, or a cousin comes to you, give her to eat and drink; eat, drink and be merry! But do not let yourself desire to take her (sexually)! It is not right. Because of such a thing they certainly die. So do not plan it! If someone wants to mislead you into such behaviour, don't listen and don't do it! That is imposed upon you by oath.
>
> (*CTH* 42; Friedrich 1930 no. 6 §§29–30)

This is followed by yet more prohibitions with respect to sexual encounters when Hukkana visits Hattusa, illustrated by a cautionary tale of what might happen if the rules were transgressed. Further, Hukkana is not only forbidden sexual intercourse with his wife's female relations, but also with the women-folk of his brothers, and he is expressly enjoined not to take a local woman as an additional wife.

The essential glue holding the empire together lay in the obligations of loyalty imposed by the Great King on his subjects, be they his personal servants, such as the bodyguard or palace-cooks, or local dynasts ruling with his blessing. In the case of subject-rulers, loyalty was demanded in a number of ways, although specific terms varied: foremost was the injunction to ensure that the royal succession proceed in the legally determined way; other regular demands were to supply troops and fight with the king when he went to war, to hand over fugitives, to report anything that might endanger the safety of the kingdom, to supply persons to carry out labour-obligations when required and provide items for the Hittite cults. To this could be added the order that the local king present himself annually at the Hittite court with his tribute, usually consisting of stipulated quantities of precious metals, as well as specific valuable gifts, which could include coloured cloth and special garments. The terms of the agreement were sanctified by oaths, and the oath sections of the treaties (where preserved) are often extremely long, showing that oaths were sworn by all the gods of both sides, including physical features, such as 'heaven (and) earth, the great sea, the mountains, rivers (and) springs of Hatti and country x'. The treaty was also witnessed by the highest court and military functionaries, identified by name. The text was inscribed on tablets of metal, sometimes precious, as in the case of the treaty with Egypt which was engraved on a tablet of silver (although this was not a 'vassal-treaty'). An archive copy was also made as a record. Until the finding of the bronze tablet with the complete text of the Tudhaliya IV-Kurunta treaty, only such archival copies on clay had been recovered. The bronze tablet gives us a good idea of how treaty texts would have looked: the tablet measures 35 cm x 23.5 cm with a thickness of 8–10 mm, and weighs 5 kg. It has been carefully engraved on both sides, and holes bored at the top of the obverse, through which bronze chains were threaded; to them were probably attached originally the divine seals, with which the treaty was sealed, as shown by the concluding sentences:

> This tablet (has been) made as the seventh copy and sealed with the seal of the sun-goddess of Arinna and with the seal of the weather-god of Hatti. One tablet has been placed before the sun-goddess of Arinna, one tablet before the weather-god of Hatti, one tablet before Lelwani, one tablet before Hepat of Kizzuwadni, one tablet before the *pihassassi* weather-god, one tablet in the royal palace before Zithariya; but Kurunta, king of Tarhuntassa, holds one tablet in his house.
>
> (Otten 1988 §28; Lebrun 1992 §21)

So the majority of copies was kept within sanctuaries under the direct control of the Great King, as well as in his palace. They were deposited before the statues of the major gods, by whom the oaths had been sworn and with whose seals the text was sealed; only one was given to the subject ruler to remind him of his obligations. A duty, sometimes laid upon a client ruler by the terms of the treaty, was to have the treaty read out to him and to his subjects (e.g. Weidner 1923 no. 2, rev. 7–8), suggesting that regularly staged readings were held in public, in which all were reminded of their dependence on the Great King in Hattusa.

The Great King and his officials

The rules imposed on palace and military officers and servants, as well as cult-officials (*CTH* 251–275), were specific to the particular function fulfilled, and consisted of detailed instructions on how they were to be performed in each case (von Schuler 1957; Güterbock and van den Hout 1991). The formal structure, even the Hittite term for the instructions, is identical to that of the 'vassal-treaties', i.e. *ishiul* (= 'bond', 'contract'). It implies that the manner in which royal servants were tied to the throne was conceived to be no different in essence from that of client-kings: *all* received their position and area of competence from the Great King, and owed him the service and duties imposed. The terminology shows that a system, initially used to extract obedience from the king's servants, was extended, as the Hittite realm grew, to representatives of new subjects, i.e. the client-kings. Loyalty was ensured by having the officials swear oaths to keep to the regulations by the same gods that are found in the treaties. Thus, for example, soldiers were sworn into their duties (Oettinger 1976). The officials connected with any kind of divine service were instructed in detail in their responsibilities, beginning with the basic need for them to be clean and moving on to precise details of how to handle the supplies for cultic meals. The manner in which the rule for cleanliness is explained to them is by comparing their role to that of a slave before his master:

> Furthermore let those who prepare the daily bread be clean; let them be washed (and) cleansed(?); let their hair(?) (be cut) and fingernails be pared, and let them have on clean clothes. If not, let them not prepare (it). Let those who propitiate the heart and soul of the gods prepare them (i.e. the loaves of bread). And let the baker's house in which they prepare them be swept(?) and sprinkled(?). Furthermore let not a pig or a dog approach the door of the place where the bread is broken. Is the disposition of men and of the gods at all different? No! Even in this (matter) somewhat (different)? No; their disposition is quite the same. When a slave stands before his master, he is washed and he has on clean (clothes); and either he gives him to eat, or he gives him to drink. And he, his master, eats (and) drinks something and he is relaxed in spirit and he is favourably inclined(?) to him. If, however, he (i.e. the slave)

is ever careless(?) and is not observant(?), there is a different disposition toward him.

(*CTH* 264; Sturtevant and Bechtel 1935 no. 4; *ANET* 207–210)

The 'instructions' give us valuable insights into the administration of the Hittite realm. Thus we know from instruction texts that there was a mayor (*HAZANNU*) of Hattusa, who was ordered by the king to control the city-guards and ensure that order reigned within the city. His officials had the duty to inspect the seals of the gates, which were locked at night, each morning to make sure they had not been broken, then remove the bullae and have the gates opened to allow traffic to pass in and out (*CTH* 257; Otten 1964; 1983; Daddi 1975). Other cities also had mayors with similar respons-ibilities, all accountable for the performance of their duties to the Great King. Garrison commanders and officers in control of frontiers similarly had their duties described and explained (*CTH* 260–261). At the head of the state administration were two groups, 'the great ones', an aristocracy formed by the great families of the realm and 'the king's sons', who were royal relatives in varying degrees. All the major court appointments, the administration of frontier regions, the government of some important client-kingdoms (Car-chemish, Tarhuntassa, Hakpis) and the high army commands, were in the hands of members of these groups. The loyalty oaths that linked each individual official to the king were cemented by marriages, so that the two groups became ever more intertwined – in effect, most ended up being in some sense members of the royal family. One outcome was the creation of a cohesive ruling élite, marked by internal competition for individual advantage among its members. The sort of rewards that went with the holding of high office, aside from a politically advantageous marriage, were shares of tribute, such as fine metal vessels and cloth (cf. the Ugarit treaty, p. 308; *CTH* 47), and of war booty, such as deportees (cf. Mursili Annals, p. 255) to work the estates granted by the king to retainers (Riemschneider 1958; *RLA* 6: 468–470):

> Arnuwanda, the great king, Asmunnikal, the great queen, and Tud-haliya, the king's son, the *tuhkanti* (crown-prince), have taken (property and personnel) and given it as a gift to Kuwatalla, the hierodule, their servant. No-one may dispute it with the sons or grandsons of Kuwatalla. The words of Arnuwanda, great king, Asmunnikal, great queen, Tud-haliya *tuhkanti*, are of iron: do not throw (them) away, do not break (them); whosoever twists them will be beheaded.
>
> (*CTH* 223; Haase 1984: 70–71)

The personnel assigned to holders of land-grants were liable to be used as soldiers and workers by the central authority, unless the Great King granted specific exemptions from such service (Haase 1984: 64–65). Some exemptions to individual landowners are known (e.g. *CTH* 224–225); but the most commonly attested ones in longer historical texts concern the exemptions of people attached to sanctuaries (Otten and Souček 1965). Keeping the cults supplied with workers and provisions was an important duty of the Great King, so the exemptions can be seen as a way for him to meet his manifold obligations in this respect.

The land of Hatti

In addition to the landed estates granted to royal functionaries, Hittite Anatolia was dotted with towns, some of which were quite large, such as Alaca Hüyük, with its substantial fortifications, and Tarhuntassa which was built up into a royal centre by Muwatalli. The great cult-centres, which must have been the size of cities, such as Samuha (Lebrun 1976), Nerik (Haas 1970), and Sallapa (possibly Gordion), have to be added to the roster. Many towns in Anatolia contained palaces and storehouses, called by the Hittites 'seal-houses'. Some of the royal storehouse centres are listed in a fairly well preserved annual festival text (KI.LAM, Singer 1983–4): one of the ceremonies involved the administrators of the royal storehouses of various towns standing by a pile of items brought out from their respective stores; when the king approached, the herald introduced each one to the king and named their towns. Ten names are preserved, although the list was much longer than this, and indicates that the 'seal-houses' were distributed throughout the realm. A number of documents reveal that the storehouse administrators were extremely important officials. The movement of goods through the empire was monitored in the storehouses; they served as collecting-points for royal income, both for grain and other agricultural products, and for textiles and metals, both precious and base. A study of inventory texts has shown that the Hittites had extensive business links not only with Babylonia and Egypt, but also with Lycia, Cyprus, Ahhiyawa, and the north Syrian states (Košak 1982). The imports of grain organised by the merchants of Ura (perhaps Gilindere, near Aydınak in Cilicia, Beal 1992; chapter 6b) have been known for some time; the evidence from the inventory texts has now revealed a little more of the mercantile structure of the realm. It is as well to stress, once again, that the Hittite inventories show that iron was only used by the Hittites for ornamental purposes; the techniques for producing useful tools and weapons of iron were not yet fully developed. The Hittites were *not* innovators in iron technology, they did *not* disseminate it and they certainly held no monopoly in it (Muhly *et al.* 1985).

There were also much smaller places, villages and hamlets, in which local community affairs were handled by village elders, who also represented their community to the central authority and its officials. Most of the information of this side of Hittite life comes from the collection of Hittite laws (*CTH* 291–292; Friedrich 1959; *ANET*: 188ff.; *TUAT* I: 96ff.; Haase 1979), which present some of the same problems that beset understanding of other 'codes', such as the Hammurabi laws (see chapter 2e). They are of Old Kingdom date, re-copied down to the empire period, when their general applicability is in question. Some clauses suggest that they derived from specific royal legal decisions, since they refer to what the consequence of a particular action used to be 'in former times' and what it is 'now' (Hoffner 1965) – a phrase reminiscent of some of the preserved royal decrees.

The agricultural base of Anatolia emerges vividly from the laws, and supplements scattered remarks in other texts. The main cereals produced were barley and emmer, used to make bread and beer, orchards and vineyards were extensively cultivated, and bees were kept in hives for honey (for food in Hittite Antolia, Hoffner 1974). The plots of cultivated land seem to have been small, separated by fences from each other, and dotted within and around the villages. Large cattle and horses were the high-value animals, as is also clear from some of the accounts of Hittite booty. Goats and sheep were more common. They were herded in a reverse pattern to that found in the Syrian and Mesopotamian plains: animals were taken to upland pastures in the summer and brought down into the valleys during the harsh winters. The treaty of Tudhaliya IV (Otten 1988) has revealed particularly clearly the importance of upland summer pastures: Kurunta is specifically granted extensive mountain grazing rights. The same document provides the interesting evidence that saltlicks existed and rights to use them were specified, as was the right to take salt. Pigs were kept very widely, perhaps because of the then more wooded nature of Anatolia, as were dogs. Both animals can cause quarrels between neighbours (hence they figure in the laws): pigs by wandering around in fields and gardens, wreaking havoc with crops, dogs by scavenging. Three types of dog are defined in the laws: sheepdogs (the most highly valued), hunting dogs and guard dogs.

The 'instructions' and a royal letter indicate that the many different communities in Anatolia lived according to a variety of local laws, and that this was recognised and provided for by the central authority. To the frontier commanders (*BEL MADGALTI*), the king issued the following instructions:

> The frontier commander and *maškim* (officials) and elders shall decide cases carefully and complete them. And as from of old in the lands the law determines against evil deeds: in the towns where one used to execute them, they should continue to be executed. But in a town where one used to exile them, one should continue to exile them. The town shall later purify itself. If someone produces a sealed wooden tablet or clay tablet in relation to a case, the frontier commander shall decide very carefully and put everything in order. But if the legal matter is too enormous, he shall refer it to his majesty. But he shall not decide in favour of his lord, nor his brother, his wife or his friend. And no-one shall accept a bribe. A good case shall not lose and a bad one shall not win. Do that which is just! Into whatever city you come – call the

inhabitants together: and whoever has a legal matter, decide for him and end it. Do the same for a male or female dependant, or for a single woman. . .

(*CTH* 261; von Schuler 1957: 36ff.; Haase 1984: 59–60)

The fine ideals which the king held up for his administrators in legal matters are very precisely delineated here: co-operation with the local authorities; respect for local norms; careful evaluation of complex cases; the transmission of very complicated matters to the Great King himself; no favouritism for the powerful or family members and connections; no bribes; justice available for all in their area of jurisdiction, including the weakest members of society. What cannot be assessed, in the absence of private documents, is to what extent this rosy image was a reality, although appeals to the Great King are attested (cf. the Emar letter, quoted p. 267). The only preserved legal cases (apparently sometimes recorded verbatim) concern the stealing of royal and cult property; they can hardly be considered typical (Haase 1984: 66–67; Werner 1967).

Pollution and purification, guilt and penitence

A mass of evidence shows that violent death was thought to cause cultic impurity for the community where it had occurred, and that purification rituals to rid it from blood guilt had to be performed. It is not always easy to understand what such a 'cleansing' involved. One scholar has argued that in a purification ritual for murder (KUB XXX 34) groups of men were divided into two teams, called 'men of Hatti' and 'men of Masa'; the Hatti team were given bronze weapons while the Masa team received reed weapons. The two teams then engaged in a 'battle' and the men of Hatti (naturally) won. A prisoner-of-war was then taken and dedicated to the god (Kümmel 1967: 150–162). But another scholar has interpreted the same text as connected to a particular autumn festival, during which a legendary battle was re-enacted (Gurney 1977: 27; 1990: 129). So the relationship of the ritual to purification remains uncertain. Any sort of death, in fact, carried the risk of contamination with it, although natural deaths only polluted close members of the family who had been in physical contact with the body, and had not yet buried the body or rid the house of items used by the dead person. As, for example, here:

His son has died. The bed on which he slept he did not burn, but sleeps on it night after night.

(KUB XVI 83 vs. 26ff.; Otten 1958: 9)

Concern with cultic purity is a recurring motif in Hittite texts, and could be caused by any number of acts and circumstances. Ignoring possible sources of pollution was extremely dangerous, as they could manifest themselves in the form of plagues that might devastate the whole population. Despite the great might of the Hittite army, for which generally only victories are reported, the Hittites did sustain defeats and a defeated army was considered to represent a serious impurity from which it must be cleansed before it could re-enter the country:

> When the troops have been defeated by the enemy, then a sacrifice should be arranged 'behind' the river thus: Behind the river one cuts a person, a kid, a puppy, and a piglet through the middle and places one half on one side and one on the other. In front of it one makes a gate out of (some kind of) wood and stretches a string(?) across it. Then one lights a fire on either side of the gate. The troops go through this, but as soon as they have arrived at the bank of the river, one sprinkles water over them.
>
> (Bo. 2039 + Bo. 2864 IV 45–56; Kümmel 1967: 151; Haase 1984: 90)

The most rigid rules and rituals to avert pollution were reserved for the king himself, who was hedged about with an elaborate series of protocols for his spiritual and physical safety, since he embodied the well-being of the whole realm. In instances where the army was defeated and a plague broke out (despite its initial cleansing), then a male prisoner-of-war and a woman were seized. The king himself stood on the road leading towards the country of the enemy, and was approached by officials leading the man and woman decked in royal robes. The king then spoke to each one: 'If a god (and to the woman: 'goddess') of the enemy has caused the plague, here is a man/woman decked out as a substitute. Be satisfied with him/her; he shall take the plague back to the enemy.' Then the substitute royal pair were sent into the country of the enemy with a bull and ewe, both decorated, driven before them (Kümmel 1967: 112ff.). The responsibility for defeat and plague was, in this instance, thought to reside in the person of the king and queen: only figures resembling the royal pair would prove acceptable to the gods of the enemy country, whose potential for doing evil in Hatti had been strengthened by victory.

In a case where plague broke out despite a victory, it was assumed that the king must have committed some crime that had gone undetected. When Suppiluliuma I's victorious soldiers brought back a virulent epidemic from Syria (p. 254), which decimated the population for twenty years as well as carrying off the Great King and his successor, Mursili II established, from ancient texts, that this was a divine punishment because his father had broken an oath and the kings of Hatti had failed to make offerings to the river Mala in the east. Although Mursili II himself was not personally guilty, he accepted that the burden of his predecessors' crimes and omissions had descended on his shoulders, and that only he could act to rid the country of the fearful pestilence. The 'plague prayers' of Mursili II movingly present the desperation of the grief-stricken king:

> What is this that you (sc. the gods) have done? A plague you have let

into the land. The Hatti land has been cruelly afflicted by the plague. For twenty years now men have been dying in my father's days, in my brother's days, and in my own since I have become the priest of the gods. When men are dying in the Hatti land like this, the plague is certainly not over. As for me, the agony of my heart and the anguish of my soul I cannot endure any more.

. . .

See! I lay the matter of the plague before the storm-god of Hatti, my lord. Hear me, storm-god of Hatti, and save my life! This is what I [have to remind] you: The bird takes refuge in (its) nest, and the nest saves its life. Again: if anything becomes too much for a servant, he appeals to his lord. His lord hears him and takes pity on him. Whatever had become too much for him, he sets right for him. Again: if the servant has incurred guilt, but confesses his guilt to his lord, his lord may do with him whatever he pleases. But, because (he) has confessed his guilt to his lord, his lord's soul is pacified, and his lord will not punish the servant. I have now confessed my father's sin. It is only too true, I have done it. If there is to be restitution, it seems clear that with all the gifts that have already been given because of this plague, with all the prisoners that have been brought home, in short with all the restitution that Hattusa has made because of the plague, it has already made restitution twenty-fold. But if you demand from me additional restitution, tell me of it in a dream and I will give it to you.

(KUB XIV 8; ANET 394–396)

King, court and ceremonial

The 'plague prayers' encapsulate perfectly the centrality of the king to the state, and one of the features of the Hittite kings (like others) was their extraordinarily intense personal involvement and concern in running their kingdom. The royal presence was marked throughout the realm by his palaces, storehouses and domains (on which subjects not exempted had to work for specified days). His commands were sealed with the great royal seal; the treaties imposing obligations and granting rights to subject kings were read aloud on certain occasions. Those accused of treachery or any very serious crime were ordered into his presence ('the wheel', cf. Apology of Hattusili III, p. 260). The highest officials ran the risk of losing all their property and labouring as peasants if they were found guilty (cf. Edict of Telepinu, p. 246). Commanders who did not heed the royal order to appear before the king were blinded (Alp 1980).

The Great King travelled regularly through the central area of the empire, celebrating a series of festivals, such as the great spring festival (AN.TAH.ŠUM; Güterbock 1960; Gurney 1977: 31 ff.) lasting all of thirty-two days, and the autumn festival (*nuntariyasha*; Güterbock 1964) which

lasted twenty-one days, to mention only the longest. The king even performed festivals while on campaign (Annals of Mursili, p. 255). While several
ceremonies had to be performed in particular towns, some of the major cults
were concentrated within Hattusa itself, such as those of the storm-god of
Hatti and the sun-goddess of Arinna. The festivals held in the capital drew
people to the royal city, such as the royal storehouse administrators (see
p. 272) who came to Hattusa for the three-day KI.LAM festival. This
particular ceremony seems to have taken place in and around the palace itself.
It included a foot race, the first two winners of which were presented with
prizes by the king, and culminated in a gathering at the *huwasi* stone of the
storm-god of Hatti. This cult-object may have been located at Yazılıkaya, in
which case a festive procession moving along the ceremonial way to this great
rock sanctuary perhaps formed the climax of the festival (Singer 1983–4).
Elaborate cult-statues of the deities certainly existed, but they could also be
represented by animals associated with them (e.g. the bull of the storm-god),
a shaped stone (e.g the *huwasi* stone), or even gold and silver discs (Werner
1967: 56 and 57, ll. 9–10).

The king was officially the main priest of all the gods of Hatti (cf. the
'plague prayer', pp. 275–276). He himself was not divine, although his
relationship to the gods was exceptionally close, and a late Hittite king,
Tudhaliya IV, was depicted in the Yazılıkaya shrine closely embraced by a
god – a scene shown in miniature on several royal seals, too. In the Empire
period, the king was regularly referred to, and referred to himself, as 'my sun',
which was a verbal echo of the royal symbol of the winged sun used, for
example, on seals, where it formed a small canopy floating above his name
rendered in Hittite hieroglyphs (see fig. 23); but the exact significance of
symbol and phrase remains enigmatic (Güterbock 1954). He was also
regularly described as 'the hero', descended from Suppiluliuma I, and, of
course, 'Great King' to mark his superiority to the many subject kings he
ruled over. The term 't/labarna', commonly used in the Old Kingdom period,
seems to have been used less and less, although it did not disappear completely
as shown by the 'Apology of Hattusili' and the Kurunta seals (see pp. 259;
265). Hattusili III also, interestingly, harks back to very ancient traditions by
defining himself as a member of the Kussara dynasty and ultimately descended from Hattusili I. This may have been dictated by the irregular circumstances that brought him to the throne, but shows nevertheless how alive the
traditions about the early history of Hatti were.

Only when he died did the king 'become a god' – the standard phrase to
express a royal death. His body was burnt and the remains taken to the 'stone-
house', where they were placed in a chamber equipped with a bed and a lamp
and fed with meat and drink (Otten 1958). A cult was set up there for the
dead king, equipped with personnel appointed to care for the dead ruler;
they were forbidden to marry people outside the cult community (Haase
1984: 69–70).

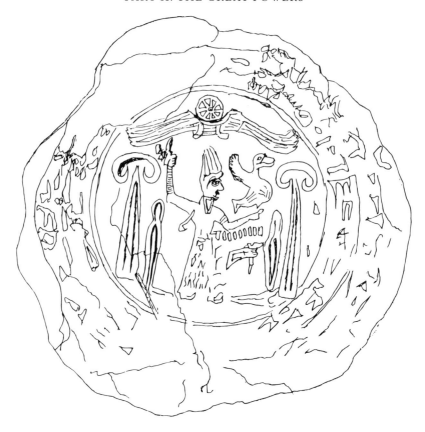

Figure 23 Seal impression of Arnuwanda III, Hattusa (drawing by D. Saxon)

The rules of succession (pp. 246–247) were carefully regulated and seem to have been adhered to until the very end of the empire (pp. 249–250). Ideally, the eldest son of the reigning king was designated crown-prince (*tuḫkanti*), and occupied a position second only to his father. His pre-eminent status is illustrated by references in the Kurunta treaty (p. 264) and the prominent role he is occasionally attested as playing in royal campaigns. The new king was anointed, as part of his role as a priest of the major cults; a gift of anointing oil and royal robes was expected as an appropriate gesture of honour to a new king on his accession (*CTH* 173). In the course of a formal ceremony, the king and queen sat upon the throne for the first time, and his royal name, sometimes different from his personal name, was called. It is likely that he and the queen then proceeded to make sacrifices.

From then on the king was subject to rigorous rules regulating palace protocol and ensuring his constant purity as behoved a priest of the major gods. The servants in whose hands was the physical day-to-day care of the king were warned, on pain of death for them and their families, against any kind of carelessness; nor need they think that no one would know, because 'the gods of the king are observing you. They will turn you into goats and chase you into the mountains' (*CTH* 265; *ANET*: 207; *TUAT* I: 124). A more humane note, showing the king's kindness to servants who confess misdeeds, also appears:

> You, who (are) the leather-workers from the house of the charioteer, the house of the store-administrator and of the inspector of ten charioteers, and who construct the king's chariots, which he enters, always take cowhide and goathide (only) from the kitchen. Other (hide) you may not take. But if you do take other (hide), then tell the king, and (then it is) not a crime for you. I, the king, can send (the chariot) to a foreigner or give it to a servant.
>
> (CTH 265 III 9–17; TUAT I: 125)

Regulations – about the order in which court-officials were to bow to the king when he descended from his chariot (Jakob-Rost 1966), what a body-guard was to do if he needed to urinate or defecate during a royal inspection, about avoiding contact with palace-women – abounded, controlling the movement of everyone in the interests of the king's safety. The ranks of the chief dignitaries surrounding the king can be deduced from a number of texts: their titles are derived from particular palace functions, which in themselves provide only scant indication of what specific services they performed. Some, such as the commander of the bodyguard and 'leader of ten', were obviously military, while others, like the chief scribe and the storehouse administrators (^{lú}AGRIG), were concerned with the administration of the empire. But others, such as the 'chief of the wine', the cupbearer, 'chief scribe of the kitchen', are harder to understand. It is probably a mistake to seek for enlightenment from the titles themselves, since it is likely that their powers were of a wide-ranging nature not reflected by their labels (cf. some of the titles in use in the British court, e.g. 'Companion of the Bath').

The position of the queen presents some problems as yet not completely resolved. Until the late fourteenth century, the title *tawananna* is regularly used of a royal woman associated with the king. She performed a number of important rituals alongside the king, and acted as a priestess in cults where he was priest. She was not, however, invariably his wife. It appears that the position of *tawananna* was handed down separately from the kingship. Usually she was the king's wife, but if the king died before her she retained her position and title until her death, when the king's wife succeeded her. It is possible that in instances where the king's wife was not *tawananna*, she held instead the title of 'great princess' (DUMU.SAL.GAL). But it must be admitted that many aspects of the position of king's wife, *tawananna* and other palace women remain very poorly understood (for discussion, see Bin-Nun 1975). The king and queen appear in quite a number of texts as acting in concert: making grants of property (Tudhaliya and Asmunikkal, p. 271), sealing treaties (Ugarit treaty, see chapter 6b), linked in perfect love (Hattusili Apology, p. 261); or the queen complements her husband's act of installing a subject ruler by selecting a woman to be his wife (Kurunta treaty, p. 268). The significance of her role is shown by the fact that she, too, was frequently included in the cult of the royal dead. The queen could also assign individuals, such as prisoners of war, to carry out work for Hittite widows with children who could not perform their duties for a cult-foundation (e.g. Puduhepa; Otten and Souček 1965); or she could provide cult-personnel with 'families':

> A girl, Titai is her name, I gave to Apallu as bride. A boy, Tatili, the brother of Titai, I gave to Apallu to bring up . . . a female baby, Pitati is her name, and a boy, Temetti, have been given to SUM-ia, the son of Pitan[. . .]ia, to bring up.
>
> (Otten and Souček 1965: 21)

This positive image of the queens is balanced by a number of famous court scandals: the 'wicked' sister of Hattusili I ('that snake', see p. 238) was said to have plotted treason; the Babylonian wife of Suppiluliuma I was accused of causing the death of Mursili II's wife by witchcraft (*CTH* 70); a complex and dire intrigue, probably played out at the court of Tudhaliya IV, involved the 'great princess' (Ünal 1978). But the preserved number of such incidents is relatively small, when spread over four hundred years; they say perhaps more about the general tendency to suspect figures, whose gender (or other characteristics) preclude them from ever wielding political power directly, but who are nevertheless intimately involved in the reproduction and continuity of the political framework. This must surely have been the situation for the Hittite queens and princesses.

One of the most important roles of the king was, of course, that of chief commander in war. All the Hittite kings appear to have campaigned regularly, and to have repeatedly led their armies in person. Even the tiring and frustrating wars where no great prizes in terms of booty, territory or glory could be won, such as the endless routine campaigns waged against the Gasga, were conducted by the kings themselves. Commands were only delegated when the king was engaged simultaneously on several fronts. The wars were of course a major source of income for the Hittite king: victories brought tribute pouring in, much needed manpower that could be used to extend and maintain the agricultural base on which the state rested, and land which could be given out to high-level functionaries, such as the captains of the golden grooms, members of the royal family and cults. Success in war also signalled that the gods of Hatti favoured the king and were prepared to bless his reign. The return from campaign of a triumphant king to Hattusa was marked by celebrations in honour of the gods and an assembly of the 'whole population of Hatti' to pay homage to the victorious ruler. But such a gathering could also present an opportunity for airing popular grievances and obtaining a generous royal settlement (von Schuler 1959; Haase 1984: 56–57). Despite the king's protected and hemmed-in existence, the public ceremonies and fest-ivals, the royal journeys through his realm on cultic or military duties were fully exploited by the population of Hatti to present petitions and complaints about injustices to him and provided opportunities for direct contact between king and quite humble subjects.

✻ ✻ ✻

While the Hittite state has often been presented as a rather ramshackle collection of motley peoples that flew apart when threatened by a serious attack, it is perhaps more appropriate to stress the remarkable strength of a system that held together so effectively for over four hundred years, during the last one hundred and fifty of which it controlled a very extensive territory. Continuity of social forms and practices from the Old Kingdom to the Empire, as seen in various texts, implies that political reverses did not drastically affect the core of the state. Much has been made of the delicately balanced mechanism of the Hittite state and its insufficiently developed infrastructure (Liverani 1987; Sandars 1978), which caused it to collapse so suddenly and totally. But that is true of many states in the ancient world. What really needs more analysis is its extraordinary resilience and ability to recover from the occasionally devastating setbacks it experienced.

Notes

1 G. Steiner argues in the *Festschrift* for Nimet Özgüç (1993) that Zalpa should be located on the Great Salt Lake in Central Turkey.

2 The three exemplars consist of one complete text and two fragmentary versions, one from the Old Hittite period (1650–1500) and one in Akkadian.

3 It is now firmly established that the Hittite form of Kanesh was 'Nesa' (cf. Otten 1973). It seems that the 'K' in the name was (or had become) silent; cf. the silent 'k' in English words such as 'knit', 'knee', 'knock' etc.

4 The texts often referred to as 'Hittite King Lists' are not chronological lists of rulers, but lists of royal ancestors to whom offerings were made. They include individuals who were never kings (e.g. queens).

5 Because of the enormous chronological uncertainties besetting the Hittite king-list, there are also confusions concerning the numbering of the Hittite kings. For example, it is not clear how many kings there were called Mursili: only two are attested – Mursili I (1620–1590) and Mursili II (1330–1295/1321–1295); but it was originally thought that there was another one, so that older books refer to the one now commonly known as Mursili II as 'Mursili III'. Similar problems exist with kings called Tudhaliya and Muwatalli, and there is a massive dispute about the number of kings called Hattusili. No certainty about any of this is possible at present.

6 A problem is the complete absence of any Mycenaean material in central Anatolia – we would expect to find some if the Hittites had contacts with Mycenaean centres. Further, a mere eight objects in the Bronze Age Aegean can, with any degree of likelihood, be given a central Anatolian origin. They constitute only

1 per cent of the Near Eastern objects found in the Bronze Age Aegean (E.H. Clines *AnSt* 41 (1991): 133ff.).

7 All texts quoted, unless otherwise stated, are from the great archives found in the city of Hattusa, especially in the Great Temple. Many are extant in a number of copies, sometimes from different dates, so that the texts represent composite versions. For details of the constituent parts of texts (up to 1970), see the cited references to *CTH*.

8 There is one definite exception now: the new king Muwatalli (I) of the Middle Hittite Kingdom (see p. 231); there may be more. We do not know his relationship to the early Empire rulers, and will have to wait until the Middle Kingdom kings are understood more clearly.

6

SYRIA AND THE LEVANT

6a Mitanni and the Hurrians

Who were the Hurrians?

Scholars first recognised the Hurrian language, as a significant cultural and political element in the ancient Near East, at the end of the nineteenth century with the discovery, in 1887, in the Amarna archive from Egypt (cf. chapter 4c), of a long letter written in cuneiform. Although written in a hitherto unknown, non-Semitic language, it was clearly sent to Egypt by Tushratta, king of Mitanni (*c.* 1370/1360). The same king had written other letters in Akkadian. On the strength of that letter the language was at first called 'Mitannian'. The Egyptian data showed that Mitanni lay somewhere to the north of the Egyptian-controlled areas of the Levant and was a powerful kingdom on a par, in terms of international politics, with Egypt. Various detailed studies of Mesopotamian personal names, from the Old Babylonian (see chapter 2) into the Kassite period (see chapter 7a), established that a good number of these 'Mitannians' (i.e. people with Mitannian-type names) were present at that time in that area too. However, their place of origin and role in this predominantly Semitic Akkadian-speaking region were obscure. The discovery of the Hittite archives at Boğazköy, and the study of their contents, added a new dimension to the problem. The archives contained numerous 'Mitannian' texts (mainly of a ritual and literary nature), but the language was called 'Hurrian' (texts in seven different languages have been found in the Boğazköy archives; the language in which texts are written is often indicated, cf. chapter 5b).

The term 'Hurrian' used by the Boğazköy archives reminds the present-day reader of the Old Testament 'Horites' (*Gen.* 14.6; 36.20; *Deut.* 2.12; 1 *Chron.* 1.38), who are mentioned as one of the population-groups of the southern Levant (south-east of the Dead Sea), predating the Israelites. In southern Mesopotamia, things 'Hurrian' are occasionally called 'Subarian' – a designation which suggests that the speakers of this language were conceived to live somewhere 'in the north' (Gelb 1944): 'Subartu' is used in Meso-

283

potamia to indicate 'north' (cf. the analogous 'Amurru' = 'west'). Because of the vagueness of the term 'Subarian', coupled with the fact that there are references to the 'Land of the Hurrians', when the state of Mitanni is meant, it has generally been considered appropriate to call the language, and any identifiable accompanying cultural traits, 'Hurrian'.

The Hurrian language is rendered in the cuneiform script, which means that a rough idea of its pronunciation is recoverable. But it is unrelated to either the Indo-European or Semitic linguistic families, and this has made it hard to analyse. Tushratta of Mitanni used a number of standard formulae in his letter, which mirror the Akkadian more regularly used in correspondence; this has provided a key for setting up a lexicon and rudimentary grammar of Hurrian. The find of a number of Hittite-Hurrian bilinguals at Boğazköy and Ugarit has also increased understanding of the language. Schooltexts, found at Ugarit (chapter 6b), list Hurrian words with their equivalents in Akkadian, Sumerian and Ugaritic – invaluable for scholars. But, despite all these 'aids', the limited number of Hurrian texts means that scholarly knowledge of the language is still imperfect (Gordon 1971: 93–95). It seems now fairly clear that Hurrian belongs to the Caucasian language group (Wilhelm 1982), and the tiny number of scholars actively engaged in studying Hurrian are constantly making progress. But unless a greater number and variety of Hurrian texts is discovered it will remain an only partially known language.

The remaining problems are enormous. For example, where were the people associated with the Hurrian language located, and when? Did a definable movement take place at some stage, bringing them into western Asia, or not? The kingdom of Mitanni seems to be the one definable political entity ruled by people who were Hurrian-speakers. But when and how exactly did it come into being? How extensive was it? Can we trace its history at all? Finally, are there any distinguishing cultural, political or legal features that we might call 'Hurrian'?

If we want to try to answer any of these questions it is essential to examine the sources for the Hurrians, which are exclusively linguistic: there are no artefacts or buildings that can with any certainty be defined as 'Hurrian' in type (Kramer 1977). One scholar (Wilhelm 1982: 8) has pointed out that a group only definable through its language does not necessarily constitute a social group. A further problem is that a lot of the evidence for Hurrians consists of personal names, which provide only a very unreliable guide to social realities. Wilhelm (1982: 18) has remarked very aptly: 'If out of one hundred personal names, fifty are Hurrian, one cannot maintain that therefore half of the population spoke, or even necessarily was, Hurrian'. Reasons for adopting particular names are multiple and complex, they are not necessarily indicative of ethno-linguistic and cultural identity.

Hurrians are not attested before the Agade empire (2340–2198): at this period, a text from Nippur mentions a gift of textiles from a woman with a Hurrian name to a recipient, also bearing a Hurrian name. This is generally interpreted as a text intended to accompany a ceremonial gift; if this is right, it suggests that the Agade rulers may have maintained diplomatic relations with a small Hurrian state on the edge of their extensive realm. From the late Agade period comes a royal inscription, written in Akkadian, but recording the founding of a temple by a man with a Hurrian name: Atalshen, of Urkish (possibly Tell Amuda in the Khabur triangle, although recently Mozan has been proposed; Buccellati and Kelly 1988) and of Nawar (in the same general area, possibly Tell Brak; D. Matthews and J. Eidem 1993); see map 4).

In the Ur III period (2112–2017), several texts in Hurrian of Tishatal, *endan* (?lord/ruler) of Urkish, confirm the Hurrian character of parts of the south-eastern region of Turkey and also the area around Nineveh:

> Tishatal, *endan* of Urkesh, has built a temple of Nerigal. May the god Lugaba protect this temple. Whosoever destroys it, may Lugaba destroy him. May the (weather)god (??) not hear his prayer(?). May the mistress of Nagar, the sun-god and the weather-god him who destroys it . . . .
>
> (Parrot and Nougayrol 1948; Wilhelm 1982: 15)

A cylinder seal suggests that Karahar, perhaps to be located in the north-east Tigris/north-west Iran region, was also a Hurrian centre at this time. There is also evidence for emissaries with Hurrian names from here, as well as other places, such as Simurrum (north Raniya plain), Urshu (north Syria/west bank of Euphrates) and Urbilum (Arbela, east bank of Tigris, modern Erbil). A number of functionaries in the Ur III empire also bear unmistakable Hurrian personal names.

The cumulative evidence of this piecemeal material shows that some centres in present-day south-east Turkey, northern Iraq and north-west Iran were ruled by kings with Hurrian names, who wrote texts in Hurrian, using the cuneiform system adopted from their Akkadian and Sumerian neighbours. Hurrians also formed a population element in the Ur III empire – they may have got there initially as prisoners-of-war; but if they arrived as captives, some of them were eventually sufficiently assimilated to become officials in the government. There were also holders of high state-office with Hurrian names in the areas of north Syria and the east Tigris.

In the Old Babylonian period (*c.* 2000–*c.* 1600), a few Hurrian personal names are attested within Babylonia. It is possible that some incantation-texts were written in Hurrian, although this is not certain (*RLA* 4. 509–310). At Mari, seven texts show strong Hurrian elements: three of these are definitely Hurrian compositions (Thureau-Dangin 1939; *RLA* 4: 510). There are also a number of Hurrian personal names, and the Mari correspondence shows that Urshu and Hashshu (both in north Syria) were ruled by Hurrian dynasties (Kupper 1957: 229–235; Sasson 1974). At the site of Shemshara (ancient Shusharra in north-east Iraq), a lot of the personal names are Hurrian in this period, as one would expect given its location; but Hurrian is not the predominant element – the evidence reflects the more general use of another language local to the region (Laessøe 1959). About 20 per cent of the personal names are Hurrian in the contemporary archives from Rimah and Chagar Bazar. Uncertainty surrounds the presence of Hurrian names in the Old Assyrian colonies in Anatolia: some scholars insist on a virtual absence (*RLA* 4: 510), while others have identified some (about fifty), including the local prince of Mama, Anum-hirbi (Garelli 1963: 155–158). About sixty to seventy years later (*c.* 1700), at Alalah VII in north-west Syria, half of the personal names are Hurrian; at the same time, the Akkadian language in use at Alalah VII shows a strong Hurrian influence, and the month-names are Hurrian.

The conclusion to be drawn from this is that, in the period between *c.* 1850 and 1600, Hurrians appear to be present in increasing numbers throughout northern Mesopotamia and Syria, as well as in the areas where they were located earlier (north-west Iran and north-east Iraq). But does this represent a movement of peoples? It is hard to say: the geographical spread of written evidence is much wider in this period than in the third millennium – so it is, at least, possible that we are simply able to see their presence more clearly at this time. A significant development that *was* taking place is that much more was being written in Hurrian, including the development of a Hurrian literature; in addition, Hurrian gods were being named and referred to much more frequently. All this may reflect the relative density and distribution of the evidence, together with an increased Hurrian 'literacy', rather than any movement of peoples. This picture may need to be revised (or adjusted) as the Ebla documents become fully available. Ebla is the only extensive possible source about Hurrian(s) in west Syria in the third millennium: the texts are not yet all published, and so far there is no evidence for Hurrian(s) there.

The Hittite Old Kingdom (*c.* 1650–*c.* 1500) contributes more material which, although vague, is important. Hattusili I (1650–1620) refers to a devastating Hurrian invasion of the eastern part of his realm (see p. 241); also, in his reign, as well as that of his successor, Mursili I (1620–1590), there were Hurrian kings in north Syria. Mursili I *may* have encountered a significant Hurrian political presence perhaps to the east of Aleppo and west of Babylonia (see p. 245). There are also fragmentary references to Hurrian attacks in the Edict of Telipinu (*c.* 1520–1500; p. 245). Although the Old Hittite texts do not refer to the kingdom of Mitanni, the evidence *could* be taken to suggest that, as a result of both the aggressive expansion of the Hittites and their destruction of the kingdom of Aleppo, the cities and people located within the bend of the Euphrates and on the north Mesopotamian plain were progressively forming a more coherent and structured political entity, which eventually crystallised into the Mitannian state.

The centuries between *c.* 1500 and *c.* 1200 provide the fullest and clearest material for the Hurrians and Mitanni, although political history, culture and society remain very problematic and the evidence is still quantitatively tiny. Two sites provide the most coherent archives connected with the kingdom of Mitanni: first, Nuzi (now Yorghan Tepe), which was part of the small principality of Arrapha (modern Kirkuk). Most of its extensive archives date *c.* 1500–1350, when Arrapha was attached to, and under the overlordship of, Mitanni. The archives found here therefore constitute an important source for political structure and social conditions within a part of the state of Mitanni. The greater part of the personal names at Nuzi are Hurrian, but the written language is Akkadian and some of the social customs comparable to Babylonia – so how typical anything of what can be reconstructed for Arrapha might be of Mitanni and the Hurrians is problematical. The same reservations apply to the virtually contemporary archives from Alalah IV, which was also subject to Mitanni, though ruled by a local dynasty. A little is known about how Alalah became a subject of Mitanni from the inscription on the statue of its ruler, Idrimi (Smith 1949; dated *c.* 1500 (1480/70 on the shorter chronology)). This text also shows that Mitanni had gained control of the city-states of Aleppo and Emar; however, the recently excavated texts from Emar (Tell Meskene) are from a later period when it was under Hittite control and are mainly literary (see chapter 6c).

There is also some evidence in this period for the 'Hurrianisation' of Qatna on the Orontes in the form of a long inventory text of the cultic furniture of a goddess (*c.* 1400; Bottéro 1949). Direct political control was probably never wielded by Mitanni over the cities in this region, but a close relationship with their large and powerful neighbour seems likely, and did exist, according to Tuthmosis III's accounts of some of his campaigns (p. 323). A large proportion of material for the the study of the Hurrian language comes from Ugarit on the coast (*c.* 1400–1200), although Ugarit was no more than briefly subject to Mitanni. We should probably assume that, because Mitanni wielded enormous political power for a time, the Hurrian literary tradition became more marked in several neighbouring places not subject to the Mitanni kingdom. A further important source is the Amarna archive (*c.* 1370–1340 (*c.* 1360–1330)), not merely because of the Tushratta letters, but because it reveals that several local dynasts in the Levant, with whom the Egyptians corresponded, bore Hurrian names. Roughly into this period fall the texts from Emar (Tell Meskene, Arnaud 1991). But the main body of Hurrian literary works (about forty texts) comes from the Hittite capital, Hattusa (Boğazköy). An indication of the extent to which we must reckon with a massive Hurrian cultural diffusion at this time is the fact that some of the Hittite kings of the Empire period (*c.* 1430/20–*c.* 1200) had Hurrian personal names (Güterbock 1954). A strong Hurrian cultic/religious influence is also definitely perceptible from *c.* 1300 on: at the great open-air shrine of Yazılıkaya (near Hattusa, cf. pp. 234–235) the leading members of the huge pantheon depicted are all Hurrian deities. Why this happened is not known – it is usually argued that Hurrian religious elements entered the Hittite court circle with the marriage of Hattusili III to Puduhepa of Kizzuwadna (in eastern Cilicia; Hattusili Apology, pp. 260–261). How precisely this is supposed to have worked remains obscure; indeed, whether all Hurrian influence in Hatti should be dated to the time of Hattusili III is rather doubtful. What *is* true is that Kizzuwadna (Cilicia) was strongly Hurrianised, although it was only briefly, and rather loosely, part of the Mitannian realm.

The conclusion we can draw from this evidence is that there was a massive increase in definable Hurrian cultural elements during the period *c.* 1500– *c.* 1200. Politically, too, we can see, though not as clearly as we should like, the existence of a distinct, large-scale, powerful state, Mitanni, which we can, with some justification, call 'Hurrian': its rulers are Hurrian; they refer to their subjects as Hurrians; they sometimes use the Hurrian language for correspondence. The politically dominant position of Mitanni probably explains the noticeable 'Hurrianisation' of the Levant and northern Meso- potamia: Hurrian culture is another element that has to be added to the already many-faceted and very complex cultures of the whole region.

We should note one further aspect: in the first millennium, the kingdom of Urartu (around Lake Van and further north) used a language which bears some similarities to earlier Hurrian (chapter 10a). Various people have, therefore, argued (e.g. Diakonoff 1972) that the Urartian language is a direct development of earlier Hurrian, and that we might understand some socio- cultural elements of Mitanni better by comparison with what we know about later Urartu. However, although Urartian and Hurrian *are* related in that they are both Caucasian languages, it is now fairly clear that the two languages developed quite independently from the third millennium onwards (Wilhelm 1982: 5). So, the linear connection between the two is broken, and Urartian culture cannot serve to throw any light on Mitanni or the Hurrians.

Can we draw any conclusions as to the affinities, origins and earlier history of the Hurrians and the development of the Hurrian state of Mitanni? North- west Iran, north Iraq, the extreme north of Syria and south-eastern areas of Turkey constituted their central area of settlement at an early date (i.e. the second half of the third millennium); nothing suggests that this situation changed later, except in terms of political developments. It is, therefore, likely that the Hurrians were a cultural-linguistic group *always* located among the foothills and mountains fringing the northern Mesopotamian and Syrian plains, stretching in an arc from east of the Tigris (north of the Diyala) to the slopes of the Taurus, west of the Euphrates (near Maraş). Following the decline of the powerful states and their system of alliances (Ashur, Eshnunna, Mari, Aleppo and Babylon), who dominated Mesopotamia and Syria in the period between *c.* 1850 and 1595 (chapter 2), a new political power emerged in northern Mesopotamia. This was the kingdom of Mitanni, whose cultural affinities, to judge by personal names and language, were Hurrian. Its focal point was probably the headwaters of the Khabur, but its political control eventually extended to the Mediterranean in the west (Emar, Aleppo and Alalah) and Iraq (Assyria and Arrapha) in the east. This picture fits quite well with two facts: a) some of the oldest Hurrian cult-centres were located in north-west Iran and north Mesopotamia (Wilhelm 1982: 69–77); and b) the Hurrian language has its own distinctive name for the Tigris. In other words, the Hurrians, as far as we can tell, were from prehistoric times connected with this region – we do not need not to visualise them as a group migrating from somewhere further north or east.

The kingdom of Mitanni

Historical outline

What do we know about the great kingdom of Mitanni – the powerful state against which Tuthmosis I (1507–1494 (1504–1491)) fought, and which blocked the great Tuthmosis III's bid for expansion (1490–1436 (1479–1425); cf. pp. 323–324)? The answer is: disappointingly little. We can date its emergence only very tentatively; there is almost no archaeological evidence from the central area of Mitanni; its capitals, Washshukanni and Taide, have not been located. The line of Mitannian kings becomes dimly discernible at the turn of the fifteenth to the fourteenth century with king Saushtatar; he appears in a date on a Nuzi tablet, together with what has been thought to be a dynastic seal mentioning his predecessors (see Stein 1989 on problems of dating). The Mitannian rulers, Kirta, Shuttarna and Parsatatar are, on this evidence, usually considered to be the predecessors of Saushtatar. All of them were preceded by Parrattarna, who was the king of Mitanni referred to on the statue of Idrimi of Alalah (c. 1500 or 1480/1470; see table 19). But this is all very imprecise: the relationship between the kings is unknown, and we do not know whether all of them actually ruled Mitanni or not. The one thing we do know for certain is that c. 1500 (or 1480/1470) Parrattarna of Mitanni was in control of Aleppo to the west. The unique and lively autobiography of Idrimi illustrates the kind of control the Mitannian king wielded over subject states. The text, composed in faulty Akkadian and inscribed on the figure of Idrimi, was found in the ruins of a temple at the site of Tell Atchana (ancient Alalah; Smith 1949; Woolley 1953). The date at which the text was placed on the statue has been assumed to be the time of Idrimi himself. But this has been questioned, and the suggestion made that it was only added to the statue about three hundred years later (Sasson 1981):

I am Idrimi, the son of Ilimilimma, servant of Teshub (storm-god), Hepat (Teshub's consort) and Shaushga (an Ishtar-like deity), the lady of Alalah, my mistress.

In Halab (Aleppo), in the house of my fathers, a crime had occurred and we fled. The lords of Emar were descended from the sisters of my mother, so we settled in Emar. My brothers, who were older than me, also lived with me. But no one considered the matters, which I was thinking about – because I thought this to myself: 'He who is in the

Table 19 Chronology of kings of Mitanni

Egypt	Mitanni	Aleppo (Alalah)	Ashur	Hatti
				Hattusili I
Amose (1552–1527)				Mursili I
Amenophis I (1527–1507)		Sharra-el		Hantili
		Abba-el		Zidanta
Tuthmosis I (1507–1494)				Telepinu
		Ilimilimma		
Tuthmosis II (1494–1490)	Parrattarna	Idrimi		
Tuthmosis III (1490–1436)	(c. 1480?) Kirta Shuttarna I			
	Parsatatar			Tudhaliya I
Amenophis II (1438–1412)	Saushtatar (Parrattarna II?)	Niqmepa	Ashur-nadin-ahhe I	Hattusili II
Tuthmosis IV (1412–1403)	Artatama I			
Amenophis III (1403–1364)	Shuttarna II			Tudhaliya II
	Artashumara		Ashur-uballit	Arnuwanda I
Amenophis IV (= Akhenaten) 1364–1347)	Tushratta (+ Artatama II Shuttarna III)			Suppiluliuma I
Tutankhamun (1345–1335)	Shattiwaza			

(This table follows the conventional chronology; all dates require lowering by *c.* 10 years for the 'low' chronology, see Wilhelm 1982.)

house of his father, he is the great son of a prince; but he who is with the people of Emar, is a slave.'

I took my horse, my chariot and my squire and went into the desert. I found shelter with the Sutaeans (nomads). Together with my groom I spent the night before the throne of Zakkar. The next day I set out and went to Canaan. In Canaan is Amiya (probably south of Tripoli, Lebanon). In Amiya there were also people from Halab, people from the land Mukish (country dominated by Alalah), people from the Land Nihi (near later Apamea-Orontes), and people of the land Amae (possibly between Aleppo and Apamea). They were living there. When they saw (and recognised) me, that I was the son of their lord, they gathered around me. So I became great (and) received the power of command. Among the *habiru*-people (see p. 320), I spent seven years. I let birds fly, carried out omen-inspections on lambs. In the seventh year Teshub turned towards me. As a result I built ships. The x-soldiers I caused to enter the ships. Across the sea I approached the country of Mukish, and reached dry land before Mount Hazzi (i.e. Mons Casius). I went up. When my country heard of me, cattle and sheep were brought to me. In a single day the country of Nihi, the country of Amae, the country of Mukish and Alalah, my city, turned towards me again like one man. My brothers heard (of this) and came to me. My brothers and I swore mutual alliance; I placed my brothers under my protection.

Further: For seven years Parrattarna, the mighty king, the king of the Hurrians, had been hostile to me. In the seventh year I sent to Parattarna the king, the king of the [Hurri]ans, Anwanda and told him about the efforts of my fathers: that my fathers had allied themselves, that our ancestors were acceptable to the kings of the Hurrians and that they had sworn a mighty oath with each other. The mighty king heard about the efforts of our ancestors and the mutual oath and was afraid of the content of the oath. Because of the wording of the oath and because of our efforts he accepted my greeting-present. In the month Kinunu, I made extensive libations. Thus I brought back to him the house which had been in flight. In my noble mind, in my loyalty, I swore him friendship. Thus I became king of Alalah.

(Smith 1949; TUAT I: 501–504)

The vivid account gives us the history of one of the sons of the royal house of Aleppo (Halab – Idrimi's father was Ilimilimma, king of Aleppo), which was subject to the king of Mitanni by the end of the sixteenth century. The territory of Aleppo included the smaller city-state of Alalah and the stretch of land to the coast that it dominated, Mukish. Following a failed revolt, Idrimi and some of his family fled to Emar (Tell Meskene) on the Euphrates ruled by his mother's family. There Idrimi realised that he would never be able to wield real power. So he went south to live with other political refugees, brigands and nomads. Here he gathered a force with which he could make an attempt to seize a city for himself. When he (and the gods) judged the moment ripe, he made a naval landing in the territory of Mukish, which formed part of his ancestral realm of Aleppo. Here he received both popular support and help from his family in Emar. In time, he was able to make overtures to Parrattarna, the king of Mitanni, who recognised his power over the territory and granted him control of it. So Idrimi ruled Alalah as a subject of the Mitannian king. He certainly had considerable independence of action (cf. treaty between Alalah and Pilliya of Kizzuwadna, Wiseman 1953 no. 3, and the war in Hittite territory he refers to in his inscription), although limited by obligations of loyalty to his overlord to whom he owed his title 'king of Alalah'. Later material from Alalah shows that the Mitannian king ultimately determined the boundaries of his subject states (Speiser 1929; Wiseman 1953 no. 14).

From the reign of Saushtatar (*c.* 1430/1420) on there is firmer evidence for Mitanni's history. The primary source is the Shattiwaza treaty. This is a Hittite 'vassal-treaty' (cf. chapter 5e), imposed by Suppiluliuma (1370–1330 (1344–1322)) on Shattiwaza,[1] a Mitannian prince, after the Hittite defeat of Mitanni. By means of this treaty, Shattiwaza was installed as Hittite client-king over the rump-state of Mitanni; in other words, he became governor on behalf of the Hittites over his paternal realm, now shorn of its more extensive possessions. The text traces some of the history of dynastic conflict in Mitanni which led to Shattiwaza seeking refuge at Hattusa; in harking back to the glories of the time of Saushtatar, it offers us glimpses of Mitannian history. The Akkadian text of the two versions of the treaty comes from an archive copy found at the Hittite capital of Hattusa (the Hittite version is only preserved in fragments, see *CTH* 51 and 52):

[Thus] (speaks) Shattiwaza, son of Tushratta, kin[g of the land] Mitanni: before [Sh]uttarna, son of Artatama, [. . .] changed . . . of the land Mitanni, Artatama, the king, his father behaved badly. The pa[lace . . . of the k]ings as well as its goods he destroyed, on the land Ashur and the land Alshe (Diyarbekr region) he besto[wed it]. Tushratta, the king, my father, built a palace, filled it with treasure. But Shuttarna destroyed it and it collapsed. And [. . .] of the kings of silver and gold, silver bowls from the treasury, he broke them, but these [. . .] of his father and his brother he gave to no one, but humbled himself before the Assyrian, the servant of his father, who had not paid tribute, and gave him his wealth as a present.

Thus (speaks) Shattiwaza, son of Tushratta, the king: a door of silver and gold which Saushtatar, the king, my great-grandfather took away from the land A[shur] for the strengthening of its power, (which) he attached in Washshukanni to his palace. I[n . . .] Shuttarna to his shame gave (them) (back) to the land Ashur. All other equipment of silver and gold he gave to the land Alshe . . . [. . .]. And the house of the king of the land Mitanni together with its goods and possessions he annihilated, covered it with earth. The palace he destroyed and eliminated the houses of the Hurri-people. And the nobles he had taken to the land Ashur and the land Alshe and delivered them. They were handed over, and at Taide they were impaled. (Thus) he destroyed them all, the Hurri-people. But Aki-Teshub fled before him, he went to the land Karduniash (Babylonia). 200 chariots fled with him. And the king of the land Karduniash took the 200 chariots and their goods away from Aki-Teshub and kept them for himself. And he pursued Aki-Teshub with his *mariyannu* (warriors), tried to kill him. And also he sought to kill me, Shattiwaza, son of Tushratta, the king, but I escaped from his hand. [T]o the gods of the sun, Suppiluliuma, the Great King, the king of the land Hatti, the hero, the beloved of Teshub, I appealed, along a path without [. . .] . . .

they led me. The gods of the king of the land Hatti and the gods of the king of the land Mitanni, allowed me to reach the sun, [Suppilu]liuma, the Great King, the king of the land Hatti, the hero, the beloved of Teshub. [And at the ri]ver Marassantiya (Halys) I fell at the feet of the sun Suppiluliuma, the Great King, the king of the land Hatti, the beloved of Teshub. [The Great King] seized me [with] his [han]d and was pleased with me. And he asked me about the situation of the land Mitanni, an[d when he] heard [. . . o]f the land Mitanni, the Great King, the hero, spoke thus: 'When I conquer Shuttarna and the land Mitanni, I shall not subject you. I shall take you to me as son, I shall come to [your] a[id], I shall let you sit on the throne of your father.' And the sun Suppiluliuma, the Great King, the king of the land Hatti, the hero, the be[loved] of Teshub, the gods know him. The word that issues from his mouth, cannot be turned back.

(the text continues with details of arrangements for Shattiwaza's return to Mitanni, oaths and curses)

(*CTH* 52; Weidner 1923 no. 2)

From the treaty we can glean the fact that Saushtatar (either Shattiwaza's great-grandfather or great-great-grandfather, see Kammenhuber 1968: 64) had conquered the city of Ashur, and taken the doors of silver and gold from the Ashur temple as booty to Washshukkanni; this event should probably be dated after Ashur-nadin-ahhe I's embassy to congratulate the Egyptian king, Amenophis II (1438–1412 (1425–1398); cf. chapter 7b). So Saushtatar emerges as an important figure, who extended Mitannian power: it is clear beyond a doubt that Ashur was included by conquest in the Mitannian political complex in his reign. Saushtatar's control over Nuzi and Alalah is confirmed by texts from both sites (Pfeiffer 1932 no. 1; Wiseman 1953 nos. 13, 14). He also claimed, at least temporarily, dominion over Ugarit on the north Syrian coast and Kizzuwadna in north-east Cilicia (Wilhelm 1982: 37).

The Amarna letters from Egypt reveal a little more. Thirteen letters in the archive (EA 17–29)[2] were sent by king Tushratta to Amenophis III (1403–1364 (1390–1352)), Tiye (Amenophis III's principal wife) and Akhenaten (Amenophis IV, 1364–1347 (1352–1336)). Some are extremely long, in particular (but not only) the texts that list the dowry gifts sent to accompany Tushratta's daughter, Taduhepa, who was married to Amenophis III. One of them is the difficult letter in Hurrian (EA 24), which first alerted scholars to the existence of this language (see p. 283). The letters frequently refer to earlier relations between the two states. The first friendly overtures were probably made in the time of Tuthmosis IV of Egypt (1412–1403 (1398–1390)) and Artatama I of Mitanni, Tushratta's grandfather, when Egypt was anxious to consolidate the gains in the Levant made by the great conqueror Pharaohs (Tuthmosis I and III, Amenophis II, see chapter 4b) and needed to reach an accommodation with Mitanni, which was now its undisputed, largest and only contiguous neighbour here. The negotiations for friendship and alliance, comfirmed by the marriage of Tushratta's aunt to Tuthmosis IV, probably took a long time, although Tushratta's statement that the Egyptian king had to ask seven times before the Mitannian princess was sent to Egypt with her wedding train should be taken with a pinch of salt; another possibility is that it is a convention for 'repeatedly':

> When [. . .], the father of Nimmureya (Amenophis III), wrote to Artatama, my grandfather, he asked for the daughter of [my grand-father, the sister] of my father. He wrote 5, 6 times, but he did not give her. When he wrote to my grandfather a seventh time, only then, was the pressure such that he gave her (to him). When Nimmureya, your father, [wro]te to Shutt[arna], my father, and asked for the daughter of my father, my own sister, he wro[te] 3 times, 4 times, but [he did] not [giv]e her. It was only when he had written 5, 6 times, that the pressure was such that he g[av]e [her] to him. Wh[en] Nimmureya, [y]our [fa]ther wrote to me and asked for my daughter, I did n[ot] say n[o]. The very first ti[me] I said to his messenger: 'Of course I shall give her.' (i.e. they trusted each other)
>
> (EA 29)

Tushratta is making the point in this letter (addressed to Akhenaten) that while his grandfather had had to be asked six times before he agreed to the marriage, and his father four to five times, he (i.e. Tushratta) had immediately agreed to give his own daughter as a bride to Amenophis III – so great was his friendship for the Egyptian king. Another sign of the friendly relations between the two states is that the statue of the goddess Shaushga of Nineveh was sent by Shuttarna II (contemporary of Amenophis III) to Egypt. This was a solemn procedure, presented (as was customary) as a journey the goddess herself wished to undertake, as Tushratta tells us:

> Thus (speaks) Shaushga of Nineveh, mistress of all the lands: 'I wish to go to Egypt, a country I love, and then to come back.' Now, given this, I send her to you and she has set out.
>
> At the time of my father . . . went to this country, and just as before, she stayed there and was honoured; now may my brother honour her ten times more than on the earlier occasion. May my brother honour her. At her wish, may he let her leave so that she can come back.
>
> May Shaushga, mistress of heaven, protect us, my brother and myself, for 100,000 years and may our mistress grant us great joy and may we behave like friends.
>
> (EA 23)

The statue of Shaushga (the Hurrian form of the Akkadian Ishtar) could have been sent to help heal the elderly, ailing Amenophis III (Wegner 1981: 65) – comparable to the way that kings sent doctors to each other (cf. chapter 7a).

But there is no evidence for this in the passage quoted, and it seems more likely that Shaushga was sent in connection with the marriage festivities between the Mitannian princesses and the Egyptian king. Tushratta repeatedly expressed the wish, in his letters dealing with the forthcoming marriage of his own daughter, Taduhepa, to Amenophis III, that Shaushga would make her pleasing to the eyes of the Egyptian ruler:

> May Shaushga, my mistress, the mistress of all the lands and of my brother, and Amun, the god of my brother, make her into the very image of the desires of my brother.

(EA 19–21)

The fact that the Mitanni rulers were able to send the statue of Shaushga (Ishtar) of Nineveh to Egypt has been thought to imply their continued control (from Saushtatar on) of Assyria, but this is not a necessary conclusion. It is just as likely that this form of the goddess was particularly revered by the Mitannians, and that the cult-statue sent to Egypt had its home in a temple in the Mitannian capital of Washshukanni (Kühne 1973a: 37, n. 176).

There is, in fact, considerable evidence against Mitannian control of Assyria at this time. The Mitanni letters from Amarna, the Shattiwaza treaty and the Assyrian evidence (see chapter 7b) point to serious problems besetting the Mitannian realm from the reign of Tushratta on, which led to its power crumbling and, eventually, the division of its territory between Assyria and the Hittites. The evidence consists of brief allusions only, which allow for varying reconstructions. A possible one runs as follows: Shuttarna II's son and heir to the throne, Artashumara, was murdered by a certain UD-hi,[3] probably not a member of the royal family. After the murder, UD-hi installed Shuttarna's younger son, Tushratta (possibly still a child), as puppet-king. Diplomatic relations between Mitanni and Egypt were clouded by this event. Only when Tushratta succeeded in executing UD-hi and his supporters, were they re-opened. As a sign of Mitanni's renewed goodwill towards Egypt, Tushratta sent the Egyptian king some of the booty taken from the Hittites, after their failed attack on Mitanni (EA 17; see p. 253). But the assassination showed up cracks in the Mitannian state, and not everyone accepted Tushratta's accession to the throne. A rival group in Mitanni supported the pretensions to the throne of one Artatama (II), who was a credible enough candidate for the Hittite king (to whom Mitanni was always a threat) to conclude a treaty with him (Weidner 1923 nos 1/2 (introduction)). Artatama (II) may have controlled a break-away part of the Mitannian kingdom (Goetze 1957), in the north-east, although another possibility is that he was simply a pretender whose ambitions were carefully fostered by the Hittites (Kühne 1973a: 19, n. 82). One reason for thinking that Artatama II did have a power-base in eastern Mitanni is that he and his son, Shuttarna (III), seem to be based there later, when the territory was dominated by the Assyrians (see chapter 7b). The victories in north Syria won by the great

Hittite king, Suppiluliuma I, in which he detached all the territory controlled there by Mitanni, and his plunder of Washshukanni, led to the gradual dismemberment of Mitanni: Artatama II's fortunes seemed to revive for a while, but his territory rapidly fell into Assyrian hands; Tushratta was murdered by his son and, in this period of anarchy, Shattiwaza, another of Tushratta's sons, fled to the Hittite court for protection. Suppiluliuma I, profiting from the chaos, decided to abandon his former ally, married Shattiwaza to one of his daughters and installed him as client-king in the western rump of Mitanni, subject to the Hittite ruler of Carchemish (a son of Suppiluliuma I). Attenuated Mitanni now formed an effective eastern buffer (for the moment) against the growing power of Assyria.

The nature of the Mitannian state

Can we pinpoint anything more about the state of Mitanni, apart from this very unsatisfactory historical outline?

Mitanni's realm between c. 1500/1480 and 1350/1340 included: Alalah (Mukish), Aleppo, Emar (Ashtata), Taide (possibly in the western headwaters of the Khabur), Alshe (around Diyarbekir), Assyria (i.e. north Iraq, perhaps only for a short time) and Arrapha (Kirkuk region). Kizzuwadna also entered the Mitannian sphere of political power in the reign of Saushtatar, as did Ugarit, although whether this control was ever as close as that wielded by Mitanni over, for example, Alalah is questionable, and it was brief. The territories forming part of the Mitanni state (and for which we have evidence) appear to have been incorporated, by treaty, as client-states under their own local rulers. They, therefore, furnish very little information on the institutional characteristics of the central Mitannian state – all we can glean from this material are aspects of its policy towards subject-states: subjects were allowed some latitude in regulating border conflicts with their immediate neighbours independently and without recourse to the Mitannian king; any moves beyond such limited and localised activity had to be referred to the overlord at Washshukkanni.

Since the evidence is so patchy, it has been suggested that Mitanni was actually a kind of federation, perhaps quite loosely structured. In support of this view, scholars have pointed to one of the titles of the king of Mitanni: 'King of the Hurrian army/warriors'; this, it is suggested, could reflect the fact that the Mitannian king primarily functioned as a war-leader of contingents furnished by the federated states who were obliged to supply soldiers, i.e. that he acted as a 'feudal' overlord. Three features have been adduced in favour of this notion and presented as characteristic of the Hurrians, and Mitanni in particular. First, the names of the Mitannian kings appear to be Indo-Iranian, and therefore it has been argued that the ruling group in the Mitannian state was an Indo-Iranian élite or warrior aristocracy dominating a Hurrian subject population. (An implicit comparison and model here would be Norman rule in England.) This is backed up by the second fact that in the long list of gods at the end of the Shattiwaza treaty, four gods familiar from the much later Vedic pantheon of India are enumerated: Varuna, Indra, Mitra and the Nasatyas. Third, the idea of a conquering, warrior aristocracy is thought to be strengthened further by the fact that in this period, and especially in relation to Mitanni, we find the possibly Indo-Iranian term *mariyannu/i* (thought by some to mean 'noble'). This describes an apparently exclusive group of chariot-fighters who owned horses and two-wheeled chariots, and held land they were not allowed to sell. It is also believed that a text from Boğazköy establishes a definite link between the horse and chariot-owners and an Indo-Iranian warrior aristocracy. The text in question gives details about horse training and is written partly in an early Indo-Iranian language (Kammenhuber 1961; see also Laroche 1979).

But all of these arguments must be modified, as research over the last twenty-five years has seriously undermined each one. First, the Indo-Iranian character of the Mitannian royal names has been challenged (Kammenhuber 1968), so that at present their linguistic classification is uncertain. Further, it seems that the Mitannian kings had personal names that were Hurrian, so that the Indo-Iranian names would only be formal throne-names and not indicative of the rulers' ethnicity. Finally, the names are so Hurrianised that, even if they do turn out to be Indo-Iranian, this cannot have been a vital linguistic ingredient in the Mitannian state. However, if they are Indo-Iranian, the very fact that they are throne-names says something about the concept of kingship and what was expected of it. Even if they are not, the names are peculiar, suggesting a distinctive element in the dynasty. But the uncertainties loom large. Secondly, only four gods out of over a hundred listed in the Shattiwaza treaty are comparable to the Vedic deities; moreover, they are listed right at the end, suggesting that they were rather minor deities and of relatively slight importance. It is possible to argue that there may have been at some stage a contact with Indo-Iranians, perhaps in the area of north-west Iran, where Hurrians are found to be located at an early stage (Diakonoff 1972). But, if such contact had resulted in some Indo-Iranian influence on Mitannian society, it formed a small element only in the kingdom by the fourteenth century.

With respect to the *mariyannu/i*, it now seems fairly certain that, linguistically, it is a Hurrian word (not Indo-Iranian). It also appears that, although the *mariyannu* were expected to see to their own horses and chariot-equipment to some degree, in certain situations (e.g. war) they could also be issued by the state with rations for themselves and their horses, and that they were given land parcels. We should also note that at Alalah it was possible to be called a *mariyannu* without owning a chariot and, conversely, to be made into a *mariyannu* by the king. This shows that they were not an exclusive group, that the king could recruit people to become *mariyannu*, who formed the chariot-regiment of the army, and that they were largely dependent on the king. It is also significant that closely comparable groups are found in all the major states of the Near East at this time: Hittite Anatolia, Kassite Babylonia, Egypt, the smaller Levant states. *Mariyannu* thus seems to be simply a way of describing the members of the trained and expert chariot-corps of the armies of this period: it is difficult for us to define the realities hidden by the term, but to see the *mariyannu* as an exclusive warrior-caste seems unwarranted. They were specialists in some of the new skills that gave better control over the horse, so that it could be harnessed and trained efficiently for chariotry. They could have been active in the Near East well before they appear in the texts (which all survive by accident).

The Boğazköy horse-training texts use elements of an Indo-Iranian language to a limited extent only (Kammenhuber 1961). The terms that *can* be analysed as such are technical ones, and it is possible that these, too, derived from north-west Iran, with which Hurrians are known to have been associated (Diakonoff 1972). If the texts are taken to mean that there were Indo-Iranians in the ancient Near East at this time, then they were probably horse-grooms and horse-trainers, but not part of a ruling élite – neither Mitanni nor the Hurrians were led or ruled by an Indo-Aryan aristocracy. Nor did the Hurrians (let alone their supposedly 'Indo-Aryan' leaders) introduce the horse, the composite bow or the two-wheeled, horse-drawn chariot (extensively used from the sixteenth century onwards) to the Near East. Their use certainly grew in significance, building on specific military techniques and items already present several hundred years earlier, which became more important with the formation of large, aggressive states in the sixteenth century (Moorey 1986).

Society

Most difficult is the question of Mitannian, or Hurrian, society and culture. It is possible to delineate something of the society of Arrapha, from the very large archives of Nuzi texts (as well as those from nearby Kirkuk and Kurruhanni), which have been extensively studied (Dosch 1993) . This small kingdom included a number of towns, several of them fortified and with palaces. In Nuzi itself the palace occupied about half the area of the walled city. The king seems to have moved to different centres with his entourage; the estates of queens, embracing whole villages, appear to have had their own administration; the palace ran an extensive textile-production centre, staffed by slaves and female-palace servants (Cassin 1974; Zaccagnini 1979). The palace may have had a monopoly in importing metals (Zaccagnini 1977), and organised the manufacture of finished metal products, but it did not play the dominant role in agricultural production. Land was held on the basis of royal grants and, by law, could not be sold, although it could be inherited. As a result, a system of fictive adoption is widely attested in the Nuzi material, whereby individuals had themselves adopted having presented their 'father' with a large gift which effectively represented the purchase price. Some people became very large landowners indeed by these means: e.g. Tehip-tilla, whose archive shows that he had an enormous number of 'fathers', who were, in effect, his paying tenants (Cassin 1938; Maidman 1976; Wilhelm 1982: 66; Dosch 1987). A practice of indenture is also attested at Nuzi, whereby an individual contracted to serve a family for a stipulated period of time, after which he was free; in return, the family of the indentured person gained access to various resources, such as grain or silver (Eichler 1973).

A number of aspects of family structure have also been illuminated by the Nuzi archive, particularly the existence of levirate marriage (Cassin 1969), the system of bridewealth and dowry (Grosz 1983), and the formal adoption of daughters, in the absence of male offspring, as 'sons' by their fathers (Grosz 1987; 1989). In this position they could act legally like male heads of families: they arranged their own marriages; they cared for the domestic gods which symbolised a family's identity; their husbands moved into the homes of their wives. The material for such social and economic analysis from Nuzi is exceptionally rich and has particularly attracted students of early Israelite society because of a number of striking analogies (see Morrison 1983 for a survey).

But we should remember that Nuzi presents a picture of this region only – the Alalah IV archives, at the western end of Mitanni's realm, reveal a different social pattern (Wilhelm 1982: 61). Moreover, both the Nuzi texts and the Alalah texts are in Akkadian not Hurrian; even the number of Hurrian texts from Emar (dating to the time after Mitanni's demise) is very small and mostly concerned with omens (Laroche 1982). So it is impossible for us to draw broad conclusions about the central state of Mitanni and its society from this material. Mitannian institutions and society thus remain elusive: its size, the precise location of its great royal cities (Washshukanni, Taide), its political structure, Mitannian kingship are simply not known nor, at present, knowable. Yet there is hope: excavations by the British School of Archaeology in Iraq at the site of Tell Brak (upper Khabur) have uncovered material from the period of Mitanni's control, including part of a public building ('palace'), and it has been tentatively suggested that, given its location, Tell Brak could be a candidate for the important Mitannian city of Taide (Oates 1985; although note now the possibility of Tell Brak = Nawar, p. 285). More material from this period has been discovered at Brak recently, including a (very fragmentary) Hurrian letter (Wilhelm 1991).

The Hurrian pantheon, some of whose members, such as the storm-god Teshub, his consort Hepat, the sun-god Shimigi, and the great goddess Shaushga are referred to in Tushratta's letters, is primarily known from slightly later material at and near Boğazköy, the Hittite capital. Details of cult and belief are unknown save for a few rituals (Haas and Thiel 1978; Haas and Wilhelm 1974; Haas and Wegner 1988), and some magnificent epics in Hurrian (the Kumarbi cycle and the 'Song of Ullikummi' (Güterbock 1946;

1951/1952)), which, again, are all known from the Hittite capital, Hattusa, and existed, indeed, in Hittite versions. The Kumarbi myth was recognised, over forty years ago, to have structural and conceptual links with Hesiod's much later poem, the *Theogony* (Güterbock 1948). Art and architecture are virtually unknown (Hrouda 1985; Muscarella 1988 [OM]), although a fine palace ware (Nuzi ware) has been found at a number of sites within the general area of Mitanni (Barrelet 1977; Stein 1984); it has even been argued that a type of porcelain may have been produced (Fritz-Münche 1984). Yet the Mitannian kings clearly commanded enormous resources and fine craftsmen, as shown by the immensely long and detailed lists of precious items which accompanied the Mitannian princess, Taduhepa, to Egypt. The beginning of one such inventory gives us a taste of this:

4 excellent horses which run (swiftly)

1 chariot, its *tulemus*, its straps, its covering, all of gold. 320 shekels of gold have been used for it.

1 whip of *pišaiš* covered in gold; its *parattitinu* (is) of genuine *hulalu*-stone; a seal of genuine *hulalu*-stone is fitted to it. 5 shekels of gold have been used for it.

2 *ša burhi*, covered in gold, 6 shekels of gold and 4 shekels of silver have been used on them.

2 *uhatati* (in leather), covered in gold and silver; the centres made of lapis lazuli. 10 shekels of gold and 20 shekels of silver have been used on them.

(and so on, for another 229 lines, including elaborate bowls, jewellery, shoes, clothes, perfumes, a complete suit of armour and weapons)

(EA 22)

6b Ugarit

See, there is no mayor's residence that can compare with that at Tyre. It is like the residence at Ugarit. Extraordinarily large are the riches there.

(EA 89)

So wrote Rib-Hadda, prince of Byblos and subject of Egypt, to the Egyptian king Akhenaten (1364–1345 (1352–1336)). To alert the pharaoh to the power of the neighbouring ruler of Tyre and warn him of his ambitions, he compared Tyre's wealth and splendour to that of Ugarit, which lay beyond Egypt's empire and was probably independent at this point. One of the Egyptian kings, Amenophis III (1403–1364 (1390–1352)), may even have numbered an Ugaritic princess among his many wives (EA 1: 39). Ugarit, modern Ras Shamra on the Syrian coast, was, until recently, the only one of the many small city-states of this region where extensive and diverse archives had been found. The texts illuminate in considerable detail the history, society and culture of a Canaanite state in the period from *c.* 1400 to just after 1200. At this time Mitanni's power was declining in the wake of repeated Hittite attacks. Suppiluliuma I (1370–1330 (1344–1322)) eventually annexed all the north Syrian territory down to Damascus to the expanding Hittite realm (chapter 5d). Ugarit itself fell under Hittite control at this point, so that its archives also shed light on how Hittite domination worked in one region. The archives postdate the Alalah IV tablets (later fifteenth century), and so help to fill a gap in the history of north Syria between c. 1400 and 1200.

A chance find in 1928 of a vaulted tomb made of hewn stone first drew the attention of French archaeologists to the site of Ras Shamra and its port at Minet el-Beida. As excavations got under way, a large stone-built palace, covering an area of a little over 1 ha (2.5 acres), was discovered. It was set in the midst of a thriving and sizeable city, its streets lined with two-storeyed houses, possibly grouped into professional quarters, and dominated by an acropolis with two temples dedicated to gods familiar to us from the Old Testament: Baal and Dagan. In the large palace, with its numerous court-yards, pillared halls, columned entrance-gates and cultivated garden area, a great number of tablets were found, covering almost all aspects of the life of Ugarit from the fourteenth to the twelfth century. Archives were also found in other buildings (van Soldt 1991). Excavation has made it clear that Ugarit existed already in the Neolithic period, and was a substantial town in the early third millennium (see generally *SDB* s.v. 'Ras Shamra'). Part of its territory continued to be a commercial centre to the third century, when it seems to have been eclipsed by Seleucia–Pieria and Laodicea-on-the-Sea (Stucky 1983; it is located a bare 11 km from modern Lataqiya).

The realm of Ugarit

The extent of the territory embraced by the state of Ugarit (as opposed to the city) is not completely certain. It dominated the coast from Ma'hadu (Minet el-Beida) to a second port, Shuksi (Tell Sukas), where an Ugaritic tablet has been found. How far it extended inland is less clear; estimates are derived from references in treaties. It may have reached as far as the Orontes, possibly even slightly beyond in the north-east: adjoining states were Mukish to the north, Nuhashshe to the east and Amurru to the south (see map 4). It also controlled two smaller states, Shiyannu and another whose name is, un fortunately, lost. Since 1975, the site of Ras Ibn Hani, situated about 5 km south-west of Ugarit, has been a focus of excavation, and two palaces set in a walled town with an orthogonal street plan have been found. Several tablets, including some in Ugaritic, confirm that this was another centre of Ugarit. The ancient name of Ras Ibn Hani was B'ir. The presence of two palaces (one belonging to a queen of Ugarit), its situation on a promontory jutting out into the sea, and the town's planned appearance, suggest that it was laid out as a royal centre, perhaps a summer residence (Bordreuil 1981).

The landscape of Ugarit was dotted with villages and small towns: agriculture, the mainstay of Ugarit (like most pre-industrial states), was the productive activity most people engaged in (Heltzer 1976; 1982). Aside from the king and his high officials and a rather small number of slaves, the population consisted of free citizens. Some of them, classified as 'king's men', were in receipt of land granted by the king in return for services performed for the state (e.g. armourers, bird-catchers, potters), while the remainder farmed their own plots. It is a mistake to think, as it has been, that the 'king's men' were in some sense wealthier or more privileged than the 'peasants'. It has now been shown convincingly that there were enormous differences of wealth within both groups, and that the classification defines the source of their land (and hence their economic relationship to the central authority) – nothing else. By granting land to some people in return for services, the court was able to meet its needs (food, weapons, furniture etc.). It was perfectly possible to find a prosperous 'peasant' and a poor 'king's man' (Vargyas 1988). In broad outline, the socio-economic pattern of Ugarit differed little from that of contemporary states.

As well as basic food (grain, wine, olives), Ugarit also produced surpluses: stacks of amphorae in warehouses at the quayside imply the production of olive oil in commercial quantities; wine and salt may also have been exported. Ugarit also had specialised craft industries: fine, purple-dyed linen and wool garments (the colour derived from murex shellfish), and bales of cloth in considerable quantities were manufactured; they were specifically demanded by the Hittites as a substantial part of the tribute from Ugarit (see p. 308). The Hittite treaty with Ugarit also shows, incidentally, that Ugarit was considered capable of raising considerable quantities of gold and silver, both in bullion and in the form of vessels made of precious metals. Some of the magnificent metal items, such as the elaborately chased gold bowl and the superb iron axe-head with its bronze collar inlaid with gold (Strommenger and Hirmer 1965 [OM] pls. 176, XXXIII, XXXIV), found at Ugarit give some idea of the level of craftsmanship. Ivory-carving and inlay was probably another skill which the king of Ugarit could command. The forests of the region supplied wood used for the production of fine furniture and luxury items, as well as for building – juniper, boxwood and pine are the types of timber known to have been used and locally available.

Merchants are a group who figure prominently in Ugarit's archives. The texts reveal that not only were the citizens of Ugarit engaged in trade, but traders from elsewhere were based in the state: the merchants of Ura in Hittite Cilicia (Beal 1992), for example, formed a small but influential merchant community; merchants from Alashiya (in Cyprus) also operated in Ugarit. The presence of Minoan and Mycenaean wares at Ugarit suggests that Aegean merchants were active there, although the exact nature and intensity of Aegean trade-links cannot be precisely gauged from this material, and they are not distinguished as a group in the Ugarit texts (for Aegean trade-links, see Morris 1992) . Ugarit was well placed for conducting a major portion of the north Syrian trade with Cyprus and further west, as well as with Cilicia and regions to the north. It was also linked by routes to Carchemish and Emar on the Euphrates, and controlled part of the route leading north through Mukish to central Anatolia. The most important known role that Ugarit played in trade at this time was that of entrepôt for grain-supplies moving from north Syria to the Hittite court (Klengel 1965–70 II; Heltzer 1978).

Given the rich documentation, both textual and archaeological, it is tempting to exaggerate Ugarit's commercial wealth and function. But it was only one of a number of similar states dotted throughout the Levant, along the coast and further inland (for Emar, see chapter 6c); scholars simply happen to know a lot about it because of the wealth of written material, but Ugarit was not unique – it was one of many, although probably among the most important and prosperous. Its large archives show that the population was, on the evidence of personal names, made up of 'Canaanites' and Hurrians. The international links of the city-state are reflected by texts written in several foreign languages: Akkadian, the diplomatic language of the time, items inscribed with Egyptian hieroglyphs, some Hittite and Hurrian, and a small number of Cypro-Minoan texts. But most important (and interesting) is the existence and extensive use of a local alphabetic script – the earliest fully known one so far (Gordon 1971: 114–124; Healey 1990: 16–26). The script records the local form of the West Semitic language, which is usually called 'Canaanite' (on the problem of this simple classification, see Millard 1973). From tiny traces at other sites (Healey 1990: 22–23) it is now virtually certain that most areas of the Levant used a variety of alphabetic scripts in the period from *c.* 1600 on. What is unusual about the Ugaritic alphabet is that it used wedge-shaped signs, superficially similar to the cuneiform system, which were impressed on clay with a stylus (see fig. 24). Because of the use of clay tablets for writing texts in Ugaritic script, rather than hide, wood or papyrus, the texts have most fortunately survived and allow this precious insight into the life of a Canaanite city. The administrative, legal and economic texts form the bulk of the documents; but there is also a substantial corpus of literary material which provides strikingly close parallels to some of the poetry found in the later Old Testament. For example:

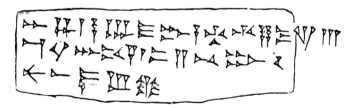

Figure 24 Tablet with Ugaritic alphabet, found in 1948 (after C. Virolleaud, *Le palais royal d'Ugarit II*, Paris, 1957)

303

'Mighty Baal is dead,
Perished the Prince, Lord of Earth.'

The beneficent El, benign,
Descended from the throne, sat on the footstool,
From footstool he sat on the ground.
He strewed straw of mourning on his head,
Dust of wallowing on his pate.
For clothing he donned loincloth.
Skin with stone he scraped,
Flint (he used) for rasp,
Plucked cheek and chin,
Harrowed upper arm,
Ploughed like a garden (his) chest,
Like a valley harrowed his body.
He lifted his voice and cried:
'Baal is dead! What of the people?
Dagan's Son! What of the multitudes?'
(5(67)6.9–24; trans. Pope 1981: 164)

The literature and Ugaritic ritual texts reveal the religion and cultic practices of the Levant, previously only known from Old Testament polemics attacking and distorting them (Caquot *et al.* 1974; 1989; Yon 1990). A particularly interesting text (discovered quite recently) concerns a ceremonial meal, organised on the occasion of the funeral of Niqmaddu III by his son 'Ammurapi II (*c.* 1210/1200?; see table 20), to which the ancestors of the dynasty were invited by invocation:

Document about the sacrificial meal for the 'shades' (i.e. the dead):
You (men) are to call the Rapi'u ('the healers', a term for dead ancestors)
    of the Und[erworld],
you shall call forth the assembly of Di[danu] (name of ancestor of
    dynasty)
(Women) call ULKN, the Rapi'u,
call TRMN, the Rapi'u,
call SDN and RDN,
call the bull 'LLMN!
(Men and women) shall call the Rapi'u of the Underworld,
you shall call forth the assembly of Didanu!
(Women) call Ammishtamru (II), the king,
call also Niqmaddu (III), the king!
Oh, the throne of Niqmaddu I shall lament!
One should lament the footstool of the king
before that lament the table of the king
and swallow the tears for him –

all of them, in their entirety!
Warm yourself, sun, yes, warm yourself,
the great light above us, the sun, call:
'Behind your lord, oh throne,
behind your lord descend into the underworld,
descend into the underworld and lie deep in the dust!
In the name of SDN and RDN!
In the name of the bull 'LLMN!
In the name of the ancient Rapi'u!
In the name of Ammishtamru, the king!
In the name – alas! – of Niqmaddu, the king!
Sacrifice once! Sacrifice twice!
Sacrifice thrice! Sacrifice four times!
Sacrifice five times! Sacrifice six times!
Sacrifice seven times!
Offer a bird!
Well-being, well-being for 'Ammurapi,
and well-being for his family!
Well-being for Sharelli (the queen or queen mother),
well-being for her family!
Well-being for Ugarit,
well-being for its gates!'

> (KTU 1.161; P. Bordreuil and D. Pardee *Syria*
> 59 (1982): 121–128; *TUAT* II: 332–333)

Ugarit's political history

An Ugaritic king-list has been found (RS 24.257 rev.; KTU 1.113; Kitchen 1977; Pardee 1988: 165–178), but it is only partly preserved, and the royal names that survive seem to be those of earlier kings of Ugarit, to whom offerings were made or who were invoked as part of the ancestral royal ceremonies (such as the funerary meal quoted). This means that none of the kings that reigned in Ugarit at the time when the archives are available are listed in this text, and the line of historically known rulers has to be reconstructed from the documents. The first attested ruler is Ammishtamru (I), although he is only known from documents outside Ugarit; one Amarna letter (EA 45) was written by him, probably to Amenophis III; kings of Ugarit mention him in their genealogies and he occasionally crops up in later texts. Exactly what the relationship of Ugarit to Egypt was in his reign is not certain – the style of address Ammishtamru uses to the pharaoh is that of a subject-ruler to his overlord; but this could merely reflect the difference in status between the two realms. There is no evidence that the Egyptian empire ever extended as far north as Ugarit (see chapter 6d).

Much more is known about Ammishtamru I's successor, Niqmaddu (II),

Table 20 Kings of Ugarit

	Ugarit	Contemporaries	
	Ammishtamru I	Amenophis III (1403–1364)	
	Niqmaddu II	Suppiluliuma I (1370–1330)	
	Arhalba		
	Niqmepa	Mursili II (1330–1295)	
Amurru		Muwatalli II (1295–1282)	*Carchemish*
Benteshina*		Hattusili III	
	Ammishtamru II	(1275–1245)	Initeshub
Shaushgamuwa		Tudhaliya IV	
	Ibiranu	(1245–1215)	
		Arnuwanda III (1215–1210)	
	Niqmaddu III		
	‘Ammurapi	Suppiluliuma II (1205–) / Ramesses III (1184–1153)	
*daughter married to Ammishtamru II			

who acceded to the throne before Suppiluliuma I's extensive Syrian campaigns (*c.* 1360 or 1335?) and probably reigned a considerable time. A letter from Niqmaddu II to the Egyptian ruler (EA 47), asking the Egyptian king to send him a doctor to serve at the Ugaritic court, shows that relations between the two courts continued to be friendly. An alabaster vessel (the 'marriage-vase'), inscribed with Niqmaddu's name and showing a scene that may reflect an Egyptian ritual used in marriages at court, also implies close relations between Ugarit and Egypt. It is possible that, either in Niqmaddu's or Amishtamru's reign, Ugarit suffered an earthquake and tidal wave, followed by fires which ruined its port and destroyed almost half the city, including part of the palace (EA 152). But recovery from the disaster seems to have been swift. During Ammishtamru's reign there had been a conflict between Ugarit and its neighbour Amurru in the region of Shiyannu, Ugarit's client state. Niqmaddu seems to have had to yield to pressure from powerful Amurru quite early in his reign, perhaps to resolve this quarrel. Possibly quite soon after this, Mukish and Nuhashshe, Ugarit's northern and eastern neighbours, tried to draw Ugarit into an anti-Hittite coalition – presumably in their role as loyal subjects of Mitanni, which was suffering repeated Hittite attacks. But Ugarit, not a subject of Mitanni, refused, and turned the tables on them by calling Suppiluliuma in to help. This gave Suppiluliuma a welcome opening, which helped in his successful conquest of north Syria.

Afterwards, the great Hittite conqueror received Niqmaddu formally at Alalah and drew up the treaty that made Ugarit henceforth into a Hittite subject-state. The Akkadian version of the treaty, covering several tablets, was recovered at Ugarit:

> Thus (speaks) my sun, Suppiluliuma, the Great King, the king of the land of Hatti, the hero: when Itur-addu, the king of Mukish, Addu-nerari, the king of Nuhashshe, and Aki-Teshub, the king of Niye, rebelled against my sun, the Great King their lord, they gathered their troops, occupied towns of Ugarit, pressurised Ugarit, took (subjects) of Niqmaddu, king of Ugarit, away as booty and destroyed the land of Ugarit.
>
> Then Niqmaddu, king of Ugarit, turned towards Suppiluliuma, the Great King and wrote as follows: 'May the sun, the Great King, my lord, save me from the hand of the enemy. I am the servant of my sun, the Great King, my lord. Against an enemy of my lord I am hostile, with an ally of my lord I am allied. The kings are pressurising me.' The Great King heard these words of Niqmaddu. Suppiluliuma, the Great King, sent princes and nobles as well as infantry (and) [chariot-figh]ters to Ugarit. . . .
>
> (broken bits mention the re-establishment of peace in Ugarit by Hittites and Niqmaddu's obeisance to Suppiluliuma in Alalah; then:)
>
> And [Suppiluliuma, the Great King,] saw Niqmaddu's loyalty.
>
> Now Suppiluliuma, the Great King, the king of Hatti-land has made a treaty with Niqmaddu, the king of Ugarit as follows:
>
> If in the future refugees from Nuhashshe or Mukish or from other lands enter the service of the king of Ugarit, the king of another land may not take them away from Niqmaddu, king of Ugarit, or from the authority of his sons and grandsons. Unto distant days! Thus has my sun, the Great King, made the treaty.
>
> (a broken passage in which the boundaries of Ugarit are carefully defined; then:)
>
> Now Suppiluliuma, the Great King, the king of Hatti, the hero, has assigned these [boundaries], places and mountains by means of a sealed document to Niqmaddu, the king of Ugarit, also to his sons (and) grandsons. For ever! Now Niqmaddu is hostile to my enemy and allied to my ally. He has done much for my sun, the Great King, his lord, and he protects the treaty (and) alliance with the land of Hatti. Now has the sun, the Great King, seen Niqmaddu's loyalty.
>
> And he who changes the words of this treaty tablet (be cursed). The thousand gods shall know (the words): the weather-god of the sky, the sun-god of heaven, the weather-god of Hatti, the sun goddess of Arinna, Hepat of Kizzuwadna, Ishtar of Alalah, Ningal of Nubanni, the weather-god of the mountain Hazzi (Mons Casius/Baal Zaphon – a peak near Ugarit of religious importance).
>
> (*CTH* 46; J. Nougayrol PRU IV (1956): 48–52)

The treaty fixed the boundaries of Ugarit in such a way that the loyal pro-Hittite state gained territory at the expense of Mukish and was enlarged in the south. Arrangements about fugitives were made, again favouring Ugarit, which needed neither to hand over fugitives from Mukish and Nuhashshe to the Hittites nor to return them to their homelands for punishment. The repeated statement that these arrangements were to hold good for Niqmaddu's descendants, too, shows that the Hittite king implicitly supported the right of the existing royal family of Ugarit to exercise power.

These very generous conditions, which make no mention of any obligation by Ugarit to support the Hittite king with troops in war, have to be set against another text which records the enormous tribute payable by Ugarit to its Hittite overlord, the only text that provides insight into details of the kinds of tribute imposed by the Hittite Great King on subject-states. Both the Akkadian and Ugaritic version of the text were preserved at Ugarit. The text begins again with Suppiluliuma's acknowledgement of Niqmaddu's support, then he says:

> Your tribute to my sun, the Great King, your lord, (is) 12 mina (1 Hittite mina = 40 shekels) 20 shekels gold (according) to the grea[t shekel-weight (18.79 gr)], a golden beaker of 1 mina weight as main tribute, 4 linen robes, a great linen dress, 500 shekel blue purple wool, 500 shekel red purple wool for my sun, the Great King, his lord.
> A golden beaker of 30 shekel weight, a linen robe, 100 shekel blue purple wool, [100 shekel] red purple wool for the queen.
> [A] gold beaker of 30 shekel weight, a linen robe, 100 (shekel) blue purple wool, 100 (shekel) red purple wool for the crown-prince.
> A silver beaker of 30 (shekel) weight, a linen robe, 100 (shekel) blue purple wool, 100 (shekel) red purple wool for the chief scribe.
> A silver beaker of 30 (shekel) weight, a linen robe, 100 (shekel) blue purple wool, 100 (shekel) red purple wool for the (high court officials of some sort)
> And for the second [store-house ad]ministrator, the same.
> [A silver beaker of 30 shekel weight] a linen robe, 100 (shekel) blue purple wool, 100 (shekel) red purple wool for the minister.
> A silver beaker, a linen robe, 100 (shekel) red purple wool, 100 (shekel) blue purple wool for the . . .
> Among the nobles with my sun, the king, his lord, there are no (further tribute-recipients). On the day that Niqmaddu brings his tribute, he is not obliged to (present an additional) present.
> (The text concludes with the statement that the Hittite gods know the content of the treaty; anyone tampering with its orders is cursed; and finally a note of the Hittite king and queen's seals attached to the agreement.)
>
> (*CTH* 47; J. Nougayrol PRU IV (1956): 40ff. (Akkadian);
> *ibid*.: 44ff.; KTU 3.1 (Ugaritic))

The quantity of gold bullion payable was around 9 kg, and an additional quantity of nearly 2 kg in the form of gold vessels. About three-quarters of the gold went directly to the Hittite king himself, while the rest was distributed to the queen and crown-prince. Other high-ranking members of the Hittite king's retinue received silver vessels, and all received linen garments and great quantities of blue and red purple-dyed wool. The tribute was assessed on the basis of the whole territory controlled by Ugarit, including Shiyannu and the territories newly added to Ugarit. Tablets, found in the palace at Ugarit, show that the tribute was raised from the local communities – their population and economic competence were calculated and listed, and they were then assigned their share of tribute to raise (Klengel 1965–70 II: 343ff.).

Niqmaddu's successor, Arhalba, probably ruled no longer than about two years before being replaced by his brother. This may mean that there was a dynastic intrigue, although that is pure speculation. Perhaps there were problems in Ugarit's relations with Hatti, because of the difficult period early in the reign of Mursili II (1330–1295 (1321–1295)), when much of Syria revolted, and the Egyptians (under king Horemheb 1332–1306 (1323–1295)) campaigned once again in north Syria. The Egyptians were obviously trying to exploit the problems caused by Suppiluliuma's sudden death in the great epidemic which swept the Levant at this time and also killed his immediate successor, Arnuwanda II, within the space of a few months (chapter 5d). The find at Ugarit of a vessel bearing the cartouche of Horemheb could be interpreted as reflecting a renewed rapprochement between Ugarit under Arhalba and Egypt at a time when the Hittite state was suffering a temporary setback. If this reconstruction is correct, then the crisis was brief, since Arhalba disappeared (perhaps into exile) and Niqmepa was installed on the throne by Mursili II (*CTH* 64; PRU IV: 63–70; Klengel 1965–70 II). Against this view we must set the will of Arhalba, which contains a clause stating that, as Arhalba had no children, his brother should marry his widow and succeed him as king. This could have been forced on him, but we do not know that it was (Curtis 1985: 45).

Niqmepa's reign is one of the longest (about fifty years: *c.* 1320–1270 (1310–1260)) and one of the most richly documented. Perhaps because Niqmepa owed his throne to the intervention of the Hittite king, perhaps because of temporary disloyalty on Ugarit's part, Niqmepa had to accept a new treaty from Mursili II that spelt out in no uncertain terms Ugarit's position as a subject of the Hittites (*CTH* 66; PRU IV: 92–101; 287ff.). Simultaneously, the territory of Shiyannu was detached and placed under the direct control of Carchemish, the centre of Hittite control in north Syria, ruled by descendants of the Hittite king as viceroys. But, at Niqmepa's request, Ugarit's tribute was reduced because of the loss of Shiyannu. Ugarit was now entirely encircled by areas under Hittite control, including Amurru to the south, one of whose princesses, Ahat-milku, was married to Niqmepa.

A Hittite royal edict (*CTH* 93; PRU IV: 103ff.), regulating the activities of the merchants of Ura (in Cilicia), who were maritime traders carrying on business in Ugarit, dates from Niqmepa's reign. The Ura merchants were responsible for grain imports into Hatti from north Syria at the order, and in the interest, of the Hittite king. Up to the time of the edict, the Ura merchants had invested their money in houses and estates within Ugarit and became involved in credit deals involving Ugarit citizens who put up their property as surety. The edict of Hattusili III (1275–1245 (1264–1239)) regulated this situation and laid down strict limits for the merchants' business transactions. Henceforth, the Ura merchants were allowed to engage in commercial activities at Ugarit in the summer months only, and had to return home in the winter. At the same time they were forbidden to buy houses and estates or invest their wealth in Ugarit. In cases of unredeemed debts contracted by Ugarit citizens, the Ura merchants were not permitted to seize the debtors' property. The situation must have been critical, perhaps even endangering Ugarit's ability to raise the tribute, for the Great King in Hattusa to intervene personally.

Ammishtamru (II)'s reign coincided with the end of the reign of Hattusili III and the larger part of the reign of Tudhaliya IV (1245–1215 (1239–1209)). This was the time when the threat from Assyria increased substantially, with the small city-states of north Syria at particular risk (see chapter 7b). In spite of this, Ugarit was able to renegotiate its treaty, and was allowed to pay a fee of 2000 shekels (over 37 kg) of gold instead of supplying men for the war. Ugarit clearly still commanded quite substantial wealth, and was more useful to the Hittites for its financial resources than any manpower it could supply.

From Ammishtamru II's reign, we gain an insight into how the Hittite viceroy at Carchemish functioned as ruler of north Syria dealing with all local affairs, although the Hittite king remained the court of last instance. A dramatic illustration of this is a set of texts dealing with Ammishtamru's divorce of his wife, the daughter of Benteshina of Amurru. The royal divorce was settled by the intervention of the Great King in Hattusa and the local ruler with responsibility for north Syria, Initeshub of Carchemish. All the texts were found in Ugarit and are in Akkadian:

1 Judgement of Hittite king, Tudhaliya IV

> Before his majesty, Tudhaliya, the Great King, king of Hatti: Ammish-tamru, king of Ugarit, made the daughter of Benteshina, king of Amurru, his wife; after (this) she deliberately made trouble for Ammish-tamru, (so that) Ammishtamru. king of Ugarit, has abandoned the daughter of Benteshina for ever; the daughter of Benteshina receives everything that she brought into the house of Ammishtamru from the hands of Ammishtamru (and) she goes her own way. Let the Amorites swear an oath concerning all that Ammishtamru may try to seize without right, so that Ammishtamru can compensate (them); and Utrisharrumma is the crown-prince in Ugarit; should Utrisharrumma say thus: 'I am

going with my mother', then let him put his coat on the footstool (i.e. abdicate) and go away, and (in that case) Ammishtamru shall appoint another of his sons as crown-prince. When Ammishtamru passes away, and (then) Utrisharrumma tries to make his mother into the queen of Ugarit again, then he must place his coat on the footstool (and) go wheresoever he will and his majesty shall then appoint another son of Ammishtamru as king. In future the daughter of Benteshina may not claim her sons, daughters and sons-in-law: they remain with Ammishtamru. If she does try to claim them, this tablet shall contradict her.

(*CTH* 107; J. Nougayrol, PRU IV (1956): 126; van Soldt 1983: 151–152)

2 Judgement of Initeshub, king of Carchemish

Before Initeshub, king of Carchemish, son of Sahurunuwa, king of Carchemish, grandson of Sharrikushuh, who (was) also king of Carchemish, the hero: everything that the daughter of Benteshina, king of Amurru, obtained in Ugarit – silver, gold, copper, bronze objects, presents received from visitors, gifts or bakshish, slaves, slave-women, garments of wool or linen – all (of it) belongs to Ammishtamru, king of Ugarit. In future the daughter of Benteshina, king of Amurru, may not lay claim to these things against Ammishtamru, against his sons and his grandsons. But if she does try to make a claim, this tablet shall contradict her.

(PRU IV: 127; van Soldt 1983: 152)

3 Judgement of Initeshub, king of Carchemish

Before Initeshub, king of Carchemish, son of Sahurunuwa, king of Carchemish, grandson of Sharrukushuh, who (was) also king of Carchemish, the hero, and before Shaushgamuwa, king of Amurru, son of Benteshina, who (was) also king of Amurru: Ammishtamru, king of Ugarit, has sent away the daughter of the Great Lady, his wife, the daughter of Benteshina, king of Amurru, from his house and land and made her return to Amurru; and Shaushgamuwa, king of Amurru, sent the daughter of the Great Lady, his sister, away from his palace in Amurru and placed her in another town. Besides she may not go up to the palace of the king of Amurru, yes, even her brother Shaushgamuwa may not speak with her, and also he may not allow her to go back to Ugarit.

If Shaushgamuwa nevertheless does speak with the daughter of the Great Lady, his sister, or brings her back to his palace, or Shaushgamuwa, king of Amurru, should begin a court case about the daughter of the Great Lady, his sister, in any way against Ammishtamru, king of Ugarit, then this tablet will contradict him.

L.R. Fisher (ed.), *The Claremont Ras Shamra Tablets* (1971): 20; van Soldt 1983: 152)

The course of events outlined by these and other texts (cf. Kühne 1973b; van Soldt 1983) was as follows: Ammishtamru rejected his wife, the daughter of his neighbour, Benteshina of Amurru and (perhaps) his principal wife, and sister of Benteshina's successor, Shaushgamuwa. The reason for the divorce is never specified, but is referred to variously as 'deliberate trouble' and a 'great evil' or 'sin'. Whether this refers to adultery or political intrigue is an open question, although the former seems likely. The Amurru princess was therefore ordered to leave Ugarit with her dowry and return home in shame. Her son, the crown-prince, was given the choice of either following her to Amurru and forfeiting his claim to the throne of Ugarit or separating himself for ever from his mother. If he opted for the latter, he was forbidden to reintroduce her to Ugarit after the death of Ammishtamru; if he should try to do so he would be deposed. The Hittite king, Tudhaliya IV, settled the case with a final verdict (above, no. 1). His decision followed initial negotiations on this tricky situation between the kings of Amurru and Ugarit (PRU IV: 128), and a series of judgements made by Initeshub, king of Carchemish (above, nos. 2 and 3), about the disposal of the queen's property and her relationship with her brother, king of Amurru, who might be tempted to use his sister as a pawn to gain political influence in Ugarit. Despite the intervention by the Hittite king, Ammishtamru still seems to have been uneasy about the possible consequences of leaving his disgraced wife in the care of his unpredictable, and sometimes hostile, neighbour. He therefore attempted at one point to recapture her with support from the king of Carchemish. Shaushgamuwa was forced to give in and hand her over, undoubtedly for execution, in return for a large sum of gold (over 26 kg), probably paid over on her death (the text, like the others, is from Ugarit):

> Thus spoke Shaushgamuwa, son of Benteshina, king of Amurru, to Ammishtamru, son of Niqmepa, king of Ugarit: 'See, the daughter of the Great Lady, your wife, who committed against you a great sin: how long must I continue to guard this villainess? So now, take the daughter of the Great Lady, the villainess, and do with her as you think fit: if you want, kill her, or if you want, throw her in the sea; but do with the daughter of the Great Lady what you want.'
>
> Shaushgamuwa, son of Benteshina, king of Amurru, spoke these words to Ammishtamru, son of Niqmepa, king of Ugarit.
>
> Now Shaushgamuwa, son of Benteshina, king of Amurru, has handed over the daughter of the Great Lady who committed the sin, to Ammishtamru, son of Niqmepa, king of Ugarit, and Ammishtamru, son of Niqmepa, king of Ugarit, has given Shaushgamuwa, son of Benteshina, king of Amurru, 1400 (shekels) gold; if Shaushgamuwa should speak again to Ammishtamru, son of Niqmepa, king of Ugarit: 'This gold is not enough, give me more gold!' then this tablet shall contradict him.'
>
> Seal of Shaushgamuwa, son of Benteshina, king of Amurru.
>
> (PRU IV: 141)

It was probably at this point that Tudhaliya intervened again to put an end once and for all to the dispute: he forbade the Amurru king and his brothers to make any attempts at further claims against Ugarit, in respect of the death of their sister (PRU IV: 147).

The series of texts (which are not always easy to arrange chronologically with any degree of certainty) provides a fascinating glimpse into the kinds of problem that could arise between two states as a result of a political marriage: misdemeanours could not be tolerated, as they might have political consequences; simply executing the wife (an option probably available to other men if the crime *was* adultery) was impossible because of her relationship to Ugarit's neighbouring king. Returning her to her home was a solution, but she could scarcely be received back into the bosom of her family if the ruler of Amurru wished to maintain friendly relations with the king of Ugarit. So she was sentenced to internal exile in Amurru in the care of her brothers at the order of the Hittite viceroy at Carchemish to whom the problem had been referred. The Hittite king approved the arrangements, and, true to the Hittite treaty with Ugarit which gave support to the local dynasty's right to rule, specifically regulated the succession in Ugarit. When later a problem (never disclosed) nevertheless arose, the viceroy in Carchemish supported the right of the Ugaritic king to recapture his former wife and, in return for an indemnity in gold for the blood of his sister, Shaushgamuwa gave in with a bad grace. The whole matter was pronounced as finally over and done with when the princess died; any attempts by the Amurru royal family to demand more satisfaction for their sister's death were declared illegal. The situation of the woman, who is never named, at the centre of this politically delicate case must have been horrific: thrown out and publicly disgraced by her husband, no contact with her children, banished by her brother to some out-of-the-way place where she was held under guard, forbidden to communicate with him, and finally handed over to her former husband for execution. One thing the affair makes very clear is that the woman remained intimately linked to her own family despite the strictly 'patriarchal' structure of society.

Another problem of Ammishtamru's reign concerned his two brothers, who were accused of plotting against the king and their mother (Ahat-milku). Again the affair was settled by an edict from Initeshub and the intervention of Tudhaliya – they were given their inheritance-share (money, tools, cattle) and banished to Cyprus. Presumably they had conspired to remove Ammishtamru from the throne, which would have threatened the dynastic stability of Ugarit and so required the personal intervention of the Hittite overlord.

Two short reigns succeeded the long one of Ammishtamru, that of Ibiranu, possibly the original crown-prince (see pp. 310–311, text 1) – the different name could mask adoption of a throne name – and the very obscure one of Niqmaddu (III; possible dates for these kings range between 1220–1210 or 1215–1205). The rather limited documentation suggests that, because of the growing threat from Assyria, Ugarit was no longer able to avoid giving active military support to its Hittite overlord, and troops were urgently demanded by Carchemish (PRU IV: 291). At the same time, some light is shed on the Hittite court's dependence on the grain supply from North Syria, organised in part by the Ugarit merchants. A letter to Ibiranu charges him with protecting the transport of 450 tons of grain to Hatti from Mukish.

The last ruler of Ugarit, 'Ammurapi, may have been a usurper and, if so, it may imply a lessening of Hittite control. The sudden and rapid disappearance of the great Hittite empire early in the twelfth century implies that it was experiencing serious problems at this time, which would explain its weakening power over subject states. Many letters from this period (after 1210 (1205)) are preserved in Ugarit. They reveal that Ugarit was suffering quite extensive piratical raids; one of the groups mentioned, the Shikala, can be connected with the 'sea peoples', who appear in contemporary Egyptian inscriptions as a massive horde of looting vandals, destroying all in their wake (see chapter 8a). Whether the fall of the Hittite empire and its dependency, Ugarit, should be attributed directly to their actions is not certain, although their role in exacerbating an already difficult situation when the huge Hittite realm was crumbling cannot be denied:

> Thus the sun, the Great King: speak to the city-governor as follows: Now the king with you (is still) small. He knows nothing. (But) I, the sun, had given him an order with respect to Lunadushu, whom the Shikala-people had captured, (the Shikala), who live on boats. Now I have sent Nisahili – (he is) with me a 'horse-guide' – to you with an order. But you send Lunadushu, whom the Shikala had captured, to me! I shall question him about the affairs of Shikila. And then he can set out again for Ugarit.
>
> (RS 34.129; cf. Dietrich and Loretz 1978)

Within a few years of this letter, the magnificent palace, harbour and much of the city of Ugarit lay in ruins. The former 'summer-palace' at Ras Ibn Hani, though destroyed, was soon reoccupied, but the days of Ugarit as the flourishing centre of an important Syrian state were over.

6c Emar

As a result of French excavations (1972–82) at the site of Tell Meskene, on the bend of the Euphrates in north Syria, it is now possible to add documentary material from ancient Emar to the evidence provided by Ugarit (*RLA* 8: 83–93). Emar was the centre of the kingdom of Ashtata, which was also incorporated into the Hittite empire by Suppiluliuma I. Its material is a little more limited chronologically (late fourteenth century to the beginning of the twelfth century), and, as the texts have only been published recently, full analysis and study of their significance is still awaited. The Emar texts provide relatively little material on Hittite relations with Ashtata, unlike

Ugarit; the material informs us mainly about Emar's society, economy and culture (Arnaud 1982; 1986; 1991; Laroche 1982). One document, for example, shows a woman being appointed to the position of family-head (see p. 299), which shows that this practice, known from Nuzi, was not unique to Nuzi society. One difference here is that the wife of the testator, not his daughter, is put in charge of the household, a position called 'father-and-mother'-hood:

> Muhra-ahi, son of Abi-Ra, healthy in body and spirit, made his brother sit down and decided the fate of his house, his children and his wife. He spoke as follows:
> 'Now the daughter of Kaga, my wife, is "father-and-mother" of my house. As long as she lives, she shall dwell in the main house and no-one shall lay claim to it against her, and her son, Rashap-kabar, shall maintain her. If Rashap-ka[ba]r does not support his "father-and-mother", he loses his rights to the house and if it is really Igmulu who maintains his "father-and-mother", then half the hut shall be the share of Igmulu and if he does not maintain her, he will lose his rights to half the hut, his share.'
> (4 witnesses)
> Month of Abau, year when (the king) made the gate of the other bank of his city.
>
> (Msk 73.60; Arnaud 1982 no. 3)

The Emar evidence has confirmed, strikingly, that the wealth and sophistication of Ugarit was, despite local differences, the norm for most of the small states of this region, not something peculiar to the coastal sites. Emar commanded quite extensive territories under agricultural production (grain, vines), using irrigation; the hilly areas were used for the grazing of sheep and goats, and pastoralists probably formed an important element of the population. The evidence of names indicates that the inhabitants were 'West Semitic', with a relatively small percentage of Hurrians (but see p. 284, on the problems of using personal names as evidence). The dominant language of the preserved documents is Akkadian, but there are some Hittite and Hurrian texts (Laroche 1982), and it is clear that Emar, too, was supervised by the Hittite viceroy at Carchemish. In fact, the seal of the same Hittite prince of Carchemish is found impressed on tablets at Emar and at Ugarit. The divine names in the texts reveal the expected pantheon of Syrian deities such as Ishtar, Teshub and Hepat. An unusual text describes the consecration of the ēntu-priestess of the storm-god at length; the ceremony had links to marriage-rites (Arnaud 1982 no. 10; Fleming 1992).

Emar's commercial function was crucially important. An Old Babylonian itinerary (Hallo 1964) indicates that in the first half of the second millennium Emar was the end-point of the overland route from Babylonia north to the Jezira and across the Khabur and Balikh rivers to the mid-Euphrates. The new Emar texts now show that it continued to play a key role in trade in this period – it was here that donkey caravans arrived, and goods were then transferred onto boats sailing down the Euphrates. Emar was linked culturally, as well as economically and politically, with areas to the west (such as Ugarit) and Babylonia to the south-east. Several copies of a poem have been found at Emar (written in Sumerian, syllabic Sumerian, Akkadian), which was probably composed by a Syrian scholar, but encapsulates the essence of a much longer Sumerian original and reflects Emar's cultural links with southern Mesopotamia. Manuscripts of the same poem have also been found at Ugarit:

> Ea it is who lays out destinies,
> it is also the will of the gods which decides the shares.
> Since antiquity,
> always, in the mouth of predecessors,
> (these things) were brought to mind:
> they were not like (us),
> they were different.
> It was in the sky that their dwellings were founded,
> It was at the bottom of the earth that their cities were.
> Just like the distant sky one cannot reach them.
> Just like the bottom of the earth no-one knows them.
> Lif[e in its entirety is nothing but blindness]
> Human life [. . .].
> Where is king Alulu [who reigned 3,600 years?]
> Where is [king] En[tena who] went [up to the sky?]
> Where is Angeshtug (i.e. Gilgamesh) .[. . . who] sought eternal life [like
>   Zius]udra?
> Where is Huwaw[a . . .] in a deat[h . . . ?]
> Where is Enkidu [. . .] who made [. . .] of power in the land?
> Where is Bazi, where is Gil[gamesh?]
> Where are the great kings
> who from antiquity until now
> are no longer begotten and no longer born?
> A life without glory,
> how does it get the better of death?
> O hero, you who constantly present tribute
> to your god, overwhelm and conquer the bull!
> That will (bring you) despair and dejection (reference to the disastrous
>   consequences following Gilgamesh's destruction of the divine bull
>   sent by Ishtar to ravage Uruk).
> The ephemeral joy of a single beautiful day
> is followed by the sadness of 36,000 years.
> May the divine coffin, my son,

be your desire in affliction!
Such is the lot of humanity.

(Arnaud 1986 no. 767; 1982 no. 13)

* * *

The Emar texts, the virtually contemporary material from Ugarit, the slightly earlier texts from Alalah IV (later fifteenth century) and VII (late seventeenth century), the huge Mari archives (early eighteenth century; chapter 2d) and the Ebla evidence (c. 2450–2350; chapter 1b), present us with an extra-ordinarily vital image of a cosmopolitan and distinctive regional Syrian culture, based on independent city-states linked to each other by commerce and political alliances as well as rivalries. They were frequently dominated by the larger empires to the north, east and south, but they nevertheless preserved their individual cultural identity, which has only begun to be understood more fully over the last sixty years. As archaeological exploration continues, it is very probable that yet more pieces will be found to fill out the history of these rich centres during the third and second millennia.

6d The Egyptian empire in Syria–Palestine

Egypt dominates politically the entire period conventionally labelled 'Late Bronze Age' and the earliest part of the Iron Age (c. 1550–1150) in the region embracing Palestine, Transjordan, Lebanon and southern Syria. The Egyptians began to move into this area at the very start of dynasty XVIII, and from Tuthmosis III's reign onwards (1490–1436 (1479–1425)), they established an empire, tightening their grip over time. Only after the middle of the twelfth century (Ramesses VI of dynasty XX:1142–1134) did they lose control of the area. It is largely because of the close Egyptian involvement with the cities and peoples of Syria–Palestine that we can reconstruct some of their history and set their Late Bronze archaeological remains in context.

Sources and terminology

The evidence is extensive. The sequence of events is known from the various royal accounts of wars, which were inscribed on the temple-walls at Karnak and on stelae set up throughout Egypt and its dominions (Nubia, Palestine). We also have descriptions in Egyptian tombs of battles in which soldiers serving with the kings fought. Pictorial representations (tomb-paintings, temple-reliefs) amplify this material, showing, for example, Egyptian sieges of Canaanite cities and Canaanite people bringing items of local manufacture. Crucial for understanding the organisation of the territory under Egyptian rule are the Amarna letters, found at the site of el-Amarna (ancient Akhetaten, see chapter 4c): the vast proportion of the texts contains the correspondence between the Egyptian king(s) and local city-rulers under Egyptian control. One problem with this important source is that it is temporally very limited – it spans only about twenty to thirty years in the later eighteenth dynasty (c. 1360–1330) – yet we know that Egyptian control became much more intense in dynasty XIX. So the picture of Egyptian imperial rule derived from the Amarna letters cannot necessarily be applied to the later empire. For this period, the late-nineteenth-dynasty document Papyrus Anastasi, which contains the records of a frontier official, is more appropriate; but it is also more restricted in the information it gives.

The material from the Levant itself is mainly archaeological in nature. It allows us to plot the location of cities at different periods, to estimate population-density and settlement shifts (Gonen 1992), and to trace the presence of Egyptian cultural items, pottery and the construction of Egyptian 'residences'. There is also a little evidence from Hittite and Ugaritic documents about affairs in northern Syria, where Hittites, Mitannians and Egyptians clashed, often violently (see chapters 5d; 6a; 6b). But written evidence from the southern region is sparse: thirteen tablets (stylistically similar to the Amarna letters) have been found at Taanach (8 km southeast of Megiddo, overlooking the Jezreel valley, see map 9) slightly predating the Amarna period (Albright 1944; Malamat 1961); seven comparable clay tablets of roughly the same date as the Amarna letters have been found at Kamid-el-Loz in eastern Lebanon (Wilhelm 1983), an important Egyptian administrative centre; scattered similar finds of differing dates have been made at other sites (Shechem, Gezer, Aphek (Palestine)). The material is important, but it is very little from what must have been quite substantial local archives.

The Egyptians used a range of terms for the Levant, which they subdivided into different areas, using certain names only in particular contexts (formal inscriptions as opposed to day-to-day documents). It is, therefore, useful to clarify them before looking at the formation and development of the empire. 'Retenu' was a general, all-embracing term, which appears already in the Middle Kingdom, to describe the territories to the north of Egypt. Sometimes, the more specific 'Upper Retenu' was used, possibly to refer to the hill country of the interior. 'Djahy' is a new term in the New Kingdom, and was applied to the coastal plain, possibly Phoenicia in particular. But at times it was used in a very general sense, comparable to 'Retenu'. Another, rather older term for Phoenicia, 'Fenkhu', is used relatively seldom. All these names can be found in inscriptions. In the Amarna letters, 'Kinahni' (i.e. 'Canaan') is the more usual term to define a large part of the region. It was applied to the area extending up the coast of Palestine from Gaza to the present Israel–Lebanon border.

Within 'Canaan', the standard socio-political pattern of life was the fortified city under a prince, controlling a stretch of surrounding countryside with small villages. The cities were located along the coast, on routes leading into the interior and along rivers; few lay in the hill country. The state of

Map 9 Syria–Palestine in the Late Bronze Age

Amurru, to the south of Ugarit and west of Kadesh, may not have had an urban centre (Liverani 1979: 14–20). There were also people who followed a seasonal transhumant pattern of life, such as the Shasu of Edom (Giveon 1971), and the groups subsumed under the poorly understood term 'Sutu'. These people could, and did, create problems for the sedentary states and their rulers, and also posed difficulties (especially in dynasty XIX) to Egyptian control. The people called *'apiru* (or *habiru*) are rather different. It is unlikely that they were a culturally and linguistically coherent group. Intensive studies of contexts in which the term appears suggest that it was applied to a range of people: runaway slaves, political exiles, brigands, and landless peasants, i.e. people on the margins of society who scratched a living in a variety of ways (seasonal agricultural labour, robbery, mercenary service). It is not, therefore, surprising to find that the word could also be used as a term of abuse (Weippert 1971: 63ff.; Loretz 1984).

The Egyptian conquest

We can distinguish several phases in Egypt's imperial presence in Syria–Palestine: the first was marked by aggressive, destructive campaigns (Amose I – Hatshepsut: 1552–1469 (1550–1458)); the second one was when Egyptian control was imposed and an imperial organisation established (Tuthmosis III – Tuthmosis IV: 1469–1403 (1458–1390)); the third phase, equivalent to the 'Amarna period' in the wider sense, was the time when the empire was firmly established (Amenophis III – Horemheb: 1403–1305 (1390–1294)); finally, the fourth was the phase when, partly as a result of Hittite expansion in Syria, Egypt consolidated its control over the northern frontier, tightened its hold on the Canaanite region, but eventually lost the imperial territories (Sety I – Ramesses VI: 1305–1134 (1294–1134)).

The first phase reflects the Egyptian concern to push back the Hyksos rulers and destroy their power-centres in Palestine (see chapters 3e; 4b). The focus of campaigns was, therefore, south-western and inland Palestine, where the evidence of scarabs suggests that the strongholds of princes associated with the Hyksos were located. Several kings (Amose and Tuthmosis I, definitely; possibly Amenophis I; Tuthmosis II and Hatshepsut, more doubtful) appear to have campaigned here and further north in Syria, right up to the frontier with Mitanni, where Tuthmosis I was even able to erect a stele on the west bank of the Euphrates (Redford 1992: 153–4). The aim was primarily aggressive/defensive; there was no attempt to establish permanent control and extract continuous income. The destruction of sites in these areas and the abandonment of many, with no sign of Egyptian occupation, is probably evidence for this, although not all can be attributed to early dynasty XVIII. The two exceptions are Tell el-Ajjul (6 km south-west of Gaza), possibly Sharuhen, one of the main centres of Hyksos power, where a small fortified camp was established (Kempinski 1974), and Gaza, which seems to have been fairly solidly in Egyptian hands by the beginning of Tuthmosis III's sole reign (Redford 1967).

From Tuthmosis III's sole reign on (following Hatshepsut's death, see table 15), Egypt's relations with the Levant were fundamentally reformulated. The Egyptians now established their claim to rule and exploit the area, and they gradually defined a frontier between themselves and the Mitannians. Tuthmosis III's annals chart the emergence of Egypt's new policy. The annals are one of the longest and most important Egyptian historical inscriptions and, save for the Piye stele (cf. chapter 12a), the most complete account of the military achievements of any Egyptian king. There are direct references in the text showing that it was based on systematic records, kept in the royal archives, which gave more details of individual campaigns. For example:

All that his majesty did ... was recorded each day by the day's name, under the title of – . Then it was recorded upon a roll of leather in the temple of Amun this day.

(*Urk.* IV 667; *ARE* II §433; Lichtheim 1973–80 [OI] II: 33)

So the recording process was quite complex: a campaign diary was kept and, on return to Egypt, a record based on the diary was written on a leather scroll and deposited in the Amun-temple at Thebes. Only some highlights were extracted from the full account and worked up into a literary form for the purpose of inscription on the temple walls. This last 'edition' is what has been preserved for modern scholars. The tomb of the (probable) campaign scribe, Tjaneni (*ARE* II §392), has been excavated in western Thebes. A stele, set up far to the south at Gebel Barkal, poetically celebrates Tuthmosis III's northern victories and conquests at Egypt's extreme southern frontier (*Urk.* IV 365). There are also the 'topographical lists', which itemise captured places and were perhaps based on campaign itineraries; they, too, are inscribed at Karnak. The lists of Tuthmosis III seem, on the whole, to be reliable, but there are problems with using them as they are not always fully preserved. It is also possible that they were subject to literary rearrangement and, in addition, the geographical names are not always readily identifiable with places on the ground (Aharoni 1979 [OGd]: 162–166).

The campaign described in most detail by Tuthmosis III is the first one. It focuses on the long siege and eventual fall of Megiddo in northern Palestine, the centre for a coalition made up of a great number of local princes, including many from considerably further north. The Egyptian army set out from Memphis, moved up to Sile in the eastern delta, and marched along the coast road to Gaza, already under quite tight Egyptian control. Then they moved on, not meeting much resistance until Joppa, which had to be besieged and was, according to a later Egyptian folk-tale, only taken by a ruse dreamt up by one of Tuthmosis' soldiers, who became its governor later (Simpson 1973 [OI]: 81–84). The annals do not include this incident, perhaps because it did not provide the best opportunity for celebrating the king. But it gives us a wonderful insight into the types of story that circulated in Egypt about the king's soldiers, their exploits and rewards, which reinforced personal commitment to the dynasty (cf. Amose son of Ebana, chapter 4b).

Finally, the army reached the Carmel ridge where, at Megiddo and in its vicinity, a coalition of three hundred and thirty princes, led by the prince of Kadesh in Syria, lay in wait. This provided the perfect opportunity for exalting the king's bravery and ridiculing the enemy's humiliating discomfiture. The king is presented as overriding the caution of his councillors, charging recklessly, but bravely, into the battle although the number of people with him was not very large and, of course, emerging victorious. The enemy were forced to turn tail and make their escape into the town:

> When they saw his majesty overwhelming them, they fled headlong [to] Megiddo with faces of fear, abandoning their horses, their chariots of gold and silver, so as to be hoisted up into the town by pulling at their garments. For the people had shut the town behind them, and they now [lowered] garments to hoist them up into the town.
>
> (*Urk*. IV 659; ARE II §430; Lichtheim 1973–80 [OI] II: 32)

At this point a tactical error made by the Egyptian soldiers is admitted:

> Now, if his majesty's troops had not set their hearts to plundering the possessions of the enemies, they would have [captured] Megiddo at this moment, when the wretched foe of Kadesh and the wretched foe of this town were being pulled up hurriedly so as to admit them into their town.
>
> (*Urk*. IV 659–660; ARE II §430; Lichtheim 1973–80 [OI] II: 32)

In other words, the defences of the city were weakened because the inhabitants had to let in people fleeing from the battle, which provided an ideal opportunity for the Egyptians to penetrate; but the soldiers were so taken with the rich booty lying around in the abandoned camp that they turned their attention to that and ignored the opportunity to capture Megiddo. As a result the city had to be besieged for several months before it surrendered. At the surrender, the princes presented Tuthmosis III with gifts of precious metals and stones, horses and chariots, as well as food for his army, signifying their readiness to accept him as ruler and help him. He then selected some people to carry the gifts home, while he reaffirmed the princes in their positions of power in the local towns. A very large number of cities in Palestine was now effectively under Egyptian control: each local ruler owed his throne to the pharaoh, which he had obtained by formal protestations of loyalty, symbolised by valuable gifts and demonstrated practically by supplying the Egyptian troops. This dependent relationship had henceforth to be reaffirmed regularly, expressed concretely by the payment of tribute, provisioning the Egyptian army and sending additional troops when demanded.

The fall of Megiddo was followed by a great number of smaller forays: one was up to the region of Lake Galilee, which seems to have formed part of the territory of Kadesh, illustrating the great power of that city at the time. Damascus appears in a list of towns that were captured around this time, suggesting a widening out of the campaigning into the Syrian desert. Damascus was later near Egypt's northern frontier – its strategic location and rich resources made it an important centre for Egypt to control (Pitard 1987). Subsequent campaigns were clearly intended to consolidate Egypt's hold of the territory won in the first war and tighten the administrative arrangements. But during the fifth to seventh campaigns, the Egyptians began to look beyond the region of Palestine to north Syria. A chain of naval stations was established along the Syrian coast to receive Egyptian boats and provision the army; one of them, Ullaza (hellenistic Orthosia, on the north frontier of modern Lebanon), was garrisoned. Unfortunately, the annals do not say a lot about the campaigns of these years, just mentioning the arrival of the army at ports, their landing and march inland to campaign (against Tunip and Kadesh, cf. map 9). The northern part of this territory was dominated by Mitanni, and the smaller states outside its direct control were politically and economically in its sphere of power (see chapter 6a). Mitanni had probably supported the earlier resistance to Tuthmosis III, and so this region became the prime battleground between the two powers (Klengel 1965–70 I).

The high point in Egypt's attempt to establish its superiority here came with Tuthmosis' eighth campaign (known in some detail from the inscription of Amenemhab, one of his soldiers, *ARE* II §§574–592): a battle against the north Syrian states and a Mitannian army, led by the Mitannian king, was fought near Aleppo; the Mitannians withdrew across the Euphrates with the Egyptians in pursuit; ships built in Lebanon arrived on carts; Tuthmosis III and his army embarked in them and sailed down the Euphrates from Carchemish to Emar, ravaging the banks. The victorious river procession was preceded by the ceremonial erection of a commemorative stele next to that of Tuthmosis III's grandfather, Tuthmosis I, on the river bank. On the way back the king hunted elephants in Niya (in the Orontes valley), then marched to the port of Sumur (to the north of Ullaza), where Egypt's entry on the stage of international power politics was acknowledged by embassies bearing gifts sent from the neighbouring states of Babylonia and Hatti; Assyria had sent gifts earlier. He then moved inland to the Orontes again and is said to have captured Kadesh (modern Tell Nebi Mend), whose prince had been a ringleader in the resistance of Megiddo eight years earlier. But the defeat of Kadesh was nominal rather than real: no Egyptian garrison was left, the local ruler did not swear an oath of allegiance to Egypt, and Tuthmosis mounted at least three more campaigns into this area. The account shows that Kadesh was independent and on the side of Mitanni (Klengel 1965–70 I). By the end of Tuthmosis III's reign, the coast up to Ullaza was Egyptian, while inland it stretched not much beyond Kumidi (modern Kamid el-Loz; Hachmann

1970) and probably took in Damascus further south-east. All the territory futher north remained independent or aligned with Mitanni.

Amenophis II (1438–1412 (1425–1398)) was finally successful in imposing an oath of allegiance on the Kadesh ruler, and also hunted wild animals with his army in the Beqa valley and Niya. The texts for his wars are not nearly as informative as those for this father, but it looks as though he continued Tuthmosis III's determined policy to shake Mitanni's hold on north Syria with vigour and some success (*ARE* II §§781–798). A great rebellion in Palestine, involving seven local dynasts, was brutally crushed in Amenophis II's ninth year, and the corpses of the defeated leaders publicly displayed: they were paraded hanging upside-down from the prow of the royal ship; then six were suspended from the walls of Thebes, the seventh from those of Napata, the southern imperial frontier. Amenophis II's success in dealing with a serious threat to Egyptian control was acknowledged by embassies sent to him from Mitanni, Hatti and Babylonia. Egypt's political presence was now to be reckoned with as a permanent feature, not limited to occasional military forays to burn down a settlement and carry off booty.

Tuthmosis IV (1412–1403 (1398–1390)) seems to have followed up Amenophis II's harsh policy in Palestine, deporting people from Gezer who were settled near Thebes (*Urk.* IV 1556, 10–11; *ANET* 248; Weinstein 1981: 13–14). The increasing tightness of Egypt's control in Syria–Palestine, coupled with setbacks to Mitannian power in north Syria (e.g. the loss of Aleppo to Tudhaliya I of Hatti), was among the factors that motivated the peace negotations between the two states, sealed by the marriage of a Mitannian princess to Tuthmosis IV. At around the same time, the Egyptians seem to have come to a friendly agreement with the Hittite king about some Anatolian merchants from the far northern city of Kurustama, who were settled in the southern Beqa valley, which now lay in Egyptian territory. But, ultimately, the rapprochement between Egypt and Mitanni meant that the Hittites lost out for a while in their ambitions to dominate north Syria. The reign of Amenophis III (1403–1364 (1390–1352)) saw no royal campaigning at all in Palestine – testimony to the fact that the firm control established by the earlier kings was holding.

Canaan under Egypt's power

The number of towns and settlements destroyed in the second phase of Egypt's expansion was immense, and the decline or extinction of a number of Palestinian cities dates to this time (Gonen 1984; Weinstein 1981). The population in the hill-country and the south declined sharply, and there was a definite shift of settlement to sites on the main routes through the country, along the coast and the prime plains and valleys (e.g. Sharon, Jezreel). Accompanying the destruction was the erection of a number of military strongholds and administrative centres to control the country and cream off its profits. The Taanach letters (and the Gezer text) show the regular pattern for relations between local dynasts and Egyptian Pharaoh in place: they were obliged to greet formally any Egyptian royals or their representatives in Palestine, furnish troops and present tribute. A papyrus text gives a long list of cities in Djahy under Egyptian control, whose envoys had come to Thebes, probably on just such an occasion, and were being supplied with beer and grain (Papyrus Hermitage 1116A: Golénischeff 1913). By the time of the 'Amarna period', following the major conquests (i.e. 'phase three', see p. 320), the Amarna letters reflect a largely similar situation, but in a lot more detail. Egyptian administration in the Levant was centred on Sumur, Gaza, and Kumidi with officials (Akkadian *rabisu*) overseeing the region. Whether, as some have thought (e.g. Helck 1971), this means that the territory was neatly divided into three governmental regions is not certain; it is possible that there were more administrative centres, for example, one at Joppa. The tight Egyptian grip on the region is clearly illustrated by the letters:

> Speak to Endaruta, the man of Akshapa (near Akko): Thus (speaks) the king: He is sending this tablet to you, saying thus: 'Be on your guard! You must protect the king's place, where you are.' And now the king is sending you Hanni, the son of Maireya, overseer of the stable of the king in Canaan. Listen to everything he says very carefully so that the king will not find fault with you. Listen to every word he tells you carefully and carry it out carefully. Be on your guard! Do not be negligent! Before the arrival of the king's bowmen, prepare plenty of food, wine (and) everything else. He is on the point of reaching you very soon, and will cut off the heads of the enemies of the king. Know that the king is as well as the sun in the heavens. His soldiers and the multitude of his chariots are very well.
>
> (*EA* 367; *RA* 19 (1922): 105; Oppenheim 1967 [OI]: no. 64; *ANET*: 484)

Exhortations to protect the city for the king, demands for co-operation and total obedience to royal orders (possibly on pain of execution?) emerge very clearly here. It also tells us of the existence of an Egyptian royal establishment ('the stable of the king in Canaan') within the imperial territories. The demands to provide the king with valuable gifts (including individuals) at his wish are illustrated by another letter:

> Thus (speaks) the king. He sends you this tablet, saying thus: Be on your guard. You must protect the king's place where you are. Prepare your daughter for the king, your lord, and prepare the contributions: [2]0 first-class slaves, silver, chariots, first-class horses – so that the king, your lord, may say to you, 'This is excellent!', about what you have given as contributions to the king to accompany your daughter. Know that the king is as well as the sun in the heavens; the multitude of his soldiers and his chariots are very well.
>
> (EA 99; Oppenheim 1967 [OI]: no. 65)

The Amarna correspondence also shows that the many local dynasts were in constant competition, even conflict, with each other, a situation that could be exploited by the Egyptians (Giles 1970). Accusing each other of treachery to the Egyptian cause or deflecting such accusations by denouncing a neighbour was commonplace, while the writer drives home his own loyalty. As here:

> To the king, my lord and my sun: The message of Lab'ayu, your servant and the dust on which you tread. I fall at the feet of the king, my lord and my sun, 7 times and 7 times. I have obeyed the orders which the king wrote me. Who am I that the king should lose his land for my sake? The fact is that I am a loyal servant of the king! I am not a rebel and I am not failing in my duty; I have not held back my tribute payments, I have refused nothing of what my commissioner has demanded of me. Look, he slanders me unjustly, but the king, my lord, does not examine my (alleged) rebellion. Besides my rebellion is this: when I entered Gazru (Gezer), I said constantly: 'All that belongs to me the king takes, but where is that which belongs to Milkilu?' I know what Milkilu is doing against me! Also, the king has written for my son. I did not know that my son was the companion of the *'apiru*. So now I have handed him over to Addaya. Further, if the king when writing should request my wife, how could I keep her? If the king wrote to me: 'Plunge a bronze dagger into your heart and die!' how could I not carry out the king's command?
>
> (EA 254; Oppenheim 1967 [OI]: no. 68)

But the idea that such local rivalries indicate that the Egyptians operated a *laissez-faire* approach to the empire and took little action to control it is utterly misleading (Several 1972). The Canaanite dynasts were clearly responsible for protecting Egyptian interests locally, were carefully watched over with respect to their loyalty and had to present their tribute regularly and in full. In return they were helped with maintaining order, so that their own security depended on Egyptian support:

> Speak to the king, my lord, my god, my sun, the breath of my life: Message of Zimreddi, mayor of Sidon. I fall before the feet of my lord, god, sun, breath of my life, 7 times and 7 times. May the king, my lord, know that Sidon, the maidservant of the king, my lord, which he has placed under my protection, is safe. When I heard the words of the king, my lord, when he wrote to his servant, then my heart rejoiced, my head lifted, and my eyes shone, on hearing the words of the king, my lord. May the king know that I have made the preparations ready for the arrival of the bowmen of the king, my lord. I have prepared everything in accordance with the command of the king, my lord. May the king, my lord, know that the war against me is very severe. All the towns that the king put under my protection have joined the *'apiru*. May the king

place me under the protection of a man who commands the bowmen of the king, in order to call to account the towns who have joined the 'apiru, so that you may place them again under my protection in such a way that I may serve the king, my lord, just as my ancestors (did) earlier.

(EA 144; Oppenheim 1967 [OI]: no. 70)

An important element of Egypt's policy for controlling the region was that some of the offspring of the Cannanite princes were brought up at the Egyptian court. In this way they became familiar with Egyptian customs and court etiquette, and established links of friendship and mutual obligation with members of the ruling group. This, combined with the taking of daughters of local dynasts into the Egyptian court, tied the local rulers and their families tightly to the Egyptian authorities:

Speak to the king, my lord, my [sun]: Message of Yahtiru, your servant, the dust of your feet. I fall at the feet of the king, my lord, my god, my sun, 7 times and 7 times. Also I am certainly the loyal servant of the king my lord. I looked here and I looked there and there was no light. Then I looked towards the king, my lord, and there was light. A brick may shift from beneath its neighbour, but I shall never shift from beneath the feet of the king, my lord. May the king, my lord, enquire of Yanhamu, his commissioner. When I was young, he took me to Egypt. I served the king, my lord, and I was at the gate of the city of the king, my lord. Let the king, my lord, ask his commissioner, if I guard the city-gate of Azzatu, and the city-gate of Yapu, and wherever the bowmen of the king, my lord, go, I go with them.

(EA 296; Oppenheim 1967 [OI]: no. 69)

The strength of Egyptian control over its Levantine territories is further attested by one of the letters found at Kamid el-Loz, and addressed to the ruler of Damascus (like the Amarna archive, these are written in Akkadian on clay):

Speak to Zalaya, the man of Damascus! Thus the king. Now I send you this tablet, my message to you. Further: send me the 'apiru . . ., about whom I wrote to you as follows: 'I shall give them to towns of the land Kasha, so that they will dwell in it in place of those I have deported.

(Edzard 1970 no. 1)

The letter clearly shows that Egyptian imperial policy included deportations, and settling new peoples in areas thus depopulated. If we add the information of this letter to the evidence for the settlement of Canaanite deportees in Thebes and Nubia by Tuthmosis IV and Akhenaten respectively (see p. 324; chapter 4c), and the more general evidence for royal gifts of prisoners-of-war to work temple estates, the notion that Egyptian control in Canaan was lackadaisical (or even rather kindly) can be seen to be wrong. Although some changes in the trading patterns of Canaan can be traced in the 'Amarna period' (cf. Weinstein 1981; Merillees 1968), there is no reason and no clear evidence to assume that the Egyptians seriously loosened their hold on Canaan at this time. There are now strong hints that Akhenaten took military action in the Levant (Schulman 1978; 1988), as did his successors, Tutankhamun and Horemheb. The international scene changed profoundly at this time, as Egypt's friend and partner, Mitanni, was destroyed by the Hittite king Suppiluliuma I, whose conquests in north Syria brushed the Egyptian frontier menacingly (see chapter 5d).

The Hittite conquest of north Syria and the greater pressure of pastoralist groups, east of the Jordan and penetrating into southern Palestine, determined the action of the dynasty XIX kings (phase four). Sety I, Ramesses II and Merneptah campaigned actively in southern Canaan and established a considerable number of fortresses and governor's residences (easily identifiable, Weippert 1988 [0Gd]: 271–274). A mass of Egyptian inscribed statuary, as well as stelae and rock inscriptions, has survived in Canaan from this time. This, together with a number of smaller Egyptian-style artefacts, locally made Egyptian pottery and the evidence of Papyrus Anastasi 3, which mentions wells, fortresses and military posts named after Egyptian kings, show that Egyptian military control intensified enormously in this period; nor does it seem to have slackened until the end of Ramesses III's reign (1152). The other arena for campaigns early in dynasty XIX was the northern frontier, where the Egyptian kings tried to push back the Hittites and renewed the old Egyptian ambition to conquer Kadesh. But the success of their attempts was limited – indeed for a while, following the battle of Kadesh (1286 (1275)), the Egyptians lost control over the Damascus region. But, on the whole, the setback was not long-lasting or serious, and the situation was resolved to the satisfaction of both sides by the treaty signed between the two powers (1269 (1258); see chapter 4d). Why and how the Egyptians lost control of the Canaanite area is not clear (see chapter 4d). All that can be said is that no evidence for an Egyptian presence exists later than the reign of Ramesses VI (1144–1136).

What did the Egyptians gain from their northern empire? The most regular income from Canaan was grain and wine: estates in a number of regions were the property of the king himself, members of the royal family and temples in Egypt. Providing the basic agricultural labour needed for the Egyptian-owned estates was probably another of the obligations laid on the local rulers (EA 365). The local fine oils were prized and arrived as gifts in Egypt as well as being traded (Gonen 1992: 284). The timber resources of the Lebanon were exploited, probably royally commandeered as needed, for constructing the boats needed by the Egyptian navy and to provide fine building wood for royal building projects in Egypt. The tight control of southern Palestine allowed the Egyptians, from dynasty XIX until the reign of Ramesses VI, to work the rich copper mines of Timna in the Wadi Arabah (Rothenberg 1972). Slaves and horses were demanded from Canaan, as were chariots and trained chariot fighters. Control of the southern Levant also put Egypt into commercial contact with regions beyond its direct rule. Caravans of merchants travelled, for example, from Mesopotamia to Egypt (EA 8; see chapter 7a). The manufactured goods and fine garments, in the production of which Canaan had a long and developed tradition, were very highly valued. The detailed list of Tuthmosis III's booty after the fall of Megiddo (recorded in his 'annals', see pp. 321–322) gives an idea of the kinds of object brought into Egypt from the Levant; it also reveals incidentally the prosperity of Canaan:

> One fine bronze coat of mail belonging to the prince of Megiddo. [Leather] coats of mail belonging to his wretched army: 200. Bows: 502. Poles of *mry*-wood worked with silver from the tent of that enemy: 7. (There follows a list of cattle, people, slaves, warriors; then:) bowls of costly stone and gold, and various vessels . . . . . One large jar of Syrian workmanship. Jars, bowls, plates, various drinking vessels, large kettles, knives: [x +]17, making 1,784 *deben* (1 *deben* = 91 gr). Gold in discs skilfully crafted, and many silver discs making 966 *deben*, 1 *kite* (one tenth of a *deben*). A silver statue . . . . with a head of gold. Walking sticks with human heads (i.e. carved in the shape of human heads): 3. Carrying chairs of that enemy of ivory, ebony, and *ssndjm*-wood worked with gold: 6. Footstools belonging to them: 6. Large tables of ivory and *ssndjm*-wood: 6. One bed of *ssndjm*-wood worked with gold and all costly stones in the manner of a *krkr*, belonging to that enemy, worked with gold throughout. A statue of ebony of that enemy worked with gold with a head of lapis lazuli. . . . bronze vessels and much clothing of the enemy.
>
> (*Urk*. IV 663–664; Lichtheim 1973–80 [OI] II: 34)

A note on Egypt's empire in Nubia

It was probably in the reign of Hatshepsut and Tuthmosis III (1490–1436 (1479–1425)) that the Egyptians firmly established their control in the Dongola Reach region of Nubia and southwards to the fourth cataract (Gebel Barkal stele of Tuthmosis III, *Urk*. IV 365; Cumming 1982: 1–6). This territory was not lost to Egypt until the very end of dynasty XX (1069). It is unfortunate that we do not know nearly as much about the details of the Nubian campaigns as about the ones in the Levant, where non-Egyptian material supplements the evidence. The one-sidedness and limited nature of the documentary record can give the impression that control of Nubia was easier to establish and maintain than in the north, and that it was perhaps altogether differently managed (e.g. Trigger 1976: 109–114; Frandsen 1979). The former *must* be wrong, considering the many references to repeated Nubian campaigns during dynasty XVIII, and the fact that the corpse of one of the Palestinian rebels was exposed on the city-walls of Napata, suggesting that the horrific sight was intended to discourage local revolts.

The question of the style of Egypt's imperial control in Nubia is difficult to evaluate as nothing comparable to the Amarna letters exists for Nubia. Tight control of the region was obviously essential in order to exploit Nubia's great economic potential: it had areas that were suitable for agriculture and viticulture and some parts were particularly favourable for cattle-raising; there was also its great mineral wealth in the form of diorite, amethyst and above all, gold, which was in constant demand by Egypt's neighbours and formed a crucial element in the system of diplomatic gift-exchange; finally, Nubia provided access to areas further south whence especially highly prized exotic goods could be brought. It is, therefore, not surprising that the Egyptian kings found it necessary to install the 'King's Son of Kush' to act as viceroy of the region. He controlled the whole territory from Hierakonpolis to the third cataract and seems to have been, in effect, the ruler of Nubia. He was responsible for managing Egypt's relations with the chieftains of the various desert-groups and the princes living further up the Nile. It is not impossible that these relations were on occasion organised on the basis of gift-exchanges. In some instances, where small Nubian principalities were subject to the Egyptians, the sons of Nubian rulers were sent to the Egyptian court to be educated, as were the sons of the Canaanite princes.

At present the geographical, political and cultural complexities of Nubia are less well understood than those of the Levant, but there is no reason to think that Egypt's control here, and attitudes to subjects, were markedly different from that in the Levant (Morkot 1988). Moreover, as is becoming abundantly clear from more recent studies of Egypt's rule of Canaan, the imperial territories in the Levant were incorporated ever more tightly, and military control became, especially in the last phase, harsh and intrusive (Weinstein 1981; Singer 1988). So the idea that Egypt had 'greater respect' for the highly developed Canaanite region, and hence used a 'velvet glove' approach there as opposed to the brute force applied to 'barbarous' Nubia, is probably misconceived. Certainly, there was no equivalent to the great imperial temple of Abu Simbel in Egypt's northern imperial territories, and there will have been other differences in the details of interaction between rulers and ruled in the two regions. But it is perhaps safer to admit that such variations in the overt expressions of control reflect responses to differing local circumstances that are not as yet understood fully, than to see them as expressing fundamental differences in Egypt's approach to rule of her northern and southern subjects.

Notes

1 Because of the polyvalence of many of the Mesopotamian cuneiform signs, there are at least three possibilities for reading the name of Shattiwaza, all of which have

been propounded at different times by scholars: Kurtiwaza, Mattiwaza and Shattiwaza. Most recently, specialists in Hurrian linguistics have argued for the reading 'Shattiwaza'. Readers should be aware that this person is identical to the 'Mattiwaza' and 'Kurtiwaza' they will encounter in books published before the 1980s.

2 An attempt was made in the 1970s to narrow down the possibilities for the location of the Mitannian royal centre, Washshukanni, by subjecting the Amarna letters written by the Mitannian king to clay analysis, on the assumption that they would have been written from Washshukanni. The method contains some uncertainties, but it has shown that the now very fragmentary tablet EA 18 used a different clay from the rest of the Mitanni letters; on the basis of this, Dobel *et al.* 1977 have suggested that it is not part of the Mitanni–Egypt correspondence.

3 The signs used to write this name are 'UD' with the Hurrian suffix '-hi'. It is not known at present how 'UD' should be pronounced and for that reason the rather awkward method of giving simply the sign-name ('UD') has been adopted; writing it in capitals indicates the uncertainty.

7

MESOPOTAMIA
c. 1600–c. 900

7a Kassite Babylonia (1595–1155)

The arrival of the Kassites

Thanks to the Mari archives, it is possible to trace something of Hammurabi's struggle for power and his ultimate success in uniting the area of south Iraq and beyond under his rule (see chapter 2e). His success in maintaining overall control of his conquests proved not to last much beyond his death, and his successors ruled a steadily diminishing area, extending ultimately not much beyond Baghdad in the north and perhaps Larsa in the south. But although Hammurabi's realm was under external pressure from the start, it is as well not to over-emphasise the evanescence of his dynasty's control. It may well be significant that the next target for attack of the Hittite king, Mursili I, after his destruction of the powerful kingdom of Yamhad (centred on Aleppo) around 1600, was Babylon itself (chapter 5c). The Hittite action suggests that the political realities, about a hundred and fifty years after Hammurabi's death, were that Babylon was still an important state, which the conqueror of Yamhad had to confront.

Yet the difficulties that the Babylon kings were experiencing are evident. Shortly after Hammurabi's death, a rival dynasty of the 'Sealand' appears in the record (*RLA* 8: 6–10). Little is known about it, but clearly it controlled the swampy area and coastline of the extreme south of Iraq,[1] thus obstructing trade-links between the region to the north and the Gulf, through which the lucrative trade with South Arabia (copper from Oman) and the Indus valley had been conducted earlier. This would have had serious economic repercussions, as well as denting royal prestige. A still debated question is when the trade with the Indus valley ceased as a result of the gradual decline of the Harappan culture. The latter is not very certainly dated (Fairservis 1975 [0Gj]: 296ff.), and the succeeding phase of Indian history, before the development of the early first millennium kingdoms of Oudh, Bengal and Bihar, still needs clarification (Fairservis 1975 [0Gj]: 311). Another point, which underlines the fragility of Babylon's power, is that Mursili I would hardly have been able to bring off his lightning raid so successfully had there not been serious internal problems in the kingdom of Babylon. The Hittite attack was devastating for the realm since the dynasty came to an abrupt end almost immediately, and the raid was recorded as a climactic event in a later Babylonian chronicle (*ABC* no. 20 B. rev. 11). It is even possible that, following the Hittite raid, the cult-statue of Marduk was removed to Hana on the Euphrates (for doubts about the historicity of this, cf. Brinkman 1976). Whether true or not, Babylonians certainly believed later that the divine figure had been pillaged at this time.

The Hittites did not remain in Babylon, but withdrew up the Euphrates, leaving the country in a state of political chaos. At this crisis-point in Mesopotamian history a new people, the Kassites, emerged as the eventually dominant power of the area and established a new dynasty. Their earlier presence (*c.* 1770 onwards) in northern Babylonia is sporadically attested, usually as small groups encamped on the edges of cities and forming mercenary contingents in the Babylonian army or working as agricultural labourers. Other contingents of Kassites lived outside the Babylonian political sphere, and appear as hostile attackers (Brinkman 1980: 466; Nashef *AfO* 27 (1980): 164–168). But whence they came and how they became powerful or prominent enough to establish themselves on the Babylonian throne is shrouded in total and frustrating obscurity.

It has generally been thought that the place of origin of the Kassites was in the Zagros mountains to the north-east of Babylonia, because this appears in the first millennium as a tribal area of the Kassites. Later Graeco-Roman writers (such as Diodorus and Strabo) also mention a mountain people called *Kossaioi* living north of Khuzestan, whom it is tempting to identify as later descendants of the Kassites. Conversely, it has been suggested (e.g. by Hallo in Hallo and Simpson 1971 [OC]: 106) that the Kassites came from the region north-west of Babylonia, as a local ruler in the mid-Euphrates kingdom of Hana in the Late Old Babylonian period has a typical Kassite name; so the eastern area with which the Kassites were later associated could simply be a place in which they continued to live as an ethnic group after their political power had waned. The most recent tendency is once again to locate the 'original homeland' of the Kassites in the Zagros, as the cumulative evidence points in that direction (Nashef *AfO* 27 (1980): 167; Liverani 1988 [OC]: 607). As with many such problems, the evidence is insufficient to solve the problem conclusively. Similarly, earlier notions about the Indo-European affiliations of the preserved scraps of the Kassite language (Balkan 1954) have been seriously questioned (Mayrhofer 1966; Kammenhuber 1968; Brinkman 1980: 472–473). On the basis of what has survived, Kassite has no obvious relationship with any other known language; the possible Indo-European identity of a tiny number of divine names is inconclusive, as it may reflect no more than a temporary, possibly indirect, cultural borrowing (cf. the similar problem of the Indo-Aryan elements in Mitanni, see chapter 6a).

One approach to the Kassites that should definitely be rejected is the idea that they were as a people in some way connected with horse-breeding, and that their success in seizing power in Babylon reflects their ability to handle a superior weapon, i.e. the light, and very fast, two-wheeled horse-drawn chariot. This type of chariot, the appropriate skills used in its construction and the necessary training of horses are now known to have developed gradually in the Near East from the early second millennium onwards (Moorey 1986). Further, although some Kassite technical words describing horse colours and markings are known, no particular connection between Kassites and horses is attested in the Old Babylonian period where they appear as simple agricultural workers and soldiers. Perhaps the Kassite terms were adopted because the use of horses in war became widespread in the Near East at the time that Babylonia was under their control. The two-wheeled chariot as the most important tactical military weapon appears to have been adopted at approximately the same time, in all the major states of the ancient Near East. How the extensive use of this new military technique affected the socio-economic structure of Near Eastern states remains obscure. The appearance of the position of 'groom' (*kartappu*) as one of the most important administrative offices in Kassite Babylonia gives us a hint that it did (cf. New Kingdom Egypt, chapter 4e). But what changes did the needs of a new group of chariot-drivers and fighters introduce? How did the need for pastures and exercising areas for horses change earlier patterns of land-holding? Or did the horses simply replace the donkeys used in warfare in preceding centuries? All that is clear is the enormous importance that the chariots and horses held for states in this period; they were seen as an essential and integral part of any power worthy of the name, as illustrated by the standard greeting formula found in the Amarna letters (see chapters 4c; 5d; 6a) exchanged between kings of equal rank in the period c. 1500–c. 1200:

> To Kadashman-Enlil, king of Karduniash (Kassite name of Babylon), my brother, thus speaks Nibmuarriya (Amenophis III), the great king, king of Egypt: I am well; may you be well! Your house, your wives, your sons, your nobles, your horses, your chariots, your lands, may they be very well. I am well, my house, my wives, my sons, my nobles, my horses, my chariots, the numerous soldiers, as many as there are, are (all) well, and in my lands everything is very well.
>
> (EA 1)

The Kassite impact on Babylonia

The most remarkable feature of Kassite rule is the extraordinary length of the dynasty's domination. Although the total of '576 years 9 months' for the dynasty's life, contained in Babylonian King List A (*RLA* 6: 92 (II 16)), clearly includes Kassite leaders who never reigned in Babylonia, it did retain power there for about four hundred years (*c.* 1530–1155). There is very little evidence for serious political disruption before the thirteenth century, when outside intervention by Assyria, and then Elam, eventually destabilised the situation enough to bring about the end of Kassite control. Political stability, then, was the norm for about three hundred years; but it should be stressed that this does not mean that few wars were fought and that it was a general period of peace. Records for the period before the thirteenth century are very sparse (Brinkman 1976), limited to terse votive and building inscriptions by kings, and inscribed cylinder seals. But, for example, the eighth-century *Synchronistic History* which traces relations between Assyria and Babylonia from *c.* 1500 onwards from an Assyrian perspective (*ABC* no. 21) gives us a selective account of political ups-and-downs and battles fought in this period. The Babylonian Chronicle P (*ABC* no. 22), too, preserves some episodes of a major war between Kurigalzu II (1332–1308) and Elam – its importance is emphasised by a later historical epic (preserved only in fragments: Grayson 1975: 47–55). Year-names, which mention some political events (see chapter 1c), are a source that could help to fill in (partly) the historical framework. But, unfortunately, from around the middle of the fourteenth century onwards, the Kassite kings dropped the practice of naming each year, and instead simply counted them numerically through each reign. Before that, there is very little documentation indeed, so the crucial earlier years, when the year-names could have provided a valuable clue to what was happening, are almost totally unknown. Another serious problem in the Kassite period is that several kings have the same name, but the dated documents do not clarify to which of them the text is referring. This, combined with the dearth of earlier documentation, means that the chronology of the Kassite kings, especially in the first two centuries of their rule, is very uncertain. Sometimes even the names and very existence of certain rulers are in doubt (see table 21). The majority of dated documents, which provide insight into the economic and social life of the region, come from the later fourteenth to thirteenth century (Kurigalzu II to Kashtiliash IV). But here, too, there are problems. First, only two sites, Nippur and Ur, have produced useful archives rather than random tablets; second, the vastly larger number of texts come from one site only (Nippur: 12,000, as opposed to Ur: 75; Gurney 1983); third, only a tiny percentage of the Nippur texts has so far been published. All this makes it difficult to write a definitive study of this important period of Mesopotamian history.

Yet the sparse material available reveals some interesting features of Babylonian life, especially in the social sphere. One text, for example, records the 'purchase' of a small girl as future bride for the purchaser's son:

One young girl, a native of Babylonia, one-half cubit in size, by the name of U_4.9.KAM-belet. Rabâ-sha-Ninimma, son of Ili-Shamash, the

Table 21 Kassite kings (with approximate dates, following Brinkman 1976)

Kassites		Contemporaries
[1 Gandash	1729	
2 Agum I		
3 Kashtiliash I	1660	
kings 4–9		end of Hammurabi dynasty (1595)
(names uncertain; no regnal years)]		
10 BurnaBuriash I	(*c.* 1530–1500?)	
11–14 (uncertain)		
?15 Karaindash	*c.* 1413	
?16 Kadashman-Harbe I		
?17 Kurigalzu I		
?18 Kadashman-Enlil I	(1374)–1360	Amenophis III of Egypt
?19 Burnaburiash II	1359–1333	Akhenaten of Egypt = Ashur-uballit
?20 Kara-hardash	1333	of Assyria
?21 Nazi-Bugash	1333	(1365–1330)
22 Kurigalzu II	1332–1308	
23 Nazi-Maruttash	1307–1282	
24 Kadashman-Turgu	1281–1264	Hattusili III
25 Kadashman-Enlil II	1263–1255	" "
26 Kudur-Enlil	1254–1246	
27 Shagarakti-Shuriash	1245–1233	
28 Kashtiliash (IV)	1232–1225	
Tukulti-Ninurta of		Tukulti-Ninurta's
Assyria	1225	reign in Assyria: 1244–1208
29 Enlil-nadin-shumi	1224	
30 Kadashman-Harbe II	1223	
31 Adad-shum-iddina	1222–1217	
32 Adad-shum-usur	1216–1187	
33 Meli-Shipak	1186–1172	
34 Marduk-apla-iddina I	1171–1159	
35 Zababa-shum-iddina	1158	
36 Enlil-nadin-ahi	1157–1155	

merchant, bought her for daughter-in-law-ship (i.e. wife) for his second son, Ninimma-zera-shubshi, from her father, Kidin-Shumaliya, son of Kiautu, a Kassite from the town of Hurad-Hamatir, (and) from her mother, Agargarutu, daughter of Sin-epiranni. As her purchase price, Rabâ-sha-Ninimma gave 2 fine *muhtillû*-garments, worth 2 shekels of gold, to Kidin-Shumaliya and Agargarutu, his wife; and for the rest of the purchase price, Rabâ-sha-Ninimma shall provide Kidin-Shumaliya and Agargarutu with food.

(The next, fragmentary lines protect Rabâ-sha-Ninimma against any other relatives of the girl who might contest the transaction; then:)

They have taken an oath together by Anu, Enlil, Ninlil (?), x, Shuq-amuna, and King Kadashman-Harbe.

Witnesses: Iautu, son of Ninurta-bani; Izkur-Ninurta, son of Kidin-

Ninurta; Nusku-aha-iddina, son of Dimahdi-Urash; Rabâ-sha-Ninurta, son of Ninurta-bani. The scribe: Eriba-Marduk, son of Ili-iqisha.

Month of Kislimu, eleventh (+?) day, accession year of Kadashman-Harbe, the king.

The fingernail mark of Kidin-Shumaliya (and) fingernail mark of Agargaru(tu), his wife, serving as their seals.

> (CBS 12917; Brinkman 1976: 383–384, text no. 9)

The practice of buying young girls for a future marriage is not attested earlier in Babylonia, although it is known in approximately contemporary Nuzi (van Praag 1945: 79–84; cf. Middle Assyrian Laws A §43) and later Assyria (eighth and seventh centuries; Postgate *Iraq* 41 (1979): 96). The tiny size of the girl (about 28 cm) is probably a convention indicating her age rather than an exact measurement (Roth 1987); it suggests that she could have been a baby. Studies of this type of 'adoption-marriage' in China suggest that it was a way for poor families to avoid infanticide of a daughter, whose claim on the family-fund for a dowry was an expense not to be contemplated. The relatively small payment made for a girl in these circumstances would obviate the need for the in-laws to fork out for the expensive bridal gifts which were part of the usual marriage. While not a prestigious form of marriage (but this might be less necessary in the case of a second son), the 'adoption-marriage' did provide another pair of hands for work and a potential mother of sons for the 'buying' family at a fairly low cost. In China it even happened that a baby girl 'adopted' in this way might be suckled by the foster-mother. While not all these circumstances need necessarily have obtained in ancient Mesopotamia, the Chinese comparison provides some insights into how the practice attested by this text might have worked (Goody 1990: 29–30).

An important document form specifically associated with the Kassites (although it continued in use for centuries afterwards) is the *kudurru*. They are stones of rectangular or phallic shape, usually with unevenly rounded tips decorated with religious symbols (*RLA* 6: 268–277). The sides normally contain an inscription, which deals with such matters as the settling of a land-dispute, or the royal gift of a stretch of land, together with privileges such as exemptions from a whole range of dues and taxes to officers for distinguished services (see chapter 7d). The term *kudurru* means, literally, 'boundary', and scholars speculated initially whether these 'boundary stones' were set up actually on the land whose ownership they commemorated. Another possibilty is that they were kept in temples as guarantees of the owner's rights and claims to the land (Steinmetzer 1922). The lack of any signs of weathering, the fact that the only *kudurru* excavated in Babylonia was found in a temple, that the relief decoration and inscription extend right to the bottom of the stone and, finally, that many are small (well below 50 cm) make their erection in temples rather than open fields much more likely (Seidl 1968: 72–73). As many of the land-grants recorded in this form are concerned with exemptions and privileges, they provide an insight into the range of dues that the king normally expected to receive from his subjects.

One of the most striking features of the Kassite period is that the Kassite ruler was 'king of Babylonia', or simply 'king'. In other words, he was king of a territorial state, a country – in marked contrast to the earlier political system of contending city-states. An outstanding and enduring achievement of the Kassite kings was to weld the region, probably after their defeat of the Sealand dynasty in the fifteenth century, into a unified whole, which continued to be the political norm even under later weak governments. We can henceforth speak of south Iraq as 'Babylonia' – an anachronism before the Kassite period (Brinkman 1974). The ceremonial capital was firmly fixed at Babylon, whose patron-god, Marduk (*possibly* recovered by the early Kassite king, Agum II kakrime; Astour 1986; see p. 333), became the most important god of the Mesopotamian pantheon. It has even been argued that the composition of the famous Babylonian *Epic of Creation*, which focuses on the rise of Marduk to pre-eminence, dates to the fifteenth century and served to celebrate the unification of Babylonia after the defeat of the Sealand and the (re-)establishment of the Marduk cult in Babylon (Jacobsen 1976 [OL]: 190).

One feature of Kassite Babylonia that remains problematic is defining the 'foreignness' of the Kassites. Their names are distinctive, totally different from Babylonian ones, and reveal the existence of a specific Kassite pantheon. They obviously spoke a different language (at least initially), some preserved their traditional tribal structure and, in legal texts, they are sometimes defined as 'Kassite' to distinguish them from Babylonians (see the text on p. 336). Yet apart from the protective deities of the royal house, Shuqamuna and Shumaliya, there is no evidence that any of these gods received a cult in Babylonia or were accommodated in the existing cult-centres. Whether some kind of syncretism between Kassite and Babylonian gods occurred must remain speculative, although it is a possibility. The Kassite kings, as far as we can tell, actively patronised and promoted the traditional Babylonian cults, including installing members of the royal family in cultic offices (Brinkman and Matthews 1990). If the later story of the recovery of the Marduk statue by Agum II kakrime is historical, it suggests a very eager embracing by the Kassites of Babylonian gods; if not, it shows that, in later times, the Kassite kings were regarded as outstanding champions and defenders of Babylonian sacred tradition. Very little of the Kassite language was ever recorded (what there is seems to be scholarly exercises) and the kings used Akkadian and Sumerian for their inscriptions. It is possible that their own stories and religious practices were only transmitted orally, but that must remain a hypothesis. As far as the available evidence goes, there was little hostility towards the Kassite kings, aside from one brief reference shortly after their fall. Indeed, the last Kassite kings bore entirely Babylonian names. How the court-élite was constituted and who (ethnically) the high administrative and military personnel were is unknown. This makes it difficult to identify a Kassite ruling group, and hard to see in what sense the Kassites were experienced as foreign rulers. The evidence of the later Agum text and some scraps of epics concerning the Kassite kings Kurigalzu II and Adad-shum-usur (Grayson 1975: 47–77) imply that the Kassite rulers were more generally perceived as wholly legitimate, true Babylonian kings (cf. the Amorite dynasties earlier, chapter 2).

Babylonia among the great powers

The most revealing source for assessing the strength of Babylonia in the Kassite period comes not from Iraq but from Egypt. The great collection of letters, written in Akkadian on clay, found at the site of el-Amarna dates to the later years of Amenophis III, the whole of the reign of Akhenaten (1364–1347 (1352–1336)) and some of his successors (see chapter 4c; Moran 1987). The detailed chronology of the archive is uncertain, but during the roughly thirty years it covers the international relations of the great powers of western Asia are brilliantly illuminated. A smaller number of less well preserved letters found at Boğazköy (Hattusa), dating to the first half of the thirteenth century, show that such correspondence was a regular and continuous part of diplomatic life (*CTH* 155–178). The Amarna letters illustrate Babylonia's position as a large, internationally important state: messengers were regularly exchanged between Egypt and Babylonia, and the powerful Egyptian king expressed his recognition of Babylonia's importance by addressing the Babylonian monarch as 'brother'; the term was only used by kings who accepted each other as equals and allies.

The earliest reference to contact between the dynasty XVIII kings of Egypt and the Kassite rulers comes from the Annals of Tuthmosis III (1490–1436 (1479–1425), see chapter 6d). The climax of his military conquests was the eighth campaign, during which the Egyptians crossed the Euphrates, penetrated Mitanni, erected a commemorative stele on Mitanni's territory and encountered the Mitannian army in battle. The importance of this foray lay less in any territorial conquests made by Egypt, more in the fact that it established Egypt's claim to control the southern parts of the Levant – a claim which it was prepared to support with military force. Egypt was now a power with whom the great states needed to establish formal links and work out a political relationship. It is, therefore, not surprising that one of the results of Tuthmosis III's campaign was the arrival of embassies bearing congratulatory gifts from the Hittites and Babylonia (Assyria had welcomed the Egyptian king several years earlier). The identity of the Babylonian king who welcomed Tuthmosis III is not certain, and, given the chronological problems of the Kassite dynasty, likely to remain so. A letter written by Burnaburiash II to Akhenaten, in which the Egyptian king is reminded of the long-standing friendship between the two countries, has been thought to refer to that occasion:

> Since the time of Karaindash, since messengers of your fathers have come regularly to my fathers, until now they have been good friends.
>
> (EA 10)

The implication would certainly appear to be that diplomatic relations had been established about four generations earlier, and the Babylonian embassy to Tuthmosis III is an attractive candidate. But there are major chronological difficulties in trying to correlate Tuthmosis III and Karaindash. Perhaps an earlier Kassite ruler simply made an initial overture to the Egyptian victor, which was not followed up with a regular exchange of embassies. Formal diplomatic contacts were then instituted only towards the end of the fifteenth century, possibly as a result of Amenophis II's success in finally forcing the surrender of the important city-state of Kadesh on the Orontes (see chapter 6d).

Archaeological and other documentary evidence reveals Babylonia's wealth and influence in the fourteenth century. The 'Sealand' had been incorporated in the fifteenth century, which reopened the rich trade-route to the Gulf. Danish excavations, conducted in the 1960s, have revealed a flourishing commercial settlement and fortress on Bahrain datable to the Kassite period. Some Nippur texts and the archaeological remains on Bahrain show that the Gulf region, as far as and including Bahrain, was governed *directly* by the Kassite kings – the next time this area was politically incorporated by an outside power was eighteen hundred years later, in the Sassanian period (Potts 1990 [OGf]; Brinkman 1993). A letter from Nippur, from the reign of Burnaburiash II, might even suggest that the daughter of the Kassite governor of the Gulf was left at a school for the children of court-personnel in Nippur while her father was posted to Bahrain (Potts 1990 [OGf] I: 309).

Several important ancient Babylonian cities were also refurbished extensively in this period, generally following the old-established architectural canons for temple architecture, and frequently using Sumerian for the accompanying commemorative inscriptions. But occasionally some specific Kassite elements appear – most strikingly in the layout and moulded brick-relief decoration of a small temple at Uruk, similar to architectural reliefs found in contemporary Elam (see chapter 7c; Strommenger and Hirmer 1965 [OM], pl. 170). Generally, though, surveys conducted in south Iraq give the impression that, while some of the large old cities flourished, the number of middle-sized towns decreased, and the number of villages increased (Adams 1981; Adams and Nissen 1972). Whether this relates in some way to the small clan units that appear to have characterised Kassite society originally (Brinkman 1980: 465–466), and, if so, how, requires more study.

A particular concern of the Kassite kings was defence of the route linking Babylonia through the Diyala with the Iranian plateau and beyond, by which the lapis lazuli mined in Badakhshan in north-eastern Afghanistan reached Babylonia. The highly prized 'genuine' lapis lazuli (called 'lapis lazuli of the mountain', as opposed to 'lapis lazuli of the kiln' – a kind of glass; Oppenheim 1970) constituted one of the gifts that the Babylonian kings sent to Egypt, sometimes, it would seem, in fairly sizeable lumps (EA 7). The strategic importance of the Diyala route is shown by the care which the Kassites displayed in safeguarding their access to it against neighbouring Assyria and Elam with the creation of the new city of Dur Kurigalzu. It is located at the site of Aqar Quf, near modern Baghdad, and, as its name ('Fortress of Kurigalzu') suggests, it was founded by Kurigalzu I. The site is dominated, even today, by the ziggurat, which is preserved to a great height, and has weathered into a curious shape. The worn core of the ziggurat reveals the details of its construction, with layers of reed-matting and bitumen laid between the mud-brick courses (Baqir 1942–6). The site has never been completely explored, but enough to show that, at a considerable distance from the sacred complex, lay the ruins of an impressive palace with remains of fine painted frescoes (Tomabechi 1983; fig. 25), brick vaulting, fragments of

Figure 25 Painting from the palace at Dur Kurigalzu (Aqar Quf; after Baqir, *Iraq* 8, pl. XII)

341

exquisite realistic sculptures and coloured glass. The technique of glass production had been developed already earlier, probably in northern Mesopotamia (Oppenheim 1970), but only now is glass found in considerable quantity, used for inlays as well as vessels.

It was in Kurigalzu I's reign (early fourteenth century) that relations between Babylonia and Egypt were consolidated by the marriage of the Babylonian king's daughter and Amenophis III. The contacts between the two states became much closer as a result, especially in terms of gifts exchanged and expected (Liverani 1979: 21–33). It was assumed that valuable commodities would be sent as a matter of course, because of the family relationship established by such political marriages. The principle is clearly stated, and accepted, in a letter written by Amenophis III of Egypt to Kadashman-Enlil I of Babylonia:

> When you (sc. Kadashman-Enlil) wrote thus:
> 'My daughters, who are married to neighbouring kings, when my messengers go there, they speak with them, [and they send] me a gift, as greeting. She who is with you [is poor?]' – these are your words – (then I answer thus:) Truly, your neighbouring kings are rich and powerful; your daughters can receive anything from them and send it to you. But what has your sister who is with me? And yet, if she should acquire anything, I shall send it you. It is a nice thing to give your daughters in order to acquire a nugget of gold(?) from beyond your country.
>
> (EA 1)

Such transactions, particularly the gold sent from Egypt, which commanded an immense supply of it from the Nubian mines, primarily served to express political prestige. The close ties with neighbours also helped to facilitate and stimulate more practical economic exchanges between Babylonia and its neighbours (see EA 8; pp. 343–344). The country's commanding role in long-distance trade, probably led to gold (instead of silver) becoming the standard for business transactions for a while in the Kassite period – the only time in the three millennia of Babylonian history (Edzard 1960). The scale of the commercial and political network to which Babylonia was linked may also be reflected by the handsome, large Kassite lapis lazuli seals found at Thebes in Greece (Porada 1981–2; cf. Morris 1992: 104), and the Mycenaean copper oxhide ingot found at Dur Kurigalzu.

Precious metals were not all that came to Babylonia from Egypt: when Kadashman-Enlil I completed a palace, for example, Amenophis III sent him handsomely carved furniture made of ebony, sheathed in gold, some of it inlaid with ivory; the list of items from Egypt includes a bed, a sedan-chair, a large armchair, nine other armchairs and footstools. The Kassite rulers particularly appreciated Egyptian sculptures:

There are skilled craftsmen where you are. Let them represent a wild animal, either a land or river creature, lifelike, so that the hide is exactly like that of a live animal! Your envoy shall bring it to me! But if old ones are ready and available, then when Shindishugab, my envoy, arrives at your court let him immediately, posthaste, borrow chariots(?) and get here. Let them make some new ones for future delivery . . .

(EA 10)

What did the Babylonians send, apart from lapis lazuli? With the routes into the Zagros and Iran firmly in their grip, the Kassites were probably able to procure the fine horses from the Iranian mountains, later so highly prized by Assyrian and Persian kings. Formal gifts from Babylonia to Egypt included teams of horses, i.e. horses trained ready for use. This impression is strengthened by the fact that they are accompanied by an equivalent number of chariots. Such a present was the ancient equivalent of being sent an equipped jet-fighter.

The Amarna correspondence, particularly that between Babylonia and Egypt, makes the rules governing diplomatic contact between the great powers very clear. It was usual for several envoys to be sent, all identified by name and sometimes their position at court. They were obviously very important people who enjoyed close personal contact with the king and were in his confidence. It seems that only one of their number actually had an audience with the king at the receiving court. In the course of this meeting the king gave orders that gold, silver, oil and other necessities be dispensed to him and his fellow-envoys; the supplies were intended for their personal use. The treatment of envoys reflected the esteem in which the country they represented was held – if they were treated shabbily or left to kick their heels for any length of time without being formally received, it was tantamount to an insult to the king they represented.

Envoys often seem to have travelled with merchants engaged in commercial ventures. If the caravans were plundered, the ruler in whose territory the incident had happened was held responsible and compensation could be demanded, as shown by this Amarna letter:

Now my merchants who came up with Ahutabu (i.e. the Babylonian envoy to Egypt) stayed behind in Canaan in order to carry on their business. After Ahutabu had continued on his way to my brother, in Hinnatuna of Canaan, Shumadda, son of Balumme, and Shutatna, son of Sharatum of Akko, sent their men there, killed my merchants and took their money away. I am sending you [. . .] as fast as possible (?). Question him so that he can tell you (everything). Canaan is your land, and its kings [are your servants]. I have been robbed in your land. Bring them to account, and the money that they took, replace it! And the people who killed my servants – kill them and thus avenge their blood. If you do not execute them, they will kill again, whether it be one of my caravans or your own messengers, so that our exchange of envoys will be cut off.

(EA 8)

The royal ambassadors were charged to transmit goodwill messages and requests between the rulers; they also furnished information on their king and country, and gathered as much news as possible about the court they visited. The gifts which accompanied each embassy were expected to be displayed, and the sender acknowledged. These diplomatic presents were meticulously itemised together with the net weights of any valuable materials; as a guarantee of their weight and value, they were sealed by the sender. On receipt the inventory of items was checked and the stated weights rigorously tested. An amusing reference to this procedure is contained in an Amarna letter from Burnaburiash to Akhenaten:

> But my brother must not delegate the (handling of the) gold which he is going to send me to somebody else; my brother must check it personally, seal it and then send it to me. My brother certainly did not check the previous (cargo of) gold which my brother sent. My brother left it to someone else to seal it and dispatch it. When I put the 40 minas of gold, which had been brought to me, into a kiln, not (even) [10, I sw]ear came out.

(EA 7; Oppenheim 1967 [OI] no. 58)

During the embassy's stay, a formal reception was organised at which the envoys expected to make contact with any of their ruler's daughters or sisters (and their retinues) who had been married to the king whose court they were now visiting. This gave them the opportunity to deliver messages and presents to her from home and take greetings from her back to the king and her mother and family. They could also check that she was well and being treated in accordance with her status. The greater part of one of the Amarna letters (EA 1) is full of suspicions about how the Babylonian king's sister is being treated at the Egyptian court, whether she is still alive, and why the Babylonian ambassadors have not been able to see her.

The strict observation of protocol helped to maintain the relationship by which equality of rank was measured and which was encapsulated in the term 'brotherhood'. A new king notified 'his brothers' formally of his accession, expressed his intention of continuing the earlier good relations and sent a present as a guarantee of his goodwill, as in this letter from king Burnaburiash of Babylonia to Akhenaten:

> Just as previously you and (my) father were good friends with each other, so now you and I should be friends together. Between us nothing else whatsoever is even to be mentioned. Whatever you want from my country, write, so that it may be brought to you. And what I want from

your country, I shall write, so that it may be brought to me . . . And as a greeting-present for you [. . .] and 1 [. . .] . . . I am sending you.

(EA 6)

Regular enquiries after the health and well-being of other kings and the sending of sympathetic messages if a fellow-ruler was ill were also part of international protocol. This is beautifully illustrated by a letter in which the Babylonian king grumbles to his Egyptian 'brother' about his failure to do so:

> I have not been well ever since my brother's messenger arrived here, so none of the messengers ate food or drank beer in my company. You may ask your messenger yourself [. . .] and he will [tell you that] I was not well, and that as far as my recovery is concerned(?), I am still by no means restored [to health]. [Furthermore], since I was not well and my brother [showed me no] concern, I for my part became angry with my brother, saying: 'Has my brother not heard that I am ill? Why has he shown me no concern? Why did he not send a messenger and visit me?' My brother's envoy addressed me thus: 'Egypt is not near enough so that your brother can hear (about you) and enquire concerning your health. It is a faraway country. Who would tell your brother so that he can immediately send you greetings? Could your brother possibly hear that you are ill and still not send a messenger?' I, for my part, spoke to him, thus: 'Is the country of my brother, the great king, far away or nearby?' And he said to me as follows: 'Ask your own messenger whether the country is far away. And that is why your brother has not heard anything (about you) and did not send (anyone) to greet you.' Now, after I asked my own messenger and he told me that it was a long journey, I was no longer angry, I said no more.

(EA 7; Oppenheim 1967 [OI] no. 58)

Despite the great distances separating the states, kings expected to invite each other to any important festivals and ceremonies, signalling the occasion with a present. When Amenophis III failed to invite Kadashman-Enlil I to such an occasion (perhaps one of his jubilee festivals, cf. chapter 4e), the Babylonian king was quick to complain and, rather pointedly, invited the Egyptian king to a ceremony in Babylonia:

> When you celebrated a great festival, you did not send your messenger to me saying: 'Come, to [eat an]d drink!' and you did not send me my greeting-gift on the occasion of the festival. . . . I have built a new [hous]e. In [my house] I have built a large [. . .]. Your messengers have seen [the house and the . . . and are happy]. Now I am going to have an inauguration (ceremony) for the house. Come [yourself] to [eat] and drink with me. [I shall not do] as you did. I am sending you [25 men and] 25 women, in all 50 [who are in my service, because of the inauguration of my house].

(EA 3)

Nothing illustrates better than the Amarna letters how diligently the inter-connections between the courts of this period were fostered. Most of the correspondence naturally concerns relations with Egypt, but references both in this collection and the Hittite letters show that all the great courts of the Near East were in contact with each other. The Hittite letters, in particular, show that, in adddition to the gifts of gold, precious stones, and horses, specialist personnel was also requested to be sent from one court to another. The Hittites asked for, and received, sculptors from Babylonia on several occasions, as well as doctors and conjurors (Zaccagnini 1983). It provided an opportunity for such highly qualified experts to enrich themselves, but they often found it difficult to return to their own country, and several are known to have died at the Hittite court. This could cause friction and also gave rise to suspicions of maltreatment, as shown by this letter found at Boğazköy:

> And I (sc. Hattusili III) have more to say to my brother (Kadashman-Enlil II), concerning the physician whom my brother has dispatched here; people accepted him and he performed cures on them but a disease befell him. I took great pains with him and I performed extispicies for him, but when his time came he died. Now one of my messengers will take the physician's servants along (to Babylon) and my brother should question them, and they will tell about the cures which the physician used to perform. The presents I had given their [master] have disappeared, however; they are afraid on account of this and so they will suppress any mention of it before my brother. My brother should know that the chariot, the wagon, the horses, silver, and linen which I gave to the physician are written down [. . .] and I have sent the tablet directly to my brother so that my brother can have it read to him. But the physician died when his appointed time caught up with him. I would never have thought to detain the physician, in view of the fact that when they received during the reign of my brother Muwatalli a conjuror and a physician (from Babylon) and detained them, I was the one to argue with him saying, 'Why do you want to detain them?' telling him that it is not according to custom to detain (such people); and now I am supposed to have detained your physician? Of the former [experts] whom they had received here, only the conjuror died [. . .]. The woman he married here was of my own family and he was held . . . but if he had said, 'I want to leave for my native country,' he could have gone right away.
>
> (*CTH* 172; Oppenheim 1967 [OI]: no. 84)

* * *

With rare exceptions, the language in which the international correspondence of the Late Bronze Age was conducted was Akkadian. Even the letters exchanged between the local Canaanite dynasts and their Egyptian overlords used Akkadian, as did the king of Alashiya in Cyprus, and the Hittite and

346

Mitannian rulers. Akkadian was the *lingua franca* of western Asia. In Kassite Babylonia there was intense scribal and literary activity. Many older texts were copied, some of them edited into an enduring 'classical' form. Scribal traditions and specialisation were handed down in particular 'families', probably to be regarded as professional, rather than kinship, groups. In the late Babylonian and Hellenistic periods, many scribes described themselves as members of one of these families, the founders of which can often be shown to have been Babylonian scholars of the Kassite period (Lambert 1957). But copying and editing was not the only contribution of Kassite scholars. One of the most magnificent Babylonian literary texts, known from its first line as *ludlul bēl nēmeqi* ('Let me praise the Lord of Wisdom') was composed at this time. It is a profound, philosophical poem, posing the problem of why a pious and good man should nevertheless suffer misfortune (the 'Job' theme familiar from the Old Testament). The text presents and explores the doubts about the gods that such 'righteous suffering' presents, and ends on a note of resignation: no man can understand the ways of gods and their reasons; they are wise and almighty, beyond human questioning (Lambert 1960: 21ff.). The description of the illness afflicting the sufferer is particularly moving:

> A demon put on my body for a garment;
> Like a net, sleep has swooped down upon me.
> My eyes are open but do not see;
> My ears are open but do not hear;
> Numbness has overcome my entire body,
> Paralysis has come upon my flesh,
> Stiffness has seized my arms,
> Debility has fallen on my loins,
> My feet have forgotten how to move.
> . . .
> I took to my bed – a confinement; my leaving (the house) was sighs.
> My house was turned into a prison for me.
> My arms are locked in the fetters of my flesh,
> My feet are paralysed in the shackles of my own self.
> The blows given me are very painful, my wound is severe.
> The whip that hit me is full of thorns,
> The goad that stung me is covered with barbs
> All day long a persecutor pursues me,
> At night he does not let me breathe for an instant.
> My sinews are parted through twisting,
> My limbs are splayed and lie awry.
> I spent the nights on my litter like an ox,
> I wallowed in my excrement like a sheep.
> The exorcist shied away from my symptoms,
> And the haruspex confused my omens.

The diagnostician could not clear up the nature of my illness
And the haruspex could not set a term for my sickness.
The god did not come to help me, did not take my hand,
The goddess did not take pity on me, did not go at my side.
Open is the grave, my funerary offerings are prepared,
Before I died the wake was over.
All my land said: 'What a pity!'
My ill-wisher heard it and his face shone,
They gave the news to the woman ill-wisher and her mood brightened.
The day has become dark for my entire family,
For all my acquaintances their sun became covered over.
(Lambert 1960: 42ff., II 71–79; 95–120; Reiner 1985 [0J]: 115–116)

A posited shift in religious sentiments during the Kassite period, namely, the development of the concept of a personal god, symbolising an individual's good fortune and able to act as intermediary between human beings and the sphere of the great and powerful gods, is rather less certain (*contra* Jacobsen 1976 [0L]). But the evidence certainly suggests that important discussions and speculations about the relationship of mankind to the gods, and the place of the individual in a confusing world, were being formulated at this time.

At Amarna, three Babylonian literary texts have been found (EA 356–358; Artzi 1982) which, it has been suggested, were written in Egypt by a Babylonian scribe active there – perhaps borrowed by the Egyptian court (like the doctors, conjurors and sculptors) to help the Egyptian officials, who had to deal with the Egyptian king's correspondence, to learn Babylonian. They, and other school copies of Babylonian literary texts from the Levant and Anatolia (cf. the poem from Emar, pp. 316–317), bear witness to the wide dissemination not only of the Babylonian script and language at this time, but also of its culture (Lambert 1965).

While it remains difficult to grasp the political and socio-economic fabric of Kassite Babylonia, and a great part of its history continues to be frustratingly obscure, it is clear from the Amarna archive, the finds in the Gulf, and the evidence from Babylonia itself that this was a phase of major political and cultural importance in the history of the region. The Kassite dynasty was one of the most stable regimes ever known here, and its political unification of the country proved to be an enduring achievement. It represents one of the important turning points of Babylonian history, and further discoveries and studies should help to confirm that impression and fill out the sadly fragmentary picture.

7b Assyria in the Middle Assyrian period (*c.* 1400–*c.* 1050)

The years separating the reign of Ishme-Dagan (1781–1741, see chapter 2d) from that of Ashur-uballit (1365–1330 (1353–1318)) are very poorly attested in Assyria, constituting a sort of 'dark age'. After that, documentation (royal inscriptions and administrative, legal, economic texts) increases steadily, and is really extensive for the thirteenth and twelfth centuries. The main site of text-finds is the old city and centre of the state, Ashur (Pedersen 1985; Postgate 1986). But texts from other locations, especially Upper Mesopotamia, annexed by Assyria in the thirteenth century also exist (Saggs and Wiseman 1968; Postgate 1986 n.4; Aynard *et al.* 1980; Jas 1990). In some respects, the Middle Assyrian state is now one of the most exciting periods for study, as finds in north-east Syria have steadily revealed more and more material, and demonstrated the intensity of Assyrian control here. The term 'Middle Assyrian' is a linguistic one, defining the particular form of the Assyrian dialect used in the texts of this period.

As a result of the formation and expansion of the state of Mitanni in northern Mesopotamia, Assyria not only lost territory but for a time was even robbed of its independence (see chapter 6a). Given such serious disruptions, the continuity of local institutions is remarkable. First, the monarchy: the later Assyrian King List insists that a dynastic line persisted successfully through this period, despite challenges. Later Assyrian kings were thus in theory ultimately descended from a scarcely known king, Adasi, who reigned some time in the sixteenth century. This concept of genealogical legitimacy was maintained throughout Assyrian history, so this, to us, obscure period was of considerable ideological importance for the Assyrian state until its disintegration at the end of the seventh century. Second, the system of annual eponymous officials, the *limmu*-ship (see chapter 2b), was retained from the Old Assyrian period right through the 'dark period' to the disappearance of Assyria. Finally, the later histories of building activities refer to acts carried out by kings of this otherwise poorly documented phase. So, despite the probably often fictional character of smooth political continuity, certain important elements characteristic of Assyrian political culture survived. Ashur-nadin-ahhe I (*c.* 1440 (1430)) is known to have made diplomatic overtures to Tuthmosis III, congratulating him on his campaigns in the Levant, referred to in both Tuthmosis III's annals (see chapter 6d) and an Amarna letter (EA 16). The *Synchronistic History* (*ABC* no. 21; see chapter 7a) mentions two boundary conflicts with Babylonia to the south – one around 1500, another late in the fifteenth century (reign of Ashur-bel-nisheshu: 1417–1409 (1407–1399)) But the independence of Assyria was lost around the same time, with the extension of Mitannian power, under king Saushtatar, to include the city of Ashur, from whose temple he removed the doors of gold and silver (see Shattiwaza treaty, chapter 6a).

Ashur-uballit and his successors (1365–1245 (1353–1234))

The bare bones of Assyria's history in the fifteenth century make it very hard to understand how and why Assyria's fortunes revived dramatically in the reign of Ashur-uballit (1365–1330 (1353–1318)). The explanation must lie in part in his ability to exploit the political and dynastic chaos created in Mitanni by the devastating invasion of the Hittite king Suppiluliuma I and the assassination of the Mitannian king Tushratta (chapter 6a). This allowed Ashur-uballit to establish his independence, and annex part of the eastern area of Mitanni, including the important grain-growing areas of Nineveh, Kilizi and Arbela, while a reduced Mitannian state was governed by Tushratta's son, Shattiwaza, under close Hittite control. A change in the Assyrian royal titulary signals Ashur-uballit's achievement: a long filiation was added to the terse 'vicar of the god Ashur'. In a text from Ashur (perhaps originally inscribed on a stele), which commemorates building by a royal scribe, Ashur-uballit is even given the majestic title 'king of the universe':

> Marduk-nadin-ahhe, the royal scribe, son of Marduk-uballit, son of Ushshur-ana-Marduk, blessed by god and king, the humble, the obedient, the one who pleases his lord:
> The house which I erected in the shadow of the temple of the god Marduk, my lord, and within which I opened a well of cold water, by the excellent wisdom of the god Marduk, my lord, I caused the . . . of the house to be occupied with eminence(??). With wise understanding and the greatest care I made the rooms under it, about which no one knew, of baked bricks. I constructed (and) completed the entire house, its store-houses and its living-quarters. I did not . . .
> May the god Marduk, my lord, look upon that house and reward(?) me for my labours. May he allow it to endure in the future for my sons, my grandsons, my offspring, and the offspring of my offspring. May I and my family revere(?) the god Marduk, my lord, and the goddess Sarpanitum (Marduk's consort), my mistress, forever. (Next sentence: fragmentary) May [the god Marduk], my lord, grant to Ashur-uballit, who loves me, king of the universe, my lord, long days together with abundant prosperity.
>
> (E. Ebeling, B. Meissner, E.F. Weidner, *Die Inschriften der Altassyrischen Könige* (Leipzig 1926): XVII 2; *ARAB* I §§62f.; Grayson 1972/1976 I, LXXIII no. 2*)

Assyria's growing power and importance under Ashur-uballit is well illustrated by the two letters from him preserved among the Amarna correspondence. In the first one, the Assyrian king was obviously feeling his way cautiously:

> Say to the king of Egypt: Thus (speaks) Ashur-uballit, king of Assyria. May everything be well with you, your house, your land, your chariots and your troops. I am sending a messenger to you to visit you and to visit your country. Until now, my predecessors did not write; (but) today I am writing. I am sending you a beautiful chariot, 2 horses, and

a date-stone (i.e.bead) of authentic lapis lazuli, as your greeting-gift. Do not delay the messenger whom I have sent to you for a visit. May he pay his visit and then come back to me. May he see how you are and how your country is, and then may he come back to me.

(EA 15; Grayson 1972/1976 I, LXXIII 10*)

There is no claim to brotherhood, the hallmark of acceptance into the club of great powers, here; the Assyrian king's title is modest, as are his requests; he is sending an unsolicited, valuable gift to greet and honour the Egyptian ruler but makes no request for a present in return as was normal (see chapter 7a). The Assyrian king was simply making overtures at this point, in the hope that his messenger would be received, his gift acknowledged, and his messenger equipped and permitted to make the return journey. By the time of the next letter (EA 16), this tentativeness has been replaced by the confidence induced by military success and power: now the king of Egypt is addressed as brother, while the Assyrian king calls himself 'great king' and demands to receive gifts concomitant with his status:

When the king of Hanigalbat (Assyrian term for Mitanni) wrote to your father in Egypt, he sent him 20 talents of gold. [Now] I am the [equal] of the king of Hanigalbat, yet you only sent me [. . .] of gold, and that is not enough to pay for the outward and return journey of my messengers.

(EA 16; Grayson 1972/1976 I, LXXIII 11*)

Table 22 Middle Assyrian empire: chronology

	conventional		low
Ashur-uballit I	1365–1330		1353–1318
Enlil-nirari	1329–1320		1317–1308
Arik-den-ili	1319–1308		1307–1296
Adad-nirari I	1307–1275		1295–1264
Shalmaneser I	1274–1245		1263–1234
Tukulti-Ninurta I	1244–1208		1233–1197
Ashur-nadin-apli	1207–1204		1196–1194
Ashur-nirari III	1203–1198		1193–1188
Enlil-kudurri-usur	1197–1193		1187–1183
Ninurta-apil-Ekur	1192–1180		1182–1180
Ashur-dan I		1179–1134	
Ninurat-tulkulti-Ashur		1133	
Mutakkil-Nusku		1133	
Assur-resha-ishi I		1132–1115	
Tiglath-pileser I		1114–1076	
Ashared-apil-Ekur		1075–1074	
Ashur-bel-kala		1073–1056	
Eriba-Adad II		1055–1054	
Shamshi-Adad IV		1053–1050	
Ashur-nasir-pal I		1049–1031	

Assyria's rise to prominence rightly worried its southern neighbour, Baby-lonia, as shown by a warning sent by Burnaburiash II to Egypt. The Babylonian king tried to undermine any Assyrian claims to be worthy of being considered of equal rank to the great rulers, by referring to them as Babylonian subjects and presenting them merely as 'businessmen' (Liverani 1988 [OC], ch. 20):

> Now, as far as my Assyrian vassals are concerned, I certainly did not send them to you. Why did they come on their own authority to your country? If you love me, they will not conduct any business. Send them away to me empty-handed.
>
> (EA 9)

In spite of the tension between Babylonia and Assyria at this time, a rapprochement was reached between the two, sealed by the marriage of Karaindash, Burnaburiash II's son, and Muballitat-Sherua, the daughter of Ashur-uballit. But when their son, Karahardash, became the next king of Babylonia, the 'Kassite troops' revolted, killed him and installed Nazibugash, described as 'a Kassite, son of a nobody' on the throne. What exactly this emphasis on the 'Kassite' character of the revolt means is not known: was the revolt really caused by some threat to 'Kassite' control? Was it fear of too much Assyrian influence? Or had Karahardash been promoted to the kingship over the head of other claimants? What *is* clear is that the revolt provoked swift retribution from the now aged Ashur-uballit, who invaded Babylonia, executed Nazibugash, and possibly installed his tiny great-grandson, Kurigalzu II, on the throne. There are irresolvable contradictions between the *Synchronistic History* (*ABC* no. 21) and *Chronicle P* (*ABC* no. 22) concerning the names and filiations of the Babylonian kings. According to the former, Kurigalzu II was another son of Burnaburiash II. This makes a difference, because if Kurigalzu was indeed a tiny child and grandson of Muballitat-Sherua (*Chronicle P*), then it is likely that during his minority Babylonia must effectively have been run by his great-grandfather and grandmother, pre-sumably very much in Assyria's interests. But if Kurigalzu II was simply brother-in-law to Muballitat-Sherua he is likely to have been relatively mature and capable of taking command for himself immediately. This would make somewhat better sense of his reported conflict with Ashur-uballit's son, Enlil-nirari, at Sugagi, in which the Babylonians apparently suffered a defeat. It would also suggest that whatever power Assyria might have attempted to wield over Babylonia was extremely temporary. However we assess the confused sources, it is plain that at Ashur-uballit's death (1330 (1318)) Assyria was a first-rank power, effectively equalling the Hittite empire, Babylonia and Egypt – even if this was only grudgingly acknowledged.

Consolidation of Ashur-uballit's achievements was not easy. His immedi-ate successor, Enlil-nirari, was successful in defending his realm, but the Babylonian frontier fortresses remained dangerously close to the city of

Ashur. Arik-den-ili, the next king, seems to have fought in the mountains to the north and east, and attempted to deal with troublesome pastoralists. These wars probably served to strengthen and protect Assyria's frontiers. It was Adad-nirari I (1307–1275 (1295–1264)) who was eventually able to move the Babylonian frontier back to the Diyala area. He also began the Assyrian push westwards, conquering the Hittite client-state of Mitanni and stopping just short of Carchemish on the Euphrates. Why the Hittites, Mitanni's overlords, did not intervene (despite being asked for aid, see inscription quoted below) is puzzling, but it is possible that Adad-nirari took advantage of the Hittite king's troubles at home, with the loss of Hattusa, and abroad, with Egypt's renewed pressure on the Syrian frontier (see chapter 5d). Adad-nirari I proudly proclaimed the victory in his inscriptions:

> Adad-nirari, king of the universe, strong king, king of Assyria, son of Arik-den-ili, king of Assyria, son of Enlil-nirari, also king of Assyria. When Shattuara, king of the land Hanigalbat, rebelled against me and committed hostilities; by the command of Ashur, my lord and ally, and of the great gods who decide in my favour, I seized him and brought him to my city Ashur. I made him take an oath and then allowed him to return to his land. Annually, as long as he lived, I regularly received his tribute within my city, Ashur.
>
> After his death, Wasashatta, his son, revolted, rebelled against me, and committed hostilities. He went to the land Hatti for aid. The Hittites took his bribes but did not render him assistance. With the strong weapons of the god Ashur, my lord, with the support of the gods An, Enlil and Ea, Sin, Shamash, Adad, Ishtar, and Nergal, most powerful among the gods, the awesome gods, my lords, I captured by conquest the city Taidu, his great royal city, the cities Amasaku, Kahat, Shuru, Nabula, Hurra, Shuduhu, and Washshukannu. I took and brought to my city, Ashur, the possessions of those cities, the accumulated (wealth) of his fathers, (and) the treasure of his palace. I conquered, burnt, (and) destroyed the city [Taidu] and sowed salt (*kuddimmu*) over it. The great gods gave me to rule from the city Taidu to the city Irridu, the city Eluhat and Mount Kashiyari in its entirety, the fortress of the city Sudu, the fortress of the city Harranu, to the bank of the Euphrates. As for the remainder of his people, I imposed upon them hoe, spade and basket (i.e. labour obligations). But as for him (sc. Wasashatta), I took out from the city Irridu, his queen, his sons, his daughters, and his people. Bound I brought them and his possessions to my city, Ashur. I conquered, burnt, and destroyed the city Irridu and the cities within the district of the city Irridu.
>
> When I saw the deserted and uncultivated areas of . . . the city Ta[idu . . .] . . . I delineated its territory (and) therein founded a palace. I built (it) from top to bottom and deposited my stelae.

In the future may a later prince restore it. May he restore my inscribed name to its place. (Then) Ashur will listen to his prayers.

(E. Weidner *AfO* 5 (1928–9): 89–99; Grayson 1972/1976 I, LXXVI 3; 1987 A.0.76.3)

Assyria and the Hittite empire were now direct neighbours. In an attempt to reduce tension with the Hittites, Adad-nirari I sent a letter to Muwatalli calling him his brother and requesting to be allowed to visit the Amanus mountains which lay within Hittite-controlled territory. The response was unbelievably insulting. Muwatalli admitted that the Assyrian king was justified in calling himself a 'great king', having conquered Mitanni, but:

> as for brotherhood, and your visit to the Amanus mountains – why should I write to you about brotherhood? You and I – were we perhaps born of the same mother or father?

> (*CTH* 171)

While Adad-nirari's real achievements were undeniable, the Hittite king had no intention of pretending friendliness with his threatening new neighbour, who had just effectively deprived the empire of a substantial stretch of valuable territory.

Although Adad-nirari I built a palace at Taide[2] (cf. p. 353 and Grayson 1972/1976 I §§398–400), Assyria's control of Upper Mesopotamia was only definitively tightened in the reign of Shalmaneser I (1274–1245 (1263–1234)), when the Mitannian client-king was replaced with an Assyrian palace-official, the *sukkallu rabû* ('great vizier'), who was given the title 'king of Hanigalbat'. An administrative restructuring accompanied this development, with Assyrian governors (*šaknu*) installed in fortified manors in several Upper Mesopotamian cities and controlling a series of districts. One of the fortresses (with mud-brick walls 2.5 m thick) was recently excavated at Tell Sabi Abyad in the upper Balikh valley (Akkermans and Rossmeisl 1990); others were located at Tell Fekheriye and Tell Sheikh Hamad (ancient Dur-Katlimmu) on the Khabur (Kühne 1990). Some of the conquered people were resettled to put new, previously unexploited land into production and so extend the economic base of the state. How densely the area was settled with Assyrian colonists is hard to determine: about half the personal names of the Middle Assyrian archives from Tell Fekheriye and 'Amuda (both located around the headwaters of the Khabur) are Assyrian, but that could simply reflect the concentration of Assyrians in a provincial capital. The tablets (admittedly only two at present, cf. Jas 1990[3]) from Tell Sabi Abyad, listing men and women, show a different pattern: half the names are Hurrian, with only eight Assyrian and a possible Babylonian one – but, then, they are from a time not far removed from Shalmaneser I's reorganisation. Over the next century or so, the Assyrians remained in control of this region: their policy of colonisation and deportation, and the dense administrative network, resulted in a degree of socio-cultural assimilation. One small but significant territorial gain was made by Shalmaneser I when he conquered the state of Nihriya, on the Upper Euphrates between the Hittite and Assyrian realm, decisively defeating the Hittite army – a triumph immediately announced by letter to the Hittite client-states in north Syria (Lackenbacher 1982).

The reign of Tukulti-Ninurta I (1244–1208 (1233–1197))

If Hittite fears of Assyria's power needed comfirmation, they received it with the reign of the great warrior king, Tukulti-Ninurta I, who strengthened the Euphrates frontier with Assyrian garrisons, and fought a battle to the northwest in Hittite-controlled Paphi, during which he claimed to have taken 28,000 prisoners. The Hittite evidence for this period shows extensive military mobilisation, and attempts to prevent the north Syrian states under their control from trading with the Assyrians. Another, less spectacular, achievement of Tukulti-Ninurta I was his extensive campaigning in the mountains to the north and east, partly for security against troublesome transhumant pastoralists, partly for raw materials such as copper (from the north), and partly to force the small states in the valleys to the east to meet Assyrian needs for items such as lapis lazuli, tin and horses. The small eastern commercial centres were dependent for their stability on maintaining trade-links with larger states, who provided consumers for the materials that they could supply through their eastern trade networks. But the Assyrians were not the only state that had such needs – Babylonia and Elam were serious competitors for the Assyrians trying to gain control of this valuable commerce. It was physically impossible to impose Assyrian rule in this region, given the terrain and nature of settlement, but Tukulti-Ninurta's establishment of control along the foothills and at the terminal points of a number of important routes was no mean achievement.

But Tukulti-Ninurta's major advance was in the south. For almost two centuries Assyria had been attempting to fix a boundary to its own advantage against Babylonian encroachments. Adad-nirari I had made some headway and an Assyro-Babylonian agreement was set up that was not breached until Tukulti-Ninurta's reign. At this point, Kashtiliash IV seems to have taken advantage of the Assyrian king's preoccupation in the north and east to advance north and capture places east of the Tigris and on the mid-Euphrates which had, for about fifty years, been part of Assyrian territory. A head-on clash between the two powers was the result. The reports of this are only preserved in fragments in the *Synchronistic History* and *Chronicle P*, from which it is hard to deduce much. Fuller information comes from Tukulti-Ninurta I's own inscriptions, and Assyria's success is certain. Tukulti-Ninurta's ultimate victory over Babylonia was celebrated in a lengthy epic poem (at least 700 lines long; Machinist 1976), which commemorated the event in high-flown language as a major Assyrian triumph:

Glorious is his might, it sco[rches] the [ir]reverent in front and behind;
Blazing is his impetuosity, it burns the unsubmissive left and right;
Fearful is his splendour, it overwhelms all his enemies.
He who ... the extremities of the four winds, all kings without
    exception live in dread of him.

(Lambert *AfO* 18 (1957–8): 48–49)

The poem was read and copied in Assyria for hundreds of years. By the end of Tukulti-Ninurta's reign, Assyrian power stretched from the Euphrates in north-east Syria to southern Iraq.

A recently published text (Walker 1982) and a new analysis of all the texts relating to Tukulti-Ninurta's conquest of Babylon (Mayer 1988) make it possible to obtain a clearer picture of the course of events. After the Babylonian king had been defeated in battle, he was brought to Ashur in chains, and Tukulti-Ninurta himself assumed the Babylonian royal titles. But direct rule of Babylonia by Assyria was brief; instead, a series of puppet kings was appointed to rule (at least) northern Babylonia on behalf of their overlords. It used to be thought that the period of Assyrian control of Babylonia lasted seven years, but it is now clear that it covered thirty-two years. It was during this time, significantly, that the Elamites made their first attempts to establish control of the east Tigris area: the elimination of Babylonia by Assyria meant that Elam was in danger of finding itself squeezed out from any chance of profiting from the rich trans-Iranian trade routes that terminated in northern Babylonia. Assyrian domination of northern Babylonia was only ended by an ultimately successful challenge mounted by a Babylonian ruler who had established himself in the extreme south, Adad-shuma-usur (1216–1187). He was able to defeat and capture the new king of Assyria, Enlil-kudurri-usur (1197–1193 (1187–1183)), in battle. A crisis ensued in Assyria, during which a new ruler, not in the direct line of succession, was able to seize the throne for himself (Ninurta-apil-Ekur: 1192–1180 (1182–1180)). Adad-shuma-usur's success over the Assyrians and his liberation of Babylonia was, in its turn, also celebrated by a Babylonian epic (Grayson 1975: 56–77), which underlines the magnitude of his achievement.

It has been assumed that, in the course of his Babylonian war, Tukulti-Ninurta I took the cult-statue of Marduk away from Babylon, as the Elamites were to do later (chapter 7c). But it is possible that this is a much later (seventh century) Babylonian invention. Texts contemporary with, or close to the time of, Tukulti-Ninurta I do not mention the removal of the divine figure (always considered a major disaster by the Babylonians); only a late text mentions its return at a time that makes it impossible for the Elamites to have taken it – and their sacrilegious pillage is well-attested (Mayer 1988; chapter 7d). One thing Tukulti-Ninurta *is* said by the epic to have brought back to Assyria, apart from prisoners and booty, is collections of Babylonian tablets. Interestingly, it is precisely in this period that it is possible to see very strong Babylonian literary influences in a number of Assyrian texts. A superb prayer of Tukulti-Ninurta, composed in Akkadian and fine literary Sumerian (see also Lambert 1976), is just one example of Babylonian influence; the literary Babylonian of the Tukulti-Ninurta epic another. Babylonian culture was older and more sophisticated – Assyria could be, and probably had been, perceived as a rather provincial outpost. But as a result of Tukulti-Ninurta's conquest of Babylonia that changed, and Babylonian cultural refinements were harnessed to enhance and elaborate, in recherché literary language, the image of the Assyrian king.

Tukulti-Ninurta's foundation of a new royal city (0.6 km²) is linked to these developments in Assyrian royal ideology. It was set on the banks of the Tigris opposite Ashur, only 3 km away from the Assyrian capital, on virgin soil. It contained palaces and temples decorated with brilliantly coloured glazed tiles; it was supplied by a new canal and was certainly intended to contain ordinary residences (*RLA* 5: 456–458). Significantly, it was named Kar-Tukulti-Ninurta ('the harbour of Tukulti-Ninurta') after the king himself. A number of inscribed alabaster tablets (from Ashur and Kar-Tukulti-Ninurta itself) commemorate the royal foundation:

> At that time the god Ashur, my lord, requested of me a cult centre on the bank opposite my city, the desired object(?) of the gods, and he commanded me to build his sanctuary. At the command of the god Ashur, the god who loves me, I built before my city Ashur, a city for the god Ashur on the opposite bank, beside the Tigris, in uncultivated plains (and) meadows where there was neither house nor dwelling, where no ruin hills or rubble had accumulated, and no bricks had been laid. I called it Kar-Tukulti-Ninurta. I cut straight as a string through rocky terrain, I cleared a way through high difficult mountains with stone chisels, I cut a wide path for a stream which supports life in the land (and) which provides abundance, and I transformed the plains of my city into irrigated fields. I arranged for regular offerings to the god Ashur and the great gods, my lords, in perpetuity from the produce of the water of the canal.
>
> At that time I built in my city, Kar-Tukulti-Ninurta, the cult centre which I had constructed, a holy temple, an awesome sanctuary for the dwelling of the god Ashur, my lord. I called it Ekurmesharra. Inside it I completed a great ziggurat as the cultic chair of the god Ashur, my lord, and deposited my stelae.
> (Weidner 1959 no. 16; Grayson 1972/1976 I, LXXVIII 16; Grayson 1987 A.O.78.23)

Name and text emphasise the king's personal role in constructing the town, and the resources of the empire, the booty and labour of deported peoples from his many wars were expended in its construction. It seems, however, not to have survived for long as an Assyrian city.

Perhaps precisely because of Tukulti-Ninurta's outstanding success in consolidating Assyrian conquests, and adding the rich prize of Babylonia to Assyrian control, struggles about who might succeed to his powerful position arose. This is shown by the fact, first, that Tukulti-Ninurta was assassinated by one of his sons and, second, that he was succeeded by three rulers, two of them his sons, all in fairly rapid succession, which suggests violent rivalry between a number of royal claimants (the chronology is somewhat confused at this point). Nevertheless the Assyrian empire did not crumble immediately. Some of the great gains made in Upper Mesopotamia by the thirteenth-century Assyrian rulers may have been lost gradually, and there were serious problems, including the loss of Babylonia fifteen years after Tukulti-Ninurta I's death (on the conventional chronology), which exacerbated the dynastic problems. But the precise impact of losses, and how much the imperial territory shrank, is uncertain. When Tiglath-pileser I came to the throne nearly a century later, he still claimed control over much of Upper Mesopotamia.

Tiglath-pileser I (1114–1076)

The political situation in the period up to the reign of Tiglath-pileser I is fairly confused. A building inscription from the Ishtar temple at Nineveh shows that Ashur-resha-ishi (1132–1115), who styled himself the 'avenger of Assyria', campaigned successfully in the tradition of the great thirteenth-century rulers against the Aramaeans, an increasingly troublesome pastoralist group, and possibly against some of the people living in the Zagros. A mark of his success is that he, too, created a new royal centre at Apku (modern Abu Maryam), north-west of Mosul.

For Tiglath-pileser I the sources are quite full for the earlier part of his reign, and the chronology of events within it can be fixed more easily because an important development took place in his reign, in the form of Assyrian royal inscriptions. Earlier building texts by Assyrian kings included references to some of their military exploits among the commemorations of royal constructions and long royal titles echoing their achievements. But they were not arranged sequentially, presenting instead a panoramic survey. With Tiglath-pileser, campaigns are arranged for the first time in chronological order within the report of building work. It becomes the standard form for memorialising the achievements of Assyrian rulers until the very end of the Neo-Assyrian empire, i.e. for the next five hundred years. This genre of royal inscriptions is the famous 'Assyrian annals'. They usually begin with long royal titles and epithets, which present the king's position in relation to the Assyrian gods and to his subjects; then comes the account of his first campaign, followed (in the case of Tiglath-pileser) by a poetic refrain in his praise, before the description of the second campaign begins. The whole concludes with his collection of exotic plants, his hunting in Upper Mesopotamia and, finally, details of the royal building which the whole text was written to celebrate, and in which it was to be deposited. An extract from Tiglath-pileser's annals may serve to give a flavour of the style:

Altogether I conquered 42 lands and their rulers from the other side of the Lower Zab in distant mountainous regions to the other side of the Euphrates, the Hittites, and the Upper Sea in the west – from my accession year to my fifth regnal year. I subdued them to one authority, took hostages from them, (and) imposed upon them tribute and impost. (This) is apart from the numerous foreign campaigns which do not appear in the (account of) my victories (and) upon which I pursued my enemies by chariot in favourable terrain and on foot in rough terrain. I prevented the enemies from setting foot in my land.

Tiglath-pileser, valiant man, armed with the unrivalled bow, expert in the hunt:

The gods Ninurta and Palil gave me their fierce weapons and their exalted bow for my lordly arms. By the command of the god Ninurta, who loves me, I slew four extraordinarily strong wild virile bulls in the desert, in the land Mitanni, and at the city Araziqu which is before the land Hatti – (I slew them) with my strong, iron arrow heads, and sharp arrows. I brought their hides and horns to my city Ashur.

I killed ten strong bull elephants in the land Harran and the region of the River Khabur (and) four live elephants I captured. I brought the hides and tusks with the live elephants to my city Ashur.

By the command of the god Ninurta, who loves me, I killed on foot 120 lions with my wildly vigorous assault. In addition, 800 lions I felled from my light chariot. I have brought down every kind of wild beast and winged bird of the heavens whenever I have shot an arrow.

After I had gained complete dominion over the enemies of the god Ashur, I rebuilt (and) completed the dilapidated temple of the Assyrian Ishtar, my mistress, the temple of the god Amurru, the temple of the god Bel-labira, the temple of the Ten Gods, the temples of the gods of my city Ashur. I put in place the entrances to their temples (and) brought the great gods, my lords, inside. I pleased their great divinity. I rebuilt and completed the palaces, the royal residences of the great cult centres in the districts of my land which since the time of my forefathers during hard years had been abandoned and had fallen into ruin and decay. I repaired the weakened fortifications of my land. I caused ploughs to be hitched up all over Assyria and (thereby) piled up more grain than my forefathers. I formed herds of horses, oxen (and) asses from the booty I took when I gained dominion over lands with the support of the god Ashur, my lord. In addition I got control of, (and) formed, herds of *nayalu*-deer, *ayalu*-deer, gazelles, ibex which the gods Ashur and Ninurta, the gods who love me, had given me in the course of the hunt in high mountain ranges. I numbered them like flocks of sheep. I sacrificed yearly to the god Ashur, my lord, the young born to them as voluntary offerings together with my pure sacrifices.

I took cedar, box-tree, Kanish oak from the lands over which I had gained dominion – such trees which none among previous kings, my forefathers, had ever planted – and I planted (them) in the orchards of my land. I took rare orchard fruit which is not found in my land (and therewith) filled the orchards of Assyria.

I had in harness for the forces of my land more chariots and teams of horses than ever before. To Assyria I added land and to its people I added people. I brought contentment to my people (and) provided them with a secure abode.

Tiglath-pileser, exalted prince, the one whom the gods Ashur and Ninurta have continually guided wherever he wished (to go) and who pursued each and every one of the enemies of the god Ashur and laid low all the rebellious . . . . (and so on)

(L.W. King, *Annals of the Kings of Assyria* (1902): 27–108; Grayson 1972/1976 II, LXXXVII 1; Grayson 1991 A.O.87.1)

The annals present the entire range of qualities deemed essential for Assyrian kings, and provide an unrivalled insight into royal imagery and imperial ideology. The king is pious, blessed by the gods; he defends his people, punishes those who threaten the land and, hence, protects the arrangements made by the gods. He is strong and untiring in his military exploits, the fruits of which are used to improve life in Assyria so that the king is the provider of plenty, well-being and stability. His amazing hunting feats display his divinely granted strength, which rids the land of those fierce animals that threaten the life of people and flocks. Assyria's enemies, as well as the wild animals, are representative of the chaos always lying in wait to engulf and destroy ordered Assyrian society.

From the annals and other inscriptions, Tiglath-pileser I's extensive campaigning can be traced, especially his renowned expeditions into the mountains directly north of Assyria. The end of one campaign was marked by a rock inscription, north of Lake Van, on the upper reaches of the Euphrates. Like Tukulti-Ninurta's campaigns in the northern and eastern mountains, Tiglath-pileser's campaign aimed to discourage raids into the lowlands and to secure control of the routes along which items such as copper, the increasingly important iron, horses and timber could be transported to Assyria. Tiglath-pileser I also went on a prestige trip to the Mediterranean where, despite the military tone of his account, he was feasted along the route and on the coast by the small states located here. Their specialised manufacturing industries (wood and ivory carving, fine metalwork, textiles) and commercial expertise all depended on supplying a large-scale consumer, such as the Assyrian state now was, in order to maintain their own *status quo*:

I marched to Mount Lebanon. I cut down (and) carried off cedar beams for the temple of the gods Anu and Adad, the great gods my lords. I continued to the land Amurru (and) conquered the entire land Amurru. I received tribute from the lands Byblos, Sidon, Arvad. I rode in boats of the city Arvad, of the land Amurru, travelled successfully a distance of three double-hours from the city Arvad, an island, to the city Samuru which is in the land Amurru. I killed at sea a *nāhiru*, which is called a sea-horse.

> (V. Scheil, *Recueil des travaux* 22 (1900): 157; *ARAB* I §§299–303; *ANET*: 274–275; Grayson 1972/1976 II, LXXXVII 3; Grayson 1991 A.O.87.3)

Another text referring to this expedition adds that Tiglath-pileser was presented on the same trip with a crocodile and a female ape, possibly a gift from Egypt. The same text also describes the sculpting, in basalt, of the *nāhiru* and its erection, together with a figure of another exotic creature, on either side of the main entrance to a newly constructed royal palace in Ashur.

In one respect, however, Tiglath-pileser was much less successful. This was his southern frontier, where he fought an unsuccessful battle against Nebuchadnezzar I (1126–1105). At one point the Babylonians were even able to capture Ekallate, close to Ashur, and it took a considerable time before Tiglath-pileser was able to dislodge them and wreak vengeance by the capture of northern Babylonia, including such important centres as Babylon, Opis and Dur Kurigalzu (reign of Marduk-nadin-ahhe: 1098–1081).

An even more serious, albeit short-lived, setback experienced by Tiglath-pileser was that, despite his repeated and much vaunted campaigning against the Aramaean raiders in the Syrian steppe, the Assyrian heartland suffered for a while from Aramaean incursions, causing famine and confusion. They dislocated communications and penetrated into Assyrian villages; the village population fled to the mountains east of Arbela to escape them; harvests were destroyed; Aramaean groups advanced on Nineveh and Tiglath-pileser was himself forced to withdraw to the mountains north of Mosul (Tadmor 1958: 133–134).

Assyria, like contemporary Babylonia (see chapter 7d), faced serious problems from the Aramaean raids. Whether Tiglath-pileser was himself successful in dealing with the threat is not known. But just a few years later Ashur-bel-kala (1073–1056) was in a position, once again, to campaign in the northern mountains, to make a treaty with Babylonia and to regulate Babylonian affairs in Assyrian interests; the arrangements were sealed by his marriage to the daughter of the Babylonian king, Adad-apla-iddina (1069–1048), whom he had himself appointed. He was also able to repel the Aramaeans along Assyria's frontiers, although some continued to mount razzias into Assyrian territory. If the gift from the Egyptian king of a crocodile, a female ape and a 'river-man' (water buffalo?) is indicative of Assyria's position in international politics, it shows that it continued to be as widely respected as under Tiglath-pileser I.

But the surface normality of the royal inscriptions should not blind us to the underlying difficulties which they gloss over. The Aramaeans were now a constant and threatening presence within the empire – very few of Ashur-bel-kala's campaigns were directed against anyone else. After the reign of Ashur-nasir-pal I (1049–1031), if not earlier, virtually all the Upper Mesopotamian territory was definitively lost. The land of Assyria shrank to the immediate environs of Ashur, Nineveh, Arbela and Kilizi – not an insubstantial territory in itself, but tiny by comparison with the earlier great realm. Sparse, but important, evidence indicates that some of the Assyrian governors continued, at least for a while, to hold things together within their administrative centres. But unfortunately for over a century from about 1050 (in Babylonia too) documentation becomes very scanty, so the details of the situation escape us.

Middle Assyrian society

A number of fundamental changes and developments took place in the Middle Assyrian period, which changed Assyrian society from the original circumscribed commercial city-state of Ashur of the Old Assyrian period (see chapter 2b). Most important was that Ashur-uballit established permanent control over the whole of north Iraq; he incorporated the main cities of the region and important agricultural land to the north and east, which was never again to be lost to Assyrian control, even in the darkest days of the Aramaean raids (see chapter 8b).

Central to the political system was the king, commanding lavish and precious items produced for use at court and in the temples, as well as immense resources, both material and human, which were used to create new irrigation schemes, extend agriculture, and construct impressive buildings. Most important among the many royal building activities was the creation of new administrative centres throughout Upper Mesopotamia, the renovation of sites such as Nineveh, and the foundation of entirely new royal cities such as Kar-Tukulti-Ninurta and Apku. Shalmaneser I (1274–1245 (1263–1234)) may also have founded Kalhu (modern Nimrud), although this is not absolutely certain – some material dating to the eighteenth century (*RLA* 5: 320) has been found in excavation, and the one later reference (Ashur-nasir-pal II: 883–859), associating Kalhu with the great thirteenth-century king, does not unmistakably attribute its foundation to him (Grayson 1972/1976 II §591).

Assyrian society consisted of peasants, slaves (although what proportion of society they constituted is not known) and a powerful aristocracy, whose ranks supplied the major officials and army commanders. The traditional Assyrian system of dating each year by an eponymous official, the *limmu*, who was selected from a restricted group of powerful families, demonstrates the political importance of the Assyrian nobility. The significance of the *limmu*-ship is illustrated by the erection of rows of stelae at Ashur, each bearing simply the name of such an official. It is, unfortunately, still a moot point what exactly the *limmu*-stelae signify (Canby 1976; Miglus 1984), but they serve as a reminder of the undiminished strength of this aristocratic group within Assyrian politics: it was they who shared most directly in the fruits of royal conquest, and they may even have provided wives for the kings (if later evidence might be read back, see p. 506). The population as a whole owed service to the king which took the form of taxes (in flocks, grain and silver) and personal service (labour for public works and military service).

The collection of Middle Assyrian laws provides our clearest insight into Assyrian society (Driver and Miles 1935; *ANET*: 180–186; Cardascia 1969; *TUAT* I 80–91). They reflect a strictly patriarchal society, with women totally under the control of husband, father or father-in-law, and brutal punishments inflicted on transgressors (Saporetti 1979). Some of the excessively harsh and vile punishments aim to regulate relationships between and within families – they were not all statutory punishments actually inflicted by the state, but simply attempts to lay down what compensations were allowable in the private sphere. One stipulation, for example, left it open for a husband not to punish his adulterous wife and her lover if he so wished; on the other hand, should he desire punishment he was permitted either to kill them both, or cut off his wife's nose, castrate her lover and mutilate his face. Apart from the horrifying penalties, the laws reveal incidentally quite a lot of the day-to-day texture of Assyrian society: for example, how marriages were solemnised; the fact that a man could have a principal wife, a secondary wife and a concubine; that, while high-ranking women were to some degree secluded, they could also walk about the streets and go shopping, albeit veiled. The laws frequently refer to rumours, which suggests a society where scandals about sexual misconduct and women were spread by gossip. The frequent festivals were popular occasions where crowds gathered – it was during them that young girls ran the greatest risk of losing their virginity. Public taverns, where men met socially and heard the latest news, were an integral part of daily life, as were brothel-keepers and prostitutes. Many women sat at home for years waiting for their husbands to return from campaigns, royal missions or trading ventures. Procuring an abortion was a capital crime; neighbours suspected each other of causing misfortune through witchcraft; a murder gave the victim's family the right to exact blood vengeance. In some cases, guilt could only be established by putting the accused through the river-ordeal (see chapter 2d) or making him swear an oath by a divine statue or symbol (see chapter 2e). If families in a village or small town could not settle their differences, they had recourse to a body of elders and a mayor; if this failed or if they preferred, they could go to the gate of the royal palace and demand a decision from the king himself or his judges.

The king, as supreme judge, also strictly regulated by edict the protocol and etiquette within his palace. A Middle Assyrian collection of court edicts, issued by kings from Ashur-uballit to Tiglath-pileser I, provides a potential insight into palace life (Weidner 1956). It is very unfortunate that many of the edicts are too fragmentary for us to understand, as the ones that are more fully preserved show that a very full picture of the complex structure of the court could be recovered from them. Two practically complete examples illustrate their range and tone:

1 Tiglath-pileser, king of the universe, king of Assyria, son of Ashur-resha-ishi, also king of Assyria, decrees to the officer of the palace of the Inner City, the palace herald, the officer of the *zarīqu* of the road (function uncertain), the harem physician, and the one in charge of the palaces of the entire extent of the land:

'(Potential) royal courtiers or (potential) servants of palace personnel who wish to enter the palace may not enter the palace without examination. If (anyone) is not satisfactory(?) he will be assigned a second time for preparation(?) as courtier. If the officer of the palace of the Inner City, the palace herald, the officer of the *zarīqu* of the road, the harem physician, or the one in charge of the palaces of the entire extent of the land allow a courtier who is not satisfactory(?) to enter the palace (and) it is observed later, one foot will be cut off each of these officials.'

2 Tiglath-pileser, king of the universe, king of Assyria, son of Ashur-resha-ishi, also king of Assyria, decrees to the men, the courtiers:

'If a woman of the palace sings or quarrels with another of her rank, and one of the royal "eunuchs" (translation debated), courtiers, or servants stands listening, he will be beaten one hundred times; one of his ears will be cut off.

If a woman of the palace calls to a courtier while her hips are bare, not covered with a loin-cloth: ["...] I will send you"; (if) he turns (and) speaks with her, he will be beaten one hundred times. The one who observes him will take his (i.e. guilty man's) cloak while that (guilty) man will have his loins bound with the *sāgu*-garment (i.e. probably stripped of his office and demoted in rank).

If a courtier wishes to speak with a woman of the palace, he may not approach closer to her than seven paces(?). If someone violates this decree and the one in charge of the palace hears of it but does not punish him, the one in charge of the palace will bear the punishment. If the officials of the one in charge of the palace have not kept watch over the palace precincts, not reported offences to him, (and) later the king has heard of an offence, the one in charge of the palace will bear the responsibility for all offences.

If the *zarīqu* have a commission to perform within the palace and the women of the palace (stand) at the entrance to their quarters, it must be reported to [the one in charge of the palace] so that he might clear them away from the entrance to (their) quarters.'

(Weidner 1956; Grayson 1972/1976 II §§185–192)

In the palace the king's word was law, just as he was the court of last instance for his humbler subjects. The king also played a central role in the state cults, as he was conceived to bear ultimate responsibility for the well-being of the country through his special, lofty relationship with the gods who communicated their will to him, and to whom in turn he communicated the needs of his country through prayer. The subservience of the king to the gods, especially the national god Ashur, is strikingly illustrated by the preserved text of the coronation ceremony (Müller 1937), which also dates from the Middle Assyrian period. The royal regalia were bestowed on the king in the Ashur temple in Ashur city by the gods, who each in turn gave him specific commands, such as 'With this mace, extend the boundaries of the land.' He was then carried through the streets of the city with the cry: 'The god Ashur is king; *x* (king's name) is his deputy!' Nothing illustrates more clearly the fundamental ideology of the Assyrian king as the human servant of the country's divine overlord. Subsequently, the officials of the land surrendered their positions, which formally acknowledged their dependence on the king's will. Assyria had come a long way from the small city-state, where the king's power was balanced by the great families of Ashur.

7c Elam: the classical period (*c.* 1450–*c.* 1100)

Definition and sources

'Elam' is the name used by modern scholars for the area of modern Khuzestan (south-west Iran), centred on Susa, and called by Greek writers, such as Strabo, 'Elymais'. But, as has become clear only relatively recently, the country of Elam included much of the modern province of Fars to the east as well (see map 10) until around the end of the eighth century, although its full extent is not certain. Elam's history, culture and language are still extremely obscure, although it is plain from Mesopotamian written evidence and from archaeological finds that it was a powerful political entity with a distinctive culture. Research carried out over the last twenty to thirty years has helped enormously to elucidate aspects of Elamite history, although much remains enigmatic.

Elamite was first identified as a distinct language after Henry Rawlinson, in the 1830s and 1840s, succeeded in obtaining squeezes of the great rock-inscription of Darius I of Persia (521–186) at Behistun (see chapter 13), on the route leading from north-east Babylonia to Ecbatana (modern Hamadan). The text turned out to be trilingual: written in Old Persian, Akkadian and Elamite. The Behistun inscription not only constituted the main basis for working out Old Persian, but also provided the key necessary for deciphering Akkadian cuneiform. The Elamite version of the text turned out to be composed in a language using Akkadian cuneiform signs, but otherwise entirely unrelated to it. It is called 'Elamite' because it fitted with some short inscriptions from Susa, generally identified as the capital of Elam. It is not a

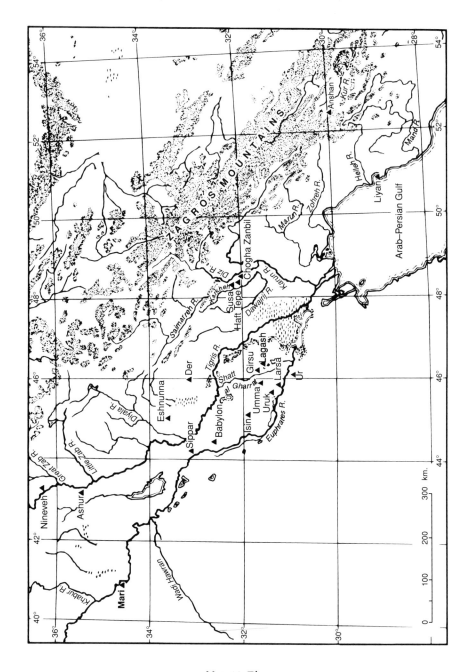

Map 10 Elam

366

Semitic language (like Akkadian) nor an Indo-European one (like Old Persian); it is not definitely related to any known language or language group (Reiner 1969; Grillot-Susini 1987). It was used by the Achaemenid Persian kings for some administrative documents in Fars during the earlier part of their rule (down to the 450s, see chapter 13), although by that time it may have been only an archival convention with Elamite no longer spoken (Gershevitch in Hallock 1971). The continued use of Elamite, and its regular employment in Achaemenid royal inscriptions (virtually all are written in Old Persian, Akkadian and Elamite), shows the strength of Elamite culture well after Elam had vanished as a significant political entity.

An obstacle in reconstructing Elamite history is that the number of published and fully understood texts in Elamite is restricted. There is a reasonable number of royal inscriptions on votive objects, monuments, statues, and bricks (König 1965), but the majority date from the period between c. 1300 and c. 1100 so their chronological span is limited. Further, many contain little in the way of hard information beyond the name and filiation of the king commemorating himself; one exception is the fragmentary Elamite treaty (found at Susa) between Naram-Sin of Agade (2254–2218) and an unknown Elamite ruler (Hinz 1967). A local script was developed and used in Elam c. 3400, 'proto-Elamite', which was contemporary with, or possibly even slightly predated, the earliest writing in Mesopotamia (Nissen 1993). But the close political and cultural links between the two areas (which sometimes resulted in direct domination by south Mesopotamian rulers of western Elam) led to the adoption of Akkadian scribal traditions and the abandonment of Elamite script. Indeed, in western Elam, many texts from Susa and adjacent regions are actually in Akkadian; this is true of legal documents and even occasional public inscriptions. Simultaneously, the evidence that has emerged more recently shows that Elamite was being regularly used for transactions in Fars (Tall-i Malyan; Stolper 1984). The main groups of documents come from the sites of Susa (Sumerian and Akkadian: several hundred; Carter and Stolper 1984: 24 and n. 169 for references), Chogha Zanbil (Paper 1955; Stève 1967 – mainly Elamite, some Akkadian: about seventy), Haft Tepe (Herrero 1976; Herrero and Glassner 1990; 1991: about 500 tablets in Akkadian) and Tall-i Malyan (Stolper 1984: about 200 tablets in Elamite). Chogha Zanbil and Haft Tepe are fairly near Susa, but Tall-i Malyan is in the region of the later Persepolis in Fars (RLA 7: 306–320). The Susa documents date between 1900 and 1500; the other texts, like many inscriptions, belong to the period c. 1300–1100. Apart from a small administrative archive from Susa dating to the early sixth century (MDP 9; Hinz 1968; Miroschedji 1982) and the Achaemenid-period ones from Persepolis (Cameron 1948; Hallock 1969), these are the only Elamite archives available at present.

Elamite history is divided, very roughly, into the 'Proto-Elamite' period (approximately contemporary with Uruk IV and III, and ED I and II in Mesopotamia: c. 3400–2600), the 'Old Elamite' period, which stretches from the Mesopotamian ED III (*c.* 2600) to just before 1500, the 'Middle Elamite' (*c.* 1500–1000) and the 'Neo-Elamite' (*c.* 1000 to mid-sixth century; Porada 1965: 45ff.). Within all these phases there are enormous gaps in knowledge, with practically no documentary information at all: in the years *c.* 2600–2200, *c.* 1750–1450 and 1100–*c.* 800 the sources are of the scantiest. But archaeological work and analysis (Carter and Stolper 1984) is introducing refinements into this very crude picture – the period of the nineteenth and earlier eighteenth century, for example, is now fairly well attested. The complexities of life in the region are also becoming evident, in particular the close links which Elam had with central and eastern Iran, and central Asia – a perspective that can be missed if Elamite history is only studied, as it so often has to be, through the medium of Mesopotamian texts.

Historical outline to *c.* 1100

But the reconstruction of Elamite history does rest very largely on Mesopotamian sources and its chronology depends on establishing synchronisms with Elam's better-documented neighbour. On that basis, it is possible to see that in ED III (*c.* 2600–2340) the picture is one of close trade-links as well as military conflicts between the south Mesopotamian cities and Elam; during the later phase of the Agade period (2340–2159), the expansionist policy of the Agade rulers brought Susa under some form of domination, but with an independent dynasty located further east in Fars. In the Ur III phase (2112–2004) Susa was included in the administrative district of the *sukkalmah*, who commanded Elamite troops. Ur itself was destroyed by the Elamites and the people of Shimashki (an area to the north of Susa), where a state and local dynasty had formed *c.* 2200 (Henrickson 1984; Steinkeller 1988; 1990), which dominated Elam, including Susa, until *c.* 1890. They may have been succeeded by the Eparti dynasty (but cf. Stolper 1982), who retained control of the region until *c.* 1520. The titles held by the rulers included that of *sukkalmah*, presumably derived from that of the Ur III regents (Carter and Stolper 1984: 24). From this period come quite a number of legal texts from Susa, written in Akkadian, that shed some light on Elamite society (inheritance, land ownership, social groups, administrative structures). How far anything of what these texts reveal might be applicable to regions beyond that dominated by Susa, or to later periods, is not certain.

When the veil of obscurity, which shrouds Elam after *c.* 1750, lifts in *c.* 1450, a new dynasty with links much further east, and whose ruler bears the title 'king of Susa and Anshan', dominates the Elamite political scene. The title 'king of Anshan' had appeared earlier in the third millennium, and for decades scholars puzzled and argued over the location of Anshan (Hansman 1972).[4] It was established finally in 1972 that Anshan is the site of Tall-i Malyan in Fars, showing that the territory embraced by Elam was much larger than had traditionally been thought (Lambert 1972; Reiner 1973; Carter and

Stolper 1976; Vallat 1980). The period beginning *c.* 1450 and extending to about 1100 constitutes a high point in Elamite history and is sometimes called Elam's 'classical' period. As a result of excavation in the 1960s and 1970s, closely followed by more intensive study of texts from various Elamite sites, a picture of this powerful period of Elamite history is gradually becoming visible.

Administrative texts and a stele from Haft Tepe show that the Elamite king, Tepti-ahar (early fourteenth century, see table 23), was in control of the Susa region and Anshan, and that a fairly sophisticated administration was in place. He was a contemporary of Kadashman-Enlil I of Babylonia (1374–1360), and the material shows that, while embassies were exchanged between the Babylonian and Elamite court (there may even have been a dynastic marriage in the reign of his predecessor, Kurigalzu I; van Dijk 1986), relations between the two states were deteriorating. The Haft Tepe stele reflects the involvement of the king in temple-building (traces of a large, probably sacred, structure have been excavated; *RLA* 4: 39–40; Negahban 1990), in regulating and supplying the cult. The impression of the Elamite state on this evidence is of

Table 23 Chronology of Elamite kings (all dates are approximate)

		Contemporaries
c. 2500–*c.* 2200:	dynasty of Awan	
c. 2200–*c.* 1900:	dynasty of Shimashki	
c. 1900–*c.* 1500:	period of *sukkalmah*s	
c. 1500–*c.* 1450:	gap in historical record	
c. 1450?:	Inshushinak-shar-ilani	
	Tan-Ruhuratire	
c. 1365:	Tepti-ahar	(= Kadashman Enlil I (1374–1360), Babylonia)
c. 1330:	Hurbatila	(= Kurigalzu II (1332–1308), Babylonia)
c. 1320:	Ige-halki	
	Pahir-ishshan	
1310–1300:	Attar-kitah	
1300–1275:	Humban-numena	
1275–1240:	Untash-napirisha	
1240–1235:	Unpahash-napirisha	
1235–1210?:	Kiden-Hutran	(= Enlil-nadin-shumi (1224); Adad-shum-iddina (1222–1217) in Babylonia; Tukulti-Ninurta I (1244–1208) in Assyria)
1205–1185:	Hallutush-Inshushinak	
1185–1155:	Shutruk-Nahhunte	(= Zababa-shum-iddina (1158); Enlil-nadin-ahi (1157–1155) in Babylonia; Ashur-dan I (1179–1134) in Assyria)
1155–1150:	Kudur-Nahhunte	
1150–1120:	Shilhak-Inshushinak	
1120–1110:	Hutelutush-Inshushinak	(= Nebuchadnezzar I (1126–1105) in Babylonia)

a powerful, highly organised political entity. According to the Babylonian *Chronicle P* (*ABC* no. 22), Kurigalzu II (1332–1308) fought against an otherwise unknown Elamite king, Hurbatila, defeated him and, according to his own inscriptions, conquered Susa and territory beyond. The reality of the Babylonian king's victory over Elam is established by some dedicatory texts of Kurigalzu II found at Susa itself. What is not known is how long this Babylonian occupation of western Elam lasted.

In the succeeding thirteenth and twelfth centuries there is far more information. This is, in part, a direct result of the rise of Elam as a political power, so that there is relatively abundant documentation in the form of more informative inscriptions in Elam itself. Because of the aggressive policy pursued by a stronger Elam – a policy possibly triggered directly by Kurigalzu II's invasion – it came into repeated conflict with Babylonia and eventually even dominated it briefly. Relations with Elam therefore figure

Figure 26 Chogha Zanbil ziggurat (courtesy of M.S. Drower)

prominently in a number of Babylonian texts of the time, which in turn helps to throw light on Elamite history.

Concrete information is only available in any quantity from the reign of Untash-napirisha (1275–1240) onwards. A large area had by then come under the direct control of the Elamite king, extending from Liyan on the Gulf (signifying maritime interests) to Anshan in Fars province, including the more northerly mountains and the Susa region. An impressive royal ceremonial centre and town with a magnificent ziggurat was founded at Chogha Zanbil (Ghirshman 1966–70; see fig. 26), called 'Al Untash-napirisha' ('city of Untash-napirisha) after the king. This may reflect a deliberate attempt by Untash-napirisha to forge closer socio-political links between the various districts under his control. Another, smaller centre, including a temple and ziggurat, was also developed by the king at Chogha Pahn East (30 km northeast of Susa; Stolper and Wright 1990). There is a hint that some conflict occurred in the east Tigris region (Der) – an area frequently disputed between Elamites, Babylonians and Assyrians, as it was the nodal point of a route which was crucial both strategically and commercially.

We should probably place into this, and the succeeding period generally, the urban development noted by excavators, including the growth of towns in the region between Khuzestan and Fars (Carter and Stolper 1984: 180). The latter were almost certainly market centres within the rural and pastoral economy. But others were linked to trading interests, and the later texts from Tall-i Malyan show that an intensive and large-scale trade in metals was a feature of the Middle Elamite period, and may be linked to the gradual expansion of the Middle Elamite kings into the northern mountains. Accompanying this shift to trade (and militarism) was a decline in the intensity of cultivation in the richest arable areas within Fars and Khuzestan (Carter and Stolper 1984: 180–181). Are the two features directly linked? Are the reasons for the changes identical in the two regions? The broadness of the archaeological phases and the lack of real precision in Elamite political and social history make it very hard to draw definite conclusions.

The next two rulers are not attested in Elamite texts, but the second, Kiden-Hutran (1235–?1210), is mentioned in Babylonian texts since, from this point on for almost a century, although not continuously, Elam became closely involved in Mesopotamian affairs. Partly at least, this was a result of Tukulti-Ninurta I's repeated campaigning in the east Tigris region, which culminated in his successful reorganisation of Babylonian affairs in Assyrian interests by controlling the Babylonian throne through personally appointed puppet kings (see chapter 7b). The extent of Elam's interests in Babylonian affairs can be gauged by the fact that the first of Tukulti-Ninurta's client-kings (Enlil-nadin-shumi: 1224) was forcibly removed by Kiden-Hutran in the course of a campaign, during which he sacked Der and its temples completely and took Nippur. In the reign of the third one, Adad-shuma-iddina (1222–1217), the Elamite king attacked again, this time taking Isin and Marad. The chaos created in Babylonia by the Elamite victory may have paved the way for the eventual overthrow of the Assyrian appointee.

The full implications of Elam's Babylonian policy remain obscure: first, because the chronology is so extraordinarily difficult; secondly, because Kiden-Hutran's reign was again followed by a period for which there is no documentation. It is possible that the vacuum in the sources is related to internal dynastic problems in Elam: it is usually assumed that the next documented king, Shutruk-Nahhunte (1185–1155), represents a new ruling family. Apart from some royal inscriptions (Grillot 1988), the main information for him and his son, Kudur-Nahhunte (1155–1150), comes from Babylonia, where, even a long time later, the devastation wrought by Shutruk-Nahhunte and Kudur-Nahhunte was remembered with great bitterness in poetic texts, of which this is an example:[5]

> [Shutruk-Nahhunte] drove away Zababa-shum-iddina, made disappear his rule [handed] over [the reign] to his first-born Kudur-Nahhunte.
> [This king . . .] whose crime was far greater than that of his forefathers, whose heavy guilt (even) exceeded theirs,
> [. . .] thought of wicked things against the land of Akkad, plotted insolence
> [installed . . . . . .] Enlil-nadin-ahi my predecessor
> [(a king) who treated Elam] as a hostile country, talked . . .,
> [Kudur-Nahhunte became angry] and swept away the whole population of Akkad like the deluge;
> [Babylon and the other] famous cult-centres he transformed [into ruin-heaps]
> The great lord Marduk, he made rise from the throne of his majesty
> [. . . . . .] the people of Sumer and Akkad he took captive [to Elam]
> [. . . . . .] he carried away Enlil-nadin-ahi [to Elam]
> [finished] his [kingdom], made disappear his rule.
> [He installed a governor,] not of Babylonian descent, an enemy [of Marduk]
>
> (Tadmor 1958: 137–138; Foster 1993 [0I]: 294)

The Elamite invasion may again have been triggered by Assyrian action in Babylonia. Shutruk-Nahhunte mounted a massive invasion of Babylonia, removed the reigning king and ransacked the country. Part of the huge booty consisted of large stone monuments, including the Hammurabi law stele and the victory stele of Naram-Sin, some of which were re-dedicated to Elamite gods, with added Elamite inscriptions, in Susa. Kudur-Nahhunte, his son, was left in control of Babylonia and added to his father's outrages (in Babylonian eyes) by removing Babylonian gods, including the centrally important cult-statue of Marduk of Babylon.

The devastation of Babylonia marks the acme of Elamite political power, as far as is known at present and always bearing the primarily Babylonian perspective in mind. Kudur-Nahhunte's successor, his brother Shilhak-Inshushinak (1150–1120), left a very large number of inscriptions, which show that he retained control of the east Tigris region and that he penetrated north into the Zagros and the Assyrian heartland. Other evidence suggests that he may also have attempted to expand into the Iranian interior. The quite substantial realm that Elam had become seems to have been maintained intact by his successor, Hutelutush-Inshushinak (1120–1100). Administrative Elamite texts from Hutelutush-Inshushinak's reign found at Tall-i Malyan reflect the material wealth and resources available to the king. Neither Shilhak-Inshushinak nor Hutelutush-Inshushinak attempted to retain direct political control of Babylonia. The reasons for this change in policy are obscure. In the reign of Shilhak-Inshushinak, Assyria was only beginning to recover from a period of relative weakness and Babylonia was still in considerable political disarray (see chapter 7d), so the Elamite rulers perhaps felt that military interference was unnecessary. If so, they were wrong: the earlier invasion (by Kudur-Nahhunte) eventually provoked a response from the energetic Babylonian king, Nebuchadnezzar I (1126–1105). After several attempts, he mounted a successful attack some time around the middle of Hutelutush-Inshushinak's reign and brought the statue of Marduk triumphantly back to Babylon (see chapter 7d).

At this point the Elamite sources fall silent for the next three hundred years. Around the same time, or shortly afterwards, a large number of towns in Khuzestan were abandoned, while already earlier Tall-i Malyan in Fars declined in size and was totally abandoned within this general time-span. The reasons for the sudden eclipse of Elam's political fortunes are unknown: Nebuchadnezzar I's invasion is usually blamed for the decline of Elam's western region. This is possible, although there is no evidence for any serious attempt by the Babylonian king to impose control; a general crisis linked to the Aramaean raids is perhaps more likely (Carter and Stolper 1984: 188; cf. ch.8b). In Fars, the shrinking settlement and eventual abandonment of Malyan is associated by many (e.g. Miroschedji 1985; Sumner 1994) with the arrival of a group of pastoralists later known as the Persians, leading to the eventual detachment of this area from Elam. The one region that appears to have suffered least, in terms of patterns of settlement, was eastern Khuzestan which, it has been suggested, could have served as an area of refuge for Elamites from east and west (Carter and Stolper 1984: 189). Not until the late eighth century did Susa and the lowlands of Khuzestan recover and again play a role in conflicts with Assyria.

Political structure and society

Our understanding of Elam's socio-economic, political, cultural and religious structure bristles with problems and scholarly disagreements. It is still true to say that only with great difficulty, and then very partially (as is obvious from the outline above), is it possible to reconstruct a little of Elam's political history with some certainty in the second half of the second millennium. The immediately preceding period (the *sukkalmah* phase) is in many ways better documented with respect to the socio-political and economic system, and it is beginning to be much better understood. The functioning of cities, administration (royal and local), modes of agricultural exploitation, social organisation, the nature of kingship and details of cult (aside from divine names) remain extraordinarily elusive. Arguments have been advanced, for example, for seeing Elam as a 'federal state' (*RLA* 2: 325–326). Some have thought that there was, certainly within the royal family, regular brother– sister marriage; that the succession went from brother to brother (or sister's son), rather than the more usual pattern of father to son, and that Elamite society displays signs of a kind of 'matriarchy' (König 1926; Hinz 1972). Some of these ideas evaporate on closer examination (Grillot 1988), although it is true that at certain times in its history Elam's government was diffused among a number of power-holders. This is most strikingly the case in the earlier second millennium when power was held by members of two generations of the royal family in a kind of 'triad' system (Carter and Stolper 1984: 24ff.), with hints of very complex succession arrangements 'up the ladder' from 'junior' to 'supreme' ruler. Some level of regional variation in government, styles of existence and modes of land-use seem likely given the great variation in climate and landscape of the areas included within the Elamite state at different times. Such regional variations had cultural repercussions, too, of which pottery (and to some extent burials) is at present the only clear indicator (Carter and Stolper 1984). There *is* a tangible Elamite culture definable from early in its history in motifs used on seals, styles of building, architectural decoration and rock reliefs (Porada 1965: 45–74; Amiet 1966; 1988). Rock reliefs in particular contain important hints of Elamite cult practices and royal ceremonies, although the details remain frustratingly obscure (Seidl 1986; de Waele 1989). The extent of our ignorance about Elam has been strikingly demonstrated by the identification of Anshan; the rich material from the site is only now being gradually published (Stolper 1984; Zeder 1991) and made available for scholarly consideration. But what is already clear from the excavations at Tall-i Malyan is that the city there was much larger (150 ha) during the earlier second millennium than in the Middle Elamite phase, when its area shrank by two-thirds to 50 ha. As publication and analysis of finds progress it may well be that the term 'classical Elamite' will have to be shifted to the time contemporary with the Old Babylonian period in Mesopotamia.

7d Babylonia: the end of the Kassites and succeeding dynasties (1158–c. 905)

As we saw (chapter 7a), it is very hard to define in what sense the Kassites were perceived as an ethnic entity distinct from 'Babylonians', although sufficient hints exist that they were. By the thirteenth century most of the kings included in the Kassite dynasty by Babylonian King List A bear purely Babylonian names. Signs of a 'nationalist' animosity towards the Kassites, after the end of the dynasty, are almost totally absent. The epics celebrating the victories of individual Kassite rulers over Elam remained in the repertoire of Babylonian literature for centuries. The Kassite gods associated with kingship continued to play a minor role in the Babylonian pantheon, and appear among the divine symbols carved on later *kudurrus* (boundary stones). Many of the administrative and socio-economic changes that began under the Kassites continued and the territory of Babylonia generally maintained its cohesion – it did not fall apart into rival city-states.

The evidence for studying the last period of Kassite rule and the next two hundred and fifty years is very scanty: there are only about twenty contemporary administrative texts for the whole time-span. Royal inscriptions and, especially, the *kudurrus* add more information. The thread of a historical outline depends on chronicles and king-lists – all of them late, often very fragmentary, and usually selective (e.g. the *Synchronistic History* (*ABC* no. 21)). The material is insufficient to allow us to trace events much beyond the bare list of kings (see table 24). The decades of conflict, essentially between Assyria and Elam, on Babylonian soil seem to have destabilised the Kassite dynasty and hastened its collapse. Royal power was next claimed by a dynasty based on Isin ('Second Dynasty of Isin': 1158–1027). Significantly, Isin lies in southern Babylonia, so the dynasty was located some distance from the main arena of war and perhaps escaped Elamite overlordship. Nebuchadnezzar I (1126–1105) had considerable success against Elam (see chapter 7c) and, to a lesser degree, Assyria (see chapter 7b). But Aramaean raids appear to have become ever more destructive towards the end of his reign and during those of his successors (see chapter 8b). It is not, therefore, surprising that the second dynasty of Isin was succeeded by three very short-lived dynasties, including, for about twenty years, a separate dynasty in the 'Sealand' (*RLA* 8: 6–10; see table 24) – a region always hard to control. From 1070 onwards, Babylonia was experiencing a serious crisis. The king-lists note a line of kings from 979 on, but it is uncertain whether they formed a coherent dynasty, and documentation is nil. Not until the reign of Shamash-mudammiq (c. 905), when Assyrian annals begin to shed light on events in Babylonia, is it possible to grasp events in south Iraq once more.

The main event of the period (apart from the devastating Elamite invasions, see chapter 7c), which we can reconstruct, is the attack on Elam by Nebuchadnezzar I (1126–1105). Firm evidence for it comes from a *kudurru* recording a grant of land made by the king to the Kassite noble and commander of the chariot-regiment, Lahti-Shihu (or Lahti-Shipak, sometimes read Sh/Ritti-Marduk) for his services during the Elamite campaign. The text is very long and recounts part of the campaign; the description of the long and wearisome march right up to Susa in the heat of the summer is particularly graphic:

> In the month Dumuzu (June–July), he launched the campaign. . . . With the heatglare scorching like fire, the surfaces of the roads were burning like open flames. In the wells, there was no water; the drinking supply was cut off. The finest of the powerful horses gave out, the legs of even the strong man faltered. On goes the pre-eminent king with the gods for his support, Nebuchadnezzar presses on, nor has he rival. He does not fear the difficult terrain, he stretches the daily march.
>
> (L.W. King, *Babylonian Boundary Stones and Memorial Tablets in the British Museum*, London, 1912 no. 6; Foster 1993 [0I]: 297–298; cf. Brinkman 1968: 107)

Table 24 Babylonian chronology 1155–*c.* 905 (following Brinkman 1968)

end of Kassite dynasty	1155	
Second dynasty of Isin	(1155–1027)	
Marduk-kabit-ahheshu	1154–1141	
Itti-Marduk-balatu	1140–1133	
Ninurta-nadin-shumi	1132–1127	
Nebuchadnezzar I	1126–1105	Tiglath-pileser I
Enlil-nadin-apli	1104–1101	of Assyria
Marduk-nadin-ahhe	1100–1083	(1114–1076)
Marduk-shapik-zeri	1082–1070	
Adad-apla-iddina	1069–1048	
Marduk-ahhe-eriba	1047	
Marduk-zer-x	1046–1035	
Nabu-shum-libur	1034–1027	
Second dynasty of Sealand	(1026–1006)	
Simbar-Shipak	1026–1009	
Ea-mukin-zeri	1009	
Kashshu-nadin-ahi	1008–1006	
house of Bazi	(1005–986)	
Eulmash-shakin-shumi	1005–989	
Ninurta-kudurri-usur I	988–986	
Shirikti-Shuqamuna	986	
Elamite dynasty		
Mar-biti-apla-usur	985–980	
dynasty of E	(979–732)	
Nabu-mukin-apli	979–944	
Ninurta-kudurri-usur II	944	
Mar-biti-ahhe-iddina	943–	
Shamash-mudammiq	*c.* 905	Adad-nirari II of Assyria (911–891)

This document is not only a superb example of Babylonian literature, it is also an important source for Babylonian administrative and social history of the period. The Nebchadnezzar *kudurru* and the few other surviving documents give us the names of some court-offices, such as the 'groom', herald and cupbearer, although their specific functions remain obscure. Babylonia was divided into fifteen provinces each under a governor (*šaknu*) with an assistant (*bēl pī/āhāti*). East of the Tigris a tribal organisation seems to have prevailed, grouped under tribal heads (*bēl bīti*), which formed enclaves within larger provinces subject to the provincial governor. At village level the important figure, as earlier, was the mayor (*hazannu*), also answerable to the *šaknu*. Most interesting are the *maššû*, who were local experts knowledgeable about the traditional associations of particular localities, and the circumstances of ancient gifts and sales of pieces of land: consulting them was obviously important so that a land-grant, for example, should not be challenged later; they are perhaps comparable to the 'remembrancers' known from other periods and places (Thomas 1992: 69–71). To what degree royal grants of land to officials, like the one recorded in the Nebuchadnezzar *kudurru*, were heritable tax-free holdings in perpetuity is uncertain. But the revenues accruing from such land were certainly turned over to the holder by royal command. The gifted land included villages and small towns located within the district granted, although that is not necessarily equivalent to giving the population into the possession of the new landlord as 'serfs'. The text also allows us to deduce the usual taxes levied on the population: unsurprisingly, they consisted of a percentage of harvest yields and flocks, providing manpower for labour and military duties, and supplying the local governor and garrison troops with essential supplies.

Several literary texts (only partially preserved: Tadmor 1958; Foster 1993 [OI] ch. III B 11 and 12; see the text quoted p. 372) and this *kudurru* imply that Kudur-Nahhunte's successor, Shilhak-Inshushinak, had remained in undisputed control over the whole eastern fringe of Mesopotamia, including the Diyala route. But Babylonian resistance was fierce and persistent: the last Kassite king, Enlil-nadin-ahi (1157–1155), had led a rebellion against Kudur-Nahhunte, in which the Babylonian king met his death and so extinguished the Kassite dynasty. The new leaders of resistance came from Isin, further south, and formed the new Babylonian dynasty (Isin II: 1158–1027). Lasting success against Elamite occupation was not achieved until the reign of Nebucchadnezzar I (1126–1105). His anti-Elamite offensive was probably only crowned with victory after several campaigns, and the triumphant climax was the return of the statue of Marduk from Susa. The importance of Nebuchadnezzar's achievement is emphasised by a spate of literary texts, apart from the *kudurru* text already discussed. There is, first, a poetic text (quoted in part, p. 372), in which Nebuchadnezzar vilifies the Elamites and traces their outrages; second, the 'Marduk prophecy' (Borger 1971; Foster 1993 [OI] ch. III B 13), stylistically a combination of hymn and royal inscription, concerns an Elamite campaign and Marduk's return and is probably to be connected with Nebuchadnezzar's Elamite war; third, there is a later epic about Nebuchadnezzar I, only fragmentarily preserved, which also seems to focus on his defeat of Elam (CT 13: 48; Brinkman 1968: 328 s.v. 4.3.8; Grayson 1975: 42–43). Significantly, Nebuchadnezzar I's victories entered the omen-literature (Weidner 1928–9: 238–239): signs associated with him came to signify success, like those of the great Sargon of Agade (see chapter 1c). Nebuchadnezzar himself also deliberately fostered the image of his greatness following the Elamite triumph, by adopting older royal titles in the style of Sargon and Hammurabi. He also revived an antique expression of royal piety, namely, instituting his daughter as *ēntu* of the moon-god at Ur (see chapter 1c).[6] These acts illustrate, strikingly, an awareness of earlier Mesopotamian history, and how it could be used to stress continuity with a more glorious past, which must have found a response among the population at large. Nebuchadnezzar I's victory over Elam was the high point in an otherwise politically and militarily undistinguished period, and seems to have become a model of Babylonian resistance for later generations.

The argument that the Babylonian Creation Story (*Enūma Eliš*; cf. Foster 1993 [OI] ch. III C 17) should be dated to the reign of Nebuchadnezzar I is strongly supported by some scholars, although others disagree. The point in favour of associating it with Nebuchadnezzar I is that, far from being a creation story, the function of *Enūma Eliš* was actually to elevate Marduk to the position of undisputed head and omnipotent ruler of the Babylonian pantheon (Lambert 1963; Roberts 1976). Together with the elevation of the local god of Babylon, Babylon itself now became for the Babylonians 'the eternal city', 'the holy city'. It was the royal capital *par excellence*, residence of the Babylonian king, one of whose most important cultic functions was the regular performance of the New Year festival, for which all the divine statues from other cities assembled in Babylon, and in the course of which *Enūma Eliš* was recited (Black 1981; Kuhrt 1987). Nebuchadnezzar I's victorious return of the Marduk statue from Susa therefore seems an appropriate occasion when this development took place. But the view has been challenged, and an attractive case has been made for associating the magnificent poem with the Kassite kings and their defeat of the Sealand rulers, and thus the elevation of Babylon and final triumph of Marduk with that period (see chapter 7a; Jacobsen 1976 [OL]: 165–191). Such an interpretation fits quite well with the little we know (although the language of *Enūma Eliš* suggests a date late in the second millennium), and the debate warns us how slender the basis for understanding the political context of literary texts is. For the moment, the question must remain open, although evidence in favour of the earlier date is increasing (Dalley 1989 [OI]: 228–230). What is indisputable is that Nebuchadnezzar I's victory over Elam and the return of Marduk marked an important revival in Babylonia's fortunes long remembered and celebrated.

The other important feature of the time is the incursions of a people called Aramaeans (see chapter 8b), sometimes associated with another group, the Suteans. The darkness shrouding Babylonian (like Assyrian and Elamite) history in the period from *c.* 1050 to *c.* 900 is very probably to be attributed to the devastation and havoc created by their raids. Tiglath-pileser I of Assyria (1114–1076) fought against them repeatedly (see chapter 7b), and Nebuchadnezzar I faced them in the region of Mari and perhaps even further west. But, in spite of repeated military action against them, it is clear that in the later Isin II dynasty more and more Aramaeans penetrated Babylonian territory, moving around between cities, ravaging the countryside and occasionally even attacking urban centres. Particularly catastrophic were the attacks in the reign of Adad-apla-iddina (1069–1048). He was not in the direct line of royal succession (Walker 1982), which itself may reflect the increasing political chaos in the country. In his reign the Aramaean attacks reached a climax: the Kassite royal city and fortress of Dur Kurigalzu as well as Der, Uruk and Nippur were sacked, and the temples of Sippar so thoroughly destroyed that the cult ceased for a period of about a hundred years. The picture of cultic disruption is echoed in a later chronicle (*Religious Chronicle* (*ABC* no. 17)) which shows that, *c.* 960, for nine successive years the New Year festival could not be celebrated, because it was impossible to assemble the statues of the gods in Babylon – even the god Nabu of Borsippa (a city very close to Babylon) could not be brought by the king to the capital. Communication between the various centres was obviously very difficult, and this was almost certainly due to the threats posed by the Aramaeans.

The general chaos and anarchy may have contributed some of the background for the 'Epic of Erra' (Cagni 1977). This is an unusual text, which circulated widely in different versions, very possibly including oral ones. Bits of it are found quoted in later royal inscriptions (both Assyrian and Babylonian), and extracts were inscribed on amulets intended to ward off evil powers. It describes a situation, where Marduk leaves Babylon in grumpy mood (for the apparently 'satirical' style in places, see Dalley 1989 [OI]: 283), leaving the unpredictable Erra, god of plague and the underworld, in charge and eager to impose his rule. The result is a period of turmoil: civil war, murder, disease, revolt, a world turned upside down. Although it is not possible to date the situation described precisely (indeed it is futile and inappropriate to try to do so), we may perhaps assume that the situation in Babylonia in the period between *c.* 1050 and the late tenth century approximated to that described in this obviously popular text:

> (Erra's adviser, Ishum, god of fire, is speaking:) 'O warrior Erra, you
>   have put the just to death,
> You have put the unjust to death.
> You have put to death the man who sinned against you,
> You have put to death the man who did not sin against you.

You have put to death the ēn-priest who made taklīmu-offerings promptly,
You have put to death the courtier who served the king,
You have put old men to death on the porch,
You have put young girls to death in their bedrooms.
Yet you will not rest at all,
Yet you say to yourself, "They despise me!"
Yet this is what you tell yourself, Warrior Erra,
"I shall smite the strong and terrify the weak,
I shall murder the leader of the army and rout the army,
I shall ruin the shrine in the temple, the wall's crenellations, the city's pride, I shall destroy.
I shall tear out the mooring poles and let boats drift downstream,
I shall break the rudder, so that it cannot reach the bank,
I shall rip out the mast and tear out its rigging.
I shall dry out the breast so that the baby cannot live,
I shall block springs, so that small channels cannot bring the waters of fertility.
I shall make Erkalla (i.e the Underworld) quake, and the heavens tremble,
I shall fell the rays of Shulpae (a Sumerian god identified with Jupiter) and wrench the stars from the sky,
The roots of trees shall be cut through so that their new growth will not flourish,
I shall destroy the base of the wall so that the top of it sways.
To the dwelling of the king of gods I shall go, so that counsel shall not prevail.'"
Warrior Erra listened to him,
And the words that Ishum spoke to him were as pleasing as the best oil.
And Warrior Erra spoke thus,
'Sealand shall not spare Sealand, nor Subartian (spare) Subartian, nor Assyrian Assyrian,
Nor shall Elamite spare Elamite, nor Kassite Kassite,
Nor Sutean spare Sutean, nor Gutian Gutian,
Nor shall Lullubean spare Lullubean, nor country country, nor city city,
Nor shall tribe spare tribe, nor man man, nor brother brother, and they shall slay one another.'
(Cagni 1977; Dalley 1989 [OI]: 282–315; Foster 1993 [OI] ch. IV C 16)

Notes

1 'Sealand' (*māt tamtim*) was a term regularly applied in the first millennium to the extreme south of Iraq, the area around the head of the Arab-Persian Gulf. For the idea that it extended further into Arabia, see Dougherty 1932.

2 Taide, like Washshukanni, has not yet been located with any certainty (see chapter 6a); somewhere in the headwaters of the Khabur is indicated, and Tell Brak has been tentatively proposed (but see p. 285).

3 In the 1993 season, a further fifty-three Middle Assyrian tablets were found at Tell Sabi Abyad; about half are well preserved. They date from late in the reign of Shalmaneser I to Ashur-nirari III (oral communication by F. Wiggerman at Rencontre Assyriologique Internationale in Berlin, July 1994).

4 'Anshan' also appears in the titulary of Cyrus the Great of Persia and that of his predecessors in the sixth century.

5 The exact date and context of composition of the text (K 2660) is not known. It is in the form of a royal pseudo-autobiography in poetic form; the poor state of preservation makes the identity of the protagonist uncertain, but there is a strong likelihood that it was Nebuchadnezzar I (Brinkman 1968: 328 s.v. 4.3.9).

6 The installation of a daughter of Nebuchadnezzar I at Ur as *ēntu* is only known from a text of Nabonidus (556–539: YOS I 45). He refers to finding descriptions of dress and ritual for the installation of the *ēntu* in a text of Nebuchadnezzar I recording the dedication of his daughter in office. It is, therefore, legitimate to doubt the historicity of Nebuchadnezzar I's act (Weadock 1975: 112), although most scholars accept it.